Supply Chain Management: Integrating Logistics and Operations

Supply Chain Management: Integrating Logistics and Operations

Edited by
Chester Ward

WILLFORD PRESS

www.willfordpress.com

Published by Willford Press,
118-35 Queens Blvd., Suite 400,
Forest Hills, NY 11375, USA

ISBN: 978-1-68285-434-1

Cataloging-in-Publication Data

Supply chain management : integrating logistics and operations / edited by Chester Ward.
    p. cm.
Includes bibliographical references and index.
ISBN 978-1-68285-434-1
1. Business logistics. 2. Industrial management. I. Ward, Chester.
HD38.5 .S87 2018
658.7--dc23

For information on all Willford Press publications
visit our website at www.willfordpress.com

Contents

Preface

The purpose of the book is to provide a glimpse into the dynamics and to present opinions and studies of some of the scientists engaged in the development of new ideas in the field from very different standpoints. This book will prove useful to students and researchers owing to its high content quality.

The entire set of processes involved in the movement of products from the manufacturers to the end consumers fall under the umbrella of supply chain. It involves the supply of raw materials, the maintenance of supply for demand, etc. This book unravels the recent studies in the field of supply chain management and its integration with logistics and business operations. It traces the progress of this field and highlights some of its key concepts and applications. For all readers who are interested in supply chain management, the case studies included in this book will serve as an excellent guide to develop a comprehensive understanding.

At the end, I would like to appreciate all the efforts made by the authors in completing their chapters professionally. I express my deepest gratitude to all of them for contributing to this book by sharing their valuable works. A special thanks to my family and friends for their constant support in this journey.

Editor

Trajectory of the Brazilian Semiconductor Industry and Supply Chain: Economic, Governmental, and Technological Perspectives

Ingridi Vargas Bortolaso
Unisinos
ingridibortolaso@yahoo.com.br

Alsones Balestrin
Unisinos
abalestrin@unisinos.br

Rafael Teixeira
Unisinos
rafaelte@unisinos.br

Kadigia Faccin
Unisinos
kadigia@gmail.com

ABSTRACT: This paper explores the semiconductor industry and its supply chain characteristics in order to aid understanding of its overall trajectory. How can a country like Brazil produce such an insignificant amount of semiconductor components? What has led the country to this situation? The objectives of this paper are twofold: first, to describe the semiconductor supply chain in order to understand its majors elements; and second, to delineate the trajectory of this industry. More specifically, we draw on evolutionary theory to analyze three macro trajectories: economic, governmental and technological. We collected archival data about these macro drivers and conducted interviews with professors and professionals in the semiconductor field. The results show four major events in the trajectory of the Brazilian semiconductor industry: (i) investment in microelectronic laboratories; (ii) a policy of market protection; (iii) a policy of market openness to product imports: and (iv) public policies to help the development of semiconductor companies through incentives.

Keywords: Semiconductor, trajectory, Brazil, supply chain

1. INTRODUCTION

The trajectory followed by an industry and its supply chain is directly linked to several factors, which include governmental actions, technological changes, innovations and the economic scenario in which it operates. Recently, studies have been specially focused on knowledge-intensive industries, such as the semiconductor industry. Mastering knowledge in all the productive stages of this industry has been a constant concern of industrialized countries, and understanding the development of the semiconductor industry and its supply chain has also been a constant task for researchers.

Since the starting point of this industry, which came with the creation of the first transistor (by Bell Laboratories) in 1947, besides the development of the first integrated circuit (by Texas Instruments) in 1961, the semiconductor industry has been the object of seminal studies, such as the work of Nelson (1962), Freeman, Harlow and Fuller (1965), Freeman (1982), Dosi (1984), Hippel (1977), Mowery (1978), Freeman and Soete (1987). These studies have unveiled the political, legal, economic, social and technological scenarios that have made countries, like the U.S. and Japan, become the world leaders in this industry. In addition, Brown and Linden (2005) identified some variables that may explain the migration of the development of semiconductors to Asia.

However, there are few studies analyzing the development trajectory of high technology products, such as semiconductors, especially in emerging countries like Brazil. The literature on supply chain management has placed great emphasis on the manufacturing supply chain of traditional products (e.g. Choi & Hartley, 1996; Flynn et al., 2010; Schoenherr et al., 2012), but little attention has been paid to high technology products. These tend to be more knowledge-intensive than traditional products, which have an impact on the entire supply chain because buyers and suppliers must possess knowledge-related capabilities that are not easily acquired. Beckman and Sinha (2005) drew attention to this gap in the literature on operations and supply chain management, even though few studies about this topic have been developed since then.

For more than three decades, Brazil, as an emerging country, has been trying to develop a semiconductor supply chain, since this country shows favorable market conditions for such an industry to flourish, as well as for an electronics industry to thrive. Revenue in the electrical and electronic industry in 2010 reached US$ 53.90 billion, which represented a growth of 11% compared to 2009. However, imports of electronic products grew 40% in dollar terms, from US$ 24.953 billion in 2009 to US$ 34.882 billion in 2010 (MCTI, 2011). The Brazilian institutional environment, composed of universities, research centers and governmental agencies, is another factor related to the evolution of the semiconductor industry. Despite the national effort, the current domestic production is still rather insignificant, showing a series of difficulties for both start-ups and for international groups to produce in Brazil.

In the Brazilian context, some studies have attempted to contribute to the knowledge about this industry. Silva (1985) highlighted the pattern of international competition and the possibility of including Brazil in this scenario, as, for Kimura (2005), it was aimed at identifying opportunities for the Brazilian semiconductor industry. Recently, Freitas (2012) assessed the innovation policies and their influence on the competitive advantage through the case of the Brazilian semiconductor industry. However, many questions still remain unanswered, especially those that contribute to a better understanding of the trajectory of this industry in Brazil: What macroeconomic events have impacted the current trajectory of the semiconductor industry? What government actions have influenced the development cycle of this industry? What were the main actions in the scientific-technological development of Brazil and their impacts on the national semiconductor industry?

In order to contribute to the knowledge about the current scenario of the semiconductor industry in Brazil, this study aims at understanding its development trajectory from the evolutionary trajectory (Nelson & Winter, 1982). To this end, three dimensions will be analyzed: governmental, macroeconomic and technological. To meet the objective of this article, we have chosen the following structure: Besides this introduction, an assessment of evolutionary theory is presented, as well as an assessment of the main ideas presented by researchers in this macroeconomic context, plus the technological trajectory and governmental approach. In the second part, the method is described. The third section covers discussion of the results. Finally, in the fourth section, the concluding remarks and suggestions for future research are presented.

2. LITERATURE REVIEW

2.1. Supply chain management

The supply chain has gained considerable attention from companies. So too have grown researchers' attempts to create an adequate definition that describes the field. Many of these definitions are broad (Harland, Lamming, & Cousins, 1999) or biased towards a particular theory and the work of the corresponding author (Tan, 2001). In fact, each definition varies depending upon the theoretical perspective used to address the subject (Teixeira & Lacerda, 2010). There is no general consensus on what exactly supply chain management really is or what it entails. Variation in the most recent and advanced definitions of supply chain management is a symptom of the infancy of the field. For example, the definition of supply chain management proposed by Chen and Paulraj (2004) highlights factors and activities that lead companies to create and maintain relationships with their suppliers, but it does not include the results and consequences of these practices. Moreover, Li et al. (2005) restrict the concept to the activities essential to management, and fail to include antecedents and results. In an attempt to synthesize a broad, comprehensive definition of the subject, Mentzer et al. (2001) analyzed several studies on supply chain management. According to the authors, supply chain management is defined as "the systemic, strategic coordination of the traditional business functions and the tactics across these business functions within a particular company and across businesses within the supply chain, for the

purposes of improving the long-term performance of the individual companies and the supply chain as a whole" (Mentzer et al., 2001, p.18). This definition is similar to that provided by other authors in the supply chain literature, such as Croom, Romano, and Giannakis (2001), Wong, Boon-itt, Wong (2011), and Gunawardane (2012).

A general supply chain model is shown in Figure 1. Typically, a supply chain encompasses a supplier, manufacturer, distributor, retailer, and the final customer (Chopra & Meindl, 2007; Fawcett, Ellram, & Ogden, 2007). In this illustrative chain, the flow of material moves downstream, from the suppliers to the customers, and the flow of information is upstream, from the customers to the suppliers. It is important to note this general model varies depending on the industry as well as the company characteristics. For instance, the Dell Computer supply chain model tends to be shorter than that of Figure 1, since Dell does not have distributors and retailers, selling its computers directly to the final consumer. In the case of services, the supply chain tends to be composed of suppliers, service providers, and final consumers. On the other hand, food companies sell their products through grocery stores, which indeed implies a supply chain like that presented in Figure 1.

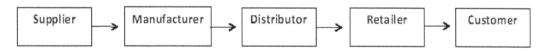

Figure 1 – A general supply chain model
Source: Adapted from Chopra and Meindl (2007)

2.2. Evolutionary theory

The evolutionary theory, also known as the neo-Schumpeterian approach, contemplates the main Schumpeter (1934) ideas. Nelson and Winter (1982) are the main articulators of this theory based on the work of Simon (1945) and Schumpeter (1934), which represents the origin of the insights on bounded rationality, innovation and ideas transposed from the evolutionary biology to explain company behavior. Other important authors are Freeman (1995), Dosi (1982, 2006), Lundvall (1992), Mowery and Rosenberg (2000), Griliches (1957) and Utterback (1996).

The term "evolutionary", according to Dosi and Nelson (1994), was used to highlight one of the main ideas presented by this theoretical mainstream, that is, the theory gains identity by allowing "explanation of why the existence of something must be closely connected to how this has become what it is" (Dosi, 1997, p.1531), emphasizing the path, the trajectory. As long as the technical shift and the industrial transformation are dependent on the trajectory, the future contains historical elements. This trajectory helps to explain the existence of different economic performances of countries, regions and sectors, as well as differences in their ability to innovate. Therefore, to assess the evolution of an industry, region or nation, it means that the study of history, which comprises the technological macro-economic and governmental trajectory, helps in understanding the current issues that stimulate the innovation process.

2.2.1. Technological trajectory

The technology comprises a set of parcels of knowledge, both practical and theoretical know-how, methods, procedures, experience of success and failure, as well as physical devices and equipment (Dosi, 2006). Thus, in analogy to scientific paradigms discussed in Thomas Kuhn's (1970) work, Dosi (2006) highlights the existence of technological paradigms, or technology research programs. Thus, the paradigm is treated as a model or a standard solution for problems related to technology (Dosi, 2006). In this way, the evolution of different technologies, incorporated in goods and/or processes for solving problems in the production system, providing progress, is what Dosi (1982; 2006) and Nelson and Winter (1982) call a technological trajectory. As time goes by, the technological directions change in order to face the new opportunities, for reasons related to the technology itself, or even issues related to economics (Dosi, 1982). And this dynamic change explains the technological leaps of an industry (Perez, 1999), or a technological paradigm shift.

In a survey conducted in the 1980s, which took into consideration the institutions that support the technical advancement of industry, Nelson (1986) points out that universities are public repository of knowledge. There are some cases that have been the objects of study of entrepreneurship linked to human capital formation and the creation of knowledge and technology for the private productive sector, such as Silicon Valley, which represents a region of high technology in the United States resulting from the interaction among universities, the government and industry (Goldstein & Drucker, 2006). Allied to this comes Dosi's argument (2006) regarding the first 10 years in the history of the semiconductor industry. For him, this period was characterized by the critical interrelationship between "science" and "technology." This interaction was able to open the way to fast generation of new technical knowledge and very successful commercial exploitation. Thus, a technological trajectory depends basically on new knowledge and its applications to solving problems, or to generating new knowledge to meet new needs; it is composed of elements and events stemming from changes and developments in technology, and it can be influenced by an economic trajectory.

2.2.2. Economic trajectory

The characteristics of the situation of an industry, or a particular sector, region or nation, economy or society are borne into the future (Nelson & Winter, 1982). In this regard, it is noteworthy that all modifications within an industry make firms adapt to their environment. In other words, any change in the structural conditions of an industry interacts with the changing patterns of corporate behavior (Dosi, 2006). These characteristics of the economic environment can also become selectors in the technological trajectory to be followed (Dosi, 1982; Perez, 1999). Thus, the institutional context can motivate or decrease the expenditure of funds for innovative activities in accordance with their expected economic returns, or when they are threatened by loss of something, some current economic benefit, or even for both reasons (Dosi, 2006).

Transitions of paradigms and technological opportunities may come from situations in which social and economic conditions are not the best (Perez, 1999). Perez (1999, p.17) emphasizes in his paper on technological change and development opportunities that it is necessary to "dance with the wolves." The author uses this analogy to explore the idea that, in a dynamic context in evolution, it is necessary for organizations to understand the conditions of access to technology according to the economic context, and that they use successive development strategies along with successive phases of paradigms. Ruttan (1997) emphasizes that the prevailing economic conditions may affect the future dimensions of knowledge and technology. Thus, successive historical events that affect the economic context of a country and ultimately influence the technological trajectories of various sectors are the macroeconomic trajectory.

2.2.3. Governmental trajectory

The laws, policies and public organizations represent an important part of the environment that shapes the private sector activities. Accordingly, the government has a central role in promoting and developing policies to support the start-up of new economic basis, as well as to generate the necessary institutions to support technological development and stimulate search for solutions to local problems that are not well solved by the market (Lundvall, 1992). So, for Nelson and Winter (1982), policies evolve partly in response to the changing demands and opportunities perceived, and such changes may result from the evolution of technologies and private market structures. So, the government role can be fruitful or unfruitful in productive innovation. Public policies are essential to ensure increased capacity for learning and dissemination of knowledge (Cooke, 2001).

Seeking to exemplify how government interventions can be crucial to the technological paradigm shift, Freeman (1989) highlights the Japanese case. The focus of the strategy was, according to Freeman (1989), the government's ability to provide integration among universities, the government and public and private industry. For Freeman (1989), the recognition of the new Japanese technological trajectory, focused on robotics, information technology and computers, was made possible by the central coordination of the government along with the *keiretsu* (conglomerates of Japanese industries.).

The importance of public policy for sectoral development was also highlighted in the work of Dosi (2006). He points out that the American supremacy in production and innovation in the semiconductor industry in the 50s and 60s was stimulated by public policies (mainly regarding the military and space). It is understood, therefore, that the use of policy instruments to extend and modify the private incentives to create new technologies, the importance of support, sectoral diversity of the situations and the complexity of the technical issues, are all combined to suggest policy interventions relating to R&D (Nelson & Winter, 1982; Dosi, 2006) and, in this way, it builds a path of governmental actions in the development of a nation, region or sector.

2.3. Theoretical model

The trajectories used in the analysis of the trajectory refer to different data sets and can be classified within the same group with similar characteristics. Anyway, the goal is to use these trajectories to guide data analysis and description of the results, allowing a more detailed understanding of the events, in particular, the historical ones that may have affected the trajectory of the industry analyzed. In order to develop this work, three trajectories were considered:

i. Macroeconomic trajectory – elements and events related to Brazilian macroeconomics and its indicators;

ii. Governmental trajectory – elements and events in the political and regulatory framework;

iii. Technological trajectory – elements and events resulting from changes and developments in technology, especially in the area of electronics and computing.

The perspectives used in the analysis of the trajectory of the Brazilian semiconductor industry involved a certain concern regarding long-term processes and progressive changes that are the result of a dynamic process. Thus, according to this dynamic view, it is necessary to know and to conjecture about the past to understand the present, as well as to see the present features that can lead to a different future, through the same dynamic process (Nelson & Winter, 1982). Figure 2 illustrates the theoretical model that guides the empirical methodology and analysis used in this study to provide understanding of the trajectory of the semiconductor industry in Brazil. Briefly, the evolutionary theory provides the theoretical foundation for understanding the phenomenon analyzed, while the semiconductor industry *per se* provides the case for review.

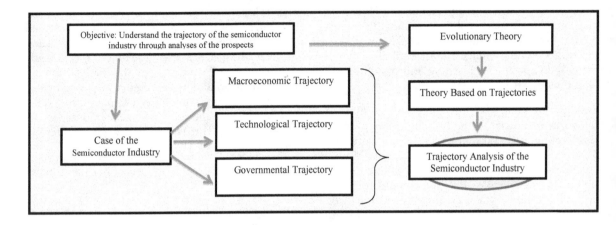

Figure 2 – Conceptual model

3. METHODS

The research design employed in this work is case study, indicated for the initial, exploratory stages of a given phenomenon (Meredith, 1998; Yin, 1989), in which the experiences of professionals are essential to the practical relevance of the results (Fisher 2007). Furthermore, a case study can provide a rich description of the phenomenon under investigation (Siggelkow, 2007), which is the Brazilian semiconductor industry. Thus, case study is the most appropriate research design because it offers the opportunity for in-depth understanding of the semiconductor industry from a historical viewpoint, outlined by three trajectories. Another justification for using this research design is based on the lack of studies that depict the development of this industry in Brazil, which ultimately hampers the use and combination of other methods.

It is worth noting that this paper aims to make the first exploration of the semiconductor industry in Brazil. Our study had the following general guidelines: i) main links in this supply chain; ii) main actors; iii) key policies governing the semiconductor industry; iv) main government assistance programs; and v) how the semiconductor industry is organized. This first study allows us to understand the current scenario of this industry.

From this scenario it is possible to trace the history of the industry and identify the events that have contributed to its development. To achieve this objective, three trajectories were defined: a) technological, b) governmental, and c) macroeconomic. The choice of these trajectories was to provide a mapping of the trajectory of the advancement of this industry in Brazil over the years, the central focus of this paper. Economic, technological,

and governmental trajectories were analyzed according to the features commonly used in each. For example, the macroeconomic trajectory analyzes characteristics, such as the inflation rate, interest rate, and the exchange rate. From a technological standpoint, the study analyzes changes in usage of technology, such as the introduction of new research laboratories or the introduction of new material used in the production process. Finally, from a governmental trajectory, our study analyzes federal government decisions that directly or indirectly affect this industry in Brazil.

Three sources were used for data collection. First, bibliographic references were used to provide initial data and information about the characteristics of the industry under analysis. This first step is essential to provide the authors of this paper with uniformity in the terminology used in the area and also information about the main features inherent in this industry. Second, documents, such as government reports and those of other institutions related to the semiconductor industry, were used. Analysis of these documents provides data and information about the characteristics of the industry over the past 30 years. This, to some extent, allows reconstruction and understanding of certain events that may be related to changes in this sector in Brazil over these years. Finally, in-depth interviews were conducted with experts, practitioners and researchers of this industry in Brazil. These were held between August and November 2012, based on a script containing semi-structured questions that served as a guide for the authors to conduct them in accordance with the research objectives. This script was pre-tested with the help of three experts in the semiconductor industry. Table 1 contains the major questions in the questionnaire.

Table 1 - Questions for in-depth interviews

1. What is the structure of the Brazilian semiconductor industry?
2. What are the main economic events that have contributed to its development?
3. What are the main technological events that have contributed to its development?
4. What are the main governmental decisions that have contributed to its development?
5. What are the main barriers to development of this industry?
6. What are the possible alternatives to overcome these barriers?

The selection of participants for the in-depth interviews was based on two criteria:

i. Experience in the semiconductor industry; and

i. Potential contribution to achieving the objectives of our study. The interviews took place in the participants' workplaces in order to make them feel comfortable enough to answer the questions. Table 2 presents some information about these participants.

Table 2 – Interviewees' characteristics

Interviewee	Institution	Highest Degree	Years in semiconductor industry
Interviewee A	Governmental agency	Doctorate	20
Interviewee B	Private company	Masters	5
Interviewee C	Private company	Bachelor	10
Interviewee D	Professor	Doctorate	25

Data from the interviews were transcribed and analyzed according to guidelines of content analysis. The content analysis was conducted based on major categories determined a priori according to our research objectives, which involve economic, technological and governmental perspectives. After transcribing the interviews, we counted and categorized the terms cited by interviwees, searching for patterns of response and classifing them in one of our three major categories: economic, technological, and governmental. In addition, as the main objective of this research was to understand the trajectory of the Brazilian semiconductor industry, a temporal logical analysis was used, in which the changes in the industry that have occurred over time were analyzed. Thus, the dates of data available were taken into account. By analyzing historical data, it was possible to identify the year to which they referred. Thus, adequate data were obtained to recreate the history of the semiconductor industry with the economic, governmental, and technological trajectories.

For the purpose of this study, a historical event is viewed as any event that has caused a significant impact on various actors, such as organizations and institutions within the industry in Brazil. These historical events are used in this study to identify possible disruptions in the structures, laws, rules, policies and existing processes in this industry. These disruptions help to highlight significant changes occurring in the industry, thereby indicating actions or decisions that have influenced its history.

4. RESULTS

All results presented in this section are based on data gathered through the interviews and documents analyzed.

4.1 The semiconductor industry and its supply chain

With a market whose figures reach US$ 248.2 billion annually worldwide (SIA, 2010), the semiconductor industry becomes a single empirical case relevant to the present study. According to Gutierrez and Leal (2004), among the leading countries in the production of integrated circuits in 2002 were China, which exports US$ 3 billion, Ireland US$ 6 billion, Malaysia US$ 13 billion and Taiwan US$ 15 billion. One reason for the rapid development of this industry in these countries may be associated with the adoption of partnerships with universities, companies, research institutes, industry federations and funding agencies.

It is worth mentioning the countries with a high level of development that also invest in attracting companies in the semiconductor industry, such as: Japan, Germany, USA and France. These countries have made huge investments in this activity, because they have identified the integrated circuit industry as strategic for maintaining the country's development, along with growth of research institutes and innovation. According to Fernandes (2010, p. 21), "The national competitiveness and economic development are closely linked with the concepts of information and knowledge economies".

It can be affirmed that the attention given to the semiconductor industry in recent years is associated with the great techno-economic revolution of society. Currently, people are immersed in a dynamic society, without borders and permeated by technology. More and more people are depending on technology to run their daily activities. As technology tools used extensively by society, one can cite, for example, computers, iPods, iPads and iPhones, which constitute facilitators of everyday activities. What might go unnoticed in the use of these new technology tools is that they all need semiconductors to work, the semiconductor also being known as a chip.

Semiconductor products, such as microchips, constitute the foundation for the development of information and communication technologies (TICs). According to Freeman and Soete (1987), these technologies can be considered a new techno-economic paradigm, as they are ubiquitous in various productive activities. In other words, they are able to "[...] revolutionize the processes of production and im-

pact all other industries and services" (Freeman & Soete, 1987, p.105).

Furthermore, the semiconductor industry has: a greatly accelerated dynamic of innovation, resulting from the combination of high rates of technological innovation (not only in product design, but also in their processes); density and complexity in its technologies (Dahmen, 1993); and also a capital intensive character and Research and Development (R&D) activities, which generate high investments and risks for manufacturers in this segment. The semiconductor chain is composed of macro-steps. They are: conception, design, front-end, back-end, test and, ultimately, customer service. The conception is the first step in the semiconductor chain and consists of idealization and activity planning. The second stage, called design, is responsible for executing the integrated circuit project. The third stage is processing/ manufacturing, which processes the physical and chemical elements of semiconductors. The packaging and testing of semiconductors refer to back-end and chip functionality testing. The customer service is the last step in the chain and corresponds to the sale and delivery of the product to the consumer.

The various steps/processes comprising the semiconductor chain can be performed by various companies located in different regions, thus allowing segment unbundling, since it makes possible the establishment of collaborative strategies in almost all parts of the chain, as can be seen in Figure 3.

Manufacturers of integrated circuits are classified according to their type of business or the way they operate in the value chain. Thus, they can be classified as integrated manufacturers, fabless companies, specialized foundries, packagers, design firms and independent intellectual property firms. Companies classified as integrated manufacturers perform the entire process of semiconductor manufacturing, from the design of the component to consumer delivery. The companies called fabless are responsible for product design and are the brand and market holders.

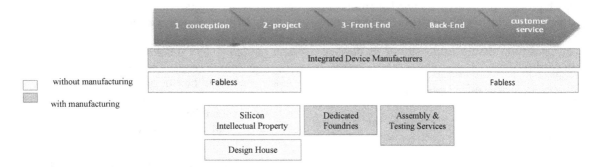

Figure 3 – General semiconductor industry supply chain
Source: Adapted from BNDES Sector (2004, p. 13)

Companies known as specialized foundries only perform the physical-chemical processing of the products. The packager is dedicated to the back-end step. Companies known as design firms (design houses) perform the integrated circuit design. And, finally, intellectual property companies design specific parts of the projects and license them to third parties, generating royalties. Although the semiconductor supply chain seems lean and organized, it is important to emphasize the need for an ecosystem to provide the enabling environment for development of the semiconductor area.

The semiconductor industry has strict infrastructure requirements regarding quality and quantity. It is important to mention the necessary availability of water, electricity and transportation, including ports and airports. Moreover, the main requirement for an integrated circuit company, whatever its form or type of business activity, is the availability of skilled labor with a range of capabilities. This allows complete integration essential to the "ecosystem" structure and specific training in microelectronics.

In this regard, long-term R&D that articulates the various government agencies must be developed, providing them with stable resources and appropriate management mechanisms. Likewise, a model truly integrated with the business environment should take into account the comparative advantages of Brazil and the joint initiatives of R&D and human resource training in the field of microelectronics.

The path taken by the semiconductor industry is only relevant and can only be understood when viewing its trajectory. Thus, the event that initiated the semiconductor industry was the discovery of the transistor in 1947, in the United States, by the company Bell Labs. The transistor constitutes the main element of the semiconductor. The intensification of studies on the transistor was driven by historical events experienced in previous years, such as the two World Wars. According to Freeman and Soete (2008), the two Wars stimulated the growth of government support for scientific research and technological development in many countries.

Due to the world conflicts, the need to improve communication among the military in combat has caused learning to advance in the telecommunications field and led to subsidized development of studies aimed at the creation of the semiconductor era postwar (Swart, 2010). The invention of the diode and triode vacuum tube, in the first two decades of the 20th century, provided the basis for the spectacular growth of the transistor, the main input of semiconductors (Adner & Kappor, 2010).

In the following years, the Bell Labs patent, licensed to other transistor manufacturers, started a cycle of intense research. In 1959, it created the first Planar process for integrated circuits. This raised the possibility of coupling various transistors to form an integrated semiconductor circuit. Shortly thereafter, in 1962, the first commercial integrated circuits reached the markets. Already in the late 60s, multiple firms were manufacturing integrated circuits in Silicon Valley.

By analyzing the process of creation and development of the semiconductor, one can see that the concept of technological development is critical. In-depth analysis of texts that highlight the emerging semiconductor demonstrates that this discovery only became feasible due to the formation of research groups that shared knowledge and generated collective learning. It seems possible to show that, according to this industry's history, technical change has been the major booster of its development worldwide.

In the 70s, there was the oil crisis, which marked the economics of global markets, forcing industrialized countries to promote adjustments in the productive sector, aiming to resume economic growth. The changes in the economic scenario forced a need to adopt coping strategies to deal with uncertainty. Because of inflation in oil prices, the oil crisis in 1973 had a significant impact on the competition and modified the trajectory of the global market. With the globalization of the world economy, there have been new patterns of international trade and competition. The main features of this process are: increased market competitiveness and uneven growth in different regions of the world. This process of globalization, access to new markets and technologies has helped other countries, such as Japan, to initiate semiconductor production. After starting production, Japan invested heavily in research and development and eventually overtook the United States, making it the largest manufacturer of these products in the world. Heavy demand for semiconductors in the late 70s and early 80s brought some ease of access to this market for incoming countries. This is the case of Germany, France and the UK, which started production in the 80s. Other countries involved in the semiconductor market started to invest in R&D, such as South Korea, Taiwan and Singapore. Until the 80s, the largest share of integrated circuit production was in the United States and Japan.

The following decades were characterized by great expansion in the countries called the "Asian Tigers", which came to dominate the global manufacture of electronic products: Hong Kong, South Korea, Singapore and Taiwan. This rapid expansion was,

among other factors, a result of the implementation of long-term government policies aimed at increasing the value of its industrial production. Brown and Linden (2005) present some factors to explain the migration of semiconductor development to the Asian continent: the existence of close contact with customers and ease of access to specialized human resources, plus relatively lower cost, implying a reduction of total production costs.

4.2. The semiconductor industry and its supply chain in Brazil

Results from analysis of interviews and documents reveal the semiconductor industry and its supply chain in Brazil, as illustrated in Figure 4. For Gutierrez and Leal (2004), Brazil is one of the few countries among the major world economies that do not have an electronics industry that includes the manufacture of integrated circuits. In the field survey, we found 22 companies operating in Brazil working in the conception and design of integrated circuits, which is the first stage in the production of semiconductors, as presented in Figure 3. At the front-end, we found 4 enterprises developing some manufacturing activities; while at the back-end, we found 7 companies performing packaging manufacturing activities. Finally, providing support for this supply chain, we found 23 training institutions promoting and generating labor and some type of knowledge to be used directly by companies in the chain. These companies and institutions are spread throughout Brazil, and receive support from the government, especially through tax incentives. It is noteworthy that there are 34 companies that supply raw materials, equipment and specialized services. We presented this model to participants of our research in order to validate the final model. Results from this validation process lead to a validated semiconductor supply chain model.

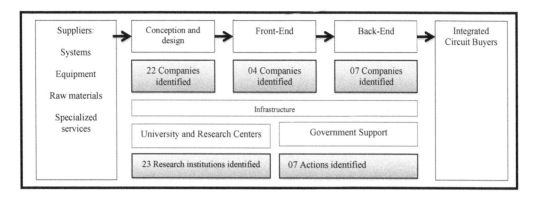

Figure 4 – Semiconductor industry supply chain in Brazil

After a thorough analysis of the path taken by the semiconductor industry, it can be said that in Brazil it has undergone various processes, marked by several technological, macroeconomic and government events. In this sense, one can understand its history, and guidance can be given by analysis of the events that make up these technological, economic and government prospects. In the following sections, these events and trajectories are discussed.

4.2.1. Technological trajectory

Results from the content analysis suggest that the technological trajectory had its starting point in the research activities conducted by the Institute of Aeronautical Technology - ITA in the 1950s. Three out of four interviewees mentioned the creation of ITA as the starting point for the technological trajectory related to the semiconductor industry. Results indicate that, although ITA was not created to foster semiconductors, it has a key role in promoting technology in several industries in Brazil, including the electronics.

Results from interviews also indicate that, in the following decade, there were several initiatives regarding the creation of microelectronics laboratories across the country, such as the assembly of microelectronics laboratories at the University of São Paulo - USP and University of Campinas - UNICAMP. These laboratories were set up in federal universities as a priority action of the government to develop the Brazilian industry. Other agencies also supported the establishment of laboratories, such as FINEP (Financier of Studies and Projects), BNDES (National Economic and Social Development Bank), CNPq (National Council for Scientific and Technological

Development), FAPESP (Foundation for Research Support in São Paulo State) and CAPES (Coordination of the Enhancement of Higher Education Personnel). It is worth noting that this action by the Brazilian government has acknowledged the important technical advance, the increased productivity and change in the economic dynamics, as quoted by the evolutionary theory of Nelson and Winter (1982).

It was a consensus among interviewees that the creation of six microeletronics laboratories during 60's, 70's and 80's were fundamental to form a skilled workforce and develop new technologies through applied research. According to Tavares (2001), the federal government made efforts to create infrastructure for research and education in science and technology by devising an information technology policy. The government role was to organize and institutionalize norms, rules and routines. Furthermore, it is important to highlight an action on the part of the private sector, namely the installation of the Philco diode and transistor factory in Sao Paulo. This is one of the very few, if not the only, technology initiative coming from the private sector.

Analysis of documents indicate that during 1990's there was a technological gap in terms of new installations, specific investments, infrastructure development laboratories and other such resources. Two interviewees suggested that this gap may have caused a rupture in the system of technological development for the electro-electronics and semiconductor industries in the country.

In the 2000s, a new initiative was incorporated into the technological trajectory of the semiconductor industry, namely the implementation of the CI Brazil program. This will be discussed in depth in the governmental trajectory section, but it is important to highlight that this program aims to develop technology aimed not only at the manufacture of components, but also geared primarily to the design of electronic components and chips used in the semiconductor industry. Table 3 presents a summary of the key initiatives that relate to the technological

perspective. In the analysis of the initiatives that make up the technological scenario, it is possible to realize that actions specifically performed by the government have been presented. In this first survey, private initiatives were not identified. The reason for the absence of these initiatives may be associated with difficulty in tracing such actions.

Table 3 - Technological trajectory

Main technological events	
1950	ITA starts research activities in semiconductors
1960	Top research activities at USP
	Philco installs diode and transistor factory in São Paulo
1970	Setting up the microelectronics lab at USP Polytechnic School
	Setting up of microelectronics lab at USP Polytechnic School
	Establishment of microelectronics lab at UNICAMP
1980	Establishment of microelectronics laboratory at UFPE Physics Institute
	Microelectronics laboratory created at UFRGS Physics Institute

4.2.2. Economic trajectory

Results based on analys of documents reveal that, in the 1960s, the country experienced the establishment of the electronics industry in Brazil and, in the 1970s, Brazil experienced a boom in consumer durables. Multiple sources mention the "miracle" of the Brazilian economy, the period of continuous economic growth. Results from interviews indicate that, during that time, Brazil was beginning to develop more effective actions for the development of the semiconductor industry, such as the implementation of a public policy to protect the market and the respective enterprises throughout the country. This protection seeks to restrict market access to international companies and ban imports of products in order to help the development of the national industry and increase internal scientific research. According to one interviewee, however, the market protection was the two sides of the coin: "It gave Brazilian companies sometime to prepare for international competition in the field of technology, however, it also created an atmosphere of protection that led companies to a confort zone, reducing their motivation for technolgy development".

From the trajectory of evolutionary theory, the market protection provided an economic shift that pro-

duced certain events in the environment, such as the establishment of 23 national and multinational companies in the semiconductor area in Brazil in the 70s. The multinationals were attracted by a market protection policy, established in 1977 (Tavares, 2001), and especially by the policies of import substitution.

During the 1980s, the country went through a turbulent economic period when three different economic plans were implemented to contain inflation, all without success, which led the country into recession.

In the 90s, the Brazilian economy was transformed by trade liberalization and the establishment of the Real Plan that brought the market into a new competitive era, since foreign competition and monetary stability had demanded new trade policies and the creation of new business strategies. The opening of the Brazilian market made it possible to import products and the implementation of new routines, which can be viewed as a paradigm shift. There was an imbalance in the trajectory of the semiconductor industry, since the import of electronic goods was facilitated, discouraging domestic production. These two events, the Real Plan and the market opening, aimed to include Brazil in the global economy, and this is what has actually ensued. However, there has been an intensification of global competition and a decline of the Brazilian semiconductor industry. This event definitively marked the history of the semiconductor industry, as the government led a process of learning and knowledge accumulation, since necessity causes adaptation. This corroborates the logic of evolutionary theory that postulates these economic changes that produce changes in the environment (Langlois and Everett, 1993). All interviewees mentioned these years as the most important from the economic perspective, suggesting that the changes in economic policy were fundamental to provoke a change in the semiconductor indsutry.

The 2000s are marked by fluctuations in the macroeconomic field. First, the continued stability of the Brazilian currency allowed investment planning, both by the government and businesses. This led the country to continuous economic growth and job creation, which, along with wages, provided the necessary input for a virtuous cycle of growth. However, the global financial crisis, which began in mid-2008, caused negative impacts on the economies of countries worldwide, including Brazil, causing a slowdown in economic growth. Table 4 summarizes the main macroeconomic events that impacted the Brazilian economy in some way.

Table 4 - Economic trajectory

Economic main events	
1960	Establishment of the electronics industry in Brazil
1970	Accelerated expansion of the market for consumer durables
	First political action for the establishment of an information technology policy
	Introduction of market protection
1980	1986 - Cruzado Monetary Plan
	1987 - Bresser Economic Plan
	1989 - Verão Economic Plan
	1981- Period of recession and unemployment
	After three failed plans, inflation gained momentum
1990	1990 - Collor Economic Plan
	1991 - Second Collor Economic Plan
	1994 - Real Monetary Plan
	1999 - Adoption of floating exchange rate
	Opening of the internal market to importation
2000	2001 - Energy blackout
	2002 - Lula Crisis
	2003 - Lula Crisis
	2005 - Corruption scandal in the federal government
	2008 - Global Financial Crisis

4.2.3. Governmental Trajectory

Results from the content analysis suggest that, after achieving an outstanding stage of development, the semiconductor industry declined at the beginning of the 90s with the end of the market protection policy. Interviewees mentioned that incentives for research and development were reduced and many of the best talents changed area or emigrated. One interviewee reported: "Some of my colleagues left Brazil searching for opportunities in other countries, it was a time of too much uncertainty and lack of resources for high technology research and development". The end of market protection suggests a rupture in the trajectory of the semiconductor industry. Government actions, such as establishing policies and incentive programs, have an influence on the characteristics and performance of the companies, which ultimately helps to delineate the path of a particular industry.

Analysis of documents shows that most multinational companies shutdown their operations in Brazil in less than six months. The end of the semiconductor industry was caused by the announcement of facilitated importation of equipment by companies, without any tax or legal restrictions, which had been imposed by the Fernando Collor de Mello government. Despite the existence of some evidence suggesting incentives for national production of electronic components (later introduced with the 2nd law of computing), there was clear evidence that importation of equipment was a decision to transfer the production of such components abroad. While Brazil was losing much of its efforts to build its own semiconductor industry, other countries were making progress in the process of establishing their semiconductor industries. The statement of one interviewee summarizes the effect of government on semiconductor industry during this time: "Brazilian Governemnt took decisions that put Brazil in a very bad position to compete in high technology because it allowed importation of eletronic devices at no cost and provide no incentive to Brazilian companies and universities to move along with research and development".

The interviewees also mentioned that the 2000s represent a shift in the government policy because Brazilian government put microelectronics industry as a priority for development. As a result, analysis of documents show that the government has created many programs, such as the Program of Integrated Circuits Brazil to foster an ecosystem suitable for the development and support of this industry. For Holbrook et al. (2000), there is no reason to believe that, without such public policies, the rate of technical advance achieved by Brazilian semiconductor industry would have been so great. This statement reinforces the need for the government as an articulator of policy and arrangements for the development of this industry.

Interviewees also called attention to the experience of other counties, which focused on attracting the integrated circuit industry. According to all four interviewees, the government should be the one the main actors in promoting the development of semiconductor indutry in Brazil. For them, public policies should involve high investments so that the minimum requirements of physical infrastructure and human resource training needed by the respective manufacturing companies are met. To a lesser or greater degree, it is possible to identify in other countries' experiences the adoption of instruments that involve subsidies, tax relief, and financial incentives in a time horizon of not less than 10 years (Gutierrez & Leal, 2004).

Currently, Brazil is one of the few among many countries that do not have an electronic industrial complex that includes the manufacturing of integrated circuits (Gutierrez & Leal, 2004). Analysis of documents reveals that, to change this situation, the Brazilian government's main objective is to make the country a player in the design and manufacturing of integrated circuits (IC). The great challenge to achieve this goal is the need to create a favorable ecosystem for this industry. It is understood as an ecosystem with the dynamism required for the correct development of the semiconductor chain. One interviewee said: "Brazil needs an ecosystem including companies, funding agencies, technology institutes, politics, entrepreneurs that are interlinked to one another by the needs of this industry". Seeking to create an ecosystem conducive to attracting more companies into the semiconductor industry and developing those already established, Brazil has taken various actions aiming at the development of this industry. The Brazilian government has developed industrial and technological policies articulated and integrated with the various institutions and government agencies, such as the PDP (Productive Development Policy) in 2008 and the PACTI (Action Plan for Science, Technology and Innovation) 2007 - 2010. Some of the key strategic actions taken by the Brazilian government should also be highlighted:

i. PADIS: This is the Support Program for Technological Development and the Industry of Semiconductor Displays. It includes a chapter dealing with the topography of integrated circuits, in line with international agreements in the intellectual property area. PADIS is developed for companies that invest in Research and Development (R&D) and are manufacturers of: information displays used as inputs for electronic equipment and technologies.

i. National Microelectronics Program: This aims to support and promote the consolidation of graduate programs through the provision of scholarships for masters and doctorate research programs related to the Microelectronics area.

Currently, nine companies operating in Brazil focus on the semiconductor industry, of which two produce power devices, three operate in the back-end, one in PV, one focuses entirely on design, and another is dedicated to the design house and foundry area (CI Brasil, 2011). In addition, 22 companies are identified as participating in the Design House Development Project for Integrated Circuits Brazil - BRAZIL CI, and 13 research institutes are involved in semiconductor studies. These institutions are scattered throughout Brazil and receive the cooperation of the government through the CI project to continue operating in the market. In 2011, collaborative action among the government, universities and private companies resulted in the installation of a company to encapsulate semiconductors (Valor Econômico,

2011), the first in Brazil.

The role played by the government is important to ensure the survival of this industry. However, the time elapsed between creation and implementation of these policies rendered survival of the semiconductor companies in the country unviable. According to Freeman and Soete (2008), a major difficulty is to promote public policies for long-lasting technologies within a globalized market economy. Therefore, technological change should be seen as a cumulative process.

Brazil is reintroducing policies, such as the National Program of Microelectronics and CI Brazil, to rebuild this industry (the government behavior seems to be aware of the adaptive types). To implement these policies, the government has made use of the knowledge acquired during the first cycle of the Brazilian semiconductor industry. To do so, the government has relied on documents, norms and institutionalized routines from that period. This statement corroborates the studies of Crossan, Lane and White (1999) with respect to the need for an institutionalization process for the validation of learning. Complementing these authors, Zawislak (2004) argues that the past experience, based on learning and competence as well as the solutions found by individuals or by a firm that builds new routines, undergoes more intensive training to face random factors, that is, situations outside the routine. Table 5 summarizes the main governmental events in the Brazil.

Table 5 - Governmental trajectory

Main governmental events	
1970	Market protectionism law
1990	Information technology law
	End of market protectionism law
2000	New information technology law
	2003 - National Microelectronics Program – Industrial Policy
	2004 - Innovation law
	2005 - BEM law
	2005 - Implementation of Design House Program - CI Brasil
	2007 - PADIS
	2008 - Plan for science, technology and innovation
2010	2010 - Governmental Purchase Law
	2011 - Plan for science, technology and innovation

4.3. Analysis through the dimension of evolutionary theory

It is worth noting that Brazil, after experiencing a golden age from the 1960s to 1990s, opted for strategies that ended up not prioritizing the preservation and development of the semiconductor industry. Thus, one can conclude that the scenario of the semiconductor industry that exists today is the result of a process of advance and setbacks caused by technological impacts, and especially by political decisions at different historical moments. This is because the essential purpose of policies supporting sustainable development is to encourage the rapid diffusion of technologies (Freeman, Soete, 2008).

Another important point to understand is the relationship of the economic, technological, governmental actions and development cycles of this industry. The explanations for this point can be obtained by analyzing the historical events that gave rise to learning and change in public policy. It can be said that the Brazilian semiconductor industry experienced its first cycle between the 60s and 80s. As a feature of this cycle, the high government investment in the development of applied research and skilled labor can be mentioned. The articulation of the government for the establishment of labs can be seen as a method of "search", "selection", "routine" procedures, "adoption" in the face of environmental uncertainty with the intention of achieving success in competitive market performance (Nelson and Winter, 2005). Table 6 presents the main historical events identified as associated with the history of the semiconductor industry.

Table 6 - Historical events during the trajectory of the semiconductor industry

Order	Period	Historical event
1st Event	1960s	The articulation of Brazil for the establishment of microelectronics laboratories.
2nd Event	1970s	Implementation of a market protection policy.
3rd Event	1990s	The opening of the Brazilian market to imports of capital goods and consumer products.
4th Event	2000s	Resumption of the Brazilian government's development of policies to revive the semiconductor industry.

However, the industry did not grow after the 1980s because Brazil was passing through a historical moment of profound change in its political structure, which had an impact on the economy. In 1985, the military government, pressured by public opinion, decided to promote democratic reform, and the first president was elected in more than 20 years since the last democratic election. This change in the political system had an influence on the economy because the president did not have the environmental conditions to minimize the uncertainty in the market. For this reason, the semiconductor industry supply chain in Brazil could not sustain its evolutionary growth process.

The second cycle of development of the semiconductor industry began in the 2000s, when the government again stressed that this industry was a priority, and promoted action to attract foreign companies and generate interest from national companies. In parallel to the evolutionary theory, one can say that the routines, norms and rules developed by the government were the genetic inheritance of the first cycle, as discussed in evolutionary theory and path dependencies. Additionally, one can add that the learning process is still viewed at an institutional level. It is this development heritage that has encouraged the government to redevelop this industry. However, it seems that, since 2007, with the creation of PADIS, the government, in a continuous process of devising public policies to guarantee development of the sector, has presented the first favorable results of attracting foreign companies.

5. CONCLUSION

In order to deepen understanding of the semiconductor industry outlook in Brazil, this study has sought to describe its development trajectory from three trajectories of analysis: scientific-technological, macroeconomic and governmental.

As for the scientific-technological trajectory, it is clear that Brazil has created an infrastructure for both the development of new products, as well for the training of human resources. The 50s marked the beginning of scientific research by the Technological Institute of Aeronautics - ITA. Especially in the 60s and 70s, new laboratories were established at the University of São Paulo - USP and the University of Campinas - UNICAMP. In the 80s, other laboratories were established at the Federal University of Rio Grande do Sul - UFRGS and the Federal University of Pernambuco - UFPE. These five institutions have formed a major center of excellence for the training of teachers and doctors, and especially for the development of basic research in the country. However, these actions were too focused on the academic field and took a long time making the technology transfer to the Brazilian industry, either through applied research or by stimulating the creation of new businesses. We can notice that, in Brazil, a further step was missed, that aimed at creating technological institutes to support the national semiconductor industry, bringing closer the basic research carried out in the centers of excellence mentioned above to the efforts of the R&D industry.

The macroeconomic trajectory was, no doubt, the dimension that had most impact on the current scenario of the Brazilian semiconductor industry. The economic instability, the lack of a robust, long-term national policy for the micro-electronic field impacted this industry in Brazil very negatively. In the 70s, Brazil created a market protection policy in order to protect the domestic industry, which represented a major initiative for the first microelectronic industrial plans to emerge. Nevertheless, because of the instability caused by the economic plans in the 80s and 90s, and the end of market protection in the 90s, the domestic industry was weakened and nearly led to extinction.

Regarding the governmental trajectory's impact on the development cycle of this industry, it is possible to notice a series of efforts, especially with the creation of the National Program of Microelectronics in 2003 and the Supporting Program for the Technological Development of the Semiconductor Industry and Displays - PADIS, in 2007. While the former program aimed to develop the academic area, especially research and postgraduate studies in Brazil, the latter aimed to assist development of the industry, especially in the R&D conducted in conjunction between industry and national research institutions.

It is also important to mention the contribution of our paper to the supply chain literature. By demonstrating the historical evolutionary path of the semiconductor industry in Brazil, we have been able to show how environmental factors, such as technology, economics and governmental actions can be related to and interfere with the development of a supply chain. By adopting an evolution theory perspective, we have been able to provide a macro perspective of the supply chain and demonstrate how it can be constrained by other factors, such those presented in this study. Thus, for a supply chain to emerge, it is necessary for there to be more than just companies capable of providing inputs for other companies.

Finally, it is important to mention that the Brazilian semiconductor industry is somewhat fragile, despite the efforts in the academic, governmental and business fields; it still has insufficient production to meet the needs of the national market. However, in the last five years, by attracting some international companies, especially from the United States and South Korea, the idea of owning a significant production of semiconductors in the following years, bringing new hope for the domestic industry, has begun to be revived.

REFERENCES

Adner, R., & Kapoor, R. (2010). Value creation in innovation ecosystems: How the structure of technological interdependence affects firm performance in new technology generations. *Strategic Management Journal, 31*, 306–333.

Brown, C., & G Linden (2005). Offshoring in the semiconductor industry: a historical trajectory. *Working Paper*, University of Berkely.

BNDES – Banco Nacional Desenvolvimento Economico e Social. (2004). *Estratégias para uma Indústria de Circuitos Integrados no Brasil.*

Chen, Injazz J., & Paulraj, Antony. (2004). Towards a theory of supply chain management: The constructs and measurements. *Journal of Operations Management, 22*, 119-150.

Choi, T. Y. & Hartley, J. L. (1996). An exploration of supplier selection practices across the supply chain. *Journal of Operations Management, 14*, 333-343.

Chopra, Sunil, & Meindl, Peter. (2007). *Supply chain management: Strategy, planning, and operation* (3th ed.). Upper Saddle River, NJ: Pearson Prentice Hall.

CI Brasil (2011). *Caderno Informativo. Secretaria de Política deInformática – SEPIN* - Ministério da Ciência, Tecnologia e Inovação. Brasilia: Letras & Artes Comunicação Integrada.

Cooke, P. (2001). Regional innovation systems, clusters, and the knowledge economy. *Industrial and Corporate Change, 10*, 945–974.

Croom, S., Romano, P. & Giannakis, M. (2000). Supply chain management: analytical framework critical literature review. *European Journal of Purchasing & Supply Chain Management, 6*, 7-83.

Crossan, M.M., Lane, H.W., & White, R.E. (1999). An organizational learning framework: from intuition to institution. *Academy of Management Review, 24*(3), 522-537.

Dahmen, D (1993). Semiconductors. In: *Developing the electronics industry*. Wellenius, B.; Miller, A; Dahman, C. World Bank Symposium, EUA.

Dosi, G (1982). Technological paradigms and technological trajectories: a suggested interpretation of the determinants and directions of technical change. *Research Policy, 11*, 147-162.

Dosi, G (1984). *Technical change and industrial transformation*. London:Macmillan

Dosi, G (1997). Opportunities, incentives and the collective patterns of technological change. *Economic Journal, 107*, 1530-1547.

Dosi, G. (2006). *Mudança Técnica e Transformação Industrial: A teoria e uma aplicação à indústria dos semicondutores*. Campinas: Editora da Unicamp.

Dosi, G., & Nelson, R. (1994). An introduction to evolutionary theories in economics. *Journal of Evolutionary Economics, 4*, 53-172.

Fawcett, S. E., Ellram, L.M., & Ogden, J.A. (2007). *Supply chain management: From vision to implementation*. Upper Saddle River, NJ: Pearson Education.

Fernandes, C. (2010). Cooperation between Knowledge Intensive Business Services and Universities: A Conceptual Model Proposal. *Advances In Management, 3*(6), 19-23.

Flynn, B. B., Huo, B. & Zhao, X. (2010). The impact of supply chain integration on performance: a contingency and configuration approach. *Journal of Operations Management, 28*, 58-71.

Freeman, C. (1982). The Economic Implications of Microeletronics. In: Agenda of Britain – 1: *Micro Policies – Choices for the 80s*, Cohen, C.D. (Ed). Londres: Philio Allen.

Freeman, C. (1989). New technology and catching up. *The European Journal of Development Research, 1*, 85-99.

Freeman, C. (1995). The national system of innovation in historical trajectory. *Cambridge Journal of Economics, 19*, 5-24.

Freeman, C., Harlow, C.J., & Fuller, J.K. (1965). Research and Development in Eletronics Capital Goods. *National Institute Economic Review, 34*, 1-14.

Freeman, C., & Perez, C. (1988). Structural crises of adjustment business cycles and investment behariour'. In: *Technical change and economic theory*, Dosi et al. (Eds.). Londres: Pinter.

Freeman, C., & Soete, L. (1987). *Technical Change And Full Employment*, Oxford: Blackwell.

Freeman, C. & Soete, L. (2008). *Economia da Inovação Industrial - Clássicos da Inovação*. Campinas: Unicamp.

Freitas, A. (2012). *Innovation Police and the Competitive Advantage of Nations: An Exploratory Case Study of Semiconductor Industry in Brazil*. MBA Thesis. Grenoble: Ecole de mangement.

Fisher, M. (2007). Strengthening the Empirical Base of Operations Management. *Manufacturing & Service Operations Management, 9*(4), 368–382.

Goldstein, H., & Drucker, J. (2006). The Economic Development Impacts of Universities on Regions: do size and distance matter? *Economic Development Quarterly, 20*; 22.

Griliches, Z. (1957). Hybrid Corn: an exploration in the economics of technological change.

Econometrics, 25(4), 501-522.

Gunawardane, G. (2012). Managing supplier to customer direct service triads in service supply chains: a case study. Journal of Supply Chain and Operations Management, 10 (2), 50-64.

Gutierrez, R. & Leal, C. (2004). *Estratégias para uma Indústria de Circuitos Integrados no Brasil. BNDES Setorial*.

Harland, Christine M., Lamming, Richard C., & Cousins, Paul D. (1999). Developing the concept of supply strategy. *International Journal of Operations & Production Management, 19*(7), 650-669.

Hippel, E. (1977). The dominant role of users in semiconductor and eletronic subassembly process innovation. In: *IEE Transactions on Enginering Management*. Massachussetts Institute of Technology.

Holbrook, D., & Cohen, C.J., Hounshell, D.A., & Klepper, S. (2000). The Nature, Sources, and Consequences of Firm Differences in the Early History of the Semiconductor Industry, *Strategic Management Journal, 21*, 1017–1041.

Kimura, A.K. (2005). Indentificação de Oportunidades para a Indústria Brasileira de Semicondutores através das teorias de vantagem competitiva e investimento Internacional. Unpublished *Dissertation*. Fundação Getúlio Vargas – FGV – Escola de Administração de Empresas de São Paulo.

Kuhn, T.S. (1970). *A Estrutura das Revoluções Científicas*. São Paulo: Editora Perspectiva.

Langlois, R., & Everett, M. (1982). What is Evolutionary Economics? In: *An evolutionary theory of economic change*. Nelson, R. and S Winter (Eds). Cambridge: Harvard University Press.

Li, Suhong, Rao, S. Subba, Ragu-Nathan, T.S., & Ragu-Nathan, Bhanu. (2005). Development and validation of a measurement instrument for studying supply chain management practices. *Journal of Operations Management, 23*, 618-641.

Lundvall, B.A. (1992). *National System of Innovation: towards a theory of innovation and interactive learning*. London: Pinter.

Mentzer, John, DeWitt, William, Keebler, James S., Min, Soonhong, Nix, Nancy W., Smith, Carlo D. (2001). Defining supply chain management. *Journal of Business Logistics, 22*(2), 1-25.

Meredith, J. (1998). Building operations management theory through case and field research. *Journal of Operations Management, 16*, 441–454

MCTI (Ministério da Ciência, tecnologia e Inovação). (2011). *CI -Brasil: Caderno Informativo*. Ministério da Ciência e Tecnologia.

Mowery, D. & Rosemberg, N. (2000). *Paths of Innovation: Technological Change in 20th-Century America*. Cambridge: Cambridge University Press.

Mowery, D. (1978). *The Semiconductor Industry*. Stanford: Stanford University.

Nelson, R.R. (1962). The Link Between Science and Invention: The case of the transistor. In: *National Bureau of Economic Research*. Cambridge: National Boureau

Nelson, R., & Winter, S. (1982). *An evolutionary theory of economic change*. Cambridge: Harvard University Press.

Nelson, R.R. 1986. Institutions Supporting Technical Advance in Industry. *The American Economic Review. 76*(2), 24-38.

Perez, C. (1999). *Technological change and opportunities for development as a moving target*. Bangkok: UNCTAD TD(X)RT.1/9.

Ruttan, V.W. (1997). Induced innovation, evolutionary theory and path dependence: sources of technical change. *Economic Journal, 107*, 1520-1529.

Schoenherr, T., Power, D., Narasimhan, R. & Samson, D. (2012). Competitive capabilities among manufacturing plants in developing, emerging, and industrialzed countries: a comparative analysis. *Decision Sciences, 43* (1), 37-71.

Schumpeter, J.A. (1934). *The theory of economic development*. Cambridge: Harvard University Press.

SIA. Semiconductor Industry Association. (2010). Disponível em: <http://www.sia-online.org/news/2010/12/03/global-sales-reports-2010/global-semiconductor-sales-flat-month-on-month>.

Siggelkow, N. (2007). Persuasion with case studies. *Academy of Management Journal, 50*, 20 - 24.

Silva, A.L.G. (1985). *A indústria de componentes eletrônicos semicondutores: Padrão de Concorrencia Internacional e Inserção do Brasil*. Unpublished Dissertation, Universidade Estadual de Campinas – UNICAMP. Instituto de Economia.

Simon, H.S. (1945). *Administrative Behavior, A study of Decision-Making Processes in Administrative Organization*. New York: The Free Press.

Swart, J. (2010). *Presentation*. International Congress of Innovation, Porto Alegre, RS.

Tan, Keah Choon. (2001). A framework f supply chain management literature. *European Journal of Purchasing and Supply Management, 7*, 39-48.

Tavares, W.M.L. (2001). *A Indústria Eletrônica no Brasil e seu Impacto Sobre A Balança Comercial*. Brasília – DF: Consultoria Legislativa.

Teixeira, R., & Lacerda, D.P. (2010). Gestão da cadeia de suprimentos: Análise dos artigos publicados em alguns periódicos acadêmicos entre os anos de 2004 e 2006. *Gestão & Produção, 17*(1), 1-14.

Valor Econômico Jornal (2011). *HT Micron dá largada à produção de chip no país*. <http://www.cwaclipping.net//sistema/newsletter/visualizar/materia.php?security=b632809e98d7.65827.476205>.

Yin, R.K. (1989) *Case Study Research: Design and Methods*. USA: Sage Publications.

Wong, C. Y., Boon-itt, S. & Wong, C. W.Y. (2011). *The contingency effects of environmental uncertainty on the relationship between supply chain integration and operational performance. Journal of Operations Management, 29*, 604–615.

Zawislak, P.A. (2004). *O estágio da Inovação no Brasil*. Update. São Paulo,15.

2

What can business learn from humanitarian supply chains? The case of the Spanish red cross in Haiti

Angel Díaz
IE Business School
angel.diaz@ie.edu

Elcio Mendonça Tachizawa
Universidad Carlos III
elcio.mendonca@uc3m.es

ABSTRACT: This paper analyzes the response of the Spanish Red Cross to the 2010 earthquake in Haiti, looking for clues of the remarkable lean-agile performance of this organization, and how they could be applied to business operations. The paper first looks into the history and organization of the Red Cross, analyzing in more detail the deployment of the Spanish Red Cross in the 2010 earthquake in Haiti. Five clues to the performance of the Red Cross are identified: a global, multi-level organization; modularity; standardization; knowledge management; and flexible funding mechanisms. These findings are then put into the framework of humanitarian logistics. Finally, the possible extension of the findings to business operations is discussed.

Keywords: Humanitarian Operations, Lean and Agile Operations

1. INTRODUCTION

Humanitarian Logistics (HL) and disaster relief (DR) have gained increasing importance over the last years. A disaster is a disruption that physically affects a system as a whole and threatens its priorities and goals, and can be man-made (war) or natural (tsunami); sudden (earthquake) or slow (draught). HL is the response to such events: "the processes and systems involved in mobilizing people, resources, skills and knowledge to help vulnerable people affected by disasters" (Van Wassenhove, 2006). There is a vast potential in research that explores the interfaces between HL and commercial Logistics (Day, Melnyk, Larson, Davis & Whybark, 2012), especially concerning how such organizations respond to critical events (Gatignon, Van Wassenhove & Charles, 2010). In particular, this paper analyzes the response of the Spanish Red Cross to the 2010 earthquake in Haiti, looking for clues of the remarkable lean-agile performance of this organization, and how they could be applied to business operations.

Sadly, there is evidence that humanitarian help is under increased demand: since 1980 natural disasters show a clear upward trend, having cost 3.8 trillion dollars (World Bank, 2013). In the last years, the number of natural and man-made disasters has increased, affecting particularly those countries less prepared to face them. For instance, the World Bank reports that the yearly number of draughts, floods, earthquakes and tropical storms has doubled from 1980-1990 to 2000-2010, affecting principally South and East Asia. In a similar period (1995-2005), the magnitude of interventions realized by the United Nations Peacekeeping Forces has tripled, requiring in 2005 an average of 5,500 people in each of the 15 simultaneous missions it deployed. Similarly, statistics on the number of countries where United Nations intervention forces are stationed show a steadily rising trend (Díaz, Claes & Borla, 2007). This extraordinary increase in demand for humanitarian relief is accompanied by increased media exposure, paradoxically linked to a reduced media attention span: it is estimated that media interest in a disaster reduces sharply after one week, reducing the window of interest for capturing funds and volunteers. In consequence, the number of agencies and non-governmental organizations (NGO) that provide humanitarian relief has greatly expanded: from an estimated 30,000 NGOs worldwide, over 3,000 were present in Haiti prior to the 2010 earthquake. While many of these NGOs are very small, at least seven have annual budgets exceeding 1,000 billion dollars (International Red Cross–including national societies, UN Development Fund, World Food Program, UN Children Fund, World Health Organization, UN High Commission for Refugees, and World Vision International – Tatham & Pettit, 2010).

In parallel to the increase in humanitarian interventions, there has been a rise in academic interest. For example, Tatham & Pettit (2010) have edited a special issue of the International Journal of Physical Distribution & Logistics Management on humanitarian logistics; Tomasini & Van Wassenhove (2009) inventoried case study research on humanitarian logistics, and there is at least a new journal specifically dedicated to humanitarian logistics (Journal of Humanitarian Logistics and Supply Chain management). There is also an increasing interest about HL in the supply chain management literature (Oloruntoba & Gray, 2006; Papadakis, 2006; Maon, Lindgreen & Vanhamme, 2009; Adivar, Athan, Oflaç & Örten, 2010; Blecken, 2010; Wild & Zhou, 2011; Kunz, Reiner & Gold, 2014; Scholten, Scott & Fynes, 2014). The increased pressure on humanitarian interventions has produced a two-fold effect: i) the emergence of HL as an academic discipline, and ii) an accelerated learning process, resulting in lean-agile organizations analyzed in this paper.

Related to this aspect, researchers agree that commercial Logistics could learn from the experience accumulated by HL organizations. For example, HL organizations are used to work in extreme conditions, e.g. high demand uncertainty and poor infrastructure (Day et al, 2012). However, there is little empirical research on how commercial Logistics could benefit from this knowledge. This study aims at tackling this research gap. In order to investigate the applications of HL experience to commercial Logistics context, we analyze in this paper the response of the Spanish Red Cross (SRC) to the 2010 earthquake in Haiti. We are particularly interested in finding clues of the remarkable lean-agile performance of this organization, and how these principles could be applied to business operations. The paper is organized as follows: firstly, we review the structure of the International Red Cross (IRC) and analyze the deployment of the organization in Haiti. Following Van Wassenhove (2006)'s cycle of four phases of the disaster management, we focus our analysis on the phases of preparedness and response, inferring the key success factors of IRC interventions. Lastly, we discuss these findings in a lean-agile framework and the applicability of these to business organizations.

The contributions of this paper are in adding to the small body of empirical studies in the field of humanitarian logistics, in increasing the body of knowledge of lean-agility, and in offering insights into the application of humanitarian organizations logistics principles to business and commercial organizations.

2. LITERATURE REVIEW

2.1 What business and commercial logistics can learn from HL

Humanitarian supply chains have several characteristics that make it different from business and commercial (in the sense of trading) ones : (1) supply and demand uncertainty are much higher; (2) the shelf life is much shorter (weeks or months); (3) the supporting systems (e.g. transportation, telecommunications) may be unstable or not functional; (4) financial flows are unilateral and uncertain; (5) the set of decision-makers is larger and procedures are less clear; (6) suppliers and partners are often unknown in advance; (7) the volume of cargo transported is not stable, with spikes of demand and large periods of inactivity; (8) the social network and physical infrastructure may be damaged or not functioning at full capacity (Balcik, Beamon. Krejci, Muramatsu & Ramirez, 2010; Charles, Lauras & Van Wassenhove, 2010; Kovacs & Spens, 2007; Holguin-Veras, Jaller, Van Wassenhove, Pérez & Wachtendorf, 2012; Day et al, 2012; Wild & Zhou, 2011). The closest commercial supply chain to this type of situation would be the launch of a new, highly-demanded product with a short lifecycle (Holguin-Veras et al, 2012). Most importantly, humanitarian supply chain objectives include not only minimizing logistics costs (e.g. transportation, inventory, etc) as in commercial supply chains, but also have to consider the deprivation costs (i.e. the loss of well-being resulting from the lack of a good or service) (Holguin-Veras et al, 2012). In order to cope with those constraints, it is argued that humanitarian supply chains present a mix of lean and agile characteristics (Oloruntoba & Gray, 2006; Cozzolino, Rossi & Conforti, 2012). Thus, understanding how humanitarian supply chains are structured can provide important insights to commercial supply chains that want to be lean and agile. The structures of humanitarian supply chains can be much more efficient than commercial ones when responding to critical events (Holguin-Veras et al, 2012). Thus, commercial SCM apparently has a lot to learn from humanitarian supply chains.

Researchers recognize that the links between research in Operations Management (OM) and HL are still incipient (Iakovou, Vlachos, Keramydas & Partsch, 2014; Heaslip, 2015; Abidi, De Leew & Klumpp, 2015). A few studies have explored the HL characteristics that make them a source of insights to commercial ones. For example, Day et al (2012) claimed that HL can teach commercial logistics how to leverage knowledge and resources generated by convergence during an emergency, and how to build social capital rapidly in such circumstances – for example, when a firm is developing a supply chain to enter a new market. Furthermore, HL can provide guidance on supply chain management in the context of extreme demand and supply uncertainty (Charles et al, 2010; Day et al, 2012; Holguin-Veras et al; 2012).

Another potential HL contribution relates to emergent organizations i.e. the management of dynamic, transient supply chain structures such as those created during disasters (Day et al, 2012; Apte, Yoho, Greenfield, & Ingram, 2013). Humanitarian supply chains have to manage highly dynamic and informal networks. Especially in the post-disaster phase, thousands of supply chains may overlap and have to be coordinated, with different levels of expertise, priorities and organizational structures. The decision-making structure of humanitarian supply chains can outperform commercial ones with respect to efficiency (Holguin-Veras et al, 2012), for example by centralizing information at Regional Logistics Units (RLU) level. This centralization allows matching supply and demand and facilitates tracking items (Gatignon et al, 2010). Furthermore, Holguin-Veras et al (2012) argue that commercial supply chains could learn from humanitarian ones how to operate with damaged social networks in the case of a disaster. The damaged physical and virtual infrastructure of humanitarian supply chains requires to operate with additional constraints, for example, to deliver the products with a reduced transportation capacity. Indeed, the surge in demand during disasters often happens when the social networks and supporting systems are at their worst condition, which provides an extreme supply chain scenario (Holguín-Veras et al, 2012).

Another potential insight from HL relates to the standardization of processes (e.g. comparing bids or emitting a purchasing order) and products (e.g. IRC has a catalog of standard emergency items) that streamline SCM in large humanitarian organizations (Gatignon et al, 2010). And lastly, there is the possibility of learning how to improve traceability, by centralizing the information about relief items at regional logistics unit (RLU) level. With standard processes and systems worldwide, it is easier to follow tracking numbers for each item, create reports or monitor key performance indicators (Gatignon et al, 2010). This standardization simultaneously facilitates cost reduction and improves agility in critical situations, as explained in the next section.

2.2 Lean-agile paradigms

Humanitarian supply chains have to equilibrate the minimization of human suffering and quick response to disasters (agility), with the cost minimization and efficiency of resources (lean) (Holguín-Veras et al, 2012). In this section, the literature on leanness, agility and potential applications to HL is reviewed.

Leanness (Womack, Jones & Roos, 1990) is defined by Lamming (1996, p. 184) as "valued-adding processes unencumbered by waste". It means developing a value stream to eliminate all waste, including buffer stocks and time, and to ensure a level schedule (Aitken, Childerhouse, Christopher & Towill, 2005). In the context of the peace-keeping operations, leanness refers to avoiding peaks and troughs in field requirements. The leanness concept resonates with the concept of efficiency of operations (Mentzer & Konrad, 1991). There is evidence to suggest that level scheduling, combined with the elimination of waste (in terms of space and in time) has successfully delivered a wide range of products to those operations where financial resources are scarce (Aitken, Christopher & Towill, 2002). Humanitarian organizations, being limited in resources, need to be lean. But, at the same time, they need to respond very rapidly to customer needs, in order to reduce deprivation costs. Thus, agility is critical as well.

Agility is defined as Sharifi & Zhang (1999) as the ability to cope with unexpected challenges, to survive unprecedented threats of business environment, and to take advantage of changes as opportunities. It is an organization-wide capability that embraces organizational structures, information systems, logistics processes, and mindsets (Christopher & Towill, 2000). In order to be agile, commercial agile supply chains require market sensitivity (demand driven rather than forecast driven), virtual supply chains (information based rather than inven-

tory based), and process alignment (joint product development, common systems, and shared information). A greater reliance on suppliers and alliance partners is inevitable and, hence, a new style of relationship is essential. Along with process integration comes joint strategy determination, buyer/supplier teams, transparency of information, and even open-book accounting (Christopher, 2005).

Humanitarian organizations, particularly when responding to sudden disasters, have agility as a vital prerequisite for responsiveness. For example, one of the techniques used by humanitarian organizations to achieve agility is the pre-positioning of inventories. It consists in positioning supplies near where they are likely to be required, in order to better satisfy uncertain demand (Gatignon et al, 2010). It can be implemented together with postponement of committed inventory until customer orders are received (Bowersox et al, 1996), which allows the use of more accurate data about real demand. Postponement of recipient-specific deliveries has a positive impact on the speed of response and flexibility (Oloruntoba & Gray, 2006).

Agility can benefit several humanitarian supply chain flows (i.e. material, financial, information). For example, Oloruntoba & Gray (2006) argue that humanitarian supply chains can be agile with financial flows e.g. when attracting and managing funds from donors in disasters. Whereas information flow agility means making information about a disaster needs flow rapidly in the supply chain, material flow agility implies making aid get rapidly to where it is needed, in the correct quantity and quality.

The literature supports the notion that the concepts of leanness and agility can be combined. This notion applies to HL, as well. For example, Oloruntoba & Grey (2006) propose a 'leagility' model for humanitarian supply chains. According to this model, humanitarian supply chains should be lean for upstream activities (e.g. sourcing, disaster preparation and planning), and agile for downstream activities (e.g. aid distribution). Agility and leanness also depend on the stage of HL life cycle. In disaster response and short-term recovery phases, the focus is on agility, because of the chaotic context and high urgency, whereas in the long-term recovery phase the focus is on leanness, because of the stable context and low urgency (Holguín-Veras et al, 2012). For that reason, large humanitarian organizations that actuate in all phases of a disaster are potential candidates to provide relevant knowledge on how to manage leanness and agility aspects of SCM.

3. METHODOLOGY

In order to gather data for the study, we used a case study methodology, grounded on interviews and archival research (Yin, 2014). There is a growing trend of using qualitative studies in top journals in Operations Management (Barratt et al, 2011; Ketokivi & Choi, 2014). In spite of that, the number of empirical studies in HL is "pitifully small" (Holguin-Veras et al, 2012). We used a single-case methodology, in order to gather data with sufficient depth to meaningful conclusions. Eisenhardt (1989) and Yin (2014) argue that case study research uses a theoretical or biased sampling approach, where cases are chosen for theoretical reasons rather than statistical sampling. In particular, the selected organization is one of the largest and most efficient humanitarian organizations in the world. Since the objective of the study was to collect information that could be applied in commercial supply chains, the focus on a single case is indicated, because it allows an in-depth exploration of the particularities that make this firm particularly successful. Furthermore, single case studies are recommended if they represent opportunities for unusual research access (Yin, 2014). In the present study, Haiti was the focal organization's largest humanitarian operation ever, and thus offered an ideal opportunity to investigate the concepts proposed in the research design.

Several data sources were used in this study: mainly, structured interviews and archival sources (documents, organizational charts, and historical records). This allowed the triangulation of multiple data sources, increasing the reliability of the conclusions (Eisenhardt, 1989).

Based on the literature analysis on lean-agility and humanitarian operations, question guidelines were prepared concerning the organization of the IRC and its deployment practices in case of intervention, focusing on the experience of the earthquake in Haiti. An extensive interview took place in October 2013 with the Deputy Director if international cooperation and an emergency specialist who participated in the operation in Haiti. This data was then triangulated against archival record, in particular those in the extensive on-line library of IRC, and also published academic papers. The sources consulted are detailed in the reference section, specifying web references in a separate section. Following Glaser & Strauss (1967), data analysis was done in parallel with data collection, and adjustments were made from the addition of data sources in existing case studies (Burgelman, 1983).

Finally, with respect to the organization of results, a descriptive case write-up was prepared, following the recommendations of Yin (2014). This procedure is critical to the creation of insights, by making researchers think about 'what the emerging issues are and how they should be captured' (Barratt, Choi & Li, 2011, p. 331). The case write-up is described in the next section.

4. CASE WRITE-UP

4.1 A brief history of the Red Cross: the remarkable achievement of Henri Dunant

In 1859 a young Swiss man, Henri Dunant, traveled to northern Italy trying to obtain some business documents he needed from the French Emperor Napoleon III. What he saw after his arrival at the little village of Solferino changed his life, and resulted in a remarkable humanitarian institution.

On June 24 of that year the joint armies of France battled the forces of the Austrian army engaged in a long and gruesome battle, in which close to 300,000 men were involved, resulted in thousands of casualties. The suffering was witnessed by Dunant in the aftermath of the battle. This terrible experience moved Dunant to write an account of the battle, "*Un Souvenir de Solferino*", published in 1862, in which he describes the chaos and suffering of the wounded, and proposes the creation of a neutral organization to provide care for wounded soldiers. By the following year a committee of five members met for the first time, thus marking 2013 as the 150th anniversary of the Red Cross. A year later, 12 states signed the First Geneva Convention in a diplomatic conference organized by the Swiss Parliament. Henri Dunant's efforts were recognized in 1901, when he became the first winner of the Nobel Prize for Peace (jointly with Frédéric Passy, co-founder of the Inter-Parliamentary Union).

The Red Cross became a truly international organization through the terrible ordeals of the 20th century: World War I and II and numerous regional conflicts (Turkish-Greek, Upper Silesia, Manchuria and Shanghai, the Chaco war, Spanish civil war). In the second half of the 20th century the organization expanded geographically to its current presence in 188 countries, and also extended its intervention scope to disaster relief and prevention, as described in this paper: the World Disaster Report of the Red Cross references over 500 disasters per year.

The Spanish Red Cross was already present in the French-Prussian war in 1870, and was very active in the Spanish Civil War of 1936–1939, honoring the principle of impartiality. The Spanish Red Cross is active in the fields of healthcare, environment, social exclusion and international cooperation, which includes the humanitarian activities analyzed in this paper. Remarkably, and in spite of the recent economic crisis and a stagnated budget, the Spanish Red Cross has been able to increase activities.

4.2 SCM & Logistics organization of the IRC

The IRCRC is organized in multiple regional levels. At the highest level is the International Committee of the Red Cross (ICRC): the original institution founded in 1863 in Geneva, Switzerland, by Henry Dunant and Gustave Moynier, a three times Nobel Prize winner institution and currently a policy making body with a 25-member committee. The ICRC is an impartial, neutral and independent organization with the exclusively humanitarian mission to protect the lives and dignity of victims of war and internal violence and to provide assistance. Its main tasks are to direct and coordinate the international relief activities of the International Movement and to prevent suffering by promoting and strengthening humanitarian law and universal humanitarian principles.

At an executive level is the International Federation of Red Cross and Red Crescent Societies (IFRC), founded in 1919 and which today coordinates the activities of the 188 National Red Cross and Red Crescent Societies. Founded in 1919 in Paris, it brings together the different national societies of the Red Cross and Red Crescent in cooperation and help. Its main tasks are to provide humanitarian assistance to affected populations in emergency situations caused by natural disasters or humanitarian crises, facilitating cooperation between National Societies and contributing to the development of local capacities of these companies through development. Finally, at the local level there are 188 National Societies recognized by the ICRC, volunteer relief agencies that cooperate with local authorities. Their tasks are to offer local and immediate support in accidents, emergency and social services and assistance to people affected by war and disasters.

Tomasini & Van Wassenhove (2009) proposed a cycle of four sequential phases of disaster management: preparedness, response, rehabilitation, and mitigation. The activities of the International Red Cross (IRC) fall under all these categories, as it engages not only in preventive activities and primary health care, but also in disaster preparedness and response. Prevention can have a significant role in reducing the aftermaths of disasters. For instance, the earthquake that struck Chile recently, in spite of being 500 times higher in intensity than the one in Haiti did a fraction of the damage due to much better prevention measures in Chile (Swiss Re, 2014). However, in this paper we focus on the first two phases (preparation for disasters and response).

This hierarchical and global organization is supported in humanitarian interventions by two specialized groups. The first one is the Field Assessment Coordination Team (FACT), which is formed by small international teams of highly trained professionals in specific areas such as logistics, health, communication and finance and who are deployed between 12 and 24 hours after the onset of the disaster and kept in the field from 2 to 4 weeks. The second type of group is the Emergency Response Unit (ERU), which corresponds to a modular system for rapid intervention in case of disaster, composed of teams of highly specialized resources. The idea of the ERU evolved from the growing complexity and demand of humanitarian operations, and was first deployed in 1994. It is noteworthy that Spain contributes to five of the seven ERU, in spite of having the lowest GDP per capita of all contributing countries (OECD, 2012). The current ERU, their functions and contributing countries are listed in Table 1 below.

Table 1: IRC Emergency response units

ERU	Function	Location
Logistics	Procurement of relief items, clearance, storage and distribution	Denmark, France, Spain, Switzerland, and UK
Water & sanitation	Treatment & distribution of water. 3 modules: up to 15,000 and 40,000 beneficiaries; and sanitation facilities for up to 20,000 people	Austria, Germany, Spain, Sweden, and UK
Basic health care	Immediate healthcare, mostly outpatient for up to 30,000 people	Finland, France, Germany, Japan, Norway, Spain plus staff support from Australia, Canada, Hong Kong, Iceland and Switzerland
Referral hospital	Inpatient first level referral hospital for up to 250,000 people	Finland, Germany and Norway
IT & Telecommunications	Links field & secretariat to assist operational coordination using satellite phones and high frequency & very high frequency radio systems	Austria, Denmark, Spain and USA
Relief	Distribution of relief items	Benelux, Denmark, Spain and USA
Base Camp	Provides acceptable living conditions for RC personnel	Denmark

In cases of disaster or humanitarian emergency, the Red Cross applies the following protocol:

1. The IFRC deploys the FACT teams. These perform a field evaluation and prepare a Relief Mobilization Table, with an initial estimation of required resources.

2. As a result of the evaluation, the IFRC in Geneva calls the National Societies mobilization and releases an emergency funds appeal to potential donors. The information form FACT is also used to determine the ERU required.

3. Based on the FACT report the National Societies with ERU evaluate their availability and inform the IFRC, who takes the final deployment decision.

4. Once in the field, the ERU contacts the National Society concerned, which provides services to the extent of its possibilities.

The IRC must at all moments act according to its entrenched principles: respect for the State sovereignty (who may decide not to allow entrance to humanitarian aid); to ensure an equal distribution of the relief, and neutrality and impartiality (fundamental in cases of civil war).

4.3 January 12, 2010: Earthquake in Haiti

On January 12, 2010 at 17:00 an earthquake of magnitude 7.3 hit Haiti, the poorest country in the Americas. Over 220,000 people died, 300,000 were wounded, more than 1 million people were left homeless, and all major infrastructures in the country were destroyed. The major cities, including the Capital, Port Au Prince, were seriously damaged. At least 105,000 houses were entirely destroyed; 60 percent of the Government and administrative buildings were damaged; total loss has been estimated at $7.8 billion, more than 120 percent of Haiti's 2009 gross domestic product (Battini et al, 2014).

The Spanish Red Cross (SRC), as other national societies, already had representatives in Haiti carrying development and disaster awareness projects.

They expected, from the feedback provided by these employees, and from their years of experience, that such a big earthquake will have devastating consequences in a fragile country like Haiti.

Amid the chaos, Haiti's national Red Cross society appealed to the International Federation of Red Cross Societies (IFRC) for help (interventions are triggered by the national societies). That night in Geneva, one hour after the news of the earthquake arrives, a first meeting of the field assessment coordination team (FACT) is held, and a FACT team is deployed within 10 hours. In less than 72 hours, an emergency funds appeal was launched, containing a preliminary evaluation of damages.

The SRC was one of the national societies answering to this call. News of the earthquake arrived at Madrid at approximately 22:00 hours. The members of the humanitarian intervention teams in the SRC hurried to their quarters, where they waited for further information and instructions from the IFRC in Geneva. In Madrid, two members of the SRC humanitarian intervention team went to Barajas airport and got into the first flight leaving for Dominican Republic, the neighboring country to Haiti.

Within a day, the SRC sent to Haiti further experts and equipment, in coordination with the IFRC. Other national societies, humanitarian NGOs and international organizations were also present in the field. The SRC, acting in coordination with the IFRC, then deployed three Emergency Response Units (water, sanitation and telecommunications), which were field-operative in less than 72 hours.

5. DISCUSSION

The following success factors of the IRC operations in Haiti have been inferred from the case analysis and archival research:

5.1 Global multi-echelon organization

Governance of large, decentralized organizations is a complex issue. The IRC addresses these issues through a hierarchical organization at three levels (local, regional and central, as described in the previous section), that mimics the global and hierarchical nature of many multinational companies and which allows for centralized coordination combined with local intervention. Appeals for help and information flows bottom-up (from the national societies), while large scale support for intervention flows top-down.

It is noteworthy that in the case of Haiti the local society suffered considerable damage (including the death of some members and their families) which complicated the initial appraisal of the situation.

On the field, governance must frequently adopt a relational model (Zaheer & Venkatraman, 1995), but this is complicated by the large number of involved actors. Kovacs & Spens (2007) cite as the main actors in humanitarian supply chains the aid agencies, logistics providers, donors, other NGO (non-governmental organizations), local governments and the military forces. Accordingly, field coordination among the many actors deployed in disasters is systematically cited as one of the main difficulties found. In a documented case (Tatham & Pettit, 2010) a coordination meeting of the water and sanitation cluster was attended by representatives from 172 organizations. Clearly, effective coordination and decision making is impossible under such circumstances. Analyzing the lessons of nephrology relief in Haiti, Portilla, Shaffer, Okusa, Mehrhotra, Molitoris, Bunchman & Ibrahim (2010) conclude that "centralized coordination between multiple responding entities at the disaster site and around the world will facilitate disaster relief efforts". As large scale crisis, such as Haiti, receive wider exposure thanks to new communications means (internet, tweeter), the fast reaction of many uncoordinated groups create serious confusion and overload of resources in the field. For instance, unrequested donations can rapidly overwhelm limited or damaged logistic infrastructures. Interaction with local governments can be also tricky, as the IRC has to respect the principle of sovereignty; and the relation among different NGOs can be reportedly competitive (as they compete for the same donor resources). To make matters worse, a growing number of well-wishing but not professionally trained collaborators that have to be accommodated, sheltered and protected.

Clearly, humanitarian operations could profit from additional coordination of supra-organizational mechanisms. That role is increasingly taken by the United Nations Office for the Coordination of Humanitarian Affairs (UNOCHA), which serves as the secretariat for inter-agency coordination with other UN units, such as the Inter-Agency Standing Committee, such as the United Nations Disaster Assessment and Coordination system, and the International Search and Rescue Advisory Group (the two latter units are rapid-response tools). Information technology can also play a role in facilitating coordination mechanisms. Figure 1 shows some of these actors in the context of the Red Cross.

Figure 1. Complexities of field coordination of humanitarian interventions

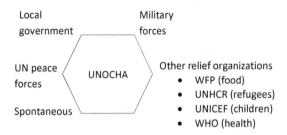

5.2 Standardization

The IRC adopts two kinds of standardization: product and process. *Product standardization* means that the same products are purchased at a global level, no matter the geographic region where it is going to be used. It is reflected in the number of stock keeping units (SKU), which are kept low at about 4,000 (Tatham & Pettit, 2010). That figure is significantly lower than a regular retailer (about 50,000), but comparable to convenience chains such as Seven-Eleven. The reduction in SKU carries the well-known advantage of risk pooling (resulting in less stock) and better relations with suppliers (the IRC has a standardized purchasing catalog that facilitates purchasing power and coordination). Product standardization contributes to leanness by allowing economies of scale in material acquisition and stochastic economies. In parallel, economies of scope increase process productivity. Product standardization, combined with supplier certification, also contributes to reducing purchasing lead time, increasing the capacity of responding quickly to demand.

In parallel, *process standardization* means that the procedures (e.g. shipping, warehousing) are defined at a global level and do not change significantly for each geographical area. The IRC has developed extensive Standard Operations procedures (SOP) and developed the Emergency Response Units (ERU) described in Table 1. The process standardization contributes to leanness because it accelerates the learning curve in the organization, reducing the costs of operation. At the same time, it has an indirect effect over agility, because the same team may be instantly assigned to different geographical areas, reducing the time of response.

The ERU are designed to fill the gaps created by the collapse or overload of a country existing systems. They can

be dispatched within 24 hours, and be field-operational within a week. Each ERU is self-contained in specially designed color-coded containers, and includes the necessary survival equipment for a staff of 3 to 25 people. The IFRC uses multiple criteria to decide on the deployment of the ERU (for example, the magnitude of the disaster and its evolution; needs of victims; capacity of the RC in the country concerned; and the inadequacy of local resources to adequately address the disaster).

Although standardization has been traditionally seen in the OM literature as an approach to achieve cost effectiveness, it seems to be highly dependent on the organizational context (Kwon, 2008). The observation of the experience of RC illustrates how the particular context of humanitarian global operations can affect standardization strategies. More importantly, it shows how a firm can obtain both cost effectiveness and agility in a global organization context by combining product and process standardization.

5.3 Modularity

Modularity is the possibility of combining a limited set of components, so that multiple product configurations can be obtained (Salvador, 2007). This allows simultaneously addressing heterogeneous customer needs (Hsuan & Skjøtt-Larsen) and component standardization (Sanchez, 1999). Although there has been considerable research about modularity in the production of goods, little is known about it in the context of services (De Blok, Meijboom, Luijkx, Schols & Schroeder, 2014).

Of particular interest for this study are the definitions of *component* i.e. 'the smallest elements in which a service offering can be meaningfully divided', and *service package* i.e. 'one or more components that together provide a complete service offering to the customer' (De Blok et al, 2014, p. 176). In this context, the ERU can be considered a 'component', and its different combinations represent 'service packages', which are customized according to particular needs (e.g. a disaster situation may require sanitation services, whereas another may prioritize food supplies). Thus, the ERU emulates the typical modular design systems used in manufacturing, but applied in the context of service management.

Accordingly, the use of ERUs allows the postponement of final product configuration according to specific need detected by the FACT, which improves the capacity of response. At the same time, costs are kept low (since the ERU are standardized). Accordingly, it has many similitudes with a Build-To-Order (BTO) production system, in which the final product is configured from different combination of basic modules (e.g. ERU), in order to satisfy a particular request (e.g. disaster-related needs). Thus, this example illustrates how BTO and postponement strategies can be applied in service operations.

5.3 Knowledge management

Knowledge management has received increasing attention from SCM researchers, who suggest that its effectiveness is highly dependent on supply chain partners' experiences, languages and contexts (Capó-Vicedo, Mula & Capó, 2011). In particular, there is need for empirical studies that describe the contexts that affect knowledge management in supply chains, notably the industry sector influence.

With that respect, the humanitarian operations context provides some particular features that may be useful to OM researches. For example, uncertainty concerning the moment, location and impact of disasters (due to confusion in the field) make forecasting and planning in humanitarian organizations very complex. The Red Cross has created mechanisms oriented to the systematic creation of an organizational memory that can facilitate more precise forecasting for deployment and budgeting processes. Knowledge management is handled internally, through the identification of projects and interventions that represent good practices; and externally, through the disclosure of this internal knowledge to the rest of society (as was the case of this investigation), and also through numerous publications, conferences and training courses offered to the general population.

5.4 Funding mechanisms

Although global supply chains increasingly rely on financial processes to coordinate the flow of goods, services and money, the implementation of financial supply chains has not been fully addressed in the SCM literature (Blackman, Holland & Westcott, 2013). Thus, it is very important to analyze supply chains that are able to provide useful insights on such coordination mechanisms. The studied company faces considerable challenges with that respect, having to coordinate several global financial flows, in conditions of extreme uncertainty of demand, supply and financial resources. Thus, it provides some interesting insights that could be used in a commercial Logistics context.

For example, the IRC has developed funding mechanisms that permit the maintenance of a basic, buffer budget, while quickly obtaining larger funds for specific actuations. The funds raised by the Red Cross originate from donations and voluntary contributions from governments (contributing to over 80% of all funds); national societies; supranational organizations (e.g. European Community) and public and private sources (companies, foundations and individuals –many of whom contribute by participating in the Red Cross lotteries). A form of non-monetary funding is the voluntary work of thousands of specialists (known as financing in kind–"*financiación en especie*", in Spain)

The Red Cross has two types of funding mechanisms: the Annual Appeal, sent at the beginning of each year to fund programs and that is used to cover the basic operations, and the Emergency Appeals, published throughout the year in response to disasters and that represent the large majority of the funding received. It is noteworthy that at peaks the emergency funds, obtained in response to specific disaster appeals can be 3 to 4 times larger than the regular funds (Tattham & Pettit, 2010).

Therefore, with respect to financial flows, the IRC can be characterized as being simultaneously agile at the funding process (helped to a great degree by the prestige of the organization), and lean (operational costs are reduced, due to product and process standardization, support from local governments and extensive voluntary work).

5.5 Leanness-agility

There has been much debate during the last decade with respect to the relative merits of the so-called "lean" and "agile" paradigms in SCM. Combining leanness and agility means, for example, having volume flexibility i.e. 'the ability to increase capacity up or down to meet demand for a single service' (Kesavan, Staats & Gilland, 2014, p. 1884), with minimal increment in costs. Although increasingly valued in several sectors, there are few empirical studies on volume flexibility in the services context (Kevasan et al, 2014). Our case analysis shows that volume flexibility is achieved by RC through the use of voluntary workforce, which is activated in case of emergencies. Before the disaster, the professional workforce is kept at minimal levels. When a disaster strikes, the workforce increases suddenly, mainly with volunteers. Furthermore, facilities cost of operation is minimal, because they are often donated by local governments. This combination of factors allows achieving minimal cost and volume flexibility simultaneously.

In addition, moving from 'lean' to 'agile' state is facilitated by maintaining a 'dormant capacity' in disaster-prone areas, through development programs. Actually, IRC is dedicated not only to disaster response, but also to long-term development activities in the affected areas. Thus, there are often trained personnel in the area, who can be instantly activated, speeding up the response process in the case of a disaster (Day et al, 2012).

'Leagility' is also achieved through the use of financial and material buffers: *Material buffers* are represented by the pre-positioning of stocks in Regional Logistics Units. They help stabilize supply and thus contribute to the level scheduling approach. *Financial buffers* are represented by the Disaster Relief Emergency Fund (DREF), centralized by the IFRC. The DREF is a fund with no specific allocation, used as a buffer to ensure the availability of financial support for immediate response to emergencies. In 2012, CHF 23 million of DREF were allocated. Funding allocations may be authorized and issued within 24 hours. Funds to launch local operations are considered loans that must be repaid with contributions received once the Emergency appeal has produced results. This financial buffer helps stabilize financial flow and reduce funding uncertainty, contributing to the leanness of operations. Another mechanism for lean-agility in deployment is through public-private partnerships (PPP). The Disaster Response Team (DRT) of DHL, developed in coordination with the UNOCHA is one of such emerging partnerships (DHL, 2014).

Being agile at the upstream side of supply chains is also a matter of concern to RC. Broadly speaking, the pre-positioning of stock, the use of ERU modules, supplier certification and standardization of products have contributed to reduce supply uncertainty. Rather than attempting to forecast a demand that is naturally hard to predict, the 'leagile' approach described in this study is characterized by increasing the speed of response by using postponement of deliveries. Moreover, it relies on 'supplier hubs'

(i.e. logistics centers near final assembly). In particular, the RC has Regional Logistics Units that are located close to disaster-prone areas (Canary Islands, Panama, Kuala Lampur, and Dubai) and that keep pre-positioned stocks of the main emergency items.

These principles illustrate how HL knowledge can be useful for commercial Logistics that want to achieve leanness and agility simultaneously. For example, we learn from the RC experience that such firms should struggle to be lean by keeping fixed costs at a minimal level. At the same time, firms should build a diversified set of buffers of 'quickly-activating' resources (e.g. material, workforce and financial), in order to be prepared in case of surges of demand. Furthermore, they should keep a 'dormant capacity' (i.e. marginal but constant operations) close to sites where demand surges are most likely to occur. Finally, we observe from the RC experience how many of manufacturing concepts such as modularization and standardization can also be applied to service operations.

6. Conclusion

This study aimed at contributing to the nascent body of empirical studies in the field of humanitarian logistics. In particular, it has analyzed the utilization of logistics principles of a global humanitarian organization to business and commercial firms. More specifically, we concluded that the IRC has developed innovative solutions to the problems posed by an environment characterized by the uncertainty and scarcity of resources. On the demand side, it is responsive, thanks to the pre-positioning of strategic stocks and to the development of the ERUs, both facilitated by its global, multilevel organization. On the supply side, it is resilient, thanks to process and product standardization, global coordination and the development of flexible mechanisms for emergency funding. The governance mechanisms of the IRC are internally hierarchical, but become relational while on the field. The latter mechanisms are especially problematic, due to the complexity of field interactions, and have attracted considerable interest in recent literature. Table 2 summarizes some of the characteristics and practices that facilitate leagility in the IRC, and that can in many case resonate with private organizations.

Table 2: SCM and logistics characteristics and practices of the IRC

Red Cross characteristics	
Global multi-level organization	A multi-level global organization allows bottom-up flow of information and a top-down global and fast deployment of resources
Standardization	The standardization of SOP and ERU, and SKU and supplier reduction facilitate risk pooling, purchasing power and fast deployment
Knowledge management	Internal and external mechanisms of archival and diffusion of experiences facilitate preparedness in face of extremely uncertain demand
Funding mechanisms	The multi-level organization and the credibility of the institution facilitate maintaining lean levels of a basic, operating budget, and an agile access to emergency funds
Coordination and governance	Hierarchical coordination mechanisms implicit in the multilevel global organization, and emerging relational governance mechanisms through UNOCHA
Lean-agile principles	Leanness implicit in basic funding and in rationalization of logistics (SKU, ERU); agility facilitated by ERU and a global organization. PPP can contribute to both

In a global business environment characterized by increased uncertainty brought by globalization and technological change, and by market-driven reduced life-cycles, the solutions developed by the RC and other humanitarian organizations can bring many managerial insights: for example, how to develop organizations that are both resources-lean and capable of fast adaptation. This can be applied in an analogous context, e.g. during the introduction of new products, or in conditions of extreme supply or demand uncertainty. In these situations, there are many strategies that could be considered, based on the RC experience (e.g. maintain a dormant capacity with easily accessible resources, to standardize processes and products worldwide). Similarly, the important issue of material convergence, present in humanitarian supply chains, resembles the typical problem of disposal of returned products in reverse logistics. Firms struggle with trying to combine both direct and reverse logistics flows. Lastly, we have verified that the application of HL to service context presents many research opportunities. Actually, recent studies recognize that there is a need for a re-conceptualization of HL to include services, and particularly there is a dramatic lack of studies on how services OM theories can be adapted for humanitarian OM research (Heaslip, 2015).

The application of humanitarian supply chain knowledge to this issue is a fertile ground for more empirical studies. These examples illustrate the many opportunities related to exploring such links between HL and commercial Logistics. Overall, we hope that empirical studies like this will help develop knowledge on this promising area of research.

Coda: the never ending story. In November 2013 Typhoon Haiyan hits the Philippines affecting 10 million people. In coordination with the IFR and the national RC, the Spanish Red Cross deploys its water and sanitation ERU (WATSAN) and estimates that will have to stay in the country for up to two years…

We acknowledge the generous support of Jaime Bará Viñas and Cristina Castillo of the Spanish

Red Cross in the realization of this research.

7. REFERENCES

Abidi, H., de Leeuw, S. & Klumpp, M. (2015). The value of fourth-party logistics services in the humanitarian supply chain. *Journal of Humanitarian Logistics & Supply Chain Management*, 5(1), 35-60.

Adivar, B., Atan, T., Oflaç, B. S. & Örten, T. (2010). Improving social welfare chain using optimal planning model. *Supply Chain Management: An International Journal*, 15(4), 290-305.

Aitken, J., Christopher, M., & Towill, D. (2002). Understanding, implementing and exploiting agility and leanness. *International Journal of Logistics, Research and Applications*, 5(3), 59-74.

Aitken J., Childerhouse, P., Christopher M., & Towill D. (2005). Designing and Managing Multiple Pipelines. *Journal of Business Logistic*, 26(2), 73-96.

Apte, A, Yoho, K., Greenfield, C. & Ingram, C. (2013). Selecting Maritime Disaster Response Capabilities. *Journal of Operations and Supply Chain Management*, 6(2), 40-58.

Balcik, B., Beamon, B. M., Krejci, C. C., Muramatsu, K. M., & Ramirez, M. (2010). Coordination in humanitarian relief chains: practices, challenges and opportunities. *International Journal of Production Economics*, 126(1), 22-34.

Barratt, M., Choi, T. Y., & Li, M. (2011). Qualitative case studies in operations management: trends, research outcomes and future research implications. *Journal of Operations Management*, 29(4), 329-342.

Battini, D., Peretti, U., Persona, A. & Sgarbossa, F. (2014). Application of humanitarian last mile distribution model. *Journal of Humanitarian Logistics & Supply Chain Management*, 4(1), 131-148.

Blecken, A. (2010). Supply chain process modeling for humanitarian organizations. *International Journal of Physical Distribution & Logistics Management*, 40(8/9), 675-692.

Blackman, I. D., Holland, C. P. & Westcott, T. (2013). Motorola's global financial supply chain strategy. *Supply Chain Management: An International Journal*, 18(2), 132-147.

Bowersox, D. J., Closs, D. J., & Helferich, O. K. (1996). *Logistical management*. New York, NY: McGraw-Hill.

Burgelman, R. (1983). A process model of internal corporate venturing in a major diversified firm. *Administrative Science Quarterly*, 28(2), 223–244.

Capó-Vicedo, J., Mula, J. & Capó, J. (2011). A social network-based organizational model for improving knowledge management in supply chains. *Supply Chain Management: An International Journal*, 16(4), 284-293.

Charles, A., Lauras, M., & Van Wassenhove, L. (2010). A model to define and assess the agility of supply chains: building on humanitarian experience. *International Journal of Physical Distribution & Logistics Management*, 40(8/9), 722-741.

Christopher M. & Towill D. (2000). Supply chain migration from lean and functional to agile and customized". *International Journal of Supply Chain Management*, 5(4), 206-213.

Christopher, M. (2005). *Logistics and supply chain management: creating value-adding networks.* Financial Times Prentice Hall, Upper Saddle River, NJ

Cozzolino, A., Rossi, S., & Conforti, A. (2012). Agile and lean principles in the humanitarian supply chain: the case of the United Nations World Food Programme. *Journal of Humanitarian Logistics & Supply Chain Management*,

Day, J. M., Melnyk, S. A., Larson, P. D., Davis, E. W., & Whybark, D. C. (2012). Humanitarian and disaster relief supply chains: A matter of life and death, *Journal of Supply Chain Management*, 48(2), 21-36.

De Blok, C., Meijboom, B., Luijkx, K., Schols, J., & Schroeder, R. (2014). Interfaces in service modularity: A typology developed in modular health care provision. *Journal of Operations Management*, 32(4), 175-189.

Díaz, A., Claes, B., & Borla, G. (2007). Streamlining Humanitarian Relief Operations. The Case of United Nations Peace Keeping Operations. *Proceedings of the POMS Conference*, Dallas.

Eisenhardt, K. M. (1989). Building theories from case study research. *Academy of management review*, 14 (4), 532-550.

Gatignon, A., Van Wassenhove, L. N., & Charles, A. (2010). The Yogyakarta earthquake: Humanitarian relief through IFRC's decentralized supply chain. *International Journal of Production Economics*, 126(1), 102-110.

Glaser, B., & Strauss, A. (1967). *The Discovery of Grounded Theory: Strategies For Qualitative Research.* Wiedenfeld & Nicholson, London.

Heaslip, G. (2015)- Humanitarian Logistics: An opportunity for service research. *Journal of Humanitarian Logistics & Supply Chain Management*, 5(1), 2-11.

Holguín-Veras, J., Jaller, M., Van Wassenhove, L. N., Pérez, N., & Wachtendorf, T. (2012). On the unique features of post-disaster humanitarian logistics. *Journal of Operations Management*, 30(7), 494-506.

Hsuan, J., & Skjøtt-Larsen, T. (2004). Supply chain integration: implications for mass customization, modularization & postponement strategies. *Production Planning Control*, 15(4), 352–361.

Iakovou, E., Vlachos, D., Keramydas, C. & Partsch, D. (2014). Dual sourcing for mitigating humanitarian supply chain disruptions. *Journal of Humanitarian Logistics and Supply Chain Management*, 4(2), 245-264.

Kesavan, S., Staats, B. R. & Gilland, W. (2014). Volume flexibility in services: The costs & benefits of flexible labor resources. *Management Science*, 60(8), 1884-1906.

Ketokivi, M., & Choi, T. (2014). Renaissance of case research as a scientific method. *Journal of Operations Management*, 32(5), 232-240.

Kovacs, G. & Spens, K. (2007). Humanitarian logistics in disaster relief operations. *International Journal of Physical Distribution & Logistics Management*, 37(2), 99-114.

Kunz, N.; Reiner, G. & Gold, S. (2014). Investing in disaster management capabilities versus pre-positioning inventory: A new approach to disaster preparedness. *International Journal of Production Economics*, 157(1), 261-272.

Kwon, S. W. (2008). Does the standardization process matter? A study of cost effectiveness in hospital drug formularies. *Management Science*, 54(6), 1065-1079.

Lamming, R. (1996). Squaring lean supply with supply chain management. *International Journal of Operations & Production Management*, 16(2), 183-196.

Maon, F., Lindgreen, A., & Vanhamme, J. (2009). Developing supply chains in disaster relief operations through cross-sector socially oriented collaborations: a theoretical model. *Supply Chain Management: An International Journal*, 14(2), 149-164.

Mentzer J., & Konrad, B. (1991). An Efficiency/Effectiveness approach to Logistics Performance Measurement. *Journal of Business Logistics*, 19(2), 33-62.

Oloruntoba, R. & Gray, R. (2006). Humanitarian aid: an agile supply chain? *Supply Chain Management: An International Journal*, 11(2), 115-120.

Papadakis, I. S. (2006). Financial performance of supply chains after disruptions: an event study. *Supply Chain Management: An International Journal*, 11(1), 25-33.

Portilla, D., Shaffer, R., Okusa, M., Mehrotra, R., Molitoris, B., Bunchman, T., & Ibrahim, T. (2010). Lessons from Haiti on Disaster Relief. *Clinical Journal of the American Society of Nephrology*, 5(11), 2122-2129.

Salvador, F. (2007). Toward a product system modularity construct: literature review and reconceptualization. *IEEE Transactions on Engineering Management*, 54(2), 219–240.

Sanchez, R. (1999). Modular architectures in the marketing process. *Journal of Marketing*, 63(4), 92–111.

Scholten, K., Scott, P., & Fynes, B. (2014). Mitigation processes–antecedents for building supply chain resilience. *Supply Chain Management: An International Journal*, 19(2), 211-228.

Sharifi, H. & Zhang, Z. (1999). A methodology for achieving agility in manufacturing organisations: an introduction. *International Journal of Production Economics*, 62(1), 7–22.

Tatham, P. & Pettit, S. (2010). Transforming humanitarian logistics: the journey to supply network management. *International Journal of Physical Distribution & Logistics Management*, 40(8/9), 609-622.

Tomasini, R. & Van Wassenhove, L. (2009). From preparedness to partnerships: case study research on humanitarian logistics. *International Transactions in Operational Research*, 16(5), 549–559.

Van Wassenhove L. (2006). Memorial Lecture: Humanitarian aid logistics: supply chain management in high gear. *Journal of the Operational Research Society*, 57(5), 475-489.

Wild, N. & Zhou, L. (2011). Ethical procurement strategies for international aid non-government organisations. *Supply Chain Management: An International Journal*, 16(2), 110-127.

Womack, J. P., Jones, D. T. & Roos, D. (1990). *The machine that changed the world*. Simon & Schuster, New York, NY.

Yin, R. K. (2014). *Case study research: Design & methods*. Sage publications, Thousand Oaks, CA.

Zaheer, A. & Venkatraman, N. (1995). Relational governance as an interorganizational strategy: an empirical test of the role of trust in economic exchange. *Strategic Management Journal*, 16(5), 373-392.

Main archival documents consulted in the WEB:

DHL, Disaster Response Teams: http://www.dpdhl.com/en/responsibility/corporate_citizenship/disaster_management/disaster_response_drt.html

IFRC, Annual Report 2013: https://www.ifrc.org/Global/Documents/Secretariat/201411/IFRC%20Annual%20Report%202013_FINAL.pdf

IFRC, Disaster Management: http://www.ifrc.org/en/what-we-do/disaster-management/responding/

IFRC, Disaster response and contingency planning guide: https://www.ifrc.org/Global/Publications/disasters/disaster-response-en.pdf

IFRC, Disaster Risk management in Haiti RC –Midterm evaluation: www.ifrc.org/en/publications-and-reports/evaluations/

IFRC, Emergency response units (ERU): https://www.ifrc.org/Global/Publications/disasters/117600-eru-brochure-en.pdf

IFRC, Field Assessment Coordination Team (Fact): http://ifrc.org/fact

IFRC, Global logistics services: http://www.ifrc.org/what-we-do/logistics/

IFRC, Haiti earthquake 4 years progress report: https://www.ifrc.org/PageFiles/60580/Haiti%204-year%20progress%20report-EN-LR.pdf

IFRC, Haiti earthquake one year progress report: http://www.ifrc.org/Global/Publications/disasters/208400-First%20anniversary%20Haiti%20EQ%20operation%20report_16b.pdf

IFRC, Haiti emergency appeal: http://www.ifrc.org/docs/appeals/10/MDRHT008PrelimAppeal.pdf

IFRC, Haiti from tragedy to opportunity: https://www.ifrc.org/Global/Publications/disasters/192600-Haiti-report-EN.pdf

IFRC, World Disaster Report 2013: http://worlddisastersreport.org/en/

OECD Statistics 2012: http://stats.oecd.org/

Swiss Re, "Chile earthquake expected to be a major insurance event": http://www.swissre.com/rethinking/chile_earthquake_expected_to_be_a_major_insurance_event.html

World Bank, "Building resilience. Integrating Climate & Disaster Risk into Development", https://www.documentcloud.org/documents/835955-wbg-2013-building-resilience.html

3

International partnership as a tool to R&D achievements

Felipe de Mattos Zarpelon
Universidade do Vale do Rio dos Sinos – UNISINOS
fmzarp@gmail.com

Iuri Gavronski
Universidade do Vale do Rio dos Sinos – UNISINOS
iuri@proxima.adm.br

ABSTRACT: Global competition emerges with a greater need for faster innovations. R&D plays an essential role in the elaboration of new products and processes in an even shorter period. As the access to resources and knowledge inside the own country borders are restricted, firms start to go abroad looking for other options of R&D. This way, international R&D partnerships arise as an important theme for theory and practice. Through a systematic literature review of 31 papers published in management journals from 2002 to 2014, this study brings two streams of the literature. First, a description of the main concepts in international R&D partnerships. Second, the best practices for the theme proposed and the gaps in the area's knowledge. This paper contributes to both practitioners and literature by providing a research agenda with seven themes for future research, regarding in-depth studies, secondary data analysis, measure proposal and managerial implications.

Keywords: International cooperation; inter-firm collaboration; coopetition; innovation; R&D partnerships; R&D alliances; global operations; research agenda; R&D achievements.

1. INTRODUCTION

In a context of the global market with a great emphasis on knowledge-based activities and products, firms are struggling to make innovations at a faster pace. In this scenario, research and development (R&D) is placed as a centre activity to seek new products and perspectives for the market. Since the 1980's firms have increased their investments in this activity to speed up the pace of innovation and diversify their technological capabilities (Miotti and Sachwald, 2003).

Although R&D might be an internal activity, cooperative agreements in such area have been used to develop and integrate knowledge in the innovation process (Autant-Bernard et al., 2007). Cooperation is positively related to a firm's innovativeness, resulting in superior performance (Facó and Csillag, 2010). Network relationships with suppliers, customers and intermediaries such as professional and trade associations are relevant factors affecting innovation performance and productivity (Pittaway et al., 2004). Firms dealing with growing outsourcing and various types of technological partnerships have built complex networks. This is explained partially by the imperfection of knowledge transactions that leads organisations to build up several kinds of alliances (Miotti and Sachwald, 2003). Regarding these imperfections, Hagedoorn (2002) pointed up that firms would have restrictions in sharing R&D because of the risk of information spillover. Anyway, coopetition (collaborating with competing firms) could be risky or beneficial on the alliance design options firms take with respect to market rivalry and their common and specialised knowledge (Ritala, 2009). Relations of trust are essential in the decision of dealing with more complex activities, such as R&D (Schreiber and Pinheiro, 2009). This is probably one of the reasons R&D partnering has become more popular in academic and press publication in recent years.

Technological knowledge has become more dispersed in the world, so international partnerships play an important role as an additional channel to access the main flows of technology (Duysters and Lokshin, 2011). The benefits of going overseas lay on the fact that these partnerships are more likely to bring diverse resources and capabilities to the alliance, because of different technology bases presented by the participants. On the other hand, international alliances bring on higher technology transfer costs and may be less useful in the joint effort of co-ordinating respective technologies (Kim and Song, 2007). A debate must be taken to understand the importance of international R&D partnerships and the reasons that lead firms to go forward this direction.

Despite the importance of the theme, there is little research on joint knowledge creation across partners (Bouncken and Teichert, 2013), and we have found no research agenda regarding international R&D partnerships. To fill this gap, we have three related objectives: describe the main concepts in international R&D partnerships, identify the best practices for international R&D partnerships, and propose a research agenda for international R&D partnerships. To achieve such objectives, we built a systematic literature review, according to the guidelines from Seuring and Gold (2012).

The literature reviewed has provided a better understanding of the international R&D partnerships and has also identified opportunities for future research. As a research agenda, we have identified opportunities for both empirical and conceptual work. We suggest in-depth studies on commitment, previous links, definition of objectives, trust and partners' reputation, stated as primary conditions for a successful R&D partnership. We also recommend practical developments for international R&D partnerships for small and medium enterprises and for managing a complex portfolio of partners. We also advocate that measures for supplier capacity and joint patents, and the update of studies about the trends on R&D partnerships (Bojanowski, Corten and Westbrock, 2012; Hagedoorn, 2002) would complement the extant literature. This way, the study contributes to the knowledge in the area and to practitioners as well.

Our paper has six sections, including this introduction. In the next section, we provide the methodological procedures conducted throughout the study. Section 3 presents the main contributions from conceptual papers in international R&D partnerships. Section 4 shows the findings from empirical papers on best practices for international R&D partnerships. Section 5 discusses the results of our systematic literature review, and section 6 brings some conclusion about the research.

2. METHODS

Seuring and Gold (2012) conducted a literature review based on a content analysis of 22 literature reviews of seven sub-fields of supply chain management (SCM). Concerned with reliability and validity, the authors suggested a systematic procedure built on four milestones: material collection, descriptive analysis, patterns of analytic categories and material evolution and research quality. This way they could draw a consistent map of SCM and its development in recent years.

As we intend to deepen and develop a research agenda for international R&D partnerships with proper reliability and replicability, we have chosen to follow the procedures conducted by Seuring and Gold (2012): material collection, descriptive analysis, patterns of analytic categories, and refinement.

2.1. Material collection

First of all, we have selected the unit of analysis as papers published in peer-reviewed journals, as they represent a primary mode of communication among researchers (Seuring and Gold, 2012). We delimited the material selected by the year of publication (from 2002 to 2014) reflecting the recent evolution of the theme. Besides, Hagedoorn (2002) has performed an extended overview through R&D partnerships since 1960, and a study assessing papers before 2002 could incur in redundancy.

The search was performed using the following key-words: international, global, R&D, research, cooperation, partnerships, networks and collaboration. We coded these keywords accordingly to the syntax of the search engines (for example, international AND R&D AND partnership*) and we searched in two on-line databases: ISI Web of Knowledge and EBSCO. We searched these keywords in the title, keywords and abstract. Additionally, the search was restricted to the "business economy" area. As a result, 50 papers were selected in the first place. After refining the search by reading the papers and reflecting over the appropriateness to the topic studied, the sample resulted in 31 papers.

2.2. Descriptive analysis

In this second step, information about the distribution of the papers across the years and journals was assessed (Figure 1). The evolution of the number of papers over the years shows a significant concentration of papers among the years 2004 and 2007, with a decrease of publications in the past three years. This sustains the argument of a need for a research agenda to keep growing the knowledge about the theme.

Figure 1. Description of the papers per year of publication and journal.

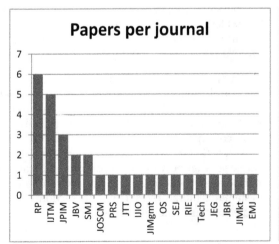

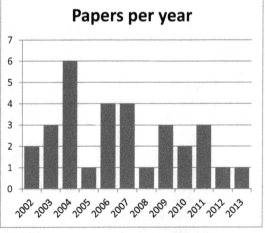

2.3. Patterns of analytic categories

In content analysis, categories must be defined to assess the data and classify the reviewed material. The options for defining categories derive from deductive paradigm – set before the analysis of the data – and inductive paradigm – categories emerge from the material assessed itself - (Eisenhardt, 1989). In our definition of categories, we accepted the suggestion of Seuring and Gold (2012) and develop two steps for categorization. First we have deductively pre-defined that papers should reflect the central concepts of international R&D partnerships and the best practices of international R&D partnerships. With this frame at hands, we intended to cover the literature on conceptual and empirical papers. Then, while analysing the material, new aspects emerged from conceptual papers and three categories were defined: benefits, eventual problems and capabilities required.

2.4. Material evolution and research quality

As we have conducted an inductive coding, it was necessary to establish a cycle of category refinement. Therefore, every time a new category emerged from the analysis, a discussion between the authors was steered, we would include this new category after reaching an agreement. Once the category was accepted, all the other papers were once again assessed.

To assure the analysis reliability, right after the assessment of the papers, the authors would meet and find a proper agreement over the interpretation of data. These procedures guarantee the reproducibility and reliability of the research.

3. THE MAIN CONCEPTS IN INTERNATIONAL R&D PARTNERSHIPS

In our literature review, we identified three main themes in the conceptual papers: benefits from international R&D partnerships, eventual problems in international R&D partnerships, and capabilities required for building and maintaining international R&D partnerships. We discuss them in the following sections.

3.1. Benefits

Strategic alliances play a significant role in developing global innovation (Zhang et al., 2010). Alliances enable firms to access capabilities and assets that are required to create, store and commercialize knowledge to generate new products (Rothaermel, Hitt and Jobe, 2006). Organisations establish relationships to access resources that they do not have themselves (Balland, Vaan and Boshma, 2013). This opportunity for combining capabilities from multiple sources is more relevant in international partnerships, because they are more likely to bring diverse resources and capabilities, which are not easy to access inside the firm's country (Kim and Song, 2007). Firms from all over the world are deliberately seeking partners with unique centres of excellence to advance their technological knowledge (Subramaniam, 2006). This way, international R&D partnerships form an additional channel to access the main flows of technology. International R&D partnerships are also seen as an alternative to access the local technology expertise (Duysters and Lokshin, 2011).

At the macro level, the international partnerships result in globe-spanning networks. Such networks can be a valuable source of international knowledge spillovers, or knowledge flows (Bojanowski, Corten and Westbrock, 2012), playing an important role in innovative R&D partnerships (Belderbos, Carree and Lokshin, 2004). Additionally, adaptation to local needs, lower costs of R&D personnel (Duysters and Lokshin, 2011) cost and risk sharing of the activity (Autant-Bernard et al., 2007) are also motivations for international R&D partnerships.

The motivations for international R&D partnerships vary among countries. American firms, for example, seek partnerships to be on the technological frontier; on the other hand, European firms pursue partnerships primarily to share R&D costs and resources (Miotti and Sachwald, 2003).

Besides proposing the motivations for international R&D partnerships, another stream of research defines a successful partnership in R&D. Kim and Song (2007), for example, suggested to measure an alliance in R&D by the number of joint patents, that is, the number of patents registered by both partners. While not all R&D efforts lead to patented intellectual property, that variable seems to be a reasonable proxy for the outcomes of the international R&D partnerships, as long as the patent registration occurs with partners from different countries.

3.2. Eventual problems

Despite all the advantages of international R&D partnerships, there are also points that require attention. Most partnerships occur among competitors in the product market. Therefore, the technology transfer cost is substantially higher as the firm develops its agreements (Kim and Song, 2007). When cooperative R&D is more successful, the higher the quality and quantity of external resources available, and the lower the transaction and coordination cost required for such arrangements (Okamuro, 2007).

Besides, the positive relationship between competition and knowledge acquisition cannot prevent, and in some cases even stimulates, opportunistic behaviour (Zhang, 2010). Opportunistic is seen as behaviour that, instead of maximizing the returns for the alliance partners, maximizes only the partner's own benefit, which is not necessarily the best interest of the partnership (Dickson, Weaver and Hoy, 2006). When the activities performed in the alliance are more extensive, interdependent, complex, and uncertain, the potential risk of opportunism is higher (Oxley and Sampson, 2004).

The literature suggests some ways to prevent opportunistic behaviours and reduce transaction and coordination costs. Commitment, previous links, the definition of objectives, trust and the partners' reputation are crucial to reduce these damages (Mora-Valentin, Montoro-Sanchez and Guerras-Martin, 2004). Opportunism is not seen as an imminent threat in industries with an institutional framework that decrease the possibility of a partner to make use of a dominant position, (Kastelli, Caloghirou and Ioannides, 2004). The experience of the firm also plays an important role, so experienced firms are more likely to be able to identify trustful collaborations and attract potential collaborators (Balland, Vaan and Boshma, 2013).

Teng (2007) propose some mechanisms to protect intellectual property. Equity arrangements, such as joint ventures or minority equity investments, are widely used to align partners' interests. Non-disclosure and non-compete agreements are contractual measures in which the partners agree to keep the intellectual property under confidentially. Also important, monitoring and auditing are ways to avoid the opportunistic behaviour.

On the contrary of what most managers think, the geographic distance is not so important to prevent opportunism. Autant-Bernard et al. (2007) suggest in their study that social distance (the number of links between each pair of firms) matters more than the geographic distance for a successful partnership.

Then, the higher the social distance, in other words, the lower the number of links between two firms, the higher will be the chance for an opportunistic behaviour.

3.3. Required capabilities

With the purpose of taking advantage of partnerships, there are some capabilities that must be reinforced and developed inside the firm. Rothaermel and Deeds (2006) suggested that the firms are pushed to establish multiple partnerships so that they have better access to resources and capabilities. On the other hand, because of the complexity of this venture, firms have to develop an alliance management capability, or the ability to manage multiple partnerships effectively. The success of a firm is directly related to this capability.

Another important ability to achieve success through international R&D partnerships is the absorptive capability (Autant-Bernard et al., 2007). Through this ability, a firm can identify the new information, assimilate it and apply it to its own process. This way, the creation of new technology can be facilitated by ensuring the positive side of the absorptive capability (Kim and Song, 2007).

The literature suggests that in order to maintain and develop successful international R&D partnerships it is necessary to have sufficiently open knowledge exchange (Bojanowski, Corten and Westbrock, 2012; Zhang et al., 2010; Kim and Song, 2007). On the other hand, it is a concern that this openness may cause opportunistic behaviour in the partnership (Dickson, Weaver and Hoy, 2006; Zhang, 2010). The trade-off between maintaining knowledge exchange between partners while controlling for unintended knowledge leakages brings an important challenge for participants in R&D partnerships. A response for that dilemma would be reducing the scope of the partnership. This way partners choose to limit the scope of alliance activities to those that can be successfully completed with limited (and carefully regulated) knowledge sharing. (Oxley and Sampson, 2004).

These main concepts bring the motivations, problems and capabilities that sustain the international R&D alliances. Table 1 summarizes the findings regarding the first objective of this paper. The next step is to show how to improve the capabilities though the best practices found in the literature.

Table 1. Main concepts from literature reviewed

Author	Year	Main concepts about international partnership for R&D
Zedtwitz and Gassmann	2002	The alliances are driven by two principal location rationales: access to market and access to science.
Miotti and Sachwald	2003	The main reasons to cooperate internationally depend on each country: Access to the technological frontier (USA), access to complementary R&D resources (France), share R&D costs (EU).
Belderbos, Caree and Lokshin	2004	The spillovers play an important role on innovative R&D partnerships.
Kastelli, I. Caloghirou, Y. Ioannides, S.	2004	In industries with a clear institutional framework with monitoring rules that reduce the possibility of a partner to make use of dominant position, opportunism does not seem to influence the benefits from cooperative R&D.
Oxley and Rachele	2004	The more extensive, interdependent, complex, and uncertain are the activities performed in the alliance, the greater is the potential risk of opportunism.
Veugelers and Cassiman	2005	Cooperating with universities is complementary to other innovation activities such as performing own R&D, sourcing public information and cooperating with other partners.
Dickson, Waever and Hoy	2006	Opportunistic behaviour is seen as behaviour that while designed to maximize the resources derived from an alliance by a participant to the alliance is not necessarily in the best interest of the alliance.
Subramaniam	2006	Firms are increasingly deliberately seeking partnerships with unique centres of excellence in order to advance their technological knowledge.
Rothaermel and Deeds	2006	The success of an international alliance for R&D depends on the alliance management capability
Kim and Song	2007	International alliances can create unique learning opportunities not typically available from the same country. On the other hand, there are higher technology transfer costs.
Autant-Bernard et. al.	2007	Geographic distance is not the main restriction to R&D partnership. Social distance is much restrictive in these matters.
Teng, B.	2007	As an output for R&D alliances, Intellectual property needs to be carefully selected and protected through mechanisms such as equity arrangement (joint ventures or minority equity investments), non-disclosure and non-compete agreements (keep intellectual property confidential), and monitoring and auditing.
Fink, M. Harms, R. Kraus, S.	2008	Self-commitment (the willingness of individuals to commit to cooperation with a partner without the safety net of controls or sanction mechanisms) is particularly important in international cooperation.
Colombo	2009	Alliance partners create an indirect link with the knowledge sources, making them more accessible to companies.

Zhang et. al.	2010	Firms can overcome resource constrains and achieve superior innovative performance not only by using internal resources but also by acquiring knowledge based capabilities from alliance partners.
Duysters and Lokshin	2011	Access to qualified R&D personnel at foreign locations, adaptation to local needs, lower costs of R&D personnel, and improved access to external knowledge at scientific competence centers located are the main motives for international alliances for R&D.
Bojanowski, Corten and Westbrock	2012	International partnerships for R&D result in a globe-spanning network that can be a valuable source of international knowledge spillovers.
Balland, Vaan and Boshma	2013	Experienced firms are more likely to be able to identify fruitful partnerships and attract potential partners.

4. BEST PRACTICES FOR INTERNATIONAL R&D PARTNERSHIPS

Literature shows the best practices for developing successful international R&D partnerships. Our review identified five of these best practices: development over previous experiences, relationship capabilities, international strategy, partner choice and governance mode. Past experience seems to be an important factor for a successful international R&D partnership. The alliance management capability is increased by recurrent experiences, making the firm more able to deal with multiple agreements (Rothaermel and Deeds, 2006). Besides, joint patents are more numerous when the partners have had previous ties (Kim and Song, 2007).

Relationship capabilities are recommended during the establishment and development stages. Managerial and organisational mechanisms must be promoted to facilitate a high degree of commitment, trust, dependence, good communication, and reduced level of conflict (Mora-Valentin, Montoro-Sanchez and Guerras-Martin, 2004). The tighter involvement of partners is determinant for sharing information and technology, but trust is the elementary variable for approaching (Petersen, Handfield and Ragartz, 2003). However, the degree of relation may vary according to the strategy, size and spread of actuation of each firm.

The international strategy adopted by multinationals suggests a local responsiveness through the development of international units of R&D. This way, the firms are able to interact with the local market and increase the knowledge exchange (Zedtwitz,

Gassmann and Boutellier, 2004). There is also a process with three stages identified by Liu, Wang and Zhang (2010) where the multinational increases the level of partnership. The first stage is called ethnocentric centralized R&D (with a dominant R&D centre serving far away markets), then evolves for a geocentric centralized R&D (where the R&D centre engages in cooperative projects with customers and other research institutes), and the last one is an R&D hub model (with the R&D centre serving as the central information and decision-making platform for all global R&D units).

International R&D partnerships are not only exclusive to multinationals and greatest firms. High-tech start-ups also take advantage of this strategy when observing two important factors: a) the partnership must involve firms located in a variety of countries, and b) these countries must be closer to the best world knowledge sources (Colombo et al. 2009). Furthermore, small and medium enterprises must pay particular attention to opportunistic behaviour in R&D partnerships, so the analysis of a potential partner should be even more exhaustive (Dickson, Weaver and Hoy, 2006).

In terms of choice of the partner, there seems to be a variety of factors that may influence this decision, but the objective of the partnership is the starting point. Once the firm has established its goal, the partner's country and the partner itself can be chosen simultaneously. This way, if a firm looks for high technology, it will choose an American or East Asian firm as a partner, especially in sectors in which these countries exhibit comparative advantage, because this way the firm is able to access complementary R&D resources close to the technological frontier (Miotti and Sachwald, 2003). Data from 40 years of international R&D partnerships shows that 99% of R&D partnerships involved at least one firm from North America, Europe or East of Asia (Hagedoorn, 2002). In a study of Chinese multinationals, Liu, Wang and Zheng (2010) identified that strategic R&D partnerships always involve at least one firm from developed or in developing countries. Therefore, it is clear that the centre of knowledge for R&D resides on developed countries and companies from less developed regions seek to begin and maintain agreements to access this core of knowledge.

In addition, the similarity of the firms, in terms of both technological and market profiles, and the familiarity through past interactions are usually regarded in the partners' choice (Vonortas and Okamura, 2009). This decision considers also R&D specific factors such as the quality of input (local talent, engaging in local scientific cooperation, etc.), the quality of expected output (cooperation with local customers and local development, market proximity, etc.), and R&D-external factors (tax optimization, reliability and stability of the local political and social system, and image enhancement) (Zedtwitz and Gassmann, 2002).

Besides partners' country, there are multiple options of partner types to be allied to, and a broad portfolio in terms of options of alliances helps innovations in R&D (Duysters and Lokshin, 2011). Competitors, suppliers, consumers, universities and research institutes are some options to build a partnership (Belderbos, Carree and Lokshin, 2004). Customers and universities are important knowledge sources for radical innovations. Further, the spillovers are more frequent when the firm is allied to universities or research institutes (Belderbos, Carree and Lokshin, 2004). The establishment of partnerships with universities is not very common in international alliances, albeit it is also sustained by the subsidized cost-sharing in public-private partnerships (Veugelers and Cassiman, 2005). Partnerships with suppliers help in development processes. This form of R&D partnership is studied mainly for its use by Japanese firms. Through cooperation, suppliers may increase their knowledge about product and processes. Moreover, sharing information and supplier involvement in internal teams result in better outcomes and technology uncertainty mitigation. Anyway, only trusted suppliers with a long experience

and proven track record are approached (Petersen, Handfield and Ragartz, 2003).

In terms of how to establish the partnership, the literature suggests mergers, acquisitions, joint ventures, or contractual agreements as strategic alternatives for joint R&D activities (Duysters and Lokshin, 2011). In the 1980's there was a trend for joint ventures, but in the 1990's on, the new trend seems to be the contractual agreements. Contractual R&D partnerships enable firms to increase their strategic flexibility through short-term joint R&D projects with a variety of partners. Another benefit from this flexibility is the cost sharing of R&D budget. (Hagedoorn, 2002). Anyway, in highly dynamic and knowledge-oriented industries (where the costs of R&D are higher), there is a substantially greater propensity for longer-term contracts than in other industries (Sytch, Tatarynowicz and Gulati, 2011). Joint ventures are the most likely governance mode when alliance objectives require partners to share complex and/or tacit knowledge, especially on innovative technology projects. When firms adopt an equity joint venture structure, the opportunistic behaviour can be mitigated due to the shared ownership (Oxley and Sampson, 2004). Zu et al. (2011) suggested another type of partnership by a research joint venture (RJV). In this partnership, the firms cooperate in R&D but compete in product markets. Also called horizontal alliances, these partnerships with competitors make a significant contribution to productivity gains in R&D (Oum et al., 2004). What is important in these ventures is a pairwise stable R&D, where both firms have the same strength in this activity. This way, opportunistic behaviour can be diminished (Zu et al., 2011). Zhang et al. (2010) added that inter-firm cooperation and competition coexist in strategic alliances and both factors increase knowledge acquisition, although from different motivational bases. A particular form of R&D partnership is studied by Geisler (2003) as an independent organisation formed by industry, government and university. The infrastructure of this cooperative organisation will affect the sustained performance of each member, by impacting the decisions to join, remain or terminate the membership.

These were the best practices identified in the literature reviewed. The partner choice depends on each objective and size of the firm. This way, a firm should first determine its goals with the partnership to be built and take self-awareness of its size to then, analyse the available options of partnering. Table 2 summarizes the main finding from the best practices.

Table 2. Best practices from literature reviewed

Author	Year	Best practices for international partnership for R&D
Hagedoorn	2002	In the 1980's there was a trend for joint ventures, but in the 1990's on the new trend are contractual agreements. Contractual R&D partnerships enable companies to increase their strategic flexibility through short-term joint R&D projects with a variety of partners. Another benefit from this flexibility is the cost sharing of R&D budget.
Miotti and Sachwald	2003	Companies must define their objectives with the international partnership. Once this is done, the partner and the country it comes from are simultaneously chosen.
Geisler, E.	2003	Industry, government and universities may form an independent organisation to coordinate joint R&D efforts. The infrastructure of cooperative organisations affects their sustained performance, by impacting the decisions to join, remain or terminate membership.
Belderbos, Caree and Lokshin	2004	Spillovers are more frequent and more powerful when the company is allied to a university or research institute.
Oxley and Rachele	2004	By adopting an equity joint venture structure, the hazards of opportunism can be mitigated because incentives are more closely aligned when ownership of the venture is shared.
Mora-Valentin, Montoro-Sanchez and Guerras-Martin	2004	Companies have to design managerial and organisational mechanisms that facilitate a high degree of commitment, trust, dependence, good communication, and reduced level of conflict.
Zedtwitz, Gassmann and Boutellier	2004	Development of units of R&D in foreign countries is a best practice for multinationals.
Oum et. al.	2004	Horizontal alliances make a significant contribution to productivity gains.
Veugelers and Cassiman	2005	This practice of allying to universities is also sustained by the subsidized cost-sharing in public-private partnerships.
Rothaermel and Deeds	2006	The alliance management capability is developed through recurrent experiences.
Colombo	2009	The greater the number of countries in which industrial partners are located and the closer these countries are to worldwide knowledge sources, the more positive the effect of the R&D alliances on firm performance.
Vonortas, N. Okamura, K.	2009	Firms are more likely to collaborate the closer they are in terms of both technological and market profiles, the higher the expected knowledge spillovers among them, the more familiar they are with each other through past interaction, and the more centrally located they are in knowledge networks
Zhang et. al.	2010	Inter-firm cooperation and competition coexist in strategic alliances and both factors increase knowledge acquisition, though from different motivational bases.

Liu, Wang and Zheng	2010	Seeking for international R&D, multinationals presented three stages: ethnocentric centralized R&D, geocentric centralized R&D and R&D hub model.
Duysters and Lokshin	2011	In international ventures, firms tend to prefer alliances to merges and acquisitions because of risk sharing. Innovators, different from imitators, tend to develop more alliances abroad.
Zu et al.	2011	Research joint ventures (RJV) where firms cooperate in R&D but compete in product markets, is an alternative type of partnership
Sytch, Tataryno-wicz and Gulati	2011	In highly dynamic and knowledge-oriented industries (where the costs of R&D are higher) there is a substantially greater propensity for extended contract than in other industries.

5. DISCUSSION AND RESEARCH AGENDA

The concepts reviewed were necessary to build a summarized knowledge on the international R&D partnerships theme. Besides, the best practices presented are mainly directed to managers who intend to go abroad into a search for potential R&D partners.

Access to and lower costs of qualified R&D personnel, adaptation to local needs and improved access to external knowledge at scientific competence centres located abroad are some of the reasons to build an international R&D partnership (Duysters and Lokshin, 2011). In some cases, the access to technological frontier (Miotti and Sachwald, 2008) and to unique opportunities of learning are only developed with partners abroad (Kim and Song, 2007). Anyhow, building an international partnership incurs in risks and costs that are not usually found in partnerships within the own country frontiers. Local taxes, reliability and stability of local political and social system (Zedtwitz and Gassmann, 2002), control, communication and hierarchy (Zedtwitz, Gassmann and Bouteller, 2004) affect the decision on international R&D partnerships. This means that the decision process of going abroad in a R&D partnership must be different from developing a R&D partnership with local companies, because they comprise different levels of complexity, risk and uncertainty.

The literature is extensive in demonstrating the main concepts about the international R&D partnership, but still, there are some gaps that were not found in the papers reviewed. Partnering with suppliers, for example, could be very positive for development, but not every supplier can be approached to the process (Petersen, Handfield and Ragartz, 2003).

Anyway, the literature does not display scientific measures to evaluate the capacity of suppliers to be allied to.

Joint patents are an important measure of R&D partnership achievements and have been increasing in recent years. Most research using joint patents as a variable had focused the pharmaceutical industry (Kim and Song, 2007). Anyway, due to the possibility to quantify the outcome of the R&D partnership, there is an excellent opportunity for further research on the theme, especially by proposing scales and applying them to a great diversity of industries.

Another gap identified regards the broadness of a portfolio of partners. It is known that a wide number of partners is beneficial to innovation ventures (Duysters and Lokshin, 2011), but this broadness, especially to firms who have partners from all over the globe, brings complexity to the management of the portfolio. The ways to deal with this complexity are not clear and need future research.

The primary conditions for success in R&D partnerships were established, but research has only started to exploit the theme. Commitment, previous links, the definition of objectives, trust and the partners' reputation are identified as main determinants of success (Mora-Valentin, Montoro-Sanchez and Guerras-Martin, 2004). Anyway, we have not identified an in-depth study on each of these factors, making this an opportunity to test what was proposed in the literature.

Furthermore, there are some longitudinal studies that show the trends of partnerships up to the beginning of the 2000's decade (Bojanowski, Corten and

Westbrock, 2012; Hagedoorn, 2002). Since then, the theme evolved substantially, and the number of partnerships has increased considerably (Kim and Song, 2007). As we have discussed here, firms are expanding their field of research to outside their country borders in a search for knowledge creation and competitiveness. Therefore, there is a good opportunity to update these studies and identify the new trends and data from international alliances of R&D.

The study over small and medium enterprises (SMEs) as international R&D partners has a long way to evolve. Research on SMEs mainly focus on strategies to avoid opportunism (Dickson, Weaver and Hoy, 2006) and transaction and coordination costs (Okamuro, 2007). It is known that high-technology start-ups are in the spotlight of R&D for small and medium enterprises (Colombo, 2009), but we have found very little literature regarding international R&D partnerships for this kind of firms. Broader studies, with an emphasis on understanding the dynamics of international R&D partnerships for SME, would contribute to the literature on international R&D partnerships.

The absorptive capability (Kim and Song, 2007; Autant-Bernard et al., 2007), or the inter-firm learning (Zhang et al., 2010) are shown as essential abilities a firm should have to take the benefits of international R&D partnerships. Nevertheless, the literature is not so clear about the best practices for developing these capabilities, making it into a gap for future studies.

To sum up, the international alliances of R&D make a fertile field for research. They are an increasingly relevant theme as the firms are in the race for innovation on a global scale. Besides, with a particular attention to the gaps in the literature, the knowledge about the field can evolve, making newer contributions to the theory and to the practitioners.

6. CONCLUSION

International R&D partnerships have become even more relevant in academic and press publication in recent years, but still we have found no research agenda in the literature. Firms can no longer treat knowledge creation only inside their borders, so by cooperation the opportunity of accessing external resources is open. An extensive literature has focused on understanding this phenomenon, but there are still gaps for future research. This way, our research has set three objectives: describe the main concepts in international R&D partnerships, identify the best

practices for international R&D partnerships, and propose a research agenda for international R&D partnerships.

As our first objective, we have described the main concepts in international R&D partnerships into three categories: benefits, eventual problems and capabilities required. The benefits stand the importance of going abroad in a search for complementary knowledge. Some of the benefits we identified are: access to state-of-the-art technology, cost sharing (Miotti and Sachwald, 2003), risk sharing (Autant-Bernard et al., 2007) and access to local technological expertise (Duysters and Lokshin, 2011). Despite those benefits, firms may face some issues in this venture, especially related to opportunism (Zhang, 2010). Capabilities to avoid opportunism and to take advantage of partnerships are relevant with a particular regard to absorptive capability (Autant-Bernard et al., 2007) and alliance management capability (Rothaermel and Deeds, 2006).

Identifying the best practices for international R&D partnerships was the second proposed objective. The exploitation of relational capabilities and experience (Rothaermel and Deeds, 2006; Mora-Valentin, Montoro-Sanchez and Guerras-Martin, 2004) were placed as some of the best practices for success in these ventures. Strategy, the choice of a partner and a country and formation of partnerships were also treated in the best practices section.

As gaps in the literature, we have found at least seven opportunities for complementary research. Although the literature suggests suppliers as a good opportunity to build R&D partnerships (Petersen, Handfield and Ragartz, 2003), no specific measures for evaluating the capacity of each supplier to contribute was proposed. Joint patents are another opportunity for scales development which little literature has covered yet. There are also some practical issues that were not fully developed in literature. For example: the ways to deal with a complex portfolio of partners, the dynamics of international R&D partnerships for SMEs and the development of absorptive capability and intra-firm learning. Also, the primary conditions for successful R&D partnerships need in-depth studies (Mora-Valentin, Montoro-Sanchez and Guerras-Martin, 2004). As a last opportunity identified, secondary data studies have shown the trend of international R&D partnerships up to the 2000's decade and must be updated.

Through these three objectives, we bring our contributions to the theory and practitioners. By defining a research agenda, we believe that future researchers have the opportunity to identify a path for complementary contributions to literature in such an important theme. Besides, practitioners may select a suitable strategic alternative among the best practices to take advantage of international R&D partnerships.

7. REFERENCES

Autant-Bernard, C., Billand P., Franchisse, D. and Massard, N. (2007) 'Social distance versus spatial distance in R&D cooperation: empirical evidence from European collaboration choices in micro and nanotechnologies', *Papers in Regional Science*, Vol. 86, No. 3, pp 495 – 519.

Balland, P-A., Vaan, M.D. and Boshma, R. (2013) 'The dynamics of interfirm networks along the industry life cycle: the case of the global video game industry, 1987–2007', *Journal of Economic Geography*, Vol. 13, No. 1, pp 741 – 765.

Belderbos, R., Carree, M. and Lokshin, B. (2004) 'Cooperative R&D and firm performance', *Research Policy*, Vol. 33, No. 1 pp 1477 – 1492.

Bojanowski, M., Corten, R. and Westbrock, B. (2012) 'The structure and dynamics of the global network of inter-firm R&D partnerships 1989–2002', *Journal of Technology Transfer*, Vol. 37, No. 1, pp 967 – 987.

Bouncken, R.B. and Teichert, T.A. (2013) 'Co-poiesis: the joint birth of knowledge across organizational boundaries', *International Journal of Innovation and Technology Management*, Vol. 10, No. 6, pp 1 – 25.

Colombo, M.G., Grilli, L., Murtino, S., Piscitello, L. and Piva, E. (2009) 'Effects of international R&D alliances on performance of high-tech start-ups: a longitudinal analysis', *Strategic Entrepreneurship Journal*, Vol. 3, No. 4, pp 346 – 368.

Dickson, P.H., Waever, K.M. and Hoy, F. (2006) 'Opportunism in R&D alliances of SMES: the roles of the institutional environment and SME size', *Journal of Business Venturing*, Vol. 21, No. 1, pp 487 – 513.

Duysters, G. and Lokshin, B. (2011) 'Determinants of alliance portfolio complexity and its effect on innovative performance of companies', *The Journal of Product Innovation Management*, Vol. 28, No. 1, pp 570 – 585.

Eisenhardt, K. (1989) 'Building theories from case study research', *Academy of Management Review*, Vol. 14 No. 4, pp 532 – 50.

Facó, J.F.B. and Csillag, J.M. (2010) 'Innovativeness of industry considering organizational slack and cooperation', *Journal of Operations and Supply Chain Management*, Vol. 3, No. 2, pp 108 – 120.

Fink, M., Harms R. and Kraus, S. (2008) 'Cooperative internationalization of SMEs: self-commitment as a success factor for international entrepreneurship', *European Management Journal*, Vol. 26, No. 1, pp 429 – 440.

Geisler, E. (2003) 'Benchmarking interorganisational technology cooperation: the link between infrastructure and sustained performance', *International Journal of Technology Management*, Vol. 25, No. 8, pp 675 – 702.

Hagedoorn, J. (2002) 'Inter-firm R&D partnerships: an overview of major trends and patters since 1960', *Research Policy*, Vol. 31, No. 1, pp 477 – 492.

Kastelli, I., Caloghirou, Y. and Ioannides, S. (2004) 'Cooperative R&D as a means for knowledge creation. Experience from European publicly funded partnerships', *International Journal of Technology Management*, Vol. 27, No. 8, pp 712 – 730.

Kim, C. and Song, J. (2007) 'Creating new technology through alliances: an empirical investigation of joint patents', *Technovation*, Vol. 27, No. 1, pp 461 – 470.

Liu, J., Wang, Y. and Zheng, G. (2010) 'Driving forces and organizational configurations of international R&D: the case of technology-intensive Chinese multinationals', *International Journal of Technology Management*, Vol. 51, No. 2/3/4, pp 409 – 426.

Miotti, L. and Sachwald F. (2003) 'Co-operative R&D: why and with whom? An integrated framework of analysis', *Research Policy*, Vol. 32, No. 1, pp 1481 – 1499.

Mora-Valentin, E.M., Montoro-Sanchez, A. and Guerras-Martin, L.A. (2004) 'Determining factors in the success of R&D cooperative agreements between firms and research organizations', *Research Policy*, Vol. 33, No. 1, pp 17 – 40.

Okamuro, H. (2007) 'Determinants of successful R&D cooperation in Japanese small businesses: The impact of organizational and contractual characteristics', *Research Policy*, Vol. 36, No.1, 1529 – 1544.

Oum, T.H., Park, J-H., Kim, K. and Yu, C. (2004) 'The effect of horizontal alliances on firm productivity and profitability: evidence from the global airline industry', *Journal of Business Research*, Vol. 57, No. 1, pp 844 – 853.

Oxley, J.E. and Sampson, R.C. (2004) 'The scope and governance of international R&D alliances', *Strategic Management Journal*, Vol. 25, No. 1, pp 723 – 749.

Petersen, K.J., Handfield, R.B. and Ragatz, G.L. (2003) 'A model of supplier integration into the new product development', *The Journal of Product Innovation Management*, Vol. 20, No. 1, pp 284 – 299.

Pittaway, L., Robertson, M., Munir, K., Denyer, D. and Neely, A. (2004) 'Networking and innovation: a systematic review of the evidence', *International Journal of Management Reviews*, Vol. 5, No. 3/4, pp 137 – 168.

Ritala, P. (2009) 'Is coopetion different from cooperation? The impact of market rivalry on value creation in alliances', *International Journal of Intellectual Property Management*, Vol. 3, No. 1, pp 39 – 55.

Rothaermel, F.T. and Deeds, D.L. (2006) 'Alliance type, alliance experience and alliance management capability in high-technology ventures', *Journal of Business Venture*, Vol. 21, No. 1, pp 429 – 460.

Rothaermel, F.T., Hitt, M.A. and Jobe, L.A. (2006) 'Balancing vertical integration and strategic outsourcing: effects on product portfolio, product success and firm performance', *Strategic Management Journal*, Vol. 21, No. 1, pp 369 – 386.

Schreiber, D. and Pinheiro, I.A. (2009) 'Outsourcing of R&D activities to Brazilian subsidiaries', *Journal of Operations and Supply Chain* Management, Vol. 2, No. 1, pp 31 – 45.

Seuring, S and Gold, S. (2012) 'Conducting content-analysis based literature review in supply chain management', *Supply Chain Management*, Vol. 17, No. 5, pp 544 – 555.

Subramaniam, M. (2006) "Integrating cross-border knowledge for transnational new product development", *Journal of Product Innovation Management*, Vol. 23, No.1, pp 541 – 555.

Sytch, M., Tatarynowicz, A. and Gulati, R. (2011) 'Toward a theory of extended contact: The incentives and opportunities for bridging across network communities', *Organization Science*, Vol. 23, No. 6, pp 1658 – 1681.

Teng, B-S. (2007) 'Managing intellectual property in R&D alliances', *International Journal of Technology Management*, Vol. 38, No. 1/2, pp 160 – 177.

Veugelers, R. and Cassiman, B. (2005) 'R&D cooperation between firms and universities. Some empirical evidence from Belgium manufacturing.' *International Journal of Industrial Organization*, Vol. 23, No.1, pp 355 – 379.

Vonortas, N.S. and Okamura, K. (2009) 'Research partners', *International Journal of Technology Management*, Vol. 46, No 3/4, pp 280 – 306.

Zedtwitz, M. and Gassmann, O. (2002) 'Market vs technology drive in R&D internationalization: four different patterns of managing research and development', *Research Policy*, Vol. 31, No. 1, pp 569 – 588.

Zedtwitz, M., Gassmann, O. and Boutellier, R. (2004) 'Organizing global R&D: challenges and dilemmas', *Journal of International Management*, Vol. 10, No. 1, pp 21-49.

Zhang, H., Shu, C., Jiang, X. and Malter A.J. (2010) 'Managing knowledge for innovation: The role of cooperation, competition and alliance nationality', *Journal of International Marketing*, Vol. 18, No. 4, pp 74 – 94.

Zu, L., Dong, B., Zhao, X. and Zhang, J. (2011) 'International R&D networks', *Review of International Economics*, Vol. 19, No. 2, pp 325 – 340.

4

Sustainable Supply Chain Management: a Literature review on Brazilian publications

Minelle Enéas da Silva
Federal University of Rio Grande do Sul
minele.adm@gmail.com

Daiane Mulling Neutzling
Universidade Feevale
daineutzling@gmail.com

Ana Paula Ferreira Alves
Federal University of Rio Grande do Sul
anapfalves@gmail.com

Patrícia Dias
Federal University of Rio Grande do Sul
patricia.pdias@gmail.com

Carlos Alberto Frantz dos Santos
Federal University of Rio Grande
carlosfrantz@hotmail.com

Luis Felipe Nascimento
Federal University of Rio Grande do Sul
lfmnascimento@ea.ufrgs.br

ABSTRACT: Based on the progress in the international research on sustainability and supply chains, this paper aims to analyze how the concept of Sustainable Supply Chain Management has been explored in papers published in major Brazilian journals and conference proceedings, especially regarding the research areas of operations management and sustainability. Recognizing the theme as incipient in Brazil, there are few published studies, mainly in relation to journals, with a total of 44 papers focused specifically on the topic. The literature review indicates that the understanding of the topic includes recurrent discussions with environmental or economic dimensions. However, a comprehensive definition of the concept, i.e., including social issues, is lacking. Therefore, this creates a research gap and an opportunity for Brazilian researchers to contribute to the gradually developing field.

Keywords: Supply Chain Management; Sustainability; Brazilian Publications.

1. INTRODUCTION

Nowadays, frequent changes have occurred in several industries and organizational environments, requiring firms to continuously adapt their strategies to remain competitive. These adaptations can be identified in the relationships that organizations establish with each other in consequence of the evident transformation related to integration, collaboration, and information sharing among these actors and their stakeholders. In fact, the importance of inter-organizational relationships for developing new features and capabilities for companies is increasingly under discussion, both from current and future perspectives.

Thus, relevance has been given to supply chain management (SCM), in which the emphasis of competitive relationships has shifted from companies to supply chains. This inter-firm integration has become a promising strategic area capable of generating value and competitiveness for those involved (Brito & Berardi, 2010). Over time, even though supply chain structures and business processes remain in their current form, the reasons why organizations sought integration along their supply chains have changed.

As indicated by Pagell and Schevchenko (2014), besides showing satisfactory economic performance, organizations have also been held accountable for upholding a positive social and environmental performance in relation to their operations and, indirectly, to their partners' and suppliers' activities. As a result, the current attention directed to supply chains is related mainly to a more efficient, innovative, and sustainable process management (Carter & Rogers, 2008; Tsoulfas & Pappis, 2006; Vachon & Mao, 2008; Vermeulen et al., 2010).

In parallel, the debates about sustainability are more widespread, since the individualistic characteristics are moving to a more collective perspective (Foladori, 2005). The inclusion of environmental and social issues in the economic debate has led to a wide range of concepts that have been applied to sustainability concerns in supply chain studies (Brito & Berardi, 2010). In many cases, focal companies have initially managed such environmental and social issues internally and over time started to involve a number of stakeholders in order to fulfill customer needs, either through networks or traditional SCM.

Discussions on the integration of sustainability strategies along the supply chain began to intensify

after the year 2000, with conceptual propositions based strongly on environmental and economic dimensions, e.g., Green Supply Chain Management (GSCM) (Sarkis, Zhu & Lai 2011; Srivastava, 2007; Zhu, Sarkis & Lai, 2007). Subsequently, the discussions were settled on the importance of considering the three dimensions of the Triple Bottom Line (TBL) (Elkington, 2002), presented alongside the concept of 'Sustainable Supply Chain Management' (Linton, Klassen & Jayaraman, 2007; Pagell & Wu, 2009; Seuring & Müller, 2008).

Their similarity has often led to a confusion regarding the use of these two concepts, mainly because it is still a new area of research and the initial studies usually refer to the terms "sustainability" and "environment" as synonymous (Ahi & Searcy, 2013; Carter & Easton, 2011; Seuring & Müller, 2008). Nevertheless, as research on "sustainability" advanced, international publications showed more clarity in using the TBL studies on supply chains (Ashby, Leat & Hudson-Smith, 2012; Beske, 2012; Carter & Easton, 2011; Carter & Rogers, 2008; Faisal, 2010; Markley & Davis, 2007; Pagell & Wu, 2009; Seuring & Müller, 2008; 2010).

Following the international debate, Brazil has also placed importance on sustainability management in the supply chain field. In the last years, a few researches have explored the importance of companies having projects on socio-environmental management integrated to their supply chains. To better analyze which issues in sustainability management have been explored in Brazilian supply chains, our paper presents the following research question: how have researchers explored the topic of sustainable supply chain management in major Brazilian academic conferences and journals so far?

The paper aims to analyze how the concept of Sustainable Supply Chain Management has been explored in papers published in major Brazilian journals and conference proceedings, especially regarding the research areas of operations management and sustainability.

We conducted a literature review on publications in selected national journals during a period of 15 years (2000-2014), totaling 37 Brazilian journals. Additionally, the proceedings of three national conferences related to operations management and sustainability were selected from a period of seven years (2008-2014).

As observed in the international scenario, this topic has increased in importance along the last years. New socio-environmental policies, stakeholders' requirements and consumer concerns about companies' actions are presented in most markets. This is also a result of supply chains being increasingly stablished in a global configuration. Many Brazilian companies are also part of these global supply chains and, therefore, it is natural that sustainability management will be part of their strategies over time. Studies exploring this empirical reality are in early stages and there is still much to be investigated. Thus, it is important to investigate what has been done and what is the potential for future research in the next years.

This paper is structured as follows: after this brief introduction, chapter two presents the concept of Sustainable Supply Chain Management and the main discussions in the field. In chapter three (method), we describe in detail how the literature review was carried out. In chapter four, we show the results and discussions. Finally, the conclusions from the analysis of data are revealed.

2. SUSTAINABLE SUPPLY CHAIN MANAGEMENT

Based on the current debates in operations research, supply chain management (SCM) and its relation to sustainability principles constitute a leading topic. Researchers have discussed the need for companies to manage aspects that go beyond the economic dimension, such as operational profitability and costs reduction. However, competitiveness and, in certain aspects, the availability of business, have to take into account the management of social and environmental aspects. Thus, by taking the precepts of the Triple Bottom Line (TBL) into SCM, the concept of Sustainable Supply Chain Management (SSCM) is derived(Linton et al., 2007; Seuring & Müller, 2008; Beske & Seuring, 2014; Seuring, 2011).

From discussions about sustainable supply chain management, the efficient management of processes along the supply chain should consider that sustainability needs to be analyzed not only on the basis of economic performance of the business but also of environmental and social performance (Ahi & Searcy, 2013; Beske, 2012; Beske & Seuring, 2014; Pagell & Schevchenko, 2014; Wolf, 2011). The evolution of supply chain management in relation to sustainability has shown greater clarification and con-

cern for the macroeconomic context of change, since businesses have become more complex in dealing with resources scarcity, greenhouse gas emissions, and consumers' awareness about labor issues.

The SSCM concept was widespread by Seuring and Müller's paper published in 2008. Based on an extensive literature review, the authors identified the need to address the strategic integration of the TBL dimensions into business. Thus, sustainable supply chain management is conceptualized as "the management of capital flows, materials and information, as well as cooperation between companies along the supply chain, seeking targets for the three dimensions: economic, environmental and social, which are requirements of customers and stakeholders" (Seuring & Müller, 2008, p.1700).

In the same vein, Pagell and Wu (2009, p.8) presented their contributions to the concept stating that a "sustainable supply chain should consider a good performance both in traditional measures of profit and loss, such as in the expanded conceptualization of performance with the inclusion of social and environmental dimensions". If a sustainable supply chain is one that performs well in all elements of the TBL, then SSCM refers to specific actions in terms of decision making and behavior changes towards the integration of social and environmental dimensions into the business management process, seeking to establish a more sustainable supply chain (Pagell & Wu, 2009).

Based on this understanding, in order to integrate sustainability objectives on the organizational and supply chain level, the initial impulse for corporate decisions comes from external pressures and stakeholder incentives (particularly customers and governments) (Seuring & Müller, 2008). According to these authors, when companies are under pressure, they tend to transfer part of it along their supply chains. Therefore, companies make use of two groups of strategies, which are: "supplier management for risks and performance" and "supply chain management for sustainable products" (Seuring & Müller, 2008).

On the one hand, companies will initially create sustainable strategies focused on the management of economic risks, long-term relationships and reduction of suppliers' base, creating win-win situations and positive performance in all the dimensions of the TBL along the supply chain (Beske, 2012). On the other hand, focal companies can also develop conditions to produce sustainable products, including all activities and inputs based on environmental and social standards in the manufacturing process (Seuring & Müller, 2008). The requirements based on a Life Cycle Analysis (LCA) also involve efficiency in the process of communication, integration, and cooperation with suppliers in the supply chain.

Regarding the introduction of practices of sustainability in supply chains, Pagell and Wu (2009) proposed a model based on the integration of new values and capabilities, as well as the development of new behaviors along the supply chain. Thus the organizational capacity to innovate linked to a sustainability orientation reflect new values internally, which should be incorporated into the SCM. In line with these considerations, companies will be considered proactive and committed if their business model is aligned with environmental and social elements of sustainability (Pagell & Wu, 2009; Wolf, 2011).

According to Pagell and Wu (2009), from a new orientation the emergence of new behaviors lead to a re-conceptualization of the supply chain and relationship continuity with suppliers. The authors highlight the integration of environmental agents, Non-Governmental Organizations (NGOs), community leaders, government agencies, and even competitors to evaluate opportunities and necessary changes along the chain. Regarding the continuity of relationships with suppliers, Pagell and Wu (2009) point out that long-term relationships facilitate transparency, traceability, certification and process of de-commoditization. Thus, the effective implementation of sustainability objectives in supply chains pervades the managerial decisions of the focal firm, responsible for defining action plans in different levels of interactions with its stakeholders.

Beske (2012) elucidated four main categories comprising the Sustainable Supply Chain Management concept, as follows: managerial orientation, continuity of the supply chain, risk management, and pro-activity. Following this research, Beske, Land and Seuring (2014) suggested a different approach to these categories. For them, a redefinition is necessary: strategic orientation, continuity, collaboration, risk management, and pro-activity (for sustainability). This change was conducted from a literature review including papers focused on the food industry. After that, Beske and Seuring (2014) presented a more advanced framework related to these categories. Now they are: orientation, continuity, collaboration, risk management, and pro-activity.

Also, three hierarchic levels are involved in the analysis of SSCM: strategic value, structure and processes. Beske and Seuring (2014) proposed to enhance the

analysis of sustainability in SCM, indicating theoretical consistence. Considering these discussions, it is clear that we have a sequence of international studies that demonstrate the advances in research on this topic. From all the previous considerations, in this study SSCM is understood as the management of capital flows, material, and information, as well as the cooperation between companies along the supply chain to achieve good performance in all elements of the TBL (economic, environmental, and social), as proposed by Elkington (2002), and to ultimately improve the sustainability of the supply chain.

In Brazil, many studies have discussed the importance of sustainability management in business (Junqueira, Maior & Pinheiro, 2011; Pereira et al., 2011; Silva et al., 2011). However, when it comes to linking sustainability dimensions to SCM, only a few studies address this topic (Abdalla & Barbieri, 2014; Adaime, Carvalho & Monzoni, 2011; Gonçalves-Dias, Labegalini & Csillag, 2012; Rocha et al., 2012). Considering this, our paper seeks to contribute to current discussions by analyzing the publications that approximate sustainability management to SCM. Also, this analysis allows us to identify the most studied issues in the Brazilian literature and contribute to future research on the topic.

3. METHOD

This paper aims to analyze how the concept of Sustainable Supply Chain Management has been explored in papers published in major Brazilian journals and conference proceedings, especially regarding the research areas of operations management and sustainability. The research consists in a literature review conducted in two steps. First, suitable material was collected. Second, using a qualitative approach, we analyzed how conformable the concepts presented in the selected papers were to the SSCM concept. We employed a bibliometric approach because it is a research design that can indicate the scientific contributions to a certain subject (Araújo, 2006).

We also used a descriptive analysis approach by means of discussions and reflexive analysis of the researchers involved. The data was collected from journals in the fields of Management, Accounting, and Tourism graded A2, B1, and B2, according to the Brazilian journal classification (Qualis Capes 2012), graded as totaling 37 journals, all published in Portuguese (see Table 1). It is noteworthy that there was no national journal with Qualis A1 available for selection.

Table 1: List of selected journals and their Qualis Classification 2012

Journal	Qualis	Journal	Qualis
Brazilian Business Review (Português)	A2	Revista de Negócios (Online)	B1
Gestão & Produção	A2	Revista Eletrônica de Administração	B1
Organização & Sociedade	A2	Revista Portuguesa e Brasileira de Gestão	B1
Revista de Administração Contemporânea	A2	Análise (PUCRS)	B2
Revista de Administração (SP)	A2	Base (UNISINOS)	B2
Revista de Administração de Empresas	A2	Contextus (Fortaleza)	B2
Revista de Administração Pública	A2	Economia & Gestão	B2
Cadernos EBAPE.BR (FGV)	B1	Pretexto (Belo Horizonte)	B2
Faces: Revista de Administração	B1	Revista Alcance	B2
Gestão & Regionalidade	B1	Revista Brasileira de Estratégia (REBRAE)	B2
Organizações Rurais e Agroindustriais	B1	Revista de Administração da UFSM	B2
Produção (São Paulo)	B1	Revista de Agronegócio e Meio Ambiente	B2
Revista Brasileira Gestão de Negócios	B1	Revista de Gestão (REGE USP)	B2
Revista Brasileira Gestão e Desenvolvimento Regional	B1	Revista de Gestão Organizacional (RGO)	B2
Revista de Administração e Inovação	B1	Revista de Gestão Socioambiental (RGSA)	B2
Revista de Administração Mackenzie (RAM)	B1	Revista Eletrônica de Ciências Administrativa (RECADM)	B2
Revista de Administração da Unimep	B1	Revista Iberoamericana de Estratégia (RIAE)	B2
Revista de Ciências da Administração (CAD/UFSC)	B1	Revista Produção Online	B2
Revista de Economia e Sociologia Rural	B1		

Besides the journals, additional material was collected from three major national conferences on the research topic. The selected conferences are:

• Simpósio de Administração da Produção, Logística e Operações Internacionais – SIMPOI (Production Management, Logistics and International Operations Symposium);

• Encontro Nacional da Associação Nacional de Pós-Graduação em Administração – EnANPAD (Nacional Meeting of the National Association of Graduate Studies in Business Administration);

• Encontro Nacional de Gestão Empresarial e Meio Ambiente – ENGEMA (Business Management and Environment National Meeting).

The decision of using these data sources is justified by the relevance of the selected conferences and academic publications in Brazil, in which it is possible to identify papers that are related to Operations and Sustainability topics. Also, the journal publications were explored for a period of 15 years (2000-2014). We used this period trying to capture how the issue of SSCM has evolved since the 2000s. Concerning publications from conferences, a period of 7 years (2008-2014) was explored. Because of the international context, we decided that 2008 can be considered a milestone in SSCM research.

During data collection, papers were selected if they actually mentioned the topic of this study. The stated journals and conference proceedings were searched by the following keywords: 'supply chain', 'supply chain management', 'sustainability', 'sustainability and supply chain', and 'sustainable supply chain management'. This search resulted in 86 papers. In a new filtering process, abstracts were scanned and, if necessary, the introduction. After this scanning process, 44 papers were selected. From this selection, all items were properly analyzed by the researchers, seeking to identify the relationship or proximity of the information found in the papers with the SSCM concept.

To analyze the data, a content analysis (Bardin, 2009) was performed, aiming to identify how sustainability has been applied in the supply chain and the impact of discussions around these themes. Furthermore, an analysis was conducted regarding the methods of research. For this purpose, we used the categories identified by Seuring and Müller (2008): (a) theoretical and conceptual, (b) case studies, (c) surveys, (d) modeling papers, and (e) literature review. Thus, by carrying out a literature review, it is possible to understand the contributions of Brazilian publications and identify the implications for future research.

4. RESULTS AND DISCUSSION

To develop the analysis, we divided it in two phases. First, we present a discussion about SSCM publications in the selected conference proceedings and academic journals in order to specify what the focus of our research is and how academics position themselves in the current debate, aiming to build a pervasive discourse. Subsequently, in order to meet the objective of the proposed research and achieve a better understanding of the concept of SSCM in the Brazilian context, a more integrated discussion is brought forth between the reviewed papers and the items constituting SSCM, as previously discussed in this paper. In the following section, discourses and practices are discussed.

5. BRAZILIAN PUBLICATIONS ON SSCM WITHIN THE ANALYZED TIME FRAME

First, we carried out a review of major academic publications means in Brazil to verify the existence of papers on the theme of sustainable supply chain management. A total of 37 papers that somehow contribute to the understanding of sustainability in supply chains were identified in the three conferences analyzed. An overview of the selected papers is presented in Table 2. It is noteworthy to point out that in some papers; only certain aspects of SSCM could be identified. Furthermore, only seven papers were found in the analyzed journals.

Concerning sustainability, papers were identified in different areas at the EnANPAD conference. One out of eight papers was published in 2008, related to 'Public Administration and Social Management'. Among the papers published between 2009 and 2014, six were found in the area of 'Operations Management and Logistics', addressing production and supply chains, SSCM in small and medium enterprises, the relationship between the external pressures and environmental practices in sustainable supply chain management, and relationships in the customer-supplier dyad or logistics integration. Two papers were related to 'Strategy in Organizations', one to corporate social responsibility with suppliers, and the other to environmental practices and competitiveness. Finally, one article was published in the area of 'Science, Technology and Innovation'.

At the SIMPOI conference, the fourteen papers analyzed were published under the topic of 'Sustainability in Operations Management'. Besides this topic, SIMPOI suggested for the first time a central theme for the conference of 2008, named 'Sustainability and Operations'. It aimed at discussing sustainable supply chains, consolidating the theme in the conference. Four of the selected papers were published in 2011. Two other studies were presented in the 2010 and 2012 editions, which focused on 'Global Operations and International Networks'. Two studies were identified in 2013 and address sustainability and environmental responsibility in the supply chain. In 2014 the theme of the conference was 'Humanitarian operations and sustainable chains', and five papers were published.

The ENGEMA conference is associated with topics on 'Social and Environmental Strategy'. From the total of thirteen papers analyzed, nine were presented under the theme strategy and published in 2011, 2012, and 2013. While seven studies concentrated on supply chains (five empirical and two theoretical), one of them focused on production chain and the other on the customer-supplier dyad. Only three of these papers were related to concepts and practices aimed at sustainability in the supply chain. The other article published in 2010, which was presented under the topic 'Technical Approach and Environmental Management', addressed reverse logistics in the supplier-customer dyad. Three other studies were presented in the 2014 edition: two papers were presented under the theme 'Sustainable Operations' and another was found in the area 'Sustainable Innovations'. In short, these three conferences have specific, focused research areas relating to parts of the concept of sustainable supply chain management.

Table 2: List of papers identified in conference proceedings during the research

Conferences	Year of publication	Paper Title Translation[1]	Authors
SIMPOI[2]	2008	The search for sustainable management in supply chains: initiatives and challenges	M. Dalmoro; D. Marconatto; V. Estivalete
SIMPOI	2010	Analysis of the incorporation of sustainability in industrial supply chains in RS - Brazil	L. B. Dalé; P. Hansen; L. Roldan
SIMPOI	2011	Analysis of a organic supply chain oriented to sustainable development: a complex vision	L. C. Zucatto; E. Pedrozo
SIMPOI	2011	Social responsibility in relations between buyer and suppliers in the supply chain of organic products in Brazil	S. B. Silva; L. M. Vieira
SIMPOI	2011	Social and environmental issues and supply chain management: a case study on the productive chain of soybean in the Brazilian Amazon	P. Adaime; A. P. Carvalho; M. Monzoni
SIMPOI	2011	Evaluation of Brazilian cash operation by approach of sustainable supply chains	O. Cattini Jr; D. Okino
SIMPOI	2012	Closed-loop supply chain: rethinking the way we do the things	R. Bergel; U. Tortato
SIMPOI	2013	Sustainable Beef - How different stakeholders of the beef production chain are involved in practices for sustainability in RS - Brazil?	M. E. Silva; A. P. F. Alves; M. D. Barcellos

SIMPOI	2013	Governance in Sustainable Supply Chains: a conceptual discussion associated with Coordination and Collaboration	D. M. Neutzling; L. F. M. Nascimento
SIMPOI	2014	Sustainable Supply Chain Management: Multi Case Study	D. O. C Morais; F. R. Pinto; M. G. O. Carlos
SIMPOI	2014	Social Issues In Sustainable Supply Chain Management: A Brazilian Perspective	M. E. Silva; L. F. M. Nascimento
SIMPOI	2014	Integration in Sustainable Supply Chain Management: A Theoretical Approach	D. M. Neutzling; L. F. M. Nascimento
SIMPOI	2014	Sustainable Management in means of accommodation and its Supply Chain: A Study on the Northern Coast of São Paulo State	C. M. João; J C. Barbieri
SIMPOI	2014	Determinants of Sustainable Supply Chain: An Analysis of Pressures Measurement Models and Social and Environmental Practice	E. C. Abdala; J. C. Barbieri
EnANPAD[3]	2008	Brazilian organic meat from the Sustainability perspective	A. M. Abicht; A. C. Ceolin
EnANPAD	2009	Sustainability in Supply Chains: A comparative perspective of national and international publications	S. Gonçalves-Dias; L. Labegalini; G. Polidório
EnANPAD	2010	An analysis of the relationships between Buyer and Supplier in the supply chain of organic products in Brazil	S. B. Silva; L. M. Vieira
EnANPAD	2010	Innovations in Production Chain and the Consumption of PET Packaging	L. F. Nascimento; M. Trevisan; P. S. Figueiró; M. Bossle
EnANPAD	2010	Social Responsibility actions in relation to Supplier: A Case Study Based on the Ethos Indicatorsat O Boticário company	R. Nakayama; R. Teixeira
EnANPAD	2010	Environmental and Social Responsibility as part of Integrated Logistics: The Case of Export of Soy Complex by Bunge Alimentos S / A.	L. T. Robles; F. G. Borger; T. R. Machado
EnANPAD	2011	Criteria for Corporate Social Responsibility in the Supply Chain of Oil and Natural Gas industry: The Case of Pernambuco Suppliers of Petrobrás	E. Melo; M. Primo; C. Gómez; R. Amaro
EnANPAD	2012	Environmental Practices and their relationship with Competitiveness and Sustainability: a case study in an agribusiness company	M. F. Barbosa; G. A. Cândido
EnANPAD	2014	Sustainable Supply Chain: Management in SMEs	D. O. C. Morais; F. R. Pinto; M. G. O. Carlos

EnANPAD	2014	Pressures and Environmental Practices in the Context of Supply Chain Management: A case study of the relationship between determinants and sustainable actions in Minas Gerais industries	E. C. Abdala; J. C. Barbieri
ENGEMA[4]	2010	Post-Consumer Reverse Logistics : relations between an industry and its suppliers	P. Figueiró; L. F. Nascimento; M. Trevisan; M. Bossle
ENGEMA	2011	Inter-organizational relationships at Rede Justa Trama as a success factor in the production and marketing of eco-cotton products	M. Bossle; L. F. M. Nascimento
ENGEMA	2011	Sustainability management in the broiler supply chain in Mato Grosso, Brazil	D. M. Neutzling; E. A. Pedrozo
ENGEMA	2012	Supply Chain Management and Sustainability: A bibliometric study of publications in the Web of Science database	A. C. Rocha; L. Rosa; J. Zamberlan; C. Camargo
ENGEMA	2012	Social and environmental aspects of the Brazilian beef chain	O. Faro; R. C. Calia
ENGEMA	2012	Selection of green suppliers: literature review, classification and analysis	T. F. Quilice; J. Salvini; C. J. Jabbour
ENGEMA	2012	Building a supply chain of the future: a case study of Wal-Mart Brazil	I. Teixeira; R. C. Calia; M. F. Neves
ENGEMA	2013	Reflections and approaches between Sustainability and Supply Chain	M. E. Silva; L. F. M. Nascimento
ENGEMA	2013	The case of a Cleaning Industry and its Sustainable Supply Chain Management within the framework of Seuring and Muller (2008)	D. O. C. Morais; F. R. Pinto; M. G. O. Carlos
ENGEMA	2013	Repositioning the floodlights of proactive behaviour: from an environmental focus to sustainable practices	A. P. F. Alves; M. E. Silva
ENGEMA	2014	Assessment Tool for Sustainable Supply Chain Management a Multicase Study	D. O. C. Morais; M. G. O. Carlos; F. R. Pinto
ENGEMA	2014	Sustainable Innovation in Supply Chain Management	P. Dias
ENGEMA	2014	Sustainable Supply Chain Practices of a Manufacturing Industry	C. Dullius; P. R. Schaeffer; C. L. Viana

[1] The titles presented here were free translated by the authors of this paper. The original titles in Portuguese are presented in the appendix (Table 4)

[2] Simpósio de Administração da Produção, Logística e Operações Internacionais (SIMPOI); [3] Encontro Nacional da Associação Nacional da Pós-Graduação em Administração (EnANPAD), and [4] Encontro Nacional de Gestão Empresarial e Meio Ambiente – (ENGEMA)

The analysis revealed that SIMPOI and ENGEMA stand out for the largest number of papers focusing on sustainability and environmental responsibility in the supply chain. It can be justified by the subject areas covered at these conferences; the first is related to operations management and the second to the relationship between organizational and environmental management. When it comes to the EnANPAD conference, only few studies (as presented in Table 2) address the customer-supplier dyad or the relationship with stakeholders, or adopt a supply chain approach. Moreover, some studies addressed only one sustainability dimension with chain actors, social or environmental. Furthermore, only seven papers were identified in national journals. They are presented in Table 3.

Table 3: List of papers identified in journals during the research

Journal	Year of publication	Paper Title Translation[1]	Authors
Revista de Administração da USP	2007	Reverse supply sustainability: a case study of the Plasma Project	M. Pedroso; R. Zwicker
Gestão & Regionalidade	2008	Socio-Environmental Responsibility in the Tobacco Supply Chain in Brazil	S. M. Santos; C. Ferrari; G. Giacomini Filho
Revista de Administração de Empresas	2010	Competitive advantage and sustainable supply chain management: a meta-analysis	R. Brito; P. Berardi.
Revista de Administração da Unimep	2012	The role of logistics operators in Sustainability actions	M. Vivaldini
Produção	2012	Sustainability in supply chains: a comparative perspective in domestic and international journals	S. Gonçalves-Dias; L. Labegalini; J. M. Csillag
Revista de Administração e Inovação	2013	Social and Environmental innovations in Supply Chain: A case study on the role of focal company	A. P. Carvalho; J. C. Barbieri
Gestão & Produção	2014	Analysis of sustainability practices used in supply chain management: a field research in the Brazilian automotive sector	R. M. Vanalle; L. B. Santos

[1] These titles were presented both in English and Portuguese. The original titles in Portuguese are shown in the appendix (Table 5)

Therefore, we can notice a difference between national and international discussions regarding the use of TBL. This fact can be explained as follows: in the 2000s, a limited number of seven papers were published in the 37 Brazilian journals. In 2008, Seuring and Müller's (2008) literature review on SSCM marked a milestone in the research area. In fact, until this moment, it is the most cited paper in the Journal of Cleaner Production. Nevertheless, the most significant studies in Brazil have only emerged after 2010. If new researchers use a more critical analysis in their publications, a better contribution can be created to improve the matching between the previously developed and future research on the SSCM concept.

6. THE BRAZILIAN VIEW ON SUSTAINABLE SUPPLY CHAIN MANAGEMENT

The study of SSCM requires a clear understanding of some theoretical issues, such as sustainability, supply chains and strategy. Thus, we highlight our comprehension about sustainability, which goes beyond the concept reported in the Brundtland Report. From the TBL perspective, we understand that sustainability takes into consideration what has been discussed by Hopwood, Mellor and O'Brien (2005). These authors believe that sustainability should be seen under a macro transformation framework, despite being a slow process, which is related to the non-maintenance of the *status quo* in terms of economy and society organization.

An in-depth analysis of the selected papers shows us that there is a misunderstanding related to sustainable practices that focus only on the environmental dimension. This finding can be related to the argument presented by Carter and Easton (2011) when discussing the continuing confusion between the environmental dimension and sustainability in general. According to the authors, the confusion can be observed in many papers. However, the finding relates to the argument presented by Ashby et al. (2012). These authors hypothesized that the environmental dimension of sustainability is substantially more represented than the social dimension, as its principles and practices are covered more in the literature.

Aiming to solve such misunderstanding, we highlight that the concept of Green Supply Chain Management (GSCM) can be used as the concept that directly represents a discussion of the environmental dimension in supply chains. In fact, GSCM was presented in some of the analyzed papers. Nevertheless, it would be necessary to observe the overlap of authors who discuss the topic (i.e. GSCM and SSCM) separately. For instance, some of the papers discuss Sustainable Supply Chain Management but use the concept of Green Supply Chain Management as a translation of SSCM to Portuguese, which indicates that there is a lack of theoretical and epistemological alignment of these themes. Actually, a deeper understanding is needed. For GSCM and SSCM, it is necessary to reach an effective comprehension of the subject.

Also, the analysis revealed the prominence of sustainability as a rather separate topic, lacking a stronger emphasis on the supply chain concept itself. More specifically, the article published at 'Revista de Administração da Unimep' by Pedroso and Zwicker (2007) was the one closest to the discussion related to sustainability and clearly relevant concepts in the operations area. Another paper that should be highlighted was published by Brito and Berardi (2010) at 'Revista de Administração de Empresas'. This paper presented a discussion about SSCM from a competitive advantage perspective, centering the discussion around the study of Seuring and Müller (2008). This article (third in Table 3) as well as the paper published at 'Revista de Administração e Inovação' by Carvalho and Barbieri (2013) used the concept of sustainable supply chain management.

Some of these papers have translation problems, where it is necessary to observe the motivation as well as the objective of the research. This argument shows that the discourse on the subject is not yet aligned with sustainability because there are some comprehension problems, but it is in a process of change. In the international debate, there are advances on such discussions. However, from the SSCM perspective, the main contribution should be towards fully understanding the theme in emerging countries (including Brazil), especially with regard to social aspects. Thus, what would be the understanding of SSCM? It could be said that the understanding is in the observation of TBL aspects since the focus is both on environmental and social dimensions.

In addition to understanding what and how Brazilian researchers carry out their research, we identified the need for analyzing the search process. In this context, the methodological approach of the papers was analyzed. Regarding the methodological type of the papers, analysis revealed a predominance of research classified as case studies (26 papers). Within this category of publication, topics on supply chains, organic food products and commodities were emphasized. Also, a total of 15 conceptual studies, including literature review and/or theoretical papers, were identified, and more than half of these papers were published during 2012. Moreover, we observed that in 2013, three (out of 15) of the published papers are considered as conceptual/theoretical. In 2014, three of the selected papers conducted a survey, showing that this is an emerging method of analysis within the topic area.

Given these considerations, we can see that researchers started to understand the theoretical background of the subject. Furthermore, with an analysis of the nature of the research, there is a concentration of case study research papers (59.09%), corresponding to a total of 26 papers, which is a finding already explained by the prior choice of article type. Also, conceptual/theoretical and literature review research (34.09%) was featured in 15 papers, and three surveys (6.82%) were identified. Therefore, national papers using secondary type techniques, focus group, experiment, and action research could contribute to future advances in the field of Sustainable Supply Chain Management.

This analysis highlights the concentration of studies in methodological terms (case studies) and in relation to the object of the studies (supply chains in the primary sector). The analysis also confirms that the methodological concentration partly explains the development of the research field, with Brazil still being in the initial stage of SSCM research. Recognizing that Brazil is still in the early stages of SSCM research justifies the use of bibliographical studies and literature reviews. In this circumstance, the results show the issues that have been discussed relating to SSCM in order to build a national discourse in Portuguese. When performing a search for publications of Brazilian researchers in English, different results may arise because there are studies that are directed accordingly. Thus, debates about the academic implications of this analysis are valid.

7. ACADEMIC IMPLICATIONS

Considering the arguments used so far, a broad field of research on Sustainable Supply Chain Management clearly exists. It should be clear to researchers in the area which field of research they contribute to, meaning operations or corporate strategy. The former focuses on improvements of operational aspects – which is the quest for direct results and with the least possible impact – while the latter field considers sustainability from a strategic perspective, which understands sustainability as a means to reach a certain result, thus taking a performance view regardless of the field.

As discussed by Ashby et al. (2012), the second perspective is the one that can reach further progress. This perspective considers that sustainability can be examined from organizational relationships, referring to human aspects (social) and environmental factors that are part of the whole process and not just the result generated by a specific vision. From a more operational perspective, there is still a focus on organizational development and performance (Rocha et al., 2012). As mentioned in the theoretical discussion, Seuring and Müller (2008) present the

possibility of changes in the relations of the supply chain according to strategies for suppliers and products (Seuring & Müller, 2008).

Furthermore, another research approach on the subject is based on the theoretical categories presented by Beske (2012), namely: continuity in supply chains, guidance, risk management, and proactivity. Although Beske (2012) presented a more focused discussion on the idea of dynamic capabilities and focused on the contribution of innovation strategies to deal with sustainability, such categories can guide new research as well. By the same logic, Pagell and Wu (2009) demonstrate a more consistent theory on the subject, in which it is clear to understand how it should be treated in the chain, the supply chain's re-conceptualization, and its total contribution in a changing scenario.

Recent examples of a national research are two groups, as follows: (1) Fundação Getúlio Vargas, in São Paulo (FGV/SP), in which in the last years at least two thesis were presented using specifically the SSCM theme; (2) Federal University of Rio Grande do Sul, in Porto Alegre, in which only in 2014 one doctoral thesis and one master's dissertation were presented. Therefore, in 2013 both groups were engaged in projects with Professor Dr. Stefan Seuring, a renowned author in the field who conducted a workshop on Sustainable Supply Chain Management, demonstrating an alignment with the field of research and involving researchers from all over Brazil in the discussion of this area.

Therefore, in addition to the required theoretical approaches, the use of alternative methods for carrying out research – besides case studies and literature reviews presented in the previous section - is still needed in order to bring new studies and approaches to the area (Pagell & Schevchenko, 2014). Furthermore, we believe that research should be conducted not only with a primary focus on sectors or in accordance with simple relationships. Research needs to be encouraged on issues involving supply chains with demands of different sectors according to energy resources, materials and also the potential impact on the three dimensions of TBL. Thus, the subject needs to be further discussed in order to improve Brazil's representativeness in relation to the world.

8. FINAL REMARKS

Increasingly more studies discussing sustainability have been conducted in the Business Administralion field. The same is true regarding SCM research. However, the effective contribution of the studies on the development or the essence of the topic to incorporating this theme in the SSCM research is not yet clear-cut. It was possible to see that in Brazil there have been publications on this topic mostly because it is an "emerging" topic, which can lead to misunderstandings, particularly in the distinction of what has been discussed in an environmental sphere or/ and in a sustainable sphere. As indicated by Carter and Easton (2011), sustainability can be considered a "license" to operate a business in the 21st century but requires a consistent theoretical outline to this end.

According to Gold, Seuring and Beske (2010), the literature on the subject still has limitations, which does not leave Brazilian research too far from a possible breakthrough in the coming years. If national researchers became more involved in the field, Brazil could play a prominent role in the international debate. Therefore, the actual introduction of the SSCM concept needs to be performed since only one of the identified papers (Brito & Berardi, 2010) showed a relationship between management, sustainability, and supply chain in relation to SSCM and the theoretical discussion presented earlier.

When we seek to understand the relation of sustainability management in the integration of members in a supply chain, such a discussion should be held. It is necessary to think about what is meant by empirical applications and how it can contribute to academic discussions. Based on this, an in-depth discussion on Brazilian publications and a reflexive analysis were performed, seeking to understand the context of Brazilian academic publications and indicating potential topics of research.

It is noteworthy to mention that when collecting papers we could see many studies addressing specific points in supply chains; however they were not selected because they were directly related to environmental aspects (i.e. ISO 14000, Life Cycle Analysis, Reverse Logistics) and did not mention the focus of this research, namely sustainability. Thus, the search was constrained to the theme of sustainability and operations. Moreover, considering the fact that not all journals ranked by Qualis Capes 2012 were scanned for potential papers to be reviewed is yet another limitation, as additional discussions could have been brought forth. Also, the inclusion of other conferences as a source for papers could have extended the results of the research.

Therefore, the research contributions of this study include the following: (1) recognizing previous academic contributions to the subject in the Brazilian context, (2) discussing the existence of alignment with the SSCM in the researches, (3) demonstrating the main methodological research designs, and (4) emphasizing the need for a more fully developed introduction to the topic, seeking to achieve more consistent research. Thus, further studies may be based on considerations of academic implications as previously presented. Moreover, from this type of research, companies may better recognize existing gaps that can be worked on throughout the supply chain.

9. REFERENCES

Abdalla, E. C. & Barbieri, J. C. (2014). Determinants of Sustainable Supply Chain: an analysis of mensuration models of pressures and socio-environmental practices. *Journal of Operations and Supply Chain Management*, 7 (2), 110-122.

Adaime, P. P., Carvalho, A. P. & Monzoni, M. P. (2011). Temas Socioambientais e Gestão de Cadeia de Suprimento: Um estudo de caso sobre a cadeia produtiva de soja na amazônia brasileira. Presented at *Simpósio de Administração da Produção, Logística e Operações Internacionais*, São Paulo, SP, Brasil.

Ahi, P. & Searcy, C. (2013). A comparative literature analysis of definitions for green and sustainable supply chain management, *Journal of Cleaner Production*, 52.

Araújo, C. A. (2006). Bibliometria: Evolução histórica e questões atuais. *Em questão*, 12 (1), 11-33.

Ashby, A., Leat, M., & Hudson-Smith, M. (2012). Making connections: A review of supply chain management and sustainability literature. *Supply Chain Management: an International Journal*, 17 (5), 497-516.

Bardin, L. (2009). *Análise de Conteúdo* (4a ed.). Lisboa: Edições 70.

Beske, P. (2012). Dynamic capabilities and sustainable supply chain management. *International Journal of Physical Distribution & Logistics Management*, 42 (4), 372-387.

Beske P., Land A. & Seuring S. (2014). Sustainable supply chain management practices and dynamic capabilities in the food industry: A critical analysis of the literature. *International Journal of Production Economics*, 152, 131-143.

Beske, P. & Seuring, S. (2014). Putting sustainability into supply chain management, *Supply Chain Management: an international journal*, 19 (3), 322-331.

Brito, R. P. & Berardi, P. C. (2010). Vantagem Competitiva na Gestão Sustentável da Cadeia de Suprimentos: um metaestudo. *Revista de Administração Eletrônica – RAE*, 50 (2), 155-169.

Carter, C. R. & Easton, P. L. (2011). Sustainable supply chain management: Evolution and future directions. *International Journal of Physical Distribution & Logistics Management*, 41 (1), 46-62.

Carter, C. R. & Rogers, D. S. (2008). A framework of sustainable supply chain management: moving toward new theory. *International Journal of Physical Distribution & Logistics Management*, 38 (5), 360-387.

Elkington, J. (eds.) (2002), *Cannibals with forks: the triple bottom line of 21st century business* [reprint]. Oxford: Capstone.

Epstein, M. J. & Roy, M. (2001). Sustainability in action: identifying and measuring the key Performance drivers. *Long Range Planning*, 34 (5), 585-604.

Faisal, M. N. (2010). Sustainable supply chains: a study of interaction among the enablers. *Business Process Management Journal*, 16 (3), 508-529.

Foladori, G. (2005). Por uma sustentabilidad alternativa. Uruguai: Colección Cabichui.

Gold, S., Seuring, S. & Beske, P. (2010). Sustainable Supply Chain Management and Inter-Organizational Resources: A literature review. *Corporate Social Responsibility and Environmental Management*, 17 (4), 230-245.

Gonçalves-Dias, S. L. F., Labegalini, L. & Csillag, J. M. (2012). Sustentabilidade e cadeia de suprimentos: uma perspectiva comparada de publicações nacionais e internacionais, *Produção*, 22 (3), 517-533.

Hopwood, B., Mellor, M. & O'brien, G. (2005). Sustainable Development: Mapping Different Approaches. *Sustainable Development*, 13.

Linton, J. D., Klassen, R. & Jayaraman, V. (2007). Sustainable Supply Chains: An introduction, *Journal of Operations Management*, 1075-1082.

Junqueira, L. A. P., Maior, J. S. & Pinheiro, F. P. (2011). Sustentabilidade: A produção científica brasileira entre os anos de 2000 e 2009. *Revista de Gestão Social e Ambiental – RGSA*, 5 (3).

Markley, M. & Davis, L. (2007). Exploring future competitive advantage through sustainable supply chains. *International Journal of Physical Distribution & Logistics Management*, 37 (9), 763-774.

Pagell, M. & Shevchenko, A. (2014). Why research in Sustainable Supply Chain Management should have no future, *Journal of Supply Chain Management*, 50 (1).

Pagell, M. & Wu, Z. (2009). Building a More Complete Theory of Sustainable Supply Chain Management Using Case Studies of 10 Exemplars. *Journal of Supply Chain Management*, April.

Pereira, G. M. C., Yen-Tsang, C., Manzini, R. B. & Almeida, N. V. (2011). Sustentabilidade Socioambiental: Um estudo bibliométrico da evolução do conceito na área de gestão de operações. *Produção*.

Rocha, A. C., Rosa, L. A. B., Zamberlan, J. F. & Camargo, C. R. (2012). Gestão da Cadeia de Suprimentos e Sustentabilidade: um estudo bibliométrico da produção científica na base Web of Science. Presented at *XII Encontro Nacional de Gestão Empresarial e Meio Ambiente – ENGEMA*. São Paulo, SP, Brazil.

Sarkis, J, Zhu Q. H., Lai, K. (2011). An organizational theoretic review of green supply chain management literature, *International Journal of Production Economics*, 130 (1).

Seuring, S. (2011). Supply Chain Management for sustainable products – insights from research applying mixed methodologies, *Business and Strategy and the Environment*, 20, 471-484.

Seuring, S. & Müller, M. (2008). From a literature review to a conceptual framework for sustainable supply chain management. *Journal of Cleaner Production*, 16, 1699-1710.

Silva, M. Z., Dani, A. C., Beuren, I. M. & Kloeppel, N. R. (2011). Características bibliométricas e sociométricas de publicações da área ambiental em congressos e periódicos nacionais. Presented at *XIII Encontro Nacional de Gestão Empresarial e Meio Ambiente – ENGEMA*. São Paulo, SP, Brazil.

Tsoulfas, G.T. & Pappis, C. P. (2006). Environmental principles applied to supply chains design and operation. *Journal of Cleaner Production*, 18 (14), 1593-1602.

Vachon, S. & Mao, Z. (2008). Linking supply chain strength to sustainable development: a country-level analysis. *Journal of Cleaner Production*, 16 (15), 1552–1560.

Vermeulen, W. J. V., Uitenboogaart, Y., Pesqueira, L. D. L., Metselaar, J. & Kok, M. T. J. (2010). *Roles of Governments in Multi-Actor Sustainable Supply Chain Governance Systems and the effectiveness of their interventions: An exploratory study*. Netherlands Environmental Assessment Agency (PBL). Utrecht University.

Wolf, J. (2011). Sustainable Supply Chain Management Integration: A Qualitative Analysis of the German Manufacturing Industry. *Journal of Business Ethics*, 102, 221-235.

Zhu, Q. H., Sarkis, J., Lai, K. H. (2007). Green supply chain management: pressures, practices and performance within the Chinese automobile industry. *Journal of Cleaner Production*, 15 (11-12), 1041-1052.

Appendix

Table 4: List in Portuguese of papers identified in conference proceedings during the research

Conferences	Year of publication	Paper Title in Portuguese
SIMPOI[1]	2008	A busca de uma gestão sustentável em cadeias de suprimentos: iniciativas e desafios
SIMPOI	2010	Análise da incorporação da sustentabilidade em cadeias de suprimentos industriais do RS
SIMPOI	2011	Análise de uma cadeia de suprimentos orgânica orientada para o desenvolvimento sustentável: uma visão complexa
SIMPOI	2011	Responsabilidade social nas relações entre comprador e fornecedores na cadeia de suprimentos de produtos orgânicos no Brasil
SIMPOI	2011	Temas socioambientais e gestão de cadeia de suprimento: um estudo de caso sobre a cadeia produtiva de soja na Amazônia brasileira
SIMPOI	2011	Avaliação da operação de numerário brasileira pela abordagem de cadeias de suprimento sustentáveis
SIMPOI	2012	*Closed-loop supply chain* repensando a maneira como fazemos as coisas
SIMPOI	2013	*Sustainable Beef* – Como diferentes *stakeholders* da cadeia de carne bovina gaúcha estão envolvidos com práticas para a sustentabilidade?
SIMPOI	2013	Governança Em Cadeias de Suprimento Sustentáveis: uma discussão conceitual associada aos aspectos da Coordenação e Colaboração
SIMPOI	2014	Gestão da Cadeia de Suprimento Sustentável Estudo Multicaso
SIMPOI	2014	Social Issues In Sustainable Supply Chain Management: A Brazilian Perspective
SIMPOI	2014	Integração na Gestão de Cadeias de Suprimentos Sustentáveis: Uma Abordagem Teórica
SIMPOI	2014	A Gestão Sustentável em Meios de Hospedagem e Sua Cadeia de Suprimentos – Um Estudo no Litoral Norte do Estado de SP
SIMPOI	2014	Determinantes da Cadeia de Suprimentos Sustentável: Uma Análise de Modelos de Mensuração de Pressões e Práticas Socioambientais
EnANPAD[2]	2008	A Carne Orgânica Brasileira Sob a Ótica da Sustentabilidade
EnANPAD	2009	Sustentabilidade em cadeias de suprimentos: Uma perspectiva comparada de publicações nacionais e internacionais
EnANPAD	2010	Uma análise dos relacionamentos entre Comprador e Fornecedores na cadeia de suprimentos de produtos orgânicos no Brasil
EnANPAD	2010	Inovações na Cadeia de Produção e Consumo de Embalagens PET
EnANPAD	2010	Ações de Responsabilidade Social com Relação ao *Stakeholder* Fornecedor: Estudo de Caso Baseado nos Indicadores Ethos na Empresa O Boticário

EnANPAD	2010	A Responsabilidade Socioambiental como Componente da Logística Integrada: O Caso da Exportação do Complexo Soja pela Bunge Alimentos S/A.
EnANPAD	2011	Critérios de Responsabilidade Social Corporativa na Cadeia de Suprimentos do Setor de Petróleo e Gás Natural: O Caso dos Fornecedores Pernambucanos da Petrobrás
EnANPAD	2012	Práticas Ambientais e suas Relações com a Competitividade e a Sustentabilidade: um estudo de caso em empresa agroindustrial
EnANPAD	2014	Cadeia de Suprimento Sustentável: Gestão em PMEs
EnANPAD	2014	Pressões e Práticas Socioambientais no Contexto da Gestão da Cadeia de Suprimentos: Um Estudo da Relação Entre os Determinantes e as Ações Sustentáveis em Indústrias de Minas Gerais
ENGEMA[3]	2010	Logística Reversa de Pós-Consumo: relações entre uma indústria e seus fornecedores
ENGEMA	2011	As relações interorganizacionais na Rede Justa Trama como um fator de sucesso na produção e comercialização dos produtos do algodão ecológico
ENGEMA	2011	Gestão da sustentabilidade na cadeia de suprimentos do frango de corte em Mato Grosso
ENGEMA	2012	Gestão da Cadeia de Suprimentos e Sustentabilidade: Um estudo bibliométrico da produção científica na base *Web of Science*
ENGEMA	2012	Aspectos socioambientais da cadeia de suprimentos da carne bovina brasileira
ENGEMA	2012	Seleção de fornecedores verdes: revisão da literatura, classificação e análise
ENGEMA	2012	Construindo a cadeia de suprimentos do futuro: um estudo de caso do Walmart Brasil
ENGEMA	2013	Reflexões e aproximações entre Sustentabilidade e Cadeia de Suprimentos
ENGEMA	2013	O caso de uma Indústria de Limpeza e sua Gestão da Cadeia de Suprimentos Sustentável à luz do *framework* de Seuring e Muller (2008)
ENGEMA	2013	Reposicionando os Holofotes do Comportamento Proativo: de um foco ambiental para práticas sustentáveis
ENGEMA	2014	Ferramenta de Avaliação para a Gestão da Cadeia de Suprimentos Sustentável: Estudo Multicaso
ENGEMA	2014	Inovação Sustentável na Cadeia de Suprimentos
ENGEMA	2014	Práticas de Gestão Sustentável na Cadeia de Suprimentos de uma Indústria de Transformação

[1]Simpósio de Administração da Produção, Logística e Operações Internacionais (SIMPOI); [2] Encontro Nacional da Associação Nacional da Pós-Graduação em Administração (EnANPAD) and [3] Encontro Nacional de Gestão Empresarial e Meio Ambiente – (ENGEMA)

Table 5: List in Portuguese of papers identified in journals during the research

Journal	Year of publication	Paper Title in Portuguese
Revista de Administração da USP	2007	Sustentabilidade na cadeia reversa de suprimentos: um estudo de caso do Projeto Plasma
Gestão & Regionalidade	2008	Responsabilidade socioambiental na cadeia de suprimentos do Tabaco no Brasil
Revista de Administração de Empresas	2010	Vantagem Competitiva na gestão sustentável da cadeia de suprimentos: um metaestudo
Revista de Administração da Unimep	2012	O papel de Operadores logísticos em ações de sustentabilidade
Produção	2012	Sustentabilidade e Cadeia de Suprimentos: uma perspectiva comparada de publicações nacionais e internacionais
Revista de Administração e Inovação	2013	Inovações Socioambientais em cadeias de suprimentos: um estudo de caso sobre o papel da empresa focal
Gestão & Produção	2014	Análise das práticas de sustentabilidade utilizadas na gestão da cadeia de suprimentos: pesquisa de campo no setor automotivo brasileiro

5

Is There a Bitter Flavor in Sustainability for the Sugar-Alcohol Industry?

Ely Laureano Paiva
FGV-EAESP
ely.paiva@fgv.br

Cristiane Biazzin
FGV-EAESP
cristiane.biazzin@fgv.br

Luiz Carlos Di Serio
FGV-EAESP
luiz.diserio@fgv.br

Marta Cleia Ferreira de Andrade
Faculdade de Ciências e Educação de Rubiataba
marta.cleia@hotmail.com

ABSTRACT: Biofuel has been pointed out as one "green" option for traditional fossil fuels like petroleum. Brazil is one the leading countries within this proposal competing globally with its sugar ethanol.. Nevertheless, there is a debate between corn ethanol and sugar ethanol .regarding the appropriateness to produce fuel instead of food in highly fertile regions. This industry is also severely criticized regarding its socio-environmental practices. We analyzed three cases identified as featuring best practices in this industry in Brazil. Two of the companies are located in the state of São Paulo, Southeastern Brazil, the most important region in sugar-ethanol production. The third is situated in the Brazilian Midwest, a region with fast growth in this industry. In this region, cattle, soy and corn have been substitute by sugarcane plantation. The results suggest that, when a company in this industry pursues a sustainable approach to its operations, it is possible to mitigate environmental impacts and to improve local social conditions. Such practices are potential sources of competitive advantage. However, clear gaps are still present regarding integration and collaboration along the supply chain. Nevertheless, sustainable business policies have also created new business opportunities. The continuous challenge is to develop synergetic operational capabilities that are able to mitigate environmental impacts, to decrease operational costs and to add value to the products.

Keywords: *green supply chain, sustainability, integration, ethanol, biofuel.*

1. INTRODUCTION

One of the current challenges in the sugar-ethanol industry is to deal with the question of sustainability, while taking into account the characteristics of this economic activity. It is known that this sector has sought to achieve new levels of operational performance in the last few years (Krajnc et al., 2007). At the same time, there is a need for improving its competitiveness, as much in the domestic market as in the international (Farinelli et al., 2009). Nevertheless, the present policies of this sector in Brazil have constantly been criticized internationally in the business press (Kozloff, 2010). Brazilian companies that focus on large scale production treat social issues as a secondary concern (see for example, Hall et al., 2009), and not as a sustained process in the long term (Pereira and Ortega, 2010).

Generally the industry has sustainability at the extend people involved want to. In the case of sugar-ethanol a lot of effort has been made in different ways around all the countries that produce sugar cane, sugar and ethanol. Sugar-ethanol industry is particularly challenging due to interdependencies of climate uncertain and political-economic decisions, what directly impacts its value chain (Everingham et al, 2002) .

This study focuses on the Brazilian sugarcane production in order to observe its challenges toward sustainability, based on triple-bottom line (economic, social and environmental perspectives). Brazil is the world's largest sugar producer and second largest ethanol producer, behind the United States. In 2010, the total sugar cane production of 620 million tons led to 38 million tons of sugar and 27.4 billion liters of ethanol. Sugarcane is grown primarily in the South-Central and Northeastern regions with different harvesting periods: in South-Central Brazil, the harvest runs from April to December, and, in the Northeast, from September to March. The South-Central region produces over 85% of Brazil's sugarcane, São Paulo State alone accounting for 60% of it.

Brazilian sugarcane cultivation today occupies 7.8 million hectares, or 2.3% of the country's total arable land. The annual revenue of the sector is around US$ 36 billion, the foreign revenue (export) component accounting for US$ 16 billion. It ranks second in Brazilian agribusiness exports, just after soya production. The industry employs 1.15 million direct workers, distributed nationwide among more than 400 mills.

2. LITERATURE REVIEW

2.1 Linking operations strategy to sustainability

The concept of the triple bottom line developed by Elkington (1997) confers broad responsibility on a company in relation to its activities.. In order to achieve a long term sustainability, a company has to manage not only its economic capital, but also those that are natural and social (Dyllick and Hockerts, 2002). It is important to stress that the concept of capital differs from the traditional vision of the economists, indeed gaining new meanings. In this case, it covers natural capital, as it is related to natural resources.

Environmental responsibility is linked to concerns, such as conservation and sustainable use of natural resources. This means adaptation of processes and development of products that utilize less material and energy, as well as limiting damage to the environment caused by the industrial activities (Kleindorfer et al., 2005).

Ecologically sustainable companies are those that only utilize natural resources that are consumed at a rate below that of natural reproduction or at a rate in accordance with the development of new resources. These do not cause emissions that accumulate in the environment beyond the capacity of the natural system to absorb and assimilate them. Finally, they are not involved in activities that degrade the social ecosystem (Dyllick and Hockerts, 2002).

It is considered that socio-environmental aspects are necessary for economic development. Such combination increases prosperity by more efficient utilization of the resources and less emissions of environmentally adverse substances. When there is integration among the partners in the Supply Chain Management (SCM), the materials are utilized more efficiently and the natural resources better conserved, providing economic advantages for the companies (Zhu and Cote, 2004, Linton et al.,2007). Thus, from an initially reactive posture, companies are gradually shifting to a more proactive one in relation to the sustainability aspects.

Social responsibility contemplates the responsibility of companies in the development of society. Ideally, companies would assume a commitment to the development of society, executing actions to boost social development, social inclusion and the improvement of the living conditions of neighboring populations (Pedroso and Zwicker, 2007, Van Der

Hejden et al., 2010). Socially sustainable companies are those that add value to the communities in which they operate, increasing the human capital of the individual partners, as well as promoting the social capital of these communities (Dyllick and Hockerts, 2002). Hutchins and Shuterland (2008) measure the social performance of a supply chain from four perspectives. They are related to labor equity, healthcare, safety and actions related to philanthropy.

2.2 Linking operations strategy and sustainability

Since Skinner seminal article of 1969, Operations strategy has discussed the strategic role of operational processes for business units. Further different authors have treated operations strategy as a business strategy deployment (for example, Wheelwright, 1984) or a capability grounded in the resource-based approach (see, for example, Schroeder et al., 2002). Wheelwright (1984) argued that operations strategy is related to the unit's business strategy, and it is operationalized through a set of decision categories: capacity, technology, facilities, vertical integration, workforce, quality and organization. The main consensus is related to the competitive criteria that include cost, delivery, flexibility and quality (Wheelwright, 1984, Miller and Roth, 1994).

Currently, new approaches, like sustainable operations, have been integrated to the operations management debate (Angell and Klassen, 1999, De Burgos and Lorente, 2001). It is possible to adapt the four stages of Wheelwright and Bowen (1996) and Hayes and Wheelwright (1984) to sustainable operations (Kleindorfer et al., 2005). According to them, a company, in the first stages, only sees the internal aspects of its operations. A company in the third stage combines their operational decisions to the business strategy. A company in the most advanced stage is able to create new capabilities from their operations, has operational issues embedded in its strategy, and creates new patterns of performance related to operations.

3. METHOD

The research method adopted was multiple case studies. Quality and depth were sought within this methodological orientation (Yin, 2009; Collis and Hussey, 2005). In order to assure internal validity, we followed the patterns indicated by the theory (Eisenhardt, 1989; Stuart et al., 2002; George and Bennett, 2004). More precisely, we selected the cases by their representativeness, as Brazil is one of the biggest

players in the sugar-ethanol industry and based on the fact that all 3 organizations chosen are known as best-practice entities. The companies studied present some singularities, such as leadership in the sugar-ethanol market and management concerned with sustainability. Their location in a traditional sugar cane region and in a more recent area for the sugar-ethanol industry in Brazil presents singular aspects when compared with each other.

For data collection, the techniques utilized were semi-structured interviews, non-participant observation and secondary data (we addressed an extensive documentary analysis through annual reports, memos and relevant documents in each organization, as well as in associations and unions). We recorded every interview for subsequent transcription. Respondents were selected based on their involvement in sustainability strategy and practices. The executives who joined the respondent group were: the Director President, the Commercial Director and Management staff from the Administrative, Operations, Purchasing, Commercial, Sustainability and Environmental Departments. On average, each interview lasted 60 minutes. Representatives of the ethanol distribution companies, Premium and Petrobras, were also interviewed. In order to improve data quality for phenomenon analysis, we sought to increase the quantity of observable information available as much as possible. In order to do so, at least two authors jointly visited, interviewed and collected data in the field. Interviews were also evaluated in real time, combining non-participant observations and field notes. Furthermore, we built a database that was shared among the authors in order to offer deeper insights and re-enact events. This strategy aimed to minimize bias and supported the robustness of the study (Eisenhardt, 1989; George and Bennett, 2004).

4. CASE STUDIES

4.1 Institutional environment influence - Sugarcane expansion in Brazil

The sugar and ethanol industries suffered significant price and volume fluctuations, as presented in Table 1. Consequently, some firms have invested in alternative product lines. The main ones have been using the bagasse for cattle feed and leavening (fermentation), and the sale of excess energy generation. Some mills have also invested on producing neutral alcohol for beverages and cosmetics products.

The main obstacle to massive investment in energy sales by the São Paulo sugar mills is lack of planning and regulation by the Federal Government, which, in turn, increases investor uncertainty. In 1993, espe- cially for the foreign market, the Group developed VHP (very high polarization) sugar, an innovation in the industry. Granulated refined, crystal and or- ganic sugar are also traded.

Table 1: Brazilian Sugarcane Harvest

	06/07	07/08	08/09	09/10	10/11	11/12
Sugarcane crushing (tons)	425,416	492,382	569,063	602,193	620,409	559,215
Sugar production (tons)	29,798	30,719	31,047	32,956	38,006	35,925
Ethanol production (million liters)	17,710	22,422	27,513	25,694	27,376	22,681
Anhydrous ethanol (million liters)	8,292	8,363	9,336	7,065	8,323	8,593
Hydrous ethanol (million liters)	9,418	14,059	18,177	18,629	19,053	14,088
Exports						
Sugar (thousand tons)	19,597	18,603	20,795	24,088	27,514	24,342
Ethanol (million liters)	3,692	3,625	4,722	3,166	1,906	3,098
Imports						
Sugar (thousand tons)	0.044	0.031	0.08	0.018	0.017	
Ethanol (million Liters)	3.808	0.568	2.441	22.971	78.076	

Source: Adapted from Unica, Mapa & Secex

At the same time, sugarcane expansion is not consid- ered a threat to the Amazon rain forest (Unica, 2008). Firstly, sugarcane expansion in the last 25 years has occurred primarily in South-Central Brazil, in areas that are significantly distant from the rain forest and other important ecological areas, such as the Panta- nal wetlands and the Cerrado. In fact, most of this expansion (currently 60% of the national output) has occurred in the populous São Paulo State on tradi- tional agricultural lands, close to established sugar and ethanol processing plants.

Second, the Amazon rain forest does not offer favor- able economic and agronomic conditions conducive to sugarcane production, alternating dry and wet sea- sons, what are not suited to grow the plant and build up sucrose levels in the cane. Moreover, the absence of a reliable transportation infrastructure to transport the final product (either sugar or ethanol, since the cane itself cannot be transported for long distances) out of the processing areas is a major limiting factor that precludes sugarcane production in the region.

Third, future expansion is anticipated to continue in South-Central Brazil, particularly in degrade pas- tures. The most promising areas for expansion are in

Western of the São Paulo state, Western of the Minas Gerais state and the Southern regions of the states of Mato Grosso do Sul and Goiás, in the Cerrado bi- ome. From 1992 to 2003,, the sugar cane areas have grown in the Center- South around 94% of the exist- ing production units. Moreover, the expansion of the sugarcane sector has not yet attracted other agricul- tural activities, such as cattle and soybean, into the rain forest (IBGE, 2008, UNICA, 2008). The dynamics of the cattle industry, which has been present in the Amazon region for the past 30 years, are unrelated to the sugarcane production. Cattle raising activities in the greater Amazon are linked to the logging indus- try, which has been the "cash crop" of the rain forest. Sugarcane for ethanol production in Brazil occupies around of 1/4 of that dedicated to corn, 1/8 of the area planted with soybeans and 1/60 of the land used for cattle farming. As a result, while sugarcane produc- tion has increased steadily in recent years, food pro- duction in Brazil has also grown dramatically with- out any material price increases for a while.

4.2 Cases: An overview

Company A is the second largest producer of eth- anol in Goias State, Midwest region of Brazil. The company has received prizes related to socio-environmental practices in the last few years. Its single plant has ISO90000 and ISO14001 certifications. It was a pioneer in Brazil in sugar-ethanol regarding socio-environmental practices. It produces organic sugar as well as traditional sugar and ethanol. Upon being enquired if the market would accept to pay a premium for a product made according to the standards of care entailed in environmental preservation, all the interviewees manifested that the Brazilian market, despite prioritizing the purchase of such a product, would still not be willing to pay more.

Company's financial data indicates that there were some losses in previous years. In 2007, the company's result was positive, totaling US$ 12.51 million. In the following years the results were negative, presenting losses of US$ 1.55 million in 2008 and US$ 24.02 million in 2009. The company explains that such results are related to the interaction of several factors: investment in new machinery and equipment for the plant, acquisition of crop machinery, hiring qualified personnel to operate them, the rising price of fertilizer used on crops and the dry weather.

Company B is the result of a joint venture between a big Brazilian sugar and ethanol exporter, and one of the biggest global players in the fuel market. This organization possesses 23 mills and is the 5th largest Brazilian corporation, based on yearly turnover.

Company B has focused on increasing sugarcane and plant productivity like other large companies in this industry. Some plants have made significant investments in industrial automation, agricultural mechanization and outsourcing, transportation logistics and sugarcane development and farming. These investments have reduced costs, increased productivity and produced residues and by-products, such as bagasse, which are used for energy co-generation, animal feed and fertilizer.

Company C is one of the largest Brazilian sugar-ethanol trader with an integrated production process based on a network configuration. Its business model concentrates 22% of the Brazilian market and plays a significant role in the global sugarcane market. The organization has a unique business model that consolidates all sugar and ethanol supply chain actors, from follow-up of the harvest in the field to the end markets, including storage, transport and trading phases.

The group now participates in the European Bonsucro standard (EU Renewable Energy Directive Production Standard), which includes fundamental requirements for the sale of biofuels in the European Union. The company also has an agreement with Eco-Energy for sales to the U.S. market. Even so, the environmental initiatives are still in their early stages. The main challenge of the Group is to engage in a sustainable approach to all the mills and partners in the network.

Even so, there is progress in this process, but the actions are still incipient. Currently they are beginning to deploy measurements procedures, sharing information and seeking mill owners' motivation to adopt best practices. Initial results already show a quick drive in this sense, but there are no significant environmental and financial results yet. While realizing the importance, a considerable part of the network members is characteristically conservative and aims to develop a sustainable culture effectively. There is an increasing pressure regarding socio-environmental impacts, and, clearly, companies in this industry are trying to respond to these pressures.

4.3 Technologies and Process

Alternative use of pesticide is one the main actions present in the cases. Company A utilizes the monitoring of termites and rationalization in the application of insecticides in infested areas have allowed an economy of US$ 500,000/year in the last few years. In the Company B the biological control of certain sugarcane pests is present. They produce spores of the Metarhizium anisopliae fungus, replacing the use of pesticides in the control of spittlebugs (Mahanarva fimbrioleta). A common pest in cane fields is the sugarcane borer (Diatraea saccharalis), which the Group controls with the Cotesia flavipes wasp, which is bred in their own laboratories. Both controls contribute to environmental preservation.

Another common action is the rationalization of the fertilization application or alternative one as well. Company A deployed several actions aimed at reducing production costs based on the utilization of the vinasse to substitute the chemical fertilizer applied to the fields. At present, the company is managing to fertilize-irrigate 20% of its plantation. The company's use of fertilizers can be observed in relation to the national average. The cost reductions have reached around US$ 1 million in the last few years. Its use of agricultural pesticides is 51.85% less than the national average. This represented a cost reduction of over US$ 2.5 million/year. The company also utilizes natural fertilizers. One example is compost, a byproduct that acts as a substitute for chemical fertilizer. Around 5%

of the residues generated in the manufacturing process are transformed into compost.

Improving industrial processes and rational use of water are two concerns in all the companies. Company B creates a program that enhances the quality of the raw material, from soil preparation through to harvesting, by reducing mineral and vegetable impurities. As a result, the sugarcane now arrives at the mill with a lower impurity content, which improves crushing efficiency and, more importantly, reduces cane washing, in turn reducing water consumption and environmental interference. Moreover, water utilization is, in general, a key factor in assessing sustainability and GSCM. Water use reduction during the industrial production process of ethanol remains a challenge for mainly mills (Schaffel and La Rovere, 2010). However, Company B has installed blower cleaning equipment in 11 mills, eliminating the use of water in their operation, and two plants have installed diffusers instead of conventional milling. This innovation improves plant crushing capacity by 0.5%.

In the company A, there are also standardized routines for all the functional areas of the plant. Periodically, an internal team audits those areas. The company explains that, for the whole process, an analysis of the environmental risk is made. With regard to seeking efficiency in the use of packaging, as suggested by Sarkis (2003), it was explained that the company utilizes plastic in its products due to its lower cost. Moreover, there is no reverse logistical flow of packaging. The company has taken actions over the years aimed at decreasing the environmental impacts caused by the residues from its industrial processes.

On the other hand, Company B adopted geo-processing technologies with utilization of satellite images to monitor plantation. The information obtained enables the company to direct actions necessary to improve its productivity rapidly and efficiently. Another geo-processing technology implemented was the SIG (Geo-Referenced Information System), which facilitates exploring the databank based on thematic maps.

Thus, Company B also decreased its water consumption by 16% from 2008-2009 to 2009-2010. There are also investments in place to obtain more concentrated vinesse, thereby reducing water. This residual water should be used to recover evaporation losses in the process, allow water consumption rationaliza-

tion and improve efficiency on the shop floor.

The first improvement mentioned by the company C is mechanized harvesting, which also leads to minimization of emissions (CO_2). To assess what would be best for nearby communities, they developed a series of joint forums and realized that the priority was to mechanize. Sugarcane burning significantly disturbed local communities directly.

Since 2011, Company C has implemented an advanced system for monitoring social, environmental and economic KPIs aligned to GRI methodology. Using EDI, all mills report, in real time, the current performance and outcomes to the entire network. The company makes significant efforts to train employees and to convince mills to adopt these methodologies, partly due to the need for competitiveness. One of the key efforts is to allocate to each mill a sustainability representative engaged in the practices, following the daily routines. Besides, Company C has also approved 40 of the 48 mills on the RFS-2. Even considering the autonomy of each member, they motivates the members of the network to share knowledge and their best practices. It highlights evidence of collaboration within the network, combining efforts on problem solving, increasing productivity and seeking better uses of natural resources like water.

4.4 Facilities

Company A has a single plant located in the Midwest of Brazil, one of the region's main producers of grains and other agricultural products. The company possesses 38,000 hectares under sugar cane cultivation, and 2,400 direct employees and 10,000 indirect. On average, the company harvests 2,800,000 tons of sugar cane, and, in the last few years, it has produced an average of 4,200,000 sacks of common sugar, 12,000 tons of which are organic. It produces around 100,000 m^3 of ethanol. Besides this, it possesses the capacity to generate 40 MW of electricity from the bagasse.

All the residues generated undergo a weighing and control process, and then accounted for. For every residue, there is an annual reduction goal of 5%. The company has also had a contract since 2001 for carbon credit trading with the Dutch government. In the period 2001 to 2007, the company contributed a reduction of 130,597 tons of CO_2, which represented revenue of € 587,686.50. The commercialization of carbon credit is possible because around 90% of the irrigation pumps used in the sugar cane fields are run on electricity produced from bagasse instead of fossil fuels like diesel.

Company B, however, is twenty times bigger than Company A in number of employees, 43,000 being direct, has a cultivated area of 605 thousand hectares, grinds 44 million tons of sugarcane, producing 4 billion tons of sugar and 2.2 billion liters of ethanol (data from 2010-2011). Their plans include expansion of its market share, and to reach a production level of 5 billion liters of ethanol by 2015.

In other hand, Company C entity is composed by 47 mills that belong to the sugar consortium by an exclusive sales regimen. These mills are located in the Southeast region of Brazil. Additionally, another 50 non-partners have occasional participation in this process too, allowed to sell non-exclusively to Company C. The main benefit of being part of this business model is to increase the competitiveness of small-size mills. Each member has the possibility of a long-term contract for the amount produced, which minimizes risks and allows investments, training and participating in projects. In the 2011-2012 harvest, Company C members were able to reach total sugar sales of 6.9 million tons. Sales in the Latin American market, including Brazil, amounted to 1.83 million tons, while global exports reached 5.12 million tons. Meanwhile, ethanol sales reached 3.7 billion liters, of which 3 billion liters represented domestic sales and the balance exports. The occasional members' mills (non-exclusive partners) represented 2.7 million tons of sugar and 400 million liters of ethanol. All these activities consolidated a net income of US$ 6 billion. For the company, exports enjoyed a premium price, but it needs to achieve socio-environmental international standards and obtain certifications.

4.5 Supply Chain

Unlike other companies in this sector in Brazil, Company A is verticalized and its activities span from the cultivation of the sugar cane to its processing. It includes bearing all the inherent costs incurred in seeding and harvesting, assuming the financial and environmental risks, providing all the equipment and labor, among other aspects. In this manner, the company aims to ensure a stable supply of the raw material.

Upon investigating if the buyers' market presents any requirement regarding productive practices

that respect the environment throughout the company's supply chain, it was detected that this occurs only in the case of organic sugar. All the production of this product is sold to foreign buyers, who seek to find out about the sustainable practices adopted by the company and the supply chain.

Company B crushed more than 39 million tons of cane in the fiscal year, 2008-2009. Its pace of growth over the past five years has forced the Group to increase its cane purchases from suppliers, which have jumped from 5.2 million tons in 2001 to more than 17 million tons in 2008-09. The company takes action to monitor and mitigate socio-environmental impacts related to the entire value chain, including suppliers and buyers. A group of 28 suppliers and 9 buyers joined in a training and development program with the objective of implementing a management approach based on the Global Reporting Initiative (GRI) model. All the participants have been involved in the search for standardized information and in the definition of needs for a software implementation.

Company B has also embarked on a joint project with several sugarcane players in order to reduce transport costs by 20%. The Group is investing around US$ 3.5 billion in building an ethanol pipeline (length 880 miles) with a capacity of 21 billion ethanol liters annually. As a result, all players will not only optimize costs, but also mitigate environmental impacts and carbon emissions.

Large buyers, like Coca-Cola, pressure the market as a whole for more advanced environmental practices because they are concerned with their whole supply chains. Next requests followed by upstream supply chain pressure indicate aspects like water consumption and re-use practices. Therefore, there is a pursuit of sustainable activities throughout the whole supply chain, from the sugarcane producer to the final client.

4.6 People

Company A moves forward through actions that contemplate concerns with society and employees which possess importance in obtaining certifications and awards, and, consequently, access to more demanding markets, such as North America and Europe. At the same time that mechanization of the reaping of the raw material, which, today, extends to 88% of the total plantation, responding to one of the main criticisms of sugar cane growing in Brazil – labor exploitation, it is viewed by the company as a potential source of social disequilibrium in the region.

Among the actions of the company to ease the loss of jobs in manual harvesting, we highlight a project that consolidates the production seedlings and provides incentives for planting rubber trees in the region. This activity needs labor for the latex collection. Currently, there are 2,700 million trees, and around 1,000 workers are employed directly. Additionally, there are actions related to community education development. Since 1994, the company has implemented a series of activities in the area of education. It provides primary and intermediate level education. Currently, more than 300 students, children of employees, are benefited.

The company invests in the qualification of its employees, providing study scholarships. The company informs that, in the last two years, it has benefited around of 380 employees with subsidization of 50% of the monthly fee at graduate and post-graduate level. The investments in education of employees reached US$ 375,000 in the last years.

Company B adopted a similar strategy who grasps its attention on training and qualification of the cane cutters and increases their remuneration, since mineral impurity content is a factor in the Profit Sharing Program. In 2007, Company B created a Program, designed to ensure that all Group employees are fully equipped to carry out the Group's agricultural activities. The partnership with HR – People and Agricultural Development resulted not only in the technical training of their workers, but also in the preparation of team leaders. The advantage is that teams are trained in technical matters by their immediate superiors and, with the help of HR, in behavioral aspects. Program results are carefully monitored in order to ensure quality, safety, and respect for the environment.

It is possible to identify a significant increase in social investments. In 2007, they invested around US$ 2 billion, followed by US$ 2.2 billion in 2008 and US$ 2.8 billion in 2009/2010. Additionally they implement a sustainable business strategy in its supply chain. It is not a simple task, because the company's database includes 33,000 suppliers, and 15,000 of them have engaged in active business with Company B in the last few years.

Specific social actions drive Company C efforts in the social dimension. Partnerships with NGOs educate more than 5,000 teenagers, aiming at improved life quality and a better future through reading, logical reasoning, problem solving, performance in learning. Other social projects take care of child health through sports initiatives, like swimming sponsorship for a group of 250 children from low-income families. Internally, there are also policies related to the improvement of job health conditions, accident reduction and workers' health.

5. Final remarks

The cases suggest that sustainability is still a challenge for the "green" biofuel even for the largest companies in Brazil. All three companies' present actions are related to sustainable practices in their operations, albeit situated in different stages.

Table 2 summarizes the decisions related to sustainability using an operations strategy perspective, and each of them are discussed in detail.

Table 2: Categories of decision and existing policies in the cases analyzed

Decision Categories	Company A	Company B	Company C
Technology and Process	Mechanization in harvesting. Rationalization in use of inputs. Re-use of byproducts (sugarcane bagasse).	Mechanization in harvesting. Advanced tools for harvesting and monitoring. Rationalization in water use. "SóPuraCana" quality system.	Mechanization in harvesting. Advanced tools for harvesting and monitoring.
Facilities	One plant. Low scale.	Multiple plants. High scale.	Network of plants. High scale.
People	Social programs for income generation. Training and development.	Training and development.	Social programs. Training and development.
Supply Chain	Low upstream integration. Increasing downstream integration. Vertical integration from plantation to processing.	Increasing upstream and downstream integration.	Increasing upstream integration.

Nevertheless, Company A is in the most advanced stage of sustainable practices, featuring simultaneous goals of cost reduction and increasing value added to its products. Apparently, this is a trade-off but a combination of quality certifications and other sustainability - related practices may create a capability in this case. For this company, sustainability is embedded in the business strategy, which influences all the decisions. Company A is characteristically in the third stage of competitiveness with a clear integration of its sustainable decisions in operations with the company's business strategy

Company B still presents actions favoring mitigation of environmental impacts in conjunction with gains in productivity and (re-)use of byproducts. The company's organic products seek to compete in higher added value markets. Similarly Company C, is in the same second stage of sustainability still following the traditional industry pattern. The mills that comprise Company C production network present initial actions related to technology and processes, but mainly for mechanized harvesting, thereby following the practices of the industry. Its products are certified commodities with potential sales in more sophisticated markets like the EU. We may state that, for these two companies, sustainability is still advancing towards higher integration with their business strategies.

We also identified that all the companies also seek to implement actions to reduce operational costs that accomplish socio-environmental standards. Thus, it is expected that companies in commodity industries, like sugar-ethanol, will develop environmental capabilities in operations that may simultaneously increase added value and decrease operational costs. In an advanced stage, we expect that is possible to create synergetic capabilities: even in a commodity market. Therefore, we may consider that companies in the sugar-ethanol industry seek to develop environmental capability in operations that enable synergy between added value and operational costs.

From the economic aspect, even though Company A presented the most advanced practices, the company has undergone a period of consolidation of its investments aimed at sustainable practices, which may explain some unsatisfactory financial results over the last few years. At the same time, Companies B and C have expanded their operations leveraged by their positive results in the last years. In the environmental dimension, several actions of the three companies have sought the reduction of residues and their reutilization, mainly for sugarcane cultivation, which demonstrates that these companies pursue improvement in their socio-environmental practices. Finally, in the social dimension, the actions are directed towards substitution of direct labor in the harvest, investments in education and training, and social actions in the society.

One of the main challenges for this industry is to add value to their commoditized products, and simultaneously decrease operational costs. Based on the cases studied, the following actions are associated to the sustainability and operations strategy approach in the sugar-ethanol sector: (i) Seeking environmental certifications and advanced technologies, (ii) Mechanization of sugarcane harvesting, (iii) Training and development for sustainable practices, (iv) Actions for input consumption reduction and reutilization, and (v) Need for supply chain integration upstream and downstream.

All these actions may decrease some trade barriers related, for example, to job safety in sugarcane harvesting and water use. At the same time, the current low risk of expansion of new cultivation areas into the Amazon rain forest region is a positive aspect for the image of this industry.

These manuscript findings were based on case studies of three Brazilian sugar-ethanol organizations. The results can be valid within this specific context. Due to the interdependencies of uncertainty, political and economic decision process, future studies may advance by comparing organizations located in different contexts.

Derived from the conclusions of this study, this paper open an opportunity of future research exploration of challenges for the trade-off of adding vale and increasing pressure for cost reduction. Also the influence of scale and organizational design in the sustainability policies deserves deeper analyses.

6. REFERENCES

Angell, L. & Klassen, R. (1999). Integrating environmental issues into the mainstream: an agenda for research in operations management. Journal of Operations Management, 17(5), 575-598.

Beamon, B. M. (1999). Designing the green supply chain. Logistics Information Management, Bingley, 12(4), 332-342.

Boyer, K. K., & Lewis, M. (2002). Competitive Priorities: Investigating the need for trade-offs in Operations Strategy. Production and Operations Management, 11(1), 9-20.

Collis, J. & Hussey, R. (2005). Business Research. New York: Macmillan.

De Burgos, J. & Lorente, J.J.C. (2001). Environmental performance as an operations objective. 2001. International Journal of Operations and Production Management. 21(12), 1553-1572.

Dyllick, T. & Hockerts, K. (2002). Beyond the business case for corporate sustainability. Business Strategy and the Environment, 11(2), 130-141.

Eisenhardt, K. (1989). Building theories from case study research. Academy of Management Review, 14(4), 532-550.

Elkington, J. (1997). Cannibals with forks: the triple bottom line of 21st century business. Oxford: Capstone.

Everingham, Y. L., Muchow, R. C., Stone, R. C., Inman-Bamber, N. G., Singels, A., & Bezuidenhout, C. N. (2002). Enhanced risk management and decision-making capability across the sugarcane industry value chain based on seasonal climate forecasts. Agricultural Systems, 74(3), 459-477.

Farinelli, B., Carter, C. A., Lin, C. & Sumner, D. A. (2009). Import demand for Brazilian ethanol: a cross-country analysis, Journal of Cleaner Production, 17, 9-17.

George, A. L., & Bennett, A. (2004). Case Studies and Theory and Theory Development in the Social Sciences. Massachusetts: MIT Press.

Hall, J., Matos, S., Severino, L. & Beltrão, N. (2009). Brazilian biofuels and social exclusion: established and concentrated ethanol versus emerging and dispersed biodiesel, Journal of Cleaner Production, 17, 77-85.

Hayes, R. & Wheelwright, S. C., (1984). Restoring Our Competitive Edge: Competing Through Manufacturing. John Wiley, New York, NY.

Hutchins, M. J. & Sutherland, J. W. (2008). An exploration of measures of social sustainability and their application to supply chain decisions, Journal of Cleaner Production. 16, 1688–1698.

Kleindorfer, P.R., Singhal, K. & Van Wassenhove, L.N. (2005). Sustainable operations management. Production and Operations Management, 14(4), 482–92.

Kozloff, N. (2010). The Dirty Underside of Lula's Clean Energy Revolution. Brazil's biofueled paradise is looking more and more like a carbon-spewing wasteland. Foreign Policy.

Krajnc, D., Mele, M. & Glavi, P. (2007). Improving the economic and environmental performances of the beet sugar industry in Slovenia: increasing fuel efficiency and using by-products for ethanol, Journal of Cleaner Production, 15, 1240-1252.

Linton, J. D., Klassen, R. & Jayaraman, V. (2007). Sustainable supply chains: An introduction. Journal of Operations Management, 25(6), 1075–1082.

Miller, J. G. & Roth, A. V. (1994). A Taxonomy of manufacturing strategies. Management Science, 40 (3), 285-304.

Pedroso, M. C. & Zwicker, R. (2007). Sustentabilidade na cadeia reversa de suprimentos: um estudo de caso do Projeto Plasma. São Paulo, RAE, 42 (4), 414-430.

Pereira, C.L.F., Ortega, E. (2010). Sustainability assessment of large-scale ethanol production from sugar cane, Journal of Cleaner Production, 18, 77-82.

Sarkis, J. (2003). A strategic decision framework for green supply chain management. Journal of Cleaner Production, 11, 397–409.

Schaffel, S.B. & La Rovere, E.L. (2010). The quest for eco-social efficiency in biofuels production in Brazil. Journal of Cleaner

Production, 18, 1663-1670.

Schroeder, R. G., Bates, K.A. & Junttila, M.A. (2002). A resource-based view of manufacturing strategy and the relationship to manufacturing performance. Strategic Management Journal, 23(2), 105-117.

Skinner, W. (1969). Manufacturing - missing link in corporate strategy. Harvard Business Review, 46 (3), 136-145.

Stuart, I., Mccutcheon, D., Handfield, R., Mclachlin, R. & Samson, D. (2002). Effective case research in operations management: a process perspective, Journal of Operations Management, 20(5), 419-433.

UNICA Report - Sugarcane Industry in Brazil. 2013. Accessed online on May/16/2013 http://www.unica.com.br/documentos/publicacoes/

Wheelwright, S. C. (1984). Manufacturing Strategy: Defining the Missing Link. Strategic Management Journal , 5(1), 77-91.

Wheelwright, S. C. & Bowen, H. K. (1996). The challenge of manufacturing advantage. Production and Operations Management, 5(1), 59–77.

Yin, Robert K. (2009). Case Study Research: Design and Methods. Thousand Oaks, California: Sage.

Zhu, Q., Cote, R. P. (2004). Integrating green supply chain management into an embryonic eco-industrial development: a case study of the Guitang Group. Journal of Cleaner Production, 12, 1025–1035.

6

Managing Complex Projects
in Multinational Enterprises

Flávio Jorge Freire D Andrade Battistuzzo

Universidade Nove de Julho

flavio@bcconsult.com.br

Marcos Roberto Piscopo

Universidade Nove de Julho

piscopomr@gmail.com

ABSTRACT: The management of complex projects has received the attention of several scholars. It is considered a process that contributes to the future success of organizations and their businesses. Within this context, Multinational Enterprises (MNEs) have specific characteristics where the correct use of the concepts of managing complex projects is a critical factor. This study was developed to analyze how capital goods manufacturing MNEs manage complex projects in the segment of Complex Products and Systems (CoPS). Based on multiple case studies, the main techniques used by MNEs representative of this market segment have been assessed. They do have some organizational practices aligned with the concept of project complexity but there is a distance between the academia and the industry.

Keywords: *Project Management; Complex Projects; Multinational Enterprises*

1. INTRODUCTION

Despite a long debate whether project management is a practice or an academic discipline, there is a convergence amongst authors regarding the increasing importance of project management (PM) within organizations. According to Kwak and Anbari (2009), based on a study of 18 top management and business journals (including *Journal of Operations Management and Academy of Management Perspectives*), project management shows connections with eight disciplines. Ranked from the most to the least appeared subjects, they are: (1) Strategy/Portfolio Management, (2) Operations Research / Decision Sciences / Operation Management / Supply Chain Management, (3) Organizational Behavior / Human Resources Management, (4) Information Technology/Information Systems; (5) Technology Applications / Innovation / New Product Development / Research and Development; (6) Performance Management/Earned Value Management; (7) Engineering and Construction; and (8) Quality Management/ Six Sigma.

Project management is perceived as a strong contributor to business become more competitive. It is also recognized as a process to enable organizations for future business success (Whitty & Maylor, 2009). Continuous demand for sustainable growth and innovation, including fast changes to technology, require companies to invest in new infrastructure intensifying the use of PM (Shenhar & Dvir, 2007). Furthermore, projects have been used as a form of work organization, comprising the need to innovate (Newell, Goussevskaia, Swan, Bresnen, & Obembe, 2008). According to Söderlund (2002), there is a *projectization* which has led to changes in the way firms organize product and process development. Finally, the use of PM system is spread along the majority of construction, product development and engineering efforts (Shenhar, 2001). Despite of this convergence regarding the use of PM as an important tool for organizations to cope with the continuous state of change, the extant PM theory is recent and needs further development. As projects become more complex, the need for more comprehensive literature and practical test of the existing theory is required. The objective is to understand the practical implications on how to effectively use the concepts of PM (Shenhar, 2001).

Approaches like the Diamond concept and the need for more qualified project managers through certification schemes like the Project Management

Institute – PMI are responses to current demands. The term complex itself has been subject to intense discussion. It may be confused with complicated (Whitty & Maylor, 2009) or perceived as a result of combined factors as per the diamond approach of Shenhar and Dvir (2007). The managerial complexity can arise from dimensions like mission, organization, delivery, stakeholders and team (MODeST dimension). Each of them with dynamic and structural complexity elements as defined by Maylor, Vidgen, and Carver (2008).

Multinational Enterprises (MNEs) are defined as organizations that own and control activities in two or more different countries. Data on MNEs show that they are responsible for about 80% of global trade (estimated at USD 19 trillion) and Foreign Direct Investments are estimated to reach USD 1.8 trillion in 2015. According to data from the Brazil Central Bank (Banco Central do Brasil, 2014) the Foreign Direct Investments (FDIs) in Brazil have reached USD 33.7 billion in 2007 with an increase of 30% in 2008 (USD 43.9 billion) and USD 30.4 in 2009. The capital goods market segment accounted for 36%, on average, for the growth over this period.

According to Dunning and Lundan (2008), MNEs engage in FDIs in order to increase the value of their assets as perceived by owners. In addition, Kalasin, Dussauge, and Rivera-Santos (2014) state that organizations expand to international markets in order to leverage their advantages in new environments. The internalization of an organization is determined according to a paradigm named as OLI (ownership, location, and internalization). This concept offers a general explanation of the extent and pattern of MNEs foreign value added activities of an organization (Dunning, 2001). Projects increase organizational innovation, facilitate the implementation of changes, and implement strategies to increase competitive advantage (Shenhar & Dvir, 2007). Therefore, in order to increase the value of their assets, companies engage in some kind of project management.

The capital goods manufacturing segment has important characteristics not only in terms of importance to MNEs but also in terms of project complexity. Based on an evaluation of Mergers and Acquisitions retrieved from data published in the UNCTAD reports from 2010 to 2013, we identified that the capital goods segment accounted for USD 530 billion in acquisition value (approximately 39% of the total amount of acquisition value – USD 1.360

billion) (UNCTAD, 2010, 2011, 2012, 2013). Regarding to complexity, manufacturing capital goods industry includes a special type of products, best known as Complex Products and Systems – CoPS. The term is used to categorize high technology and high-value capital goods (Davies & Hobday, 2005).

The main objective of this study is to explore how capital goods manufacturing MNEs manage complex projects within the CoPS market segment. More specifically, we aim at investigating three main aspects: (i) what dimensions of project complexity organizations consider, (ii) how complex projects characteristics affect organizations' project management practices, and (iii) how organization strategies are aligned with project execution.

The relevance of the theme can be highlighted by the importance of this market segment to FDI investments, mergers and acquisitions and the unique characteristics

of project complexity related to the CoPS market segment. In order to respond these questions, we initially performed a theory review covering project complexity, MNEs, capital goods (CoPS) and the management of complex projects in MNEs. Following the theoretical review, we presented the methodological procedures employed. We, then, demonstrated the results and discussed them. Finally, we made some conclusions and recommendations for further research.

2. THEORY REVIEW

Theory review was performed to cover four main topics: (i) project complexity, (ii) multinational enterprises, (iii) capital goods, CoPS, and (iv) managing complex projects in MNEs. Table 1 summarizes these topics by mentioning some relevant works related to each of them.

Table 1

Theory Review	
Project Complexity	Maylor et al. (2008), Whitty and Maylor (2009), Browning (2014), Baccarini (1996), College of Complex Project Managers (2006), Shenhar and Dvir (2007), Sauser, Reilly, and Shenhar (2009)
Multinational Enterprises	Dunning and Lundan (2008), Harris, Kim, and Schwedel (2011), D'Aveni and Gunther (1994), D'Aveni, Dagnino, and Smith (2010), Dunning (2001), Hitt, Ireland, and Hoskisson (2011), Scholes, Johnson, and Whittington (2008)
Capital Goods – Complex Products and Systems	Davies and Hobday (2005), UNCTAD (2010), UNCTAD (2011), UNCTAD (2012), UNCTAD (2013), Banco Central do Brasil (2014)
Managing Complex Projects in Multinational Enterprises	Sauser et al. (2009), Wikström, Artto, Kujala, and Söderlund (2010), Pinto and Slevin (1988), Raz, Shenhar, and Dvir (2002), Shenhar (2001), Milosevic and Srivannaboon (2006), Shenhar (2004), Hass (2009)

Source: Summary prepared by the authors

2.1 Project Complexity

The first important aspect regarding a complex project is the definition of the word *complex* and its distinction from *complicated*. Understanding the difference is an important baseline for managing this kind of undertaking. According to the Webster Dictionary, *complex* is defined as "composed of two or more parts; involving many parts" – *complicated* is something "difficult to analyze or understand". The difference relates to the interconnection between

parts. In complex parts, there is interdependency between them. In complex systems there are interactions amongst parts of the system producing neither linear nor predictable outcomes (Maylor et al., 2008). Further expanding this concept, Whitty and Maylor (2009, p. 305), states that "a complex system is a system formed out of many components whose behavior is emergent". The outcome of the complex system cannot be inferred from the behavior of its components.

Complexity is an attribute that does not depend on the observer in opposition to complicatedness. According to Browning (2014), complexity is an objective characteristic of the system and complicatedness is a subjective one. Complicated may be related to the number of stakeholders involved. In complicated projects, complication can be managed with expertise, a better understanding of the parts that constitute the system. Project complexity has been studied by a number of authors and there is a general understanding that the application of the same approach for different projects (one size fits all) is not effective (Baccarini, 1996; College of Complex Project Managers, 2006; Shenhar & Dvir, 2007). Project complexity is defined as a measure of project scope which reflects characteristics like the number and interdependency between tasks as per Shenhar and Dvir (2007).

Project complexity affects the way projects should be managed. Baccarini (1996, p. 202) defines project complexity as "consisting of many varied interrelated parts and operationalized in terms of *differentiation* and *interdependency*". Complex projects require a greater managerial effort during its execution. Therefore, project complexity can be applied to different dimensions of the project management process, like organization, technology, decision-making, and environment. In such a way, when defining project complexity, one needs to state for which dimension the concept is being used (Baccarini, 1996). Complexity is a measure of the difficult to achieve the desired understanding of a complex system. Although high levels of uncertainty are a fundamental aspect of complex projects, this is not an exclusive characteristic of complexity. Is this sense, complexity is a variable and not a qualitative concept (Whitty & Maylor, 2009).

Another approach for the management of complex projects is the adaptive model, the Diamond concept. The underlying concept in this model is that different projects should be managed in different ways. This approach contrasts to more prescriptive ones adopted by the body of knowledge framework since it requires a system to identify the basic differences between projects. These differences are related to four dimensions, NTCP: novelty, technology, complexity and pace (Shenhar & Dvir, 2007). In the contingency theory, the idea is to fit project characteristics to project management approach instead of identifying critical success factors (Sauser *et al.*, 2009).

The 'novelty' dimension is related to how new the product is and it is composed of three sub dimensions: derivative, platform and breakthrough. The 'technology' refers to how much new technology is used encompassing sub dimensions as low-tech, medium-tech, high-tech and super high-tech. 'Complexity' is related to the extent of the complexity of systems and subsystems used and is classified into sub dimensions like assembly, system and array. Last, 'pace' gives an idea of how critical the period is, involving the sub dimensions regular, fast/competitive, time-critical and blitz. These four dimensions of the adaptive model for project management form the diamond model that sustains that the greater the diamond, the greater the potential benefits of the projects and the associated risks. The combination of these characteristics provides a comprehensive set of management practices what is expected to support the organization achieving project success and business results.

2.2 Multinational Enterprises

An MNE is defined by Dunning and Lundan (2008, p. 8) as an "enterprise that engages in FDI and owns or, in some way, controls value-added activities in more than one country". In the overcoming decades, MNEs shall face macroeconomics shocks that will establish the way MNE adapt and grow in the next decades. The world Gross Domestic Product (GDP) is estimated to reach USD 90 trillion by 2020, an increase of 40 percent when compared to that of 2011 (Harris *et al.*, 2011). The sources of the economic growth will tend to come from developing and emerging economies, considering that two thirds of the growth will be generated by advanced economies (Harris *et al.*, 2011).

According to the "World Investment Report 2013" (UNCTAD, 2013), MNEs are expected to account for 80% of global trade through their networks of affiliates, partners and suppliers. Specifically in developing countries, the trade value added generated by MNEs contributes to 30% of GDP. However, participating in this global value chain involves risks for these countries since there may be a potential for them to capture only a small portion of this value added chain, remaining locked to low added value activities. Nevertheless, according to UNCTAD estimates, foreign direct investments may reach USD 1.45 trillion in 2013 and USD 1.8 trillion in 2015. Table 2 indicates the FDI in Brazil from 2005 to 2009, according to the Central Bank of Brazil.

Table 2

FDI in Brazil – Evolution (USD billion)					
Year	2005	2006	2007	2008	2009
Capital Goods	6.4	8.7	12.2	14.0	11.9
Total	21.5	22.2	33.7	43.9	30.4
% of Capital Goods	29,8%	39,3%	36,1%	31,9%	39,2%

Source: Prepared by the authors based on Brazil Central Bank (2014)

As said by Dunning and Lundan (2008), MNEs engage in FDIs and production in order to increase the value of their assets as perceived by owners. MNEs activities are defined according to an approach called eclectic paradigm or OLI-Model. In line with this paradigm, internalization of an organization is determined by the transaction cost theory: in such cases, transactions are made within the organization when the transactions costs of the market are higher than the internal ones. This paradigm offers a general explanation of the extent and pattern of MNEs foreign value added activities of firms.

According to this paradigm, three forces determine the FDI undertaken by a firm. First, *Ownership advantages*, i.e., the competitive advantages that an organization of one nationality possesses when compared to organizations of another nationality in supplying a product or service to a particular set of market – for example, economies of scale, production processes, and property rights. Second, *Location advantages*: in this case, the organization chooses to add value to its operation/processes by locating its operation in other countries (for example, the existence of raw materials, low wages, and incentives). Third, *Internalization advantages* is re-

lated to the perceived advantage of producing rather than licensing to an external company or developing a partnership for production purpose (Dunning, 2001). Complementary to this concept, internalization advantages are expected to exploit market failures, like avoiding moral hazards, and compensation for the absence of future markets (Dunning & Lundan, 2008).

In order to earn above average returns, organizations define and implement strategies at business and corporate levels. At the business level, the concern is to gain a competitive advantage using organization's core competencies in a specific market. Corporate level strategies are focused on generating competitive advantage by selecting in what markets to compete (product and businesses) and how corporate functions should manage those firms (Hitt *et al.*, 2011). Regardless of strategy level, both have the ultimate objective of adding value to the company. Although there are some questions regarding the extent to which corporate level strategies add more value when compared to the isolated value created by business units, the fact is that companies use corporate level strategies for different reasons as indicated in Table 3.

Table 3

Corporate Strategies	
Strategy	**Reasons Underpinning the Strategy**
Market penetration – consolidation* *Defense actions to protect its assets*	Retaliation from competitors; Legal constraints; Defending market share; Downsizing or divestment.
Product development	Develop new or modified products to existing markets.

Corporate Strategies	
Strategy	**Reasons Underpinning the Strategy**
Market development	Offering new existing products to new markets.
Diversification	Efficiency gains – economies of scope;
	Deployment of corporate capabilities into new markets;
	Increase of market power;
	Response to market decline;
	Spreading of the risks;
	Fulfillment of power stakeholder's expectations.

Source: Adapted by the authors from Scholes *et al.* (2008).

2.3 Capital Goods – CoPS: Complex Products and Systems

As discussed, the capital goods segment plays a fundamental role in the Mergers and Acquisitions (M&A) scenario as well as in the FDIs. In 2012, the global economic crises in the Eurozone and the reduction of growing in the emergent economies produced an impact not only on greenfield FDI as well as on M&A projects (UNCTAD, 2013). The capital expenditure on greenfield projects fell by 33% comparing to that of 2011 reaching USD 612 billion in 2012, and the cross-border M&A declined significant 45% in the same period (total of USD 308 billion in 2012). Even considering the global economic crises, FDI greenfield projects within the capital good segment (manufacturing) reached USD 264 billion in 2012 (43% of total cross-border FDIs). M&A reached USD 308 billion in 2012 as indicated in Table 4.

Table 4

FDI Greenfield and M&A Cross-border investments (USD billions)					
	FDI Greenfield			**Cross border M&A**	
Year	2012	2011		2012	2011
Services	323	385		124	214
Manufacturing	264	453		137	205
Primary	25	76		47	137
Total	612	914		308	556

Source: Adapted by the authors based on UNCTAD (2013)

A subgroup of this market segment is the Complex Products and Systems (CoPS), defined as high technology and high value capital goods. According to Davies and Hobday (2005), this definition encompasses high cost products like electricity network control systems, infrastructure and engineering constructions. In general, MNEs provide these services and products through business projects. These companies use project management concepts to handle the delivery of major capital undertakings. The typical hierarchical and management structure does not match the needs to bring the required knowledge to face the environmental dynamics of this market. A project-oriented organization is more adaptive to these needs and to comply with that of customers in a fast changing condition (Davies & Hobday, 2005).

In terms of projects, the provision of CoPS depends fundamentally on project capabilities. According to Davies and Hobday (2005), every CoPS is a new project, requiring organizations in this area to develop abilities to win bids, learn from previous projects and manage in an efficient and effective way their projects, rather than focusing on cost, scope or economies of scales advantages.

2.4 Managing Complex Projects in Multinational Enterprises

The management of projects is becoming a central concern in most organizations. Its framework and concepts are used to leverage internal resources into process improvements, product development and/ or new services (Sauser *et al.*, 2009). Organizations also engage in projects to improve their own innovative capacity, serving as a strategic process to develop new capabilities (Wikström *et al.*, 2010). Not only project-based organizations use projects to manage complex business transactions but also those in the construction business, technology-based and service providing firms. These organizations structure their operational activities in different projects. Similarly, large events like Olympic Games organize their business into multiparty projects. The management of these complex projects produces new requirements for proper control by means of portfolio and program management (Wikström *et al.*, 2010).

The need for aligning strategy with project management has received the attention of various scholars (Pinto & Slevin, 1988; Raz et al., 2002; Shenhar, 2001; Shenhar & Dvir, 2007). According to Milosevic and Srivannaboon (2006), aligning projects with organizational strategies is an important aspect to avoid costs of project termination that do not contribute to organization's goals or the resource allocation to ongoing projects not aligned with these goals. Project management may be defined as a specialized form of management used as a mechanism or process to achieve business goals, tasks in a defined time/cost basis. Its fundamental objective is to support the execution of a specific strategy. As organizations formulate their strategies to achieve their goals, it can be concluded that projects are a mechanism or tool for achieving them (Milosevic & Srivannaboon, 2006).

Following Shenhar (2004), the traditional approach to project management focused on 'getting the job done' through the control of costs/schedule/scope is not enough to cope with the current business needs. As defined by its conceptual approach, Strategic Project Leadership®, projects are strategic organizational processes developed by organizations to achieve business strategies and goals. Customer needs, strategy, and success dimensions should be the focus of these projects. A project strategy is required as a form of alignment between business strategy and project management. In this sense, project strategy is defined as guidelines and definitions on how to achieve competitive advantage from project outcomes. The project success depends on factors like efficiency, impact on customer, impact on team, business and direct success and preparation for future (Shenhar & Dvir, 2007). However, in order to be successful, the management has to consider five factors: strategy, spirit, processes, organization and tools.

Contemporary projects performed by different organizations are focused on the process of adding value through implementing breakthroughs ideas, improving process performance, and creating competitive advantage (Hass, 2009). In order to achieve these benefits, MNEs engage in some forms of projects and have to develop project capabilities (Davies & Hobday, 2005). Furthermore, complexity is associated with four dimensions: size, variety, difficulty and change. In terms of size, projects with many components tend to be more complex (Frame, 2002). Variety is associated with the excessive options (and decisions) that project managers have to face (different contractors, employees, solutions, dates, etc.). Difficulty is related to something that is hard to do. The rapidity of change is the last facet of complexity. It contributes to the complexity "...by creating moving targets" (Frame, 2002, p. 30). Even as one assumes to have understood the customer requirements, they change. Sources for this facet of complexity can come from technology change, level of competition changes, and economic forces, for instance.

These factors tend to be present when MNEs implement their strategies as they involve different countries (size of the project), variety/decisions (local or international suppliers), difficulty in managing communications, and pace of change of local conditions (market innovation, change in regulatory markets).

The question on how capital goods manufacturing MNEs manage complex projects, particularly in the CoPS, is an important aspect of project management. The manner companies handle the complexities related to the business and project management needs to be understood and explored in a deeper way. Moreover, other important market segments can use lessons learned from these organizations. Figure 1 summarizes the proposed model.

Figure 1: Schematic of the conceptual model

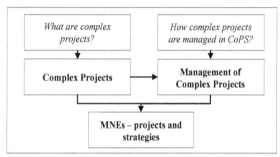

Source: Prepared by authors

3. METHODOLOGY

In order to answer the question stated in the beginning of this study – how capital goods manufacturing MNEs manage complex projects – a qualitative approach through a descriptive multiple case study was used (two MNEs). As an exploratory work, it aimed at developing and clarifying ideas and concepts for further studies or the development of hypotheses to be used by other researchers (Gil, 2008; Yin, 2010).

According to Yin (2003), a case study should be used when the main objective of the study is to answer "how" and/or "why" questions and the behavior of the participants cannot be controlled. Furthermore, the case study is indicated when it is necessary to evaluate contextual situations that are relevant to the phenomena under investigation. The nature of this study is descriptive as it is recommend when the objective is to analyze a phenomenon within its context and an emphasis is placed on the processes involved. A multiple case is justified when the researcher is interested in collecting data from different sources to draw conclusions based on empiric observations (Yin, 2003).

The unit of analysis is the organization. To select the investigated organizations we have used the following criteria. First, the organization should be a MNE. For the purpose of this study, "MNE, multinational or transnational enterprise, is an enterprise that engages in FDI and owns or, in some way, controls value-added activities in more than one coun-

try" as per Dunning and Lundan's (2008, p. 8) definition. Second, the organization (and its business unit) should be part of the capital goods segment, engaged in the manufacturing of CoPS – Complex Products and Systems (high technology and high-value capital goods (Davies & Hobday, 2005). Third, the organization would have to be project-oriented for the provision of its products and services to their customers. Last, it should be an important unit to the MNE in terms of the Brazilian operation, considering its strategic function within the group.

In order to proper evaluate the responses we defined some characteristics of the persons to be interviewed. He or she should have a deep knowledge of project management, act in a managerial position and have more than 10 years as an employee of the organization. The small number of interviewed persons (one from each organization) is justified by the focus of this study and by the representativeness of the selected persons.

The first selected organization is an European-based MNE named hereafter as Alpha. With global revenues greater than USD 40 billion in 2013 and more than 100.000 employees in the world, its business is comprised of different business units, all of them in the electrical equipment industry. Its portfolio of products includes assembly of electronics, software and system integration, and tailored suited to the customer requirements. All business units are project-oriented and most of their facilities hold ISO certifications like ISO 9001 (Quality), ISO 14001 (Environmental) and ISO 18001 (Occupational Health and Safety). This MNE operates in Brazil for more than 50 years and according to its annual report, revenues from Americas increased at a double-digit rate when comparing 2013 to 2012.

The second MNE (Beta) is an European-based corporation who is involved in the manufacturing of electric and electronic CoPS for different market segments, like civil construction and aerospace industries. These pieces of equipment are highly connected to specific software applications. The revenues of the group as a whole are greater than USD 40 billion with investments in research & development of around 20% of revenues. It operates in more than 50 countries with 60.000 employees and innovation is a driving force for both global and local operations. The Brazilian operation, although not large, plays an important role within the group, being a center of excellence of the entire group in its area of expertise. In Brazil, the business unit is part of the corporate organization for less than 10 years and holds ISO 9001 Quality Management System certification.

We used primary and secondary sources of information for data collection. As primary source, we opted for semi-structured interviews that were conducted in August 2014 and based on an script prepared considering the Shenhar and Dvir (2007)'s research and complemented with other theoretical insights. As secondary source of information we basically used the annual reports of both organizations in order to confirm the compliance to our selection criteria of MNEs. Some specific procedures on how to manage projects and regarding the process for internal qualification/certification of project managers specifically for organization Alpha (a total of 2 procedures and more than 10 specific training programs) were evaluated. For organization Beta, secondary sources of information were based only on annual reports written by the headquarters. It has to be noted that organization Beta operates in a more sensitive market in terms of confidentiality. For organization Alpha a sample record of the project managers qualification was also checked during the interview process.

As a result, the questions of the script involved the following topics: (i) characteristics of complex projects, (ii) management of complex projects in CoPS, and (iii) MNEs and their complex projects. Due to the research focus, one interview was performed with the manager responsible for the operational excellence of the processes within the business unity (Alpha). His professional experience included more than 20 years in the company, having supported the establishment of the process of project management, occupying the position of Project Manager for more than five years. In organization Beta, the interviewed was a mathematician, with a specialization in computer network and project management. The interviewed, at the time of interview, had more than 20 years in the engineering field, being 11 years in project management.

As secondary source of information, analyses were performed both in documents (procedures, records and other general documents) made available during the interview and in documents obtained in their websites, like Alpha and Beta annual reports. The content of the interviews was analyzed through the concepts of content analysis. According to Krippendorff (2012, p. 18), content analysis is "a research technique for making replicable and valid inferences from texts (or other meaningful matter) to the contexts of their use". The basic steps of this process

were based on Moraes (1999): (1) preparation of information, (2) unitization of information, (3) categorization or classification of the unities in categories, (4) description and (5) interpretation.

4. DATA ANALYSIS AND DISCUSSION

The data analysis was performed into three different aspects: (i) what dimensions of project complexity are considered by organizations, (ii) how complex projects characteristics affect organizations' project management practices, and (iii) how organization strategies are aligned with project execution.

Prior to the interview categories of analysis were defined and used as the basis for formulating the semi-structured interview script. The categories included were: (i) MNEs and the alignment between projects and strategies, (ii) project complexity and its differentiation to complicatedness, and (iii) management of complex projects in MNEs.

4.1 Complex Projects Characteristics

Organizations Alpha and Beta are project-oriented businesses what confirms the theory of organization structure of this market segment (Davies & Hobday, 2005). Alpha's projects are not the same in terms of complexity, although a general classification can be done using the Diamond approach. With regard to *Novelty*, Alpha's projects usually fit on platform (new generation in an existing product line) but a disruptive product may be developed locally or at the corporate level. In relation to *Technology*, it is medium to high technology. It has to be addressed that technology seems not to be a concern for organization Alpha. As addressed by the interviewed Alpha's executive, "We are a company of engineers; we always have someone in the group with a proper solution for an existing problem, always".

Regarding the *Complexity* dimension, Alpha's projects are a system or a matrix, a collection of scattered systems with a common mission. In respect to *Pace*, time is usually critical since Alpha's products are generally huge investments in capital goods made by their clients to increase manufacturing capacity. To Alpha, pace is one of the key aspects of their business. First, because pace is a common client complaint revealed by their customer satisfaction survey. Second, some of the delays are out of Alpha control since, to some extent, delays are caused by the client itself. As informed by the Alpha's executive interviewed, "sometimes delays or anticipations are requested by the client due to the price of the commodity, for example, energy and/or gasoline". Other external factor is the myriad of customer specific manufacturing standards for the product; what may be accepted in Europe as best practice, Brazilian customer demands a more stringent technical solution even to a higher cost. According to Alpha's executive, the third reason for delays is: "Brazilians are too optimistic ... our planning is not real ... we easily forget what happened in the past". Regarding complexity, Alpha does not identify or establish a difference between complex and complicated projects, although both factors are addressed by Alpha through different ways of managing complex projects as previously discussed in item 4.2.

Differently from Alpha's set of projects, Beta performs projects with a very similar level of complexity. Using the Diamond model, these projects can be classified as follows: (1) platform (novelty dimension), (2) high technology (technology dimension), (3) system (complexity dimension), and (4) regular (pace). In terms of project control, a different series of meetings is locally held in a monthly basis, and every four months at the corporate level.

Beta makes distinction between complex and complicatedness. All Beta projects are complicated since purchasing has more interfaces in terms of legal aspects than a normal business operation due to product reasons. The complexity comes from the process within the engineering function. For Beta, the specific characteristics of their engineering fit into the general definition of complexity made by scholars (Baccarini, 1996; Whitty & Maylor, 2009).

4.2 Management of Complex Projects

Alpha MNE follows corporate guidelines to manage projects although they may be flexible to match local procedures and needs. For instance, controlling cost is mandatory but how to do that may vary across countries. As informed by the interviewed, "It is basically an Alpha PMBoK, but including stronger considerations to safety and environmental aspects".

Alpha has a system to classify projects according to their complexity and complicatedness altogether (project complexity factor). Some of the factors involved in this classification are country of the client, involvement of state-owned companies, value of the project, existence of a joint venture between Alpha units in different countries, level of product innova-

tion and others. This set of aspects is rated in a numerical scale and depending on the number, a more skilled project manager is designated for a specific project. Alpha has a formal program to certify their project managers according to a 4-level scale and evaluate their performance through a career planning process.

Other aspect of project complexity considered by Alpha is the project review process. As the complexity factor mentioned above is higher, a different group of people makes the project review. According to the Alpha's executive interviewed, "the idea is simple: the more complex the project is, a higher level of functions is required to perform the project review".

On the execution side of projects in Alpha, there is an operations manager. Once a sale is closed, the operations manager assigns a project manager responsible for the project development. Their responsibility is to make sure the project is delivered according not only to the classic iron triangle (cost, scope, time) but also to the interface with clients in order to keep their needs under control. The project manager also participates in the commissioning of the equipment in order to understand problems that may emerge due to project management.

The project management process used by Alpha to conduct their projects does not follow the Diamond model in its full extent. However, it employs some aspects regarding the four dimensions of Shenhar and Dvir (2007) approach. Factors of *Novelty, Technology, Complexity* and *Pace* can be seen in their system for project complexity evaluation. On the other hand, despite the fact that technology is an important factor for complexity in the Diamond approach, it is not a concern for the organization Alpha. The reason for that, according to the interviewed, is one of their competitive advantages: the engineering knowledge and expertise of the Alpha team around the world.

Documentary sources of information from organization Alpha validated the qualification/certification process as well as that one used to manage projects. These documents are clear in terms of scope, detailing the steps required for managing projects like project review, interfaces with clients and control of all aspects of project execution – cost, scope and time. The documented qualification/certification process confirmed the data retrieved from the interview.

In Beta, the complicatedness of a project is managed through the basic concepts of PMBoK. Once a proposal is accepted, a project manager is designated and a project team is built. Team members are more functional rather than someone specifically designated to the project. For instance, there is no specific member responsible for the procurement process. In project review meetings, someone from purchasing participates to inform about the status of the processes. As said by the Beta's executive interviewed, "resources do not belong to project manager". In opposition to Alpha, there is no a general project manager.

In Engineering, Beta uses some specific tools for addressing the complexities of this set of activities. For instance, statistical and more probabilistic tools are used like the Graphic Evaluation and Review Technique (GERT), Monte Carlo Simulation, etc. As per the opinion expressed by the interviewed, "the current project managers do not have knowledge regarding PERT and other tools to analyze the complexities involved in projects and the interdependence of activities".

Based on the observation made, some conclusions may be drawn. Despite the fact that both organizations deal with complexity to some extent, they have the same basic level to address it as per the Diamond approach. The way both organizations deal with complexity is different and it is relevant to pointing out that, although both Alpha and Beta do not fully follow the diamond approach in terms of managing complex projects, both agree with the underlying concept of "one size does not fit all" (Shenhar & Dvir, 2007).

Organization Alpha used to have a system to financially reward the best projects. If the profit margin of the project was higher than planned part of the additional margin was distributed between team members and the project manager. There were three main reasons for Alpha to cease this financial reward. First, in some projects, an increase in the profit margin was an easy task and in most times this was not directly related to the internal capabilities of project team members. Second, the increase of margin was associated with external factors. As stated by the interviewed, "The better margin achieved was related with client mistakes rather than a good management of the project". Third, when projects were sold with known low margins, there was a tendency of the project manager to refuse to manage this project but Alpha has implemented a system to promote the best projects. Every year, all countries may indicate one successful project for each business unit to

be evaluated by the corporate committee. Based on aspects like cost, scope, time, etc., one project is selected and awarded. According to the interviewed, "It is a reward, a statue; it is an Alpha Oscar". It has to be highlighted that client perception plays a fundamental role in this process.

There is no financial award, but the project manager goes to the European headquarters and can take his wife with him and enjoys other interesting features like a formal ceremony, etc. The indication itself grants a status of an excellent project manager and can leverage their career. Finally, Alpha locally uses a small holographic statue with the project name in order to promote the project and reinforce its importance to the group. This way of promoting values aims to enhance the project meaning to the organization and it is in line with the concept of strategic project leadership by Shenhar (2004).

In Beta, the company was founded and initiated by engineers carrying out projects. In this sense, the interviewed has a perception that the employees have a great sense of self-motivation. The way the company performs businesses drives team members to an adequate level of motivation. As per the interviewed, "Project Management is our DNA".

4.3 Multinational Enterprises and Their Complex Projects

Both organizations, Alpha and Beta, have corporate offices in Europe. The FDI investments of these companies, according to their annual reports, follow the concept of the OLI paradigm (Dunning & Lundan, 2008). The strongest forces seem to be the internalization and location advantages. It is clear from their annual reports that investments in local operations explore these advantages. It also has to be addressed that for organization Beta, due to its line of products, the internalization is apparently the only option.

Organization Alpha is focused on technology innovation and business integration in order to capitalize the synergies between new companies and existing business unities. This strategy intends to increase Alpha's penetration in a market segment and develop new markets through acquisitions of other companies and product development (product innovation and improvement). This general corporate strategy does follow the concepts of the OLI paradigm of Dunning (2001), Dunning and Lundan (2008) and the Ansoff Matrix (Scholes et al., 2008).

In Alpha, the alignment goes beyond projects and corporate strategy to encompass quality, health, safety and environmental policies. The execution of the strategy is performed through a matrix organizational model. In this case, there is a manager responsible for strategy implementation who evaluates market trends. As informed by the interviewed "the business unit manager is responsible to get the businesses".

It has to be highlighted that Alpha's organizational structure has changed over the years from matrix to functional and vice-versa. According to the interviewed the matrix works better when there is a good personnel synergy between the operations manager and the business unit manager. The alignment between projects and corporate strategies is also pursued when there is a need to develop equipment and solutions to local clients. In this case, when a decision is made to enter a new market or to offer the same product to an existing market, Alpha sends their personnel to a center of excellence, for instance, in China, in order to acquire the competencies required for the business. This market strategy is in line with Ansoff's matrix as market penetration and also product development (Scholes *et al.*, 2008).

In Beta, a weaker organizational function matrix is in place. The Key Account Manager (KAM) is responsible for executing corporate strategies in terms of market penetration and product development. However, to some extent, the KAM has more autonomy to identify local opportunities and to locally work on them, what is different from Alpha's procedures. In any case, this new business or line of business has to be within the corporation portfolio of products and services and to consider potential risks for the business. Another aspect related to the alignment between projects and strategies is the corporate company request to establish a bidding process area.

The bidding process area is responsible to make sure that not only all aspects of the bidding process

have been fully considerate (profit margin, costs, cash flow, time, procurement, etc.), but also there is a proper alignment between sales proposal and corporate strategies. The initial analysis includes risk evaluation (e.g. country sensitivity), financial analysis (e.g. change fluctuation), accounting (taxes) and last, the required expertise for developing the solution to the client. This process happens before a commitment for selling is made.

Organization Alpha seems to be more mature in terms of organizational structure since it has experiencing lessons learned for longer time than Beta, who is still in the process of changing some local practices. For instance, Beta is a fully project-oriented organization and according to the interviewed person, "At corporate level, PM has complete authority".

Both Alpha and Beta manage their complex projects in a similar way. The idea of "one size does not fit all" is an underlying concept used by them to deal with the complexities of their projects and products. For Alpha, the management of complex projects is based on a corporate guideline and in this sense, complex and complicatedness are considered in the "project complexity factor". Alpha also has a strong organizational matrix structure what seems to be a consequence of a longer time under the corporate "umbrella". In Beta, the complexity and complicatedness of their projects are managed separately allowing the differentiation of both concepts and the implications of this differentiation. Beta deals with complexity in its engineering functional area and complicatedness is managed through the traditional concepts of project management like work breakdown structure.

The comparison between the two investigated companies was done in order to identify similarities and fundamental differences. Table 5 summarizes the main aspects identified.

Table 5

Alpha and Beta Comparison				
	Similarities			**Differences**
Complex Projects	Both Alpha and Beta are project-oriented organizations and conduct complex projects. Both Alpha and Beta control projects with reviews made at different levels.			Alpha deals with complex and complicatedness altogether. In BETA, complexity is within the Engineering function and complicatedness relates to the project as a whole. Alpha has a more restrictive approach do project management through guidelines from Corporate Headquarters. It uses a system for project classification. Beta does not follow specific guidelines for project management. Engineering project activities are considered complex and some probabilistic tools are used for project control and analysis.
The management of complex projects				
Multinational Enterprises	Both Alpha and Beta conduct FDI investments based on internationalization strategies and location advantages. The execution of corporate strategies is done by a specific function.			Alpha has a strong matrix organizational structure. The BU manager is responsible for aligning strategies and projects. In Beta, alignment between strategies and projects rests with KAM and the bidding process.

5. FINAL REMARKS

The main objective of this empiric study was to answer the question on how capital goods manufacturing MNEs manage complex projects, specifically within the Complex Products and Systems (CoPS) market segment. In order to properly answer this question, a descriptive case study was conducted in two capital goods MNEs, being both considered representative of the phenomenon under investigation.

Alpha and Beta MNEs consider complexity in their projects in different ways under the Diamond approach. In such a way, both MNEs have adaptive systems to manage their projects (Shenhar & Dvir, 2007). Alpha uses a complex factor calculator as the basis for managing their projects. Due to the similarities of their projects in terms of complexity,

Beta uses different probabilistic tools for controlling them in the engineering department. Therefore, both MNEs consider that "one size does not fit all".

With respect to project management, the way Alpha and Beta consider complexities in projects reveals some interesting aspects. First, the concepts of complexity and complicatedness seem not to have a clear consequence in the way Alpha manage their projects. As projects have different levels of complexity (as revealed by their complexity factors), complexity and complicatedness of the projects are taken altogether. In Beta, all projects have the same level of complexity. Alpha approach is more adaptive while Beta has a more informal way of executing their projects.

In terms of a system to pursue success within project management, Alpha seems to be more proactive.

Our analysis reveals that this mature view is possibly due to its longer project experience in Brazil. Alpha operates in Brazil for more than 50 years and have lessons learned on project motivation. Beta, however, has less than 10 years as part of the corporation and, therefore, the European culture of project management has not yet been fully absorbed by the local company. It is interesting to see that there is a real concern regarding the success of projects in both organizations although they address this aspect in different ways.

We also found that both organizations, at the corporate level, develop FDI mainly based on the internalization force (the OLI paradigm), confirming the theory proposed by Dunning and Lundan (2008). For Beta, the strongest force is clearly the internalization due to the specific characteristics of their products and client demands.

Considering how Alpha and Beta manage their complex projects, we concluded that they employ similar approaches since both are project-oriented organizations. While Alpha uses a strong organizational matrix to pursue the goals of each functional area involved Beta has the Key Account Manager (KAM) and a bidding system to assure that all proposals are aligned with corporate strategies. Therefore, Alpha and Beta follow much more 'common sense' practices rather than a specific theory of project management.

The empiric observation shows that the alignment between corporate strategies and projects, for both companies, seems to be a natural consequence of how these companies perform their business. As both companies operate in the CoPS business, investments made in research, at the corporate level, are deployed at local market depending on local conditions.

Further areas of research could be identified as a result of this study. First, an evaluation of the existing gaps between practitioners and recommendations from scholars on how to manage complex projects. This evaluation could focus on practical differences between complex and complicated projects. Second, explore how organizations can leverage the management of project complexity based on compensation (through financial and/or recognition award). Third, study how multinational project-based organizations manage complex product undertakings in the CoPS market segment and how they align them with business strategies.

Although limited in the number of MNEs studied and persons interviewed, this paper contributes in practical and academic senses. It encourages organizations involved in the CoPS business as well as in other market segment to apply the concepts largely used in managing complex projects in order to avoid the typical 'one size fits all' pitfalls. This paper has clear limitations. First, the number of the MNEs involved in the study has to be considered when extending the conclusions and recommendations. Second, the number of interviewed persons is also limited. These factors, rather than being seem only in a restrictive perspective, should be an incentive for other scholars to expand its concept in order to support theory development regarding project complexity in MNEs.

6. REFERENCES

Baccarini, D. (1996). The concept of project complexity—a review. *International Journal of Project Management, 14*(4), 3.

Banco Central do Brasil. (2014). Investimento Direto Estrangeiro. *http://www.bcb.gov.br/rex/ied/port/ingressos/htms/index3.asp?idpai=INVED*. Retrieved 17 Aug, 2014

Browning, T. R. (2014). Managing complex project process models with a process architecture framework. *International Journal of Project Management, 32*(2), 229-241.

College of Complex Project Managers, A. D. M. O. (2006). Competency Standard for Complex Project Managers Version 2.0 Sep.2006. Australia: Commonwealth of Austrlia (Department of Defense).

D'Aveni, R. A., Dagnino, G. B., & Smith, K. G. (2010). The age of temporary advantage. *Strategic Management Journal, 31*(13), 1371-1385. doi: 10.1002/smj.897

D'Aveni, R. A., & Gunther, R. (1994). *Hypercompetition Managing the Dynamics of Strategic Maneuvering*: The Free Press.

Davies, A., & Hobday, M. (2005). *The business of projects: managing innovation in complex products and systems*: Cambridge University Press.

Dunning, J. H. (2001). The eclectic (OLI) paradigm of international production: past, present and future. *International journal of the economics of business, 8*(2), 173-190.

Dunning, J. H., & Lundan, S. M. (2008). *Multinational enterprises and the global economy*: Edward Elgar Publishing.

Frame, J. D. (2002). *The new project management: tools for an age of rapid change, complexity, and other business realities* (Second Edition ed.): John Wiley & Sons.

Gil, A. C. (2008). Métodos e técnicas de pesquisa social *Métodos e técnicas de pesquisa social*: Atlas.

Harris, K., Kim, A., & Schwedel, A. (2011). THE GREAT EIGHT Trillion-Dollar Growth Trends to 2020. *Bain & Company, Inc.*, 44.

Hass, K. B. (2009). *Managing complex projects: A new model*: Management Concepts Inc.

Hitt, M. A., Ireland, D., & Hoskisson, R. E. (2011). *Strategic Management: Competitiveness and Globalization: Concepts* (9th Edition ed.): South-Western Cengage Learning.

Kalasin, K., Dussauge, P., & Rivera-Santos, M. (2014). The Expansion of Emerging Economy Firms into Advanced Markets: The Influence of Intentional Path-Breaking Change. *Global Strategy Journal, 4*(2), 75-103.

Krippendorff, K. (2012). *Content analysis: An introduction to its methodology*: Sage.

Kwak, Y. H., & Anbari, F. T. (2009). Analyzing project management research: Perspectives from top management journals. *International Journal of Project Management, 27*(5), 435-446.

Maylor, H., Vidgen, R., & Carver, S. (2008). Managerial complexity in project-based operations: A grounded model and its implications for practice. *Project Management Journal, 39*(S1), S15-S26.

Milosevic, D. Z., & Srivannaboon, S. (2006). A theoretical framework for aligning project management with business strategy. *Project Management Journal, 37*, 98-110.

Moraes, R. (1999). Análise de conteúdo. *Educação, 22*(37), 7-32.

Newell, S., Goussevskaia, A., Swan, J., Bresnen, M., & Obembe, A. (2008). Interdependencies in Complex Project Ecologies: The Case of Biomedical Innovation. *Long Range Planning, 41*(1), 33-54.

Pinto, J. K., & Slevin, D. P. (1988). 20. Critical Success Factors in Effective Project implementation*. *Project management handbook, 479*.

Raz, T., Shenhar, A. J., & Dvir, D. (2002). Risk management, project success, and technological uncertainty. *R&D Management, 32*(2), 101-109.

Sauser, B. J., Reilly, R. R., & Shenhar, A. J. (2009). Why projects fail? How contingency theory can provide new insights–A comparative analysis of NASA's Mars Climate Orbiter loss.

International Journal of Project Management, 27(7), 665-679.

Scholes, K., Johnson, G., & Whittington, R. (2008). *Exploring Corporate Strategy*: Prentice Hall.

Shenhar, A. J. (2001). One size does not fit all projects: exploring classical contingency domains. *Management Science, 47*(3), 394-414.

Shenhar, A. J. (2004). Strategic Project Leadership® Toward a strategic approach to project management. *R&D Management, 34*(5), 569-578.

Shenhar, A. J., & Dvir, D. (2007). *Reinventing Project Management: The Diamond Approach to Successful Growth and Innovation* (1 ed.): Harvard Business School Press.

Söderlund, J. (2002). Managing complex development projects: arenas, knowledge processes and time. *R&D Management, 32*(2).

UNCTAD, G. (2010). World Investment Report: UNP, New York and Geneva.

UNCTAD, G. (2011). World Investment Report: UNP, New York and Geneva.

UNCTAD, G. (2012). World Investment Report: UNP, New York and Geneva.

UNCTAD, G. (2013). World Investment Report: UNP, New York and Geneva.

Whitty, S. J., & Maylor, H. (2009). And then came Complex Project Management (revised). *International Journal of Project Management, 27*(3), 304-310.

Wikström, K., Artto, K., Kujala, J., & Söderlund, J. (2010). Business models in project business. *International Journal of Project Management, 28*(8), 832-841.

Yin, R. K. (2003). Case Study Research: Design and Methods, (Applied Social Research Methods, Vol. 5).

Yin, R. K. (2010). Estudo de caso: planejando métodos: Porto Alegre: Bookman.

7

Risk Management in the Supply Chain of the Brazilian automotive industry

Edson Júnior Gomes Guedes
FGV-EAESP
edson.guedes77@gmail.com

Alexandre de Vicente Bittar
FGV-EAESP
alexandre.bittar@fgv.br

Luiz Carlos Di Serio
FGV-EAESP
luiz.diserio@fgv.br

Luciel Henrique de Oliveira
FGV-EAESP
luciel.oliveira@fgv.br

ABSTRACT: With a growth scenario found in few places in the world, the Brazilian automotive market has become attractive, jumping from investments of about 1 billion dollar in 2005 to more than 5 billion dollars in 2012. This article has the objective to give a vision of the supply chain risk management in the Brazilian automotive industry through a case study, when samples of a strong (an automaker) and a weak (a second tier supplier) links were compared based on existing theory in order to understand their limits, variables and potential new findings. Secondary data generated by Sindipeças, ANFAVEA and national institutes were used in the context of the case study, as well as semi-structured interviews with executives and experts in risk management and supply chain areas of an automaker and a second tier supplier installed in Brazil.

Keywords: *Risk management, supply chain, automotive industry, case study.*

1. INTRODUCTION

The Brazilian automotive industry is one of the most important automotive industries in the world, both from the point of view of vehicles production as of consumer market. It is currently the seventh largest producer and has the fourth largest consumer market, with 26 automakers established in the country, including the production of buses and trucks (ANFAVEA, 2013).

From 2002 to 2011 the Brazilian automotive market grew 145%, while production progressed at a slower pace, reaching 109% in the same period. This growth scenario was found in very few places in the world, which made the Brazilian automotive market attractive for investment by automakers in the country, jumping from just over $ 1 billion in 2005 to nearly $ 5.4 billion in 2012 (ANFAVEA, 2013). Thus, the Brazilian automotive industry has guaranteed presence in macroeconomic discussions of the country, with a share of the Brazilian industrial GDP of 21% and total GDP of 5%.

In an environment where internal demand was higher than local production was capable to supply, the quest for competitiveness and productivity gains became a recurring theme in the executive agenda in order to increase market share and profitability, and at the same time the search for risk reduction and its consequent losses began to be discussed in the companies.

The supply chain of the automotive industry is characterized by (1) a lot of links from raw materials to the final consumer (dealerships, automakers, auto parts manufacturers, manufacturing industries and raw material producers), (2) outsourcing, (3) increasing reliance on suppliers in the strategic procurement process, (4) use of information technology and communication tools in a cooperative way, and (5) globalization (Narasimhan & Talluri, 2009). Due to this context of high complexity, it is growing the interest in risk management in the recent literature on supply chain management.

In addition to the complexity of the automotive supply chain, Wagner and Neshat (2009) suggest the increase of natural disasters (i.e. droughts, floods, hurricanes and earthquakes) and disasters generated by human action (i.e. wars, accidents, strikes and terrorist attacks) as sources of vulnerability of supply chains. Therefore, issues such as competition based on quality, cycle time, delivery and technology (Lee, Padmanabhan & Wang, 1997; Flynn & Flynn, 2004) have been revisited under the concept of the resilience of the supply chain (Zolli, 2012; Christopher & Peck, 2004).

Despite a growing interest in supply chain risk management in developed countries, the subject is poorly treated in the Brazilian academic literature, as shown by the bibliographic reference of one of the few publications available (Di Serio, Oliveira & Schuch, 2011). In a recent field research conducted by Sodhi, Son and Tang (2012), it was concluded that this new field of business practice has three significant weaknesses: (1) supply chain risk management terms and definitions are not yet consolidated and present significant differences between researchers, (2) inadequate coverage of the responses to the risks of incidents and (3) inappropriate use of empirical methods in published research.

This article has the objective to provide a case study related to the supply chain of the Brazilian automotive industry, with particular attention to risk management, seeking to understand the supply chain risk management in the Brazilian automotive industry, considering the network of manufacturers (OEMs), systems suppliers (first tier) and mainly their suppliers (second tier). Thus, the research question is:

How is the supply chain risk management in the Brazilian automotive industry, based on a case study?

This paper is organized into five sections: the first one consists of this introduction, presenting the theme and its relevance to the business practice. In the second section, it is made a presentation of the theoretical basis, with a brief history of the evolution of risk management in the supply chain field. The third section deals with the methodology, with details of the tools used for the data collection, treatment and analysis. The fourth section brings the case study itself, followed by the fifth section, with discussions about the case and the conclusions, with its main findings and contributions to business practice.

2. LITERATURE REVIEW

The theorethical framework of this section will cover three streams of study: supply chain management, risk management, and supply chain risk management.

2.1 Supply Chain Management

There is an extensive literature related to the supply chain management. The criticality of processes and operations integration among every link has been discussed and analyzed by scholars over the past 30 years (Wheelwright & Hayes, 1985; Porter, 1986; Lee, Padmanabhan & Wang, 1997; Flynn & Flynn, 2004; Souza

Filho, Pereira, Di Serio & Martins, 2011 and 2012).

The term supply chain management (SCM) was coined in the 1980s by a group of consultants after the conclusion that problems related with materials flow had direct impact in the business, bringing to discussion the importance of this theme and proposing a management of the chain of the suppliers. The popularity of the SCM concept has been fostered by many researchs from correlated events as (Chen & Paulraj, 2004): (1) the quality revolution, (2) the discussion over materials management and integrated logistics, (3) the growing interest in industrial markets and their networks, (4) the notion of increasing focus, and (5) the publication of relevant studies on specific industries.

In terms of theoretical development, two approaches were observed. The first is to fragment the scale of management issues in the supply chain into more manageable pieces and then develop the theory in relation to this specific problem. Examples of this can be seen in the emergence of sustainable supply chain management (SSCM) and supply chain risk management (SCRM). The second one is to keep a broad conceptual approach and integrate the theories being developed from many different perspectives. This is the approach adopted in the seminal works of Mentzer et al. (2001) and Lamber and Cooper (2000).

In the automotive industry, terms such as cooperation, collaboration and competition have become common in a globalized business environment (Souza Filho et al., 2011), with technological and specialized human resources shared among manufacturers and members of the supply chain, known as systems suppliers (first tier) and their suppliers (second and third tiers).

In order to classify the different supply chains according to their scope, Mentzer et al. (2001) points out that "any organization can be part of numerous supply chains. Walmart, for example, can be part of the supply chain for candy, clothes, computers, and many other products". It can be seen then that a clear definition of a particular supply chain will depend on the company used as a reference. For this reason, Mentzer et al. (2001) proposes three definitions of supply chain complexity: a direct supply chain, an extended supply chain, and an ultimate supply chain. A direct supply chain consists of a minimum complexity, where a company and its direct supplier and customer are involved in the upstream and downstream flows of products and information. In the other extreme, an ultimate supply chain includes all the organizations involved in all the upstream and downstream flows of products, services, finances, and information.

Another classification that supply chains often receive is related with the degrees of separation from the focal company: its suppliers are called first tier and the suppliers of suppliers are called second tier (Lambert & Cooper, 2000).

Along three decades of the subject of the supply chain management, academics and professionals contributed to the consolidation of the constructs (Table 1). Unlike what is most recently seen in supply chain risk management (SCRM), the terms and definitions in SCM show little variation and can be used as a basis for understanding SCRM.

Table 1 – SCM constructs by author

SCM Literature Constructs		
Burgess, Singh & Koroglu (2006)	"Soft" Constructs	Leadership
		Intra-organization relationships
		Inter-organization relationships
	"Hard" Constructs	Logistics
		Process improvement orientation
		Information system
		Business results and outcomes
Stadtler (2005)	Integration of organizational units	Choice of partners
		Network organization and inter-organizational collaboration
		Leadership
	Flow coordination	Use of Information and communication technology
		Process orientation
		Advanced planning

Chen & Paulraj (2004)	Environmental uncertainty	-
	Customer focus	-
	Information Technology	-
	Strategic purchasing	Competitive priorities
		Purchasing strategy
	Supply network coordination	-
	Supply Management	Communication
		Supplier base reduction
		Long term relationships
		Supplier selection
		Supplier certification
		Supplier involvement
		Cross-functional teams
		Trust and commitment
	Logistics integration	Internal integration
		External integration
	Supply chain performance (Buyer and Supplier)	Financial performance
		Operational performance
		Supply chain performance
Mentzer et al. (2001)	Integrated behavior	-
	Mutual sharing of information	-
	Mutual sharing risks and rewards	-
	Cooperation	-
	The same goal and the same focus on serving customers	-
	Integration of processes	-
	Partners to build and maintain long term relationships	-
Lambert & Cooper (2000)	Physical and technical management components	Planning and control methods
		Work structure / Activity structure
		Organization structure
		Product flow facility structure
		Information flow facility structure
	Managerial and behavioral management components	Management methods
		Power and leadership structure
		Risk and reward structure
		Culture and attitude

2.2 Risk Management

The concept of risk used by IBGC (Instituto Brasileiro de Governança Corporativa - Brazilian Institute of Corporate Governance) is important for the understanding of the hypothesis and to delimit the scope:

Risk as the possibility of something does not work is a common understanding, but the current concept of risk involves the quantification and qualification of uncertainty, both with respect to losses and earnings, and with respect to the direction of the planned events, whether by individuals or by organizations. Operational risks stem from the possibility of losses (production, assets, customers, revenue) resulting from

faults, deficiencies or inadequacy of internal processes, people and systems or from external events such as natural disasters, fraud, strikes and terrorist acts. (IBGC, 2007)

Risk is defined as the potential for undesirable negative consequences which can arise from an event or activity (Rowe, 1980). Waters (2011), in turn, defines risk in a supply chain when unexpected events can interrupt the flow of materials in their journey of initial suppliers through end customers. The potential occurrence of an incident or the failure to seize opportunities can generate a financial loss for the company (Zsidisin & Smith, 2005). In a study by Kerner and Lynch (2011), more than 709% of the 300 participating companies indicated to have suffered an interruption of supply, and 50% of these companies had the experience of more than one rupture. Many of these risks are unavoidable, clearly noted when it is involved natural disasters.

It is important to note that risk management is not intended to eliminate risk completely, but to evaluate the various risk treatment alternatives, including:

a) Avoid the risk: not to act in a situation where certain risk occurs

b) Accept the risk:

b.1) Hold the risk: keep the risk at the current level of impact and probability

b.2) Reduce the risk: minimize the current level of impact and probability

b.3) Transfer / Share risk: reduce the impact and/ or probability by transfer or, in some cases, sharing part of the risk

b.4) Explore the risk: increase the degree of exposure to the extent that it enables competitive advantages

Despite the literature concentration in financial risk, most of the entrepreneurial efforts in the prevention and reduction of risks generated significant experience in the risk management, mainly operational risks, as well as in the management of adverse impacts and situations of interruption of organizations in several industries. Thus, it is possible to exemplify situations where each type of operational risk produces losses (Protiviti, 2006):

Table 2 – Operational risks (Protiviti, 2006)

OPERATIONAL RISKS (Protiviti, 2006)	
Efficiency Risk	High production cycle time generating excessive inventory
	Increase in errors during production
	Increased production costs
Capacity Risk	Underutilized productive capacity of the business unit
	Productive capacity of the business unit is not adequate to meet the customer demand
Scale Risk	Inability to operate efficiently in high volumes, preventing better recovery of costs and resulting in loss of economies of scale and better margins
	Production process equipaments are obsolete
	Operational labor not able to operate in large volumes
	Production process equipments do not support high volume production
Performance Risk	Inferior quality when compared to the competition or the best in the market
	High costs when compared to the competition or the best in the market
	High production cycle time when compared to the competition or the best in the market
Cycle time Risk	High cycle time means greater need of capital use, blocking capital release for investment in growth strategies
	Shorter cycle time allows the use of JIT (Just-in-Time), reducing the size of inventories and increasing cash flow
	Shorter cycle time enables greater flexibility of delivery, reduced costs, better communication and greater reliability
Interruption Risk	Unavailability of raw materials
	Unavailability of experienced and/or skilled workforce
	Crash of critical systems for business continuity

The impact of these risks in supply chain management will be evaluated in this study in order to show that the investment in the fixed assets of Brazilian business community must take into account not only the traditional financial return as EBIT, ROE or ROA, but also the reduction of this risk in order to not expose the company and its customers to production losses, consumers, and ultimately, revenue (IBGC, 2007).

2.3 Supply Chain Risk Management

Since the 1990s, initiatives to increase corporate profitability (ie revenue growth, cost reduction, asset impairment) occurred simultaneously with the increasing complexity of supply chains (Craighead, Blackhurst, Rungtusanatham & Handfield, 2007). Bakshi and Kleindorfer (2009) and Sodhi (2005) point to factors such as globalization of the supply chain and reducing the life cycle of products as responsibles for a greater exposure to the risk of supply chains. In addition, the increase in the number of natural disasters (ie droughts, floods, hurricanes and earthquakes) and disasters generated by human action (ie wars, accidents, strikes and terrorist attacks) are sources of vulnerability of supply chains (Wagner & Neshat, 2009). Authors like Sheffi (2005) and Tang (2006) have called attention to the need for resilience or strengthening of supply chains in order to reduce the vulnerability brought by these external factors.

Examples of supply chains disruptions cited in academic and professional publications show the diversity of risks and industries exposed to them. Ford and Land Rover, both of the automobile industry, faced significant breaks in 2001 for incidents arising from distinct risks: while Ford closed its factories for days due to the terrorist attacks of September 11, Land Rover dismissed over 1,000 employees after a bankruptcy of one supplier of its chain. The information technology and communication supply chains have also suffered disruptions, with names like Dell, Sony and Ericsson joining the list of companies with financial performance impacted by the failure of one link (Chopra & Sodhi, 2004; Martha & Subbakrishna, 2002; Sheffi, 2005; Hendricks & Singhal, 2003, 2005a, 2005b; Wagner & Bode, 2008a, 2008b).

However, few incidents infringed operational and financial impact as big as those that occurred in Fukushima, Japan, in 2011. In a series of natural and nuclear disasters, the supply chain of the Japanese automotive industry, characterized by the concept of lean manufacturing and globally known by JIT (just-in-time) practices, faced extended rupture of its production causing millions in financial losses. As an example, Toyota and Honda had losses of more than $ 3,200 million and $ 800 million respectively. Since then researchers began to distinguish the supply chain risk management studies in two research lines: the management of the supply chain to respond to risks of high probability (or occurrence) and low impact, also called operational risks (Blackhurst, Craighead, Elkins & Handfield, 2005; Tang & Tomlin, 2008; Braunscheidel & Suresh, 2009), and the management of the supply chain to respond to risks of low probability (or occurrence) and high impact, called catastrophic risks (Norrman & Jansson, 2004; Kleindorfer & Saad, 2005; Knemeyer, Zinn & Eroglu, 2009).

Wagner and Neshat (2009) report a long list of incidents and their consequences for the companies inserted in a supply chain when their vulnerabilities are not identified, assessed and mitigated. According to them, supply chain managers should be better prepared methodologically and have available tools of supply chain risk management, and not remain only in the conceptual or normative level theme.

Manu and Mentzer (2008) demonstrate illustratively the five steps for managing the process of supply chain risk management and its mitigation.

Figure 1 – 5 steps to managing the risk management process and its mitigation in the supply chain

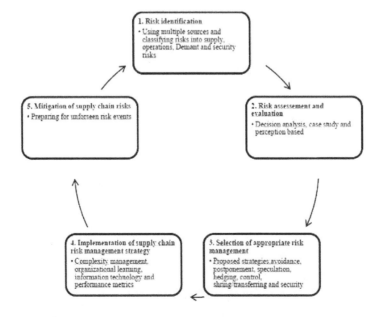

A case registered in the United States (Bednarz, 2006) shows how the supply chain risk management can support the business continuity, even in situations where the damages challenge the most sophisticated contingency plans. For Procter & Gamble, a business continuity plan was essential to the recovery of the business, which was submerged after Hurricane Katrina swept the Gulf Coast region in August 2005. In less than a month, the company had reached more than 85% of its coffee production level from third-party sources and alternative sites of the company.

Carvalho et al. (2011) reports in his article the inter-changeability of terms such as disturbance (Mason-Jones & Towill, 1998), rupture (Blackhurst et al., 2005), vulnerability (Svensson, 2004; Wagner & Neshat, 2009) and risk (Chopra & Sodhi, 2004) in the supply chain management. It appears then that this new field of administrative practice presents significant gap in the consensus on terms and definitions, and that it is necessary for the evolution of supply chain risk management the consolidation of such terms and definitions in order to minimize the significant differences between researchers.

Many studies suggest strategies such as risk assessment and mitigation in order to deal with disruptions in the supply chain (Kleindorfer & Saad, 2005). According to Ji and Zhu (2008), Norrman and Jansson (2004), Pickett (2006) and Kull (2008), strategies for risk management in the supply chain should significantly contribute to the reduction of losses, probability, speed, frequency and exposure to risk events. The sensitive point of these suggestions is the balance between the benefits and costs of supply chain risk management, since some of the proposals for risk mitigation go against cost reduction initiatives such as the sustained decrease in inventory levels by lean production (lean manufacturing concept) and JIT / JIS (Just-In-Time / Just-In-Sequence).

Azevedo et al. (2008) proposes that the management of the supply chain progresses to a level of resilience of organizations through the following variables: level of inventory, supply chain, outsourcing and information sharing level.

Di Serio, Oliveira and Schuch (2011) propose four objectives for a job focused on the supply chain risk management: (1) organizations consider risk management as an important initiative for carrying out their strategies and obtaining sustainable results; (2) organizations include formal risk analyses in their decision-making processes; (3) identification, analy-

sis and handling of financial risks is more developed than in the case of operating risks, and (4) the adoption of a structured organizational risk management system has a positive impact on performance.

Considering the growth scenario of the Brazilian automotive market boosted by high investments recorded between 2005 and 2011, there was an increase in production demand and productivity of the entire supply chain. Assuming the use of direct and indirect labor, equipment, raw materials, energy, and other resources are related with production function, the impact of risk management that senior managers have on operational decisions is relevant, as quality, cost, flexibility, reliability and cycle time are key factors to respond to a growing demand for production in an increasingly complex environment.

In a complex supply chain as in the automotive industry, there are a lot of links from raw material to the final consumer (dealerships, vehicle manufacturers, systems suppliers and parts manufacturers, manufacturing industries and raw materials producers). In addition, outsourcing, the growing dependence on suppliers in the strategic purchasing process, the cooperative use of information technology and communications tools, and globalization (Narasimhan & Talluri, 2009) should be taken into account in the risk management. These factors make this supply chain susceptible to ruptures when the weak link is not evaluated, monitored and changed to meet the requirements of quality, cycle time, delivery and technology (Lee et al., 1997; Flynn and Flynn, 2004).

3. METHODOLOGY

Considering the gap identified in the research, notably the terms and definitions of supply chain risk management not consolidated yet and significant differences among researchers, inadequate coverage of the responses to the risks of incidents and, finally, the inappropriate use of empirical methods in the published researches (Sodhi, Son & Tang, 2012), it was decided to use case study as the methodology for this paper, since it offers a suitable mean of in-depth analysis of emerging practices (Voss, Tsikriktsis & Frohlich, 2002).

Yin (2009) points three characteristics as crucial to make a case study relevant: (1) the case is not common and is of interest to the general public, (2) the subliminal problems of the case are of national importance, whether from the point of theoretical view or from a practical point of view, and (3) the case features the two characteristics above.

Taking into account that the supply chain risk management is a world emerging issue, with little treatment in academic publications and journals when compared with issues such as supply chain management or risk management, and being the chosen locus for this work the Brazilian automotive industry, relevant to the Brazilian economy, it is considered that the specifications for a case study was met.

The objective of this study is to provide a scenario that allows the reader to infer how is the supply chain risk management in the Brazilian automotive industry through a case study of two analytical units integrated into the same supply chain and exposed to the same economic and industrial macro-environment. This is done through the characterization of each individual case, before any generalizations that can be given at the conclusion of this study (Yin, 2009; Voss et al., 2002; Eisenhardt, 1989).

From the point of view of the approach, this work adopts the form of an exploratory research (Creswell, 2007) in order to verify if the characteristics of the supply chain risk management of the Brazilian automotive industry have some correlation with the different risks from this theoretical review and from the interviews based on semi-structured questionnaire used for the preparation of the case study.

The case study was conducted in two links of the Brazilian automotive supply chain industry - an automaker and a component supplier company, also called as second tier. The reason for this choice was what Flyvbjerg (2011) calls extreme cases or outliers. Systematic investigation of outliers can increase the chances of discovering new ideas. The variables of each company - number of employees, annual billing, capital source and risk management structure (Table 3) are extremely divergent, contrasting the units of analysis, which enables deeper understanding of risk management in the supply chain and open space for developing and discussing new concepts about it.

Table 3 - Comparison between Automaker and Component Supplier

	AUTOMAKER	COMPONENT SUPPLIER
Number of Employees	> 10.000 employees	< 500 employees
Total Revenue per year	> US$ 1 billion	< US$ 100 million
Capital Source	USA	Brazil
Risk Management Structure	Organized, uses assessment tools and has formal decision-making process based on risk analysis	Not organized, no use of assessment tools and has no formal decision-making process based on risk analysis

The use of multiple sources of evidence, such as secondary data generated by Sindipeças, ANFAVEA and national institutes is justified as support for the supply chain risk management context among the various participants in the Brazilian automotive market. In addition, semi-structured interviews (Flynn, Sado, Schroeder, Bates & Flynn, 1990) were held with executives and specialists in risk management and supply chain areas from the automaker and from the second tier supplier to build such case study. Any finding or conclusion of the case study is more accurate through the triangulation of data sources. Thus, it is possible to unite in one case study personal experience and extensive field research (Yin, 2009).

4. CASE STUDY IN THE BRAZILIAN AUTOMOTIVE CHAIN

The availability of components has been a recurring theme in the Brazilian automotive industry in recent years, mainly due to the production growth of motor vehicles in Brazil. The increase in the number of vehicle manufacturers in the country (ANFAVEA, 2013), the amount of investment in fixed assets in the sector (IBGE, 2010) and the increasing dependence on automakers and their suppliers on import components (Sindipeças, 2012) has raised the interest of professionals and researchers in a rising area: supply chain risk management.

4.1 Automaker Case

Installed in Brazil as the first subsidiary outside its country of origin, the automaker of this case study is listed among the top 10 in vehicle sales in Brazil and worldwide. In 1956, it began a process of nationalization of production of its vehicles through the efforts of the Automotive Industry Executive Group (Grupo Executivo da Indústria Automobilística - GEIA) for the consolidation of the Brazilian industrial park. It is an exemplary sample for the study of supply chain risk management because it has a global political governance, requiring from the subsidiaries around the world the application of procedures and attendance of legal requirements not always required by the legislation of the country where the subsidiaries are located.

After the disaster of Fukushima, Japan, in 2011, the headquarters began a series of changes aimed at integrating the various tools for the assessment, measurement and mitigation of risks. The stated goal was to prevent that low probability and high impact events could affect business continuity and to avoid that they passed unnoticed in decision-making - from the installation of a new plant to the purchase

of components from suppliers installed in regions of high risk of supply disruption.

Examples of disruption of supply chains cited in academic and professional publications show the diversity of risks and industries exposed to them (Chopra and Sodhi, 2004; Martha and Subbakrishna, 2002; Sheffi, 2005; Hendricks and Singhal, 2003, 2005a, 2005b; Wagner and Bode, 2008a).

The automaker has a Risk Management department (figure 2), a formal functional structure of supply chain risk management, with risk management managers allocated in Finance and in Operations, the last one focused at the Purchasing activity. The influence of this risk departament is not restricted to these functional areas, because Supply Chain, Logistics and Manufacturing also respond in matrix for Risk Management.

Figure 2 – Automaker risk management organizational chart

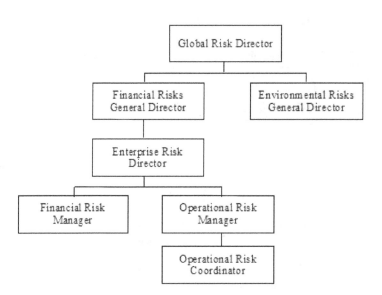

These functional areas have a group of expert analysts in the assessment, measurement and mitigation of risk as part of cross-functional teams responsible for ERM - Enterprise Risk Management. They act from the strategic plan to the implementation of activities, with the overall objective to ensure business continuity. They are supported by consultants and insurers which have operations in the country, but

whose hiring is under direct influence of the headquarters. In the interview with one of the consultants of the insurance companies that provides services to the automaker, it was detected the alignment of the Brazilian subsidiary with the governance policies of the headquarters. The attendance of local requirements occurs only when local legislation is prevalent in relation to the headquarters policies.

The risk management activity in the Financial and Purchasing areas is aimed at preventing the occurrence of incidents that result in business interruption. The analysis of the financial health of the suppliers is considered in new business, and take into account the supplier's capitalization, timely payment history, threats to break up in trade negotiations and more recently, access to credit.

For the interviewed employees in the automaker, risk management is understood as a multifunctional activity. In addition to a centralized structure (ERM) to support the different functional areas in specific risk management, each executive is responsible for supporting practices to identify, assess, manage and mitigate the material risks to business continuity or to the achievement of company goals.

The areas of Purchasing, Logistics and Supply Chain plays an important role in supply risk management as they are responsible for the procurement of parts for vehicles, machinery and equipment for factories, and products and services used globally by the Assembly. In these areas, supply chain risk management began in 2004 in response to the escalation in the number of suppliers who had chronic financial problems. According to one interviewed, "considering the complex structure of the deal, the automaker has a vast supplier base but still fragile. Moreover, our success or failure is intrinsically linked to our suppliers." It is important to notice that, in response to business requirements of the automaker, the component suppliers became to present a capital intensive business model, with higher necessity of capital to investments in development and material costs. Furthermore, these companies are exposed to long development cycles for new products.

In the Supplier Quality, Supply Chain and Logistics areas, there is no expertise in risk management. The use of assessment tools, measurement and risk mitigation at supply chain is not a regular and homogeneous activity. Although audited, the risk management in these areas is not relevant in the decision making process for new business with suppliers. The difficulty in quantifying the financial risks in quality, cycle time and delivery time (Lee et al., 1997; Flynn & Flynn, 2004) has been the biggest obstacle to these areas to influence the process of strategic purchasing. If revisited in the light of supply chain resilience (Zolli, 2012; Sheffi, 2005), such decision making processes should consider who and where the automaker will buy their components and systems, taking into account the total cost of the transaction.

It became clear during the interview that the supply chain risk management is in a higher stage of development in the areas of Finance and Purchasing than in Supplier Quality, Supply Chain and Logistics. According to one interviewee, this can occur due to internal policies related to SOX requirements (Sarbanes-Oxley) and the COSO II (Committee of Sponsoring Organizations of the Treadway Commission). These requirements, applied extensively after regulation aimed at reducing the risks of international and USA financial system, led to the development of risk management related areas in automotive companies.

The situation of a troubled supplier can be identified in many different ways, as well as by many different people. According to the Operational Risk Manager, it is imperative that the TS (Troubled Supplier) Team engages as soon as possible so that problems can be evaluated and the situation be remedied before further deterioration of the supply chain.

All cases of TS are ranked between "active management" or "proactive management". Active cases can be broadly characterized as suppliers with financial problems situations, where the TS team is actively involved in the development and implementation of a risk mitigation strategy. For proactive cases, the initial assessment of TS team can conclude that a risk mitigation strategy will be needed if the supplier become financially troubled.

Once the team is aware of a supplier with problems, a review of the situation is performed. If the team is informed of the real or potential situation on time, the automaker usually sends a team of internal operations and external financial advisers for a thorough examination of the business, including a review of operations and the viability in the short and long term. According to one interviewed, sometimes the staff is notified to the scene too late, and has not enough time to perform a thorough analysis. In such cases, the internal staff or external financial advisors, together with the greatest amount of information available, formulate a mitigation strategy for the chain rupture risk.

The goal of short term strategy is to understand the company's liquidity position and capacity to finance ongoing operations as well its working capital requirements over the next few days or weeks. In the short term, the company's cash position is the most important factor considered by the team.

The goal of long term analysis is to evaluate the company's ability to finance other demands such as payment of the outstanding debt or collection of taxes and legal deposits related to the payroll. The long term analysis includes a detailed examination of the supplier's capital structure in order to determine its viability as a going concern. Related to the analysis of the capital structure, external financial consultants also assess the company's value from the perspective of an ordered or forced liquidation in order to take appropriate decisions regarding the strategy of permanence or exit.

The financial analysis also describes the interests of other parties involved with the companies in difficulties as well as its strategic and economic interests. This list includes, but is not limited to lenders, owners, trade creditors and other clients.

Generally, operating in-depth analyzes are only possible when there is enough time. However, as far as possible, the analyzes are performed in situations of imminent break, especially in cases in which continuity of supply is involved. The primary objective of the operational analysis is to determine the company's ability to maintain the continuity of supply to the automaker.

Although the continuity of supply is directly related to the financial resources of a company, this analysis looks at the management capacity (some managers may have left the company due to bankrupt), ability and productive capacity. For example, if a company has several plants operating below capacity, there may be opportunity for consolidation, which not only improve operational performance, but also provide cost savings. This analysis becomes especially important if the launch of a new vehicle is involved or if the supplier is entering a new line of business, where there was no proven evidence of their capability.

The risk of natural disasters is also under the scope of the ERM. Brazil has not had yet systematic and integrated databases on disaster occurrences and therefore did not make available to professionals and researchers processed information about these events in historical series. In an effort Similar to the work done by the CRED (Centre for Research on the Epidemiology of Disasters) of the "Université Catholique de Louvain", the Brazilian Atlas of Natural Disasters is a product of research, a result of the cooperation agreement between the National Secretariat of Civil Defense and the University Center for Studies and Research on Disasters at Federal University of Santa Catarina.

This research compiled and made available on the site of S2ID - Integrated Disaster Information, information on disaster records occurred throughout the country in the last 20 years (1991-2010). The survey of historical records, deriving in the preparation of thematic maps and production of the Atlas, is relevant because it enables to build an overview of the occurrence and recurrence of disasters in the country and its specificities for States and Regions. Therefore, it allows support the proper planning in risk management and disaster reduction, from the extended analysis covering the country, the observed frequency patterns, the periods of high occurrence, the relationship of these events with other global phenomena and the analysis on the processes related to disasters in the country.

The Brazilian Atlas of Natural Disasters is the first nationwide work, and presents thematic maps of natural disaster occurrences in Brazil, referring to 31909 records of occurrences, which show annually the risks related to natural disasters as sudden inundation, flooding, gradual inundation, windstorm and/or cyclone, distributed in thematic maps of events, which, together with the analysis of the records and human damage, give a complete picture of disasters in the country, in order to support the planning and management of the risk minimization actions. This work represents an effort by the state and the academy for proper planning in risk management and disaster reduction. Such information may be used by various entities of the automotive industry to mitigate the losses related to the risk of interruption of the supply chain.

Among the most frequent natural disasters in Brazil, the largest impact on the automotive industry supply chain is caused by the sudden inundation and flooding. As the national logistics is mainly based on road transport, this type of event usually stop partially or totally roads and highways. In evaluating the natural disaster map from sudden inundation and flooding in Brazil in 1991 and 2010 period and its respective distribution by region, there is a significant concentration in the South and Southeast regions. If we compare this concentration of occurrences with the concentration of vehicle manufacturers systems suppliers and component suppliers in the automotive industry in the same regions, which is 91.3% (IBGE, 2010), we conclude that the assessment, management and mitigation of such risks are justified.

4.2 Component Supplier Case

The supplier of components is a national capital company, whose founders act as executives directly linked to the areas of Engineering, Finance and Sales. It has been operating for more than 60 years in the domestic market of metal components, and despite its diversification of markets (electronics and white goods), the portfolio of automotive clients represents about 70% of annual sales.

The component supplier participates in the supply chain of the automaker (second tier). Risk management has no formal structure and is in charge of functional managers, which have no formal expertise in risk management. There are no expert analysts in the assessment, measurement and risk mitigation, but it is supported by consultants and insurers whose hiring is under direct influence of the automaker. In the interview with one of the executives not related to the controlling family, it was detected the alignment with the existing governance of the client.

The use of assessment tools, measurement and risk mitigation of the supply chain is not regular and homogeneous in the company. These tools were provided by the automaker and were found in the structures of Finance, Procurement, Supplier Quality, Supply Chain and Logistics. Although audited by the automaker, risk management in these areas is not relevant in the decision making process for new business with suppliers. The difficulty in quantifying the financial risks in quality, cycle time and delivery time (Lee et al., 1997; Flynn & Flynn, 2004) has been the biggest obstacle to these areas to influence the process of strategic purchasing. If revisited in the light of resilience of the supply chain (Zolli, 2012; Sheffi, 2005), such decision-making processes should consider who and where the Component Supplier buy their inputs, taking into account the total cost of the transaction.

The functional areas are not prepared to handle with the risks described in the literature as being causes of supply disruption. The company does not act preventively over the incidents indicated by the automaker, and reacts on the occurrence of incidents that result in business interruption.

Initiatives related to cross-functional teams responsible for ERM - Enterprise Risk Management are unknown in the company. They act in the strategic plan just for investment decisions and for the operationalization of activities, with the overall objective to ensure business continuity.

5. CONCLUSION

The objective of this article was to provide a case study related to the supply chain risk management of the Brazilian automotive industry, considering the network of manufacturers, systems suppliers (first tier) and mainly their suppliers (second tier), and to answer to the research question:

How is the supply chain risk management in the Brazilian automotive industry, based on a case study?

Through a case study with two units of analysis of the Brazilian automotive chain, the present work provided an exploratory analysis that implies there is heterogeneity in the risk management between the chain links. The intentional choice of a unit of analysis considered as strong link (automaker) and another one considered as weak link (components supplier) exposed the vulnerability (Wagner & Neshat, 2009) of the supply chain of the Brazilian automotive industry due to the lack of risk management in the second tier supplier. It was found that there are gaps in the supply chain risk management in the Brazilian automotive industry when compared with its global competitors. The main reasons are:

(a) the second tier supplier is basically working with risk management to attend the necessities of the automaker or your direct customer (first tier supplier). There is no own intention to invest on risk management: it is necessary investment in specialized people and resources, and in a situation of competitive resources the company prefers to invest on other demands;

(b) the automaker does not require the analysis of risk management of the second tier suppliers in their decision making with the first tier suppliers. The difficulty in quantifying financial risks in quality, cycle time and delivery time (Lee et al., 1997; Flynn and Flynn, 2004) has been the biggest obstacle to the areas of Quality and Risk to influence the strategic purchasing process. Such decision making processes should consider from who and where the supplier will buy their inputs, taking into account the total cost of the transaction. A detailed analysis of the risk management of the suppliers of the supplier is necessary.

There are tools and processes to support the supply chain risk management, though predominantly focused at the operational level. The awareness of the importance to assess, measure and mitigate the risk of the automotive industry supply chain is growing. In response, a number of tools, processes and governmental and professional initiatives have been developed to reduce the impact of interruptions in supply chain networks and transportation. However, the tools that are applied varied for the following reasons:

(1) Significantly different levels of adoption of supply chain risk management tools between companies: in this work, the case study led to the confirmation of what the literature calls the vulnerability of the chain, characterized by its weakest link. The analyzed automaker ensures that your direct suppliers (first tier) implement risk management tools in order to minimize exposure to breakage. However, there is no systematic application of the same tools by their indirect suppliers (second and third tiers).

(2) Risk management initiatives are at the discretion of each company - considering that the automakers in Brazil are from distinct sources (American, European or Asian), the governance policy that each one takes is influenced by regulation and legal requirements of the country of source array. The automaker studied here is averse to risk exposure, a conservative feature of its management, keeping locally executives of the same nationality of the matrix to ensure adherence to the corporate governance policies. On the contrary, its first and second tiers suppliers adopt higher risk exposure management models, with greater flexibility to meet different requirements of several automakers in the country. Figure 3 demonstrates the risk management initiatives of the automaker and its second tier supplier, demonstrating that while the automaker has a strong risk management of its internal activities and with its first tier suppliers, the second tier supplier has few initiatives, usually induced by the automaker.

(3) Tools and risk mitigation processes are often designed or applied on a local or regional basis, resulting in a non-cohesive management of the global risk.

(4) There is little standardization or official certification in the supply chain risk management.

(5) Laws and available certifications are developed in a stand alone model for a industry or segment, and are not integrated into business processes.

This study has limitations regarding its locus and the specifity of the analyzed industry. It was concentrated in only one country, although Brazil is an emerging country with the fourth largest consumer market in the world, and it was focused in the automobile industry, with its own characteristics. Thus, as a proposal for future work, can consider playing the same exploratory qualitative methodology in another locus or industry.

For future research, the authors suggest some topics that should be investigated:

- The relationship between supply chain risk management and performance

- Areas close to the end customer (Sales, After Sales and Customer Service) were not part of this study

- Relationship between automaker country of origin and collaborative practices with suppliers were underexplored in this study.

Figure 3 – Risk management tools and processes

Risk Management Tools and Processes								
Internal company tool/process			Cross-company tool/process			Professional bodies		
Tool/Process	Automaker Case	Component (Second Tier) Supplier	Tool/Process	Automaker Case	Component (Second Tier) Supplier	Participation in Certified with	Automaker Case	Component (Second Tier) Supplier
Track and trace tools	Y	OC	Supplier audit collaboration	Y	N	Industry associations, e.g International Air Transport Association (IATA)	Y	N
Risk mapping/prioritization	Y	OC	Standardized certifications (e.g BSI development on supplier continuity planning)	Y	N	Supply Chain Risk Leadership Council	Y	N
Business continuity planning	Y	N	Disruption news feeds	Y	N	Professional associations, e.g Chartered Institute of Logistics; Business Continuity Institute	Y	N
Scenario planning	Y	N				Supply Chain Council and SCOR model	Y	N
Event management tools	Y	N				ISO 28000	Y	N
Centralized risk management unit/personnel	Y	N						
Centralized/standardized supplier assessments	Y	N						
Supplier codes of conduct	Y	N						
Quantification metrics	Y	N						
Employee training initiatives	Y	N						
Supply chain mapping	Y	Y						
Business impact analysis tools	Y	OC						
Legend: Y= Yes, it is used	N = No, it is not used	UI = Under Implementation	OC = Occasional use					

6. REFERENCES

ANFAVEA: Anuário da Indústria Automobilística Brasileira (2013). São Paulo: ANFAVEA.

Annual Disaster Statistical Review (2012). CRED – Centre for Research on the Epidemiology of Disasters, Université Catholique de Louvain.

Bakshi, N.; Kleindorfer, P. (2009). Co-opetition and investment for supply-chain resilience. Production and Operations Management, 18(6): 583–603.

Bednarz, A. (2006). Supply Chain Execs Share Disaster-Planning Techniques. Available at: http://www.computerworld.com/s/article/9000810/Supply_chain_execs_share_disaster_planning_techniques. Accessed in November 24th, 2013.

Blackhurst, J.; Craighead, C.; Elkins, D.; Handfield, R. (2005). An empirically derived agenda of critical research issues for managing supply-chain disruptions. International Journal of Production Research, 43 (19), 4067–4081.

Braunscheidel, M. J.; Suresh, N. C. (2009). The organizational antecedents of a firm's supply chain agility for risk mitigation and response. Journal of Operations Management, 27(2): 119–140.

Burgess, K.; Singh, P.; Koroglu, R. (2006). Supply chain management: a structured literature review and implications for future research. International Journal of Operations & Production Management, 26(7): 703–729.

Chen, I.J.; Paulraj, A. (2004). Understanding supply chain management: critical research and a theoretical framework. International Journal of Production Research, 42(1): 131–163.

Chopra, S.; Sodhi, M.S. (2004). Managing risk to avoid supply chain breakdown. MIT Sloan Management Review, 46 (1), 53–61.

Christopher, M.; Peck, H. (2004). Building the resilient supply chain. The International Journal of Logistics Management, 15 (2), 1-14.

Craighead, C. W.; Blackhurst, J.; Rungtusanatham, M. J.; Handfield, R. B. (2007). The severity of supply chain disruptions: Design characteristics and mitigation capabilities. Decision Science, 38(1):131–156.

Creswell, J. W.; Piano Clark, V. L (2007). Designing and conducting mixed methods research. Thousand Oaks, CA: Sage.

Di Serio, L. C.; Oliveira, L. H.; Schuch, L. M. S. (2011). Organizational Risk Management – A case study in companies that have won the Brazilian quality award prize. Journal of Technology Management & Innovation, v. 6, n. 2.

Eisenhardt, K. (1989). Building theories from case study research. *Academy of Management Review*, 14(4): 532–550.

Flyvbjerg, B. (2001). *Making social science matter: why social inquiry fails and how it can succeed again.* Cambridge, UK: Cambridge University Press

Flynn, B. B.; Flynn, E. J. (2004). An exploratory study of the nature of cumulative capabilities. *Journal of Operations Management*, v. 22, n. 1, p. 439–457.

Flynn, B. B., Sado, S., Schroeder, R.G., Bates, K.A.; Flynn, E.J. (1990). Empirical research methods in operations management. *Journal of Operations Management*, 9(2): 250–284.

Guia de orientação para gerenciamento de riscos corporativos (2007). São Paulo: IBGC.

Hendricks, K. B.; Singhal, V. R. (2003). The effect of supply chain glitches on shareholder wealth. *Journal of Operations Management*, 21(5): 501–522.

Hendricks, K. B.; Singhal, V. R. (2005a). An empirical analysis of the effects of supply chain disruptions on long-run stock price performance and equity risk of the firm. *Production and Operations Management*, 14(1), 35-52.

Hendricks, K. B.; Singhal, V. R. (2005b). Association between supply chain glitches and operating performance. *Management Science*, 51(5): 695–711.

Kaplan, R. S.; Mikes, A. (2012). Managing Risks: A New Framework. *Harvard Business Review*, June, 2012.

Kleindorfer, P. R.; Saad, G. H. (2005). Managing disruption risks in supply chains. *Production and Operations Management*, 14 (1), 53–68.

Knemeyer, A. M.; Zinn, W.; Eroglu, C. (2009). Proactive planning for catastrophic events in supply chains. *Journal of Operations Management*, 27(2): 141–153.

Kreps, D. (2004). *Microeconomics for Managers.* New York: W.W. Norton, 2004.

Lambert, D. M.; Cooper, M. C. (2000). Issues in supply chain management. *Industrial Marketing Management*, 29, 65–83.

Lee, H. L.; Padmanabhan, V.; Wang, S. (1997). The bullwhip effect in supply chains. *Sloan Management Review*, v.38, n. 3, p.93–102.

Manuj, I.; Mentzer, J. T. (2008a). Global supply chain risk management strategies. *International Journal of Physical Distribution & Logistics Management*, 38(3): 192–223.

Mason-Jones, R.; Towill, D.R. (1998). Time compression in the supply chain: information management is the vital ingredient. *Logistics Information Management*, vol. 11, Iss:2, pp. 93-104.

Mentzer, J. T.; DeWitt, W.; Kleeber, J. S.; Min, S.; Nix, N. W.; Smith, C. D.; Zacharia, Z. G. (2001). Defining Supply Chain Management. *Journal of Business Logistics*, v. 22, (2): 1-25.

Narasimhan, R.; Talluri, S. (2009). Perspectives on risk management in supply chains. *Journal of Operations Management*, 27(2): 114–118.

Norrman, A.; Jansson, U. (2004). Ericsson's proactive supply chain risk management approach after a serious sub-supplier accident. *International Journal of Physical Distribution & Logistics Management*, 34(5): 434–456.

PIA - Pesquisa Industrial Anual (2010), v.29, n.1, IBGE, Empresa.

PIA - Pesquisa Industrial Anual (2012), v.30, n.1, IBGE, Empresa.

Porter, M. (1986). *Estratégia competitiva: técnicas para a análise da indústria e da concorrência.* 17a.

Edição. Rio de Janeiro: Campus, 1986.

Protiviti (2006). *Definition of business risks* (2006). Protiviti – Independent Risk Consulting.

Sheffi, Y. (2005). *The resilient enterprise: overcoming vulnerability for competitive advantage.* The MIT Press, Boston, USA.

Sodhi, M. S.; Son, B. G.; Tang, C. S. (2012). Researchers' perspectives on supply chain risk management. *Production and Operations Management*, 21(1): 1-13.

Souza Filho, O.; Pereira, S.; Di Serio, L.C.; Martins, R. (2011). Collaborative practices in the management automotive chain: does the origin of automakers matter? *Conferência Anual do POMS*, April, 2011.

Souza Filho, O.; Pereira, S.; Di Serio, L.C.; Martins, R. (2012). Alinhamento de estratégias de relacionamentos fornecedor-cliente na cadeia automobilística brasileira. XXXVI EnANPAD, September, 2012.

S2ID - Sistema Integrado de Informações Sobre Desastres. Available at: http://s2id.integracao.gov.br/portal/imagens/botao_atlas.png. Accessed in January 02nd, 2014.

Stadtler, H. (2005). Supply chain management and advanced planning – basics, overview and challenge. *European Journal of Operational Research*, 163, 575–588.

Svensson, G. (2004). Key areas, causes and contingency planning of corporate vulnerability in supply chains. *International Journal of Physical Distribution & Logistics Management*, 34 (9), 728–748.

Tang, C. S. (2006). Perspectives in supply chain risk management. *International Journal of Production and Economic*, 103(2): 451–488.

Tang, C. S.; Tomlin, B. (2008). The power of flexibility for mitigating supply chain risks. *International Journal of Production and Economic*. 116(1): 12–27.

Voss, C.; Tsikriktsis, N.; Frohlich, M. (2002). Case research in operations management. *International Journal of Operations & Production Management*, 22(2): 195–219.

Wagner, S. M.; Bode, C. (2008a). An empirical examination of supply chain performance along several dimensions of risk. *Journal of Business Logistics*, 29(1): 307–325.

Wagner, S. M.; Bode, C. (2008b). Dominant risks and risk management practices in supply chains. *Journal of Business Logistics*, 32(4): 234–256.

Wagner, S. M.; Neshat, N. (2009). Assessing the vulnerability of supply chains using graph theory. *International Journal of Production Economics*. v.126, 121-129.

Wheelwright, S. C.; Hayes, R. H. (1985). Competing through manufacturing. *Harvard Business Review*, v. 63, n. 1, p. 99–109.

World Economic Forum (2013). Global Risks Report.

Yin, R. (2009). *Case study research: design and methods*. Applied social research methods series. 4rd ed. Sage Publications, Thousand Oaks, USA.

Zsidisin, G.; Smith, M. (2005). Managing supply risk with early supplier involvement: a case study and research propositions. *The Journal of Supply Chain Management*, 41 (4), 44–57.

8

The Development of Logistics Services in the United States

Yeongling H. Yang
San Diego State University
hyang@mail.sdsu.edu

ABSTRACT: This research studies third party logistics (3PL) providers in the United States to investigate how the industry has strategically developed its service offerings in response to the customers' growing needs in managing global supply chains. Logistics management has significant impacts on various aspects of supply chains such as response time, total supply chain cost, sourcing risk, customer service, security, etc. The results show that 3PL services vary based on industry served, region served, and asset ownership structure. Over the years logistics services providers have served more industry sectors, became asset light, and provided broader services. Two of the five service categories, technology services and special services, have been evolved and expanded rapidly. The development has strengthened the capabilities of the logistics service providers and sustained the growth of the industry.

1. INTRODUCTION

As companies expand into the global marketplace, logistics becomes critical in support of their global supply chains. In order to remain competitive in today's changing business environment, more and more companies focus on core competencies. Instead of developing in-house capabilities in the various logistics disciplines such as transportation planning, warehouse management, and information technology, companies are opting to outsource to third party logistics providers. Third-party logistics (3PL) is the use of contracted firm(s) to supply services in the planning, implementation and controlling of the flow and storage of raw materials, in-process inventory, finished goods, and related information throughout the supply chain. Third party logistics providers may handle all or part of the distribution of merchandise along the supply chain to the consumer. Hence the firms are able to concentrate on their own core business, while the 3PLs concentrate on inflows and outflows of the global supply chain activities.

Third party logistics was identified as a separate industry and service in the late 1980s, and started to gain market share in the U.S. only since early 1990s (Ashenbaum, et al., 2005). Since then, the third party logistics industry has grown rapidly from about US$6 billion in 1991 to US$146.4 billion in 2013. In the United States, the logistics cost was 8.5% of the GDP in 2013, and the average 3PL user paid approximately 10.5% of the company's logistics operating budget to 3PL providers. In contrast, the logistics cost was 18% of the GDP in China and the average 3PL user outsourced only 7% of the company's logistics budget on 3PL services in 2013 (Armstrong & Associates, 2015).

3PL relationships are more complex than traditional logistics supplier relationships, which are often transaction based and focus on single function (Simchi-Levi, et al., 2003, p. 149). As 3PLs become more vital to a company's operations, these arrangements require active participation by both parties. In contracting out the logistics operations, the third party provider is now an important partner which has significant impacts on the company's quality, service, and dependability. Boyson et al. (1999) showed that the outsourcing of logistics functions had proven to be effective in helping firms to achieve competitive advantages, improve their customer service levels and reduce their overall logistics costs. Berglund et al. (1999) found that 3PLs can add value by creating operational efficiencies and by sharing resources across customers. This paper investigates the strategic development of 3PL services in the United States in the last decade and studies the role of 3PLs in managing today's global supply chains.

2. LITERATURE REVIEW

In earlier years, companies chose 3PL providers mainly by cost. However Millegan (2000) noted that more meaningful relationships had been emerging since late 1990s. Bhatnagar et al. (1999) found that other than cost, customer service and flexibility/customization were the most important factors for selecting logistic outsourcing. For example, shippers are choosing their providers based on their emphasis on value, innovation and performance in an increasingly global context. This trend presents a challenge for the logistics service providers. Millegan's study (2000) indicated that customer demands for performance and sophistication had been accelerating. The 3PL providers need to keep pace in service scope.

Lieb and Bentz's (2005) surveyed the use of 3PLs services by large American manufacturing firms. They found that eighty percent of sixty *Fortune* 500 manufacturers indicated that they had used 3PL services in 2004. Major companies outsource logistics services to 3PLs are from demand sensitive, fast-moving industries such as consumer product goods, electronics, food and beverage, and automotive companies. However companies from more specialised industries, such as furniture, cosmetics, and renewable energy, are beginning to outsource logistics services (O'Reilly, 2011).

Various strategies are utilized by 3PL providers. Other than serving the needs of individual customer, some 3PLs take multiple customers within a particularly focused industry sector, yielding greater efficiencies and cost savings. Some 3PLs spend great resources to develop competitive specific channels and then use the channel throughout their customer base. Industry-specific 3PLs often use the same supply chain design and channels for clients that are competitors (Burnson, 1999). As more diverse industries use 3PLs and outsource more logistic functions, the scope of services provided by 3PLs shall be broadened.

Another strategy for 3PLs is to consolidate or form alliances with other 3PLs. As mentioned earlier, most of these 3PLs offer a variety of services from transportation management, contract carrier, ware-house management, and information technology, but no one company dominates the market share in all of these areas. Consolidation or multiple partner alliances are sometimes the only way to provide the range of diverse geographic services demanded by customers (Cook, 1998). Current trend in consolidation and strategic alliances comes from the pressure of 3PL users to extend global capabilities and provide one-stop-shopping. Cost efficiency can be improved as the benefit of scale economy. This trend changes the ownership structure of the 3PL industry. Some examples of consolidation include UPS's acquisition of Fritz, which allowed freight forwarding to be added to the expertise of the transportation and warehousing giant. Fritz was also a significant ocean non-vessel operating common carrier as well as a charter agent. Thus UPS was able to move beyond the small parcel dimension of global trade. Exel, a warehousing and freight-forwarding leader, acquired Mark VII so that it could add domestic surface transportation management to its offered services. In addition to partnerships with other service providers, 3PL providers also enhance and expand partnerships with their users.

Furthermore, as globalization escalates, the 3PL providers seek international partners for overseas coverage. Some 3PL providers target a specialized niche market to differentiate them and then form alliances with other players. HUB Group is a good example of this strategy. Hub Group has decided to focus on intermodal transportation due to its strong relationship with the nation's railroad services in the United States. When a niche player has a customer that is looking for a more comprehensive service, they may partner up with another niche player that complements their own service. HUB Group partnered up with TMM Logistics in Mexico in order to be able to increase their presence in Mexico. TMM Logistics is the dominant logistic provider in Mexico. With this strategic partnership Hub, a niche 3PL player, is able to provide cross-border transportation (Business Wire, 2002).

Most of the extant literature focuses on the perspectives from the customers/users of 3PLs services. For examples, Murphy and Poist (1998) examined *third-party logistics* usage among a group of small to large manufacturers and non-manufacturers. Vaidyanathan (2005) proposed a conceptual framework using IT as the focus to evaluate the core functionalities of 3PL providers for the users. Moberg and Speh

(2004) surveyed the warehouse customers to compare the selection criteria of a regional warehouse and a national warehouse. Some literature studies 3PLs within a specific country context. For example, Lieb and Bentz (2004, 2005) and Langley et al. (2004) repeatedly surveyed the use of 3PL services among large American manufacturers over the years. Separate studies by Piplani et al. (2004) and Wilding and Juriado (2004) investigated customers' perceptions of 3PLs in Singapore and Europe, respectively. Knemeyer and Murphy (2005) studied the users of 3PL services to investigate whether certain 3PL relationship outcomes are influenced by relationship characteristics or customer attributes. Their findings suggest that one relationship characteristic, communication with the provider, showed statistically significant influences on all outcomes. Anderson, et al. (2011) surveyed over three hundred managers responsible for purchasing logistics services and found three distinct decision models. They concluded that the drivers of 3PL selection vary greatly between customer groups.

Murphy and Poist (2000) compared the perspectives of 3PL providers and 3PL users on most commonly provided/used services. They found some overlaps and mismatches between the 3PL services offered and used. There are overlaps on five of the ten most commonly provided/used services: EDI capability, freight consolidation, warehousing, consulting, and freight bill payment. The customers tend to be interested in operational services such as customs clearance, pick and delivery, freight charge auditing, intermodal service, and order picking and packing. However, their sample size was rather small and the comparisons are not from paired samples. Yeung, et al. (2006) investigated the relationship of strategic choices on a composite measure of financial performance for 3PL providers in Hong Kong. They found that the combined strategy of cost and differentiation performing best and pure cost strategy performing the worst.

Little research is conducted from the perspective of the 3PL service provider. Hertz and Alfredsson (2003) followed the strategic development of four different types of logistics firms into 3PLs. They found that the existing network of these firms' customers, customers' customers and partners seemed to have played an important role for the development into a 3PL and also in the continued development. Larson and Gammelgaad (2001) studied Danish logistics providers and found them to be more niche firms, focusing on the domestic market and limited sets of customers by industry. Lieb and Kendrick (2003) provided some macro level insights into the *third-party logistics* industry; but their results were based on a survey of a small sample of twenty CEOs of the largest 3PL companies in the U.S. Min and Joo (2006) studied six largest 3PLs in the United States for their operational efficiency. Zhou, et al. (2008) conducted a similar study with top ten largest Chinese 3PL providers and identified some sources of inefficiency.

3. RESEARCH QUESTIONS AND HYPOTHESES

This research explores service offerings from 3PL providers in the United States in the last decade to investigate how 3PL service scope has been strategically developed in response to the customers' growing needs in global supply chain management. The goal is to provide a longitudinal investigation on the strategic development in this industry. Based on extant literature reviewed, the following hypotheses are proposed.

H1: 3PLs service scope gets broader over time.

H2: 3PLs serve more industry sectors over time.

H3: 3PLs get more global over time.

H4: Asset ownership structure of 3PLs changes over time.

H5: Service offerings vary among the asset ownership structure of 3PLs.

H6: Service offerings vary between global and North America focused 3PLs.

4. METHODOLOGY

This study uses secondary data published by Inbound Logistics on their annual survey of American 3PLs, published in its July issue every year. Unlike Lieb and Bentz's survey (2004, 2005), which focuses only on the largest American manufactures' perspectives on 3PLs, this dataset consists of a mix of large, public companies and small, niche providers from 3PL industry, reflecting a broad range of capabilities. Inbound Logistics, established in 1981, is the leading trade magazine for logistics and supply chain managers in various industries. Each year, Inbound Logistics invites companies to submit data using an online questionnaire with an extensive list of questions (Inbound Logistics Top 100 3PL Providers Questionnaire). Then the top one hundred companies are selected from a pool of over 250 companies through survey inputs, phone interviews, and online research. The selected companies offer various operational capabilities and experiences in logistics services. Their database includes information such as regions served, industry sectors served, asset ownership, possible services in five categories, and membership of three certificates-- ISO, SmartWay, and C-TPAT. Services listed on this database were much broader in scope and in industry coverage comparing to the ones listed on Lieb and Bentz's (2005) survey that contained only 26 services for sixty large manufacturing companies. Table 1 shows all five 3PL service categories and their specific services. All data in the Inbound Logistics database from five points in time—2002, 2004, 2007, 2010, and 2013 are analysed to test the hypotheses. Sample size is 100 per year. Since the number of services varies somewhat from year to year, some raw counts are converted to percentages in data analysis.

Table 1: Major 3PL services categories

Category	Service Types
Logistics Services	Inbound Logistics, Integrated Logistics, Warehousing, Lead Logistic Provider, Inventory Management, JIT, Process Re-Engineering, Vendor Management, Payment Audit Processing, Product Life Cycle Management, Global Trade Services
Transportation Services	Small Package, Air Cargo, LTL, TL, Intermodal, Ocean, Rail, Bulk, Dedicated Contract Carriage, Fleet Acquisition, Equipment/ Drivers, Final Mile
Warehousing Services	Pick/Pack Sub-Assembly, Cross docking, DC Management, Location Services, Vendor Managed Inventory, Fulfilment

Special Services	Direct to Store, Direct to Home, Import/Export/Customs, Reverse Logistics, Marketing Customer Service, Logistics/Transportation Consulting, Global Expansion (sourcing/ selling), Security Analysis, Contingency/Crisis Planning, Labor Management
Technology/ Web Services	EDI, Satellite/Wireless Communication, Enterprise Web Enablement, Product Visibility, Customer Relationship Management

Source: Inbound Logistics, various issues 2002-2013

Radar diagrams are drawn to show the levels of the five service categories over years. ANOVA tests are conducted to analyse service scope (H1) and industry breadth (H2) over years as well as the asset ownership impact on service offerings (H5). Chi-square tests are conducted to show changes on region served (H3) and asset ownership over years (H4). Lastly independent t test is used to see if 3PLs with a global focus opposed to a North America focus offer different services (H6).

5. ANALYSIS AND RESULTS

There are five strategic service categories provided by 3PLs—logistics, transportation, warehousing, special services, technology and internet-based services. Each category contains four to thirteen specific services. Figure 1 shows the average percentages of services in each category provided each year. Over the years, broader scope of 3PL services are offered. For logistics services, the most commonly offered services are inbound logistics and integrated logistics, and the least offered services are global trade service and payment audit process. For transportation services, TL, LTL, and intermodal are offered by almost all 3PLs and the last-mile delivery service is gaining ground in recent years. For warehousing services, over 80% of the companies offer cross docking and pick/pack subassembly and more companies offer vendor managed inventory and location services in recent years.

Figure 1: Services Provided by 3PLs

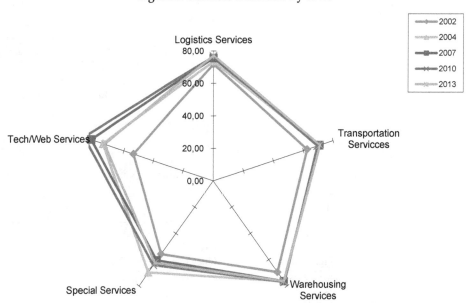

Two categories—special services and technology services clearly show expansions over time. Figure 2 and Figure 3 depict the average percentages of specific service offered in each category, respectively. Reverse logistics was offered by 78% of the companies in 2002 and 85% of the companies in 2013. Deliver directly to store service was offered by 69% in 2002 and 83% in 2013. The special service category keeps expanding. New services such as global sourcing and market expansion, security analysis, contingency & crisis planning, and logistics labor management were added to the list in 2007. On the technology service category, EDI link has been offered by almost all 3PLs since 2002. All other technology related services have shown significant growth. For examples, enterprise web enablement service was increased from 52% of the companies in 2002 to 92% of the companies in 2010; customer relationship management was increased from 24% of the companies in 2002 to 67% of the companies in 2013, while product visibility service was increased from 39% in 2002 to 92% in 2013.

Figure 2: Value-added Services Provided by 3PLs

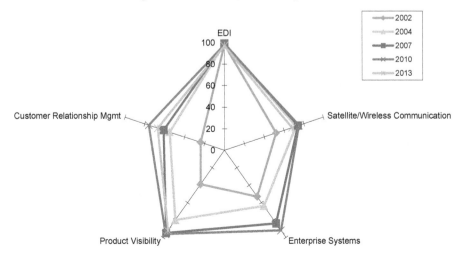

Figure 3: Tech/Web Services by 3PLS

ANOVA analysis (Table 2) on the aggregated numbers of all service categories shows significant growth at p=.000 level. Hence Hypothesis 1 is not rejected. Further analyses on each service category find that transportation service, special services, and technology based service show significant growth over the years, with p values of .025, .002, and .000, respectively. The technology related services show double digit growth in most of the years. Although not at the significant level, logistics services are also growing at a steady rate. The service categories that have even more future growth potentials are in the transportation service and special service areas. Four industry sectors—manufacturing, retail/e-tail, distributor, and services—are reported in the survey. Most 3PLs serve more than one industry sector. Table 3 shows that 3PLs are serving more industries over time. ANOVA analysis reveals that all growth comes from the retail sector, distribution sector, and service sector, with p values of .006, .040, and .004, respectively. Hence hypothesis 2 is not rejected.

Table 2: ANOVA test on service category by year

Service Category	2002	2004	2007	2010	2013	F Statistic	Sig.
All services	63.54	74.02	73.11	74.36	71.25	7.086	.000
Logistics services	71.81	73.55	75.56	76.46	77.10	1.062	.375
Transportation services	62.53	70.34	70.98	69.44	71.17	2.810	.025
Warehouse services	69.53	76.43	76.43	77.10	76.43	1.059	.376
Special services	55.72	69.70	60.49	64.14	62.50	4.434	.002
Tech/Web services	53.54	74.34	82.42	87.27	73.20	56.728	.000

Number presents the average percentage of companies providing services in each category

Table 3: ANOVA test on industry served by year

Industry served	2002	2004	2007	2010	2013	F Statistic	Sig.
Manufacturing	98	97	98	99	99	.393	.813
Retail/e-retail	77	87	92	91	91	3.640	.006
Distributor	83	89	92	96	88	2.526	.040
Service	53	71	69	78	67	3.907	.004

Number represents count

As the supply chains getting global, one would expect the 3PLs will also expand their services to global regions. Table 4 shows an increase of globally focused 3PLs over the years. However Chi-square test does not show the increase was at a significant level (p value=0.359). Hence Hypothesis 3 is rejected. Asset ownership varies among the 3PL companies. Table 4 shows significant changes (p value=0.003) on asset ownership of 3PLs over the years. Hence Hypothesis 4 is not rejected. Pure asset-owned 3PLs were going down from twenty three companies in 2002 to only eight companies in 2013. The number of 3PLs that leverage both asset and non-asset capabilities grows from thirty-two companies in 2002 to fifty-two companies in 2013.

Table 4: Chi-square tests on region and asset ownership by year

Region	2002	2004	2007	2010	2013	Chi-Square	Sig.
North America	42	51	46	40	38	4.364	0.359
Global	58	49	54	60	62		
Asset Ownership	2002	2004	2007	2010	2013	Chi-Square	Sig.
Non-Asset	44	44	49	50	40		
Asset	23	20	13	6	8	23.021	0.003
Both	32	36	38	44	52		

Number represents count

In general asset-based providers offer dedicated services, primarily through owned or leased assets. Non-asset-based providers offer administrative management services, and tend to subcontract for the necessary logistics assets which are not available in-house. ANOVA tests (Table 5) are conducted on all data and find significant difference (p=.000) in the overall service levels among the three types of asset ownership. Non-asset based 3PLs offer an average of 69.42% of all service surveyed. Asset based 3PLs offer an average of 66.08% of all services and the both non-asset and asset based 3PLs offer an average of 75.70% of all services. Hence Hypothesis 5 is accepted. In fact 3PLs that leverage on both non-asset and asset based capabilities provide more services in all service categories, the averages ranging from 68.02% in special services to 81.89% in warehouse services. This result is consistent with Stank and Maltz's study (1996), but it is different from Murphy and Poist's study (1998). Murphy and Poist (1998) concluded that there were no differences in the number of services offered by either asset-based or non-asset-based providers. However, their study compared customers' reported usage of services from asset-based and non-asset-based providers, not the actual services offered by 3PLs.

Table 5: Service category means and ANOVA tests by asset ownership

Service Category	Non-Asset based	Asset based	Both non-asset and asset based	F Statistic	Sig.
All services	69.42	66.08	75.70	10.240	.000
Logistics services	73.87	64.41	78.19	10.034	.000
Transportation services	67.95	58.81	72.15	7.242	.001
Warehouse services	66.49	83.06	81.89	18.475	.000
Special services	59.27	57.71	68.02	5.306	.005
Tech/Web services	71.81	71.61	78.53	6.467	.002

Number represents the average percentage of companies of each asset ownership type in providing each service category

Table 6 indicates that the service levels differ between the global players and North America regional players significantly (p=.000). Hence Hypothesis 6 is accepted. Global 3PL companies provide significantly broader level of services in all categories except the technology category, the averages ranging from 66.93% in special services to 79.63% in logistics services.

Table **6: Service category means and independent t tests by Region Served**

Service Category	North America	Global	t Value	Sig.
All services	66.61	74.81	-5.422	*.000*
Logistics services	68.13	79.63	-6.143	*.000*
Transportation services	61.91	73.94	-6.136	*.000*
Warehouse services	74.94	75.31	-.134	.894
Special services	56.37	66.93	-4.844	*.000*
Tech/Web services	74.47	73.78	.311	.756

Number represents the average percentage of companies of each region focus in providing each service category

6. MANAGERIAL IMPLICATIONS

As business goes global, the supply chain networks and logistics complexity increases. Outsourcing logistics functions offers the opportunity for supply chain participants to concentrate on their core capabilities. The growth of the third-party logistics industry makes both the formation and dismantling of supply chain arrangements easier.

This study shows 3PLs have served more industry sectors over the years. Third-party logistics have been commonly utilized in the manufacturing sector. As logistics outsourcing becomes a viable strategy, industry sectors such as retail and e-retail, distribution and wholesale, and service sector have also adopted the best practices, which expand 3PL service markets. The fastest growing market for 3PLs comes from the service sector and retail/e-retail sector. In 2002, 53% of 3PLs served in the service sector and the percentage was increased to 78% in 2010. Retail/e-retail sectors also had significant growth of 14% from 2002 to 2013. Some 3PLs focus on e-retailers and offer warehousing, shipping, and order-management services to support the business-to-customer (B2C) e-business model. As of 2013, the number of industry served per 3PL providers ranged from one to sixteen, with an average of ten verticals. Armstrong & Associates (2009) reported seventy-seven percent Fortune 500 companies used 3PLs for logistics and supply chain functions and many of them used more than one 3PLs provider. For examples, General Motors, Procter & Gamble,

Wal-Mart, PepsiCo, and Ford Motor each used 30 or more 3PLs (Armstrong & Associates, 2009). Similarly O'Reilly (2011) reported seventy-seven percent of more than 5000 3PLs users working with multiple 3PLs partners.

Asset based companies are typically larger firms. They usually enjoy economies of scale, own warehouse or transportation assets, have broader industry knowledge, and have a larger customer base. However non-asset based firms are more flexible and more able to tailor services with specialized industry expertise. This study finds fewer pure asset based 3PLs companies over the years. Asset-based companies have tapped into the non-asset based capabilities to serve their customers. As the customers demand more service offerings from 3PLs, the expanded service scope satisfies customer's desire for "one-stop" shopping. The transportation and logistics market in the United States is highly fragmented. Strategic merger and acquisition has become a strategy as consolidation provides a significant opportunity to build up capabilities and expand markets. Publicly traded logistics companies and private equity firms are seen as the most aggressive buyers, going after smaller private companies or specific niche areas that are highly valuable to profit and revenue (Reuters, 2011). For example, Thoma Bravo LLC, a leading private equity investment firm, acquired UPS Logistics Technologies, a business unit of UPS, in 2010. The newly independent company has been renamed Roadnet Technologies, Inc. with the goal to provide world-class transportation management applications (PEHub, 2010).

In response to the specific needs of each industry and customer, there is a proliferation of 3PLs services. This study shows that service scope gets broader over time in this industry. The results, in general, continue the trend projected by Persson and Virum (2001) and Lieb and Bentz (2003). Not only 3PL companies offer more services in all categories, the rank orders of the five service categories change also. In 2002 the rank order from the most offered services to the least offered services was logistics, warehousing, transportation, special services, and technology services. In 2010 the rank order was changed to technology services, warehousing, logistics, transportation, and special services.

Van Hoek's (2000) found that traditional third-party logistics services such as warehousing and logistics have become commoditized. To differentiate in the 3PLs market, logistics and supply chain related technologies have help created niche expertise. This is interesting because in Lieb's 2003 user survey, users of 3PLs generally did not see 3PL providers as leading edge suppliers of information technology. Lieb and Bentz (2004) indicated that 3PLs must decide upon appropriate strategies for strengthening their technology capabilities to convince potential users. This research shows that 3PLs have made consistently and significantly improvement in technology and web service offerings in the last decade. In 2002 only 53 percent of 3PLs companies offered technology services and the percentage was increased to 73.2% in 2013. Technology services related to product visibility, customer relationship management, and enterprise web enablement have shown rapid growth. Via technologies, the buyer, seller, and shipping partners can monitor the status of a shipment in real time from start to finish. For example, FedEx and UPS have modified their services quickly to accommodate their e-commerce customers for package delivery (Armstrong, 2004). Looking forward, Figure 3 shows wireless communication and customer relationship management are the two areas with more room for future growth.

Traditionally, turnover rate was high in 3PL market. Mottley (1998) showed that more than one-third

of users had cancelled at least one 3PL contract. However, a later survey by Lieb and Bentz (2004) showed seventy-two percent of the users identified in their survey had used 3PL services for more than five years, which is the highest percentage ever reported in this category in their surveys. This finding indicates that the relationships between customers and some 3PLs are stabilized over time and may be changing from adversary to partnership. However, using a proprietary database Armstrong & Associates (2009) studied 3,936 3PLs customer relationships from 2005 through 2008. It is found that only 18.5% of the relationships were considered strategic and the remaining 81.5% were classified as tactical relationships. To become a true strategic partner to its logistic outsourcer, these high value-added special services could create competitive advantages.

One way to gain reputation as 3PL leaders is through certifications. Table 7 shows three certificates to improve 3PLs' credentials. ISO is a highly regarded international standard for an established quality system in a company. ISO was first published in 1987 by International Organization for Standardization. As shown in Table 7, ISO is most adopted by 3PLs companies serving global region and service sector. Asset-based 3PLs companies do not embrace this quality certificate. In 2004, US EPA launched SmartWaySM — an innovative brand that represents environmentally cleaner, more fuel efficient transportation options. SmartWay brand identifies products and services that reduce transportation-related emissions. SmartWay partners are committed to sustainability through promoting greater energy efficiency and air quality within the freight transport sector (EPS web site). Recently many companies have developed sustainable supply chain initiatives. 3PLs with SmartWay certificate may become a strategic partner to such initiatives. C-TPAT (Customs-Trade Partnership against Terrorism) is a new certificate from the first worldwide supply chain security initiative in 2007. The voluntary government-business initiative is to build cooperative relationships that strengthen and improve overall international supply chain and U.S. border security (C-TPAT web site). C-TPAT is adopted more by global players and non-asset based 3PLs companies. Supply chain security is a growing concern in global business. More 3PLs are expected to provide special services in this area.

Table 7: Certificate adoption by industry, region, and asset ownership structure

Industry served	ISO	Smart Way	C-TPAT
Manufacturing	57.58%	65.66%	59.6%
Retail/e-retail	57.14%	68.13%	61.5%
Distributor	55.68%	63.64%	60.4%
Service	65.67%	76.12%	62.8%
Region served	**ISO**	**Smart Way**	**C-TPAT**
Domestic	50%	46.74%	45%
Global	62.90%	79.03%	70%
Asset Ownership	**ISO**	**Smart Way**	**C-TPAT**
Non-Asset	55.00%	62.50%	62%
Asset	37.50%	62.50%	50%
Both	63.46%	69.23%	59.1%

Number represents the percentage of 3PLs adopted the certificate. ISO and Smart Way numbers are from 2013 survey and C-TPAT numbers are from 2010 survey.

7. CONCLUSION AND FUTURE RESEARCH

Logistics management has significant impacts on various aspects of supply chains such as response time, total supply chain cost, sourcing risk, customer service, security, sustainability, etc. A 3PL study by three professional organizations and Georgia Institute of Technology affirms that logistics is one of the keys to company's success, and many firms give credits to logistics service providers for helping them achieve critical service, cost, and customer satisfaction goals (Lagley et al., 2004). This study proposed seven hypotheses based on extant literature to examine the strategic development of the 3PLs industry in the United Sates. Using secondary data gathered from 3PLs in the last decade, comprehensive analyses are conducted to provide a longitudinal view.

This study shows that 3PLs services vary based on industry verticals served, regions served, and asset ownership structure. Over last decade 3PLs have served more industry sectors, became asset light, and provided broader services. 3PL companies offer five service categorires—transportation, logistics, warehousing, technology, and value-added special services. The first three categories are traditional services. The last two service categories have been evolved and expanded rapidly in the last decade, and the new capabilities have strengthened the strategic position of this industry.

The limitation of this study comes from the secondary data utilized. The dichotomy nature of the data makes it hard to assess the quality and impact of 3PLs services. Moreover, the data represent the provider's view. For future studies, it will be useful to obtain paired data to get outsourcers' inputs. Obtaining financial and assessment data will provide more insights to the development of 3PLs industry. In addition, new issues in global supply chains such as supply chain risks, sustainability, and security have imposed enormous challenges. It will be interesting to conduct a detailed study on the role of 3PLs and its strategies to make profound impacts in these areas.

8. REFERENCES

Anderson, E., Coltman, T., Devinney, T. and Keating, B. (2011), "What Drives the Choice of a Third-Party Logistics Provider?" *Journal of Supply Chain Management*, Vol. 47 No. 2.

Armstrong & Associates (2015), Global 3PL Market Size Estimates, available at: http://www.3plogistics.com/3PLmarketGlobal.htm (accessed 6 Sept 2015).

Armstrong & Associates (2009) Guides & Market Research Reports, available at: http://www.3plogistics.com/PR_3PL_Customers-2009.htm, (accessed 9 April 2012).

Ashenbaum, B., Maltz, A. and Rabinovich, E. (2005), "Studies of Trends in Third-Party Logistics Usage: What Can We Conclude?" *Transportation Journal*, Vol. 44 No. 3, pp. 39-50.

Berglund, M., van Laarhoven, P., Sharman, G. and Wendel, S. (1999), "Third Party Logistics: Is There a Future?" *International Journal of Logistics Management*, Vol. 10 No. 1, pp. 59-70.

Bhatnagar, R., Sohal, A. S. and Millen, R. (1999), "Third Party Logistics Service: A Singapore Perspective", *International Journal of Physical Distribution and Logistics Management*, Vol. 29 No. 9, pp. 569-587.

Boyson, S., Corsi, T., Dresner, M. and Rabinovich, E. (1999), "Managing Effective Third Party Logistics Partnerships: What Does It Take?" *Journal of Business Logistics*, Vol. 20 No. 1, pp. 73-100.

Business Wire (2002), "Hub Group and TMM Logistics Announce Operating Partnership to Streamline Cross-Border Shipping", 29 October.

Burnson, P. (1999), "Getting Logistics in Order", *World Trade*, Vol. 12 No. 8, pp. 50-52.

Cooke, J. A. (2000), "3PLs: Riding the Wave", *Logistics Management and Distribution Report*, Vol. 39 No. 7, pp. 69.

C-TAPT, available at http://www.cbp.gov/xp/cgov/trade/cargo_security/ctpat/ (accessed on April 3, 2012)

EPA SmartWay, available at http://www.epa.gov/smartway/index.htm (accessed on April 3, 2012.)

Hertz, S. and Alfredsson, M. (2003), "Strategic development of third party logistics providers", *Industrial Marketing Management*, Vol. 32 No. 20, pp. 139.

Inbound Logistics (2002-2013), "Top 100 American 3PLs", various Issues in July, Thomas Publishing Company.

Inbound Logistics Top 100 3PL Providers Questionnaire, available at http://www.inboundlogistics.com/cms/3pl-questionnaire/ (accessed on November 21, 2105.)

Knemeyer, A. M. and Murphy, P. R. (2005), "Exploring the Potential Impact of Relationship Characteristics and Customer Attributes on the Outcomes of Third-Party Logistics Arrangements", *Transportation Journal*, Vol. 44 No. 1, pp. 5-19.

Lagley, C. J. jr., Allen, G. R. and Dale, T. A. (2004), "Third-Party Logistics: Results and Findings of the 2004 Ninth Annual Survey", in *Georgia Institute of Technology, Cap Gemini U.S., and Federal Express Corporation.*

Larson, P. D. and Gammelgaad, B. (2002), "Logistics in Denmark: A Survey of the Industry", *International Journal of Logistics: Research and Applications*, Vol. 4 No. 2, pp. 191-206.

Lieb, R. C. and Bentz, B. A. (2005), "The Use of Third-Party Logistics Services by Large American Manufacturers: The 2004 Survey", *Transportation Journal*, Vol. 44 No. 2, pp. 5-15.

Lieb, R. C. and Bentz, B. A. (2004), "The Use of Third-Party Logistics Services by Large American Manufacturers: The 2004 Survey", *Transportation Journal*, Vol. 43 No. 3, pp. 24-34.

Lieb, R. C. and Kendrick, S. (2003), "The Year 2002 Survey: CEO Perspectives on the Current Status and Future Prospects of the Third-Party Logistics Industry in the United States", *Transportation Journal*, Vol. 42 No. 3, pp. 5-17.

Millegan, B. (2000), "Third-Party Logistics Providers Told To 'Get to the Net'", *Purchasing*, Vol. 129 No. 8, pp. 91.

Min, H. and Joo, S. (2006), "Benchmarking the Operational Efficiency of Third Party Logistics Providers using Data Envelopment Analysis", *Supply Chain Management, An International Journal*, Vol. 11 No. 3, pp. 572-587.

Moberg, C. R. and Speh, T. W. (2004), "Third-Party Warehousing Selection: A Comparison of National and Regional Firms", *Mid - American Journal of Business*, Vol. 19 No. 2.

Mottley, R. (1998), "Good News, Bad News for 3rd Parties", *American Shipper*, Vol. 40 No. 12, pp. 38-40.

Murphy, P. and Poist, R. (2000), "Third-Party Logistics: Some User Versus Producer Perspectives", *Journal of Business Logistics*, Vol. 21 No. 1, pp. 121-133.

Murphy, P. R. and Poist, R. F. (1998), "Third-party logistics usage: An assessment of propositions based on previous research", *Transportation Journal*, Vol. 37 No. 4, pp. 26-36.

O'Reilly, J. (2011), "3PL Perspectives 2011", *Inbound Logistics*, July, pp. 71-86.

PEHub (2010) Thoma Bravo Closed Buy of UPS's Logistics Technologies Unit, available at http://www.pehub.com/91805/thoma-bravo-closes-buy-of-upss-logistic-technologies-unit/ (Accessed on April 12, 2012)

Persson, G. and Virum, H. (2001), "Growth Strategies for Logistics Service Providers: A Case Study", *International Journal of Logistics Management*, Vol. 12 No. 1, pp. 53-64.

Rajesh, P., Pokharel, S. and Tan, A. (2004), "Perspectives on the Use of Information Technology at Third Party Logistics Service Providers in Singapore", *Asia Pacific Journal of Marketing and Logistics*, Vol. 16 No. 1, pp. 27-43.

Reuters (2011), US Logistics M&A Expected to Pick Up, available at http://www.pehub.com/101438/reuters-us-logistics-ma-expected-to-pick-up/ (accessed on April 12, 2012)

Simchi-Levi, D., Kaminsky, P. and Simchi-Levi, E. (2003), *Designing and Managing the Supply Chain, second edition*, Irwin McGraw-Hill, Boston, MA.

Stank, T.P. and Maltz, A.B. (1996), "Some Propositions on *Third-Party* Choice: Domestic vs. International *Logistics* Providers", *Journal of Marketing Theory and Practice*, pp. 45-54.

Sowinski, L. L. (2000), "Is There a Perfect Logistics Software Product on the Market?" *World Trade*, Vol. 13 No. 2, pp. 32-36.

Vaidyanathan, G. (2005), "A Framework for Evaluating Third-Party Logistics", *Communications of the ACM*, Vol. 48 No. 1, pp. 89-95.

Van Laarhoven, P., Berglund, M. and Peters, M. (2000), "Third-Party Logistics in Europe - Five Years Later", *International Journal of Physical Distribution & Logistics Management*, Vol. 30 No. 3, pp. 425-442.

Wilding, R. and Rein, J. (2004), "Customer perceptions on logistics outsourcing in the European consumer goods industry", *International Journal of Physical Distribution & Logistics Management*, Vol. 34 No. 7/8, pp. 628.

Wilson, R. (2004), "15th Annual State of Logistics Report: Globalization", available at: http://www.nescon.org/cgi-bin/2004/index2.pl?r_wilson_presentation, (accessed 9 April 2012).

Yeung, J. Y., Selen, W., Sum, C. and Huo, B. (2006), "Linking Financial Performance to Strategic Orientation and Operations Priorities—An Empirical Study of Third-Party Logistics Providers", *International Journal of Physical Distribution & Logistics Management*, Vol. 34 No. 3, pp. 210-230.

Zhou, G., Min, H., Xu, C. and Cao, Z. (2008), "Evaluating the Comparative Efficiency of Chinese Third-Party Logistics Providers using Data Envelopment Analysis", *International Journal of Physical Distribution & Logistics management*, Vol. 38 No. 4, pp. 262-279.

9

Characterization of cross-functional integration level: A multi case study in Agribusiness Organizations

Ana Cristina Ferreira
Federal University of Uberlândia
ana-cristina18@hotmail.com

Franciele Olivo Bertan
Federal University of Uberlândia
folivo2@yahoo.com.br

Marcio Lopes Pimenta
Federal University of Uberlândia
pimenta.mp@gmail.com

ABSTRACT: A point that has generated discussion in the literature is the level of integration required for the coordination of activities between areas. However, there is a lack of theoretical definitions and field studies that explain this phenomenon in depth. Thus, this study aims to characterize the level of cross-integration, the factors that generate it and the impacts on organizational performance. For this, interviews with managers of Operations, R&D and Marketing/Commercial areas, from two multinational companies based in Minas Gerais were performed. The results indicate that the level of integration can be analyzed as a combination of three factors: 1) absence of overlapping of perceptions about integration factors over the processes, balance between formality and informality, and absence of manifest conflicts of interest. This is a setting that provides a deeper definition than those obtained in the studied literature, which basically present integration mechanisms, without detailing how these should be applied in order to generate higher levels of integration.

Keywords: Cross-functional integration; Integration level; Operations; R&D; Marketing.

1. INTRODUCTION

The integration management can help to ensure that there is harmony between organizational functions, so that they can work together (Lawrence & Lorsch, 1967). This is an important factor, as it can improve the sense of interdependence and organizational results (Stank, Daugherty & Ellinger, 1999). There are studies on this issue that address the correlation between generating mechanisms of functional integration and results (Stank *et al.* 1999; Ellinger, 2000; Daugherty, Mattioda & Grawe, 2009). This perspective represents the mainstream in the studied literature, in which, some authors identify important tools to conduct the cross-functional integration (Kahn & Mentzer, 1996; Kahn, 1996; Gimenez & Ventura, 2005; Jütnner, Christopher & Baker, 2007).

An element that has generated discussion in the literature is the level of integration, which corresponds to the intensity in which the areas relate towards the coordination of their activities (Pimenta, 2011). There is, however, a lack of theoretical definitions and field studies explaining, in depth, how this phenomenon operates. Authors such as Kahn (1996) and Gimenez and Ventura (2005) mention the importance of achieving higher levels of integration, since this element denotes strong correlation with the improvement of functional and organizational results. Pagell (2004) elaborates a little further in the practical sense, explaining that the definition of the level of integration is relative, because different managers in different contexts can interpret it in different ways. Thus, characterization should be based on semantic definition of evidence, which is often subjective.

Santos and D'Antone (2014), after conducting a review of literature, argued that it is necessary to verify if integration can have a degree of measurement, and if high levels of integration are necessary and advisable. The authors also propose new topics for further research, revealing, among them, the lack of studies dealing with the level of integration.

Pimenta (2011) identifies characteristics of three integration levels (high, medium and low) in the context of Marketing and Logistics. According to him, high levels of integration are characterized by the balance between formal and informal mechanisms of integration within the points of contact between areas. Basnet (2013) developed a scale for assessing the level of cross-functional integration, and his work is one of the first to measure this element quan-

titatively. However, the study mentioned features integration levels according to the mere presence or absence of mechanisms of integration, not correlating other elements such as: as points of contact and formality and informality of integration.

We believe that a qualitative study can help to improve the understanding about the level of cross-functional integration in order to identify a set of factors beyond the mere presence of integration mechanisms. In this sense, this study aims to characterize different levels of cross-functional integration according to its peculiarities in terms of integration factors (mechanisms), practical perceptions, formality / informality and conflicts between internal functions. Regarding these features, Santos and D'Antone (2014) found no papers dealing with the issues considered here, mainly about differences in the perception between people of the same company in relation to integration factors.

The following section presents a theoretical review about cross-functional integration and level of integration.

2. CROSS-FUNCTIONAL INTEGRATION

The increasing complexity of the competitive environment has required quick decision making and increasing harmony between demand and supply. The management of cross-functional integration can contribute to reach these needs (Silva, Lombardi & Pimenta, 2013). Integration can be defined as "the quality of the state of collaboration that exists among departments that are required to achieve unity of effort by the demands of the environment" (Lawrence & Lorsch, 1967, p.11). Thus, it contributes to improve internal cooperation and the competitiveness of the organization (Baofen, 2013).

Pagell (2004) refers to integration as a process in which functions, such as production, purchasing and logistics, work cooperatively to reach acceptable results for the organization. Stank *et al.* (1999) highlight that integration can bring many benefits such as reduced production cycles, successful new product strategies, better understanding of consumer values and also improved service levels.

Kahn and Mentzer (1996) state that cross-functional integration is practiced by processes of interaction and collaboration, consisting, respectively, in both formal and informal processes that lead to departments acting together towards a cohesive organization. To Baofen (2013) as antecedents of integration, it is necessary to exist good relationship, trust and commitment in relationships. Jin, Luo & Eksioglu (2013) established that awareness of the competitive potential that integration can provide is not enough to mobilize resources and mitigate resistance to collaboration, and it takes commitment, which is the key element.

The literature on integration presents analyses of various elements such as: integration factors (Daugherty et al 2009); contact points (Mentzer et al., 2008); formality and informality (Kahn & Mentzer, 1996; Ellinger, Keller & Hansen, 2006); integrating effects (Stank*et al.* 1999; Gimenez, 2006; Jutnner *et al.* 2007) and level of integration (Basnet, 2013). Kidron et al. (2013), claim that informal and formal mechanisms may increase the level of integration, especially the informal ones. There is also a sub-theme in this issue that discusses about antecedents and consequences of the level of integration (Basnet, 2013). This sub-theme will be specifically addressed below.

2.1 Integration Level

The level of cross-functional integration is the intensity of the involvement of functions with each other, based on the interaction frequency and on the ability to perform activities that require cooperation (Pimenta, 2011). Stank *et al.* (1999) noted that organizations with high level of integration, through cooperation, achieve higher performance than the less integrated organizations.

Kahn and Mentzer (1996) argue that not all situations require high levels of integration. For these authors, working with critical products and processes, in turbulent environments, requires high levels of internal integration, which in turn will result in higher administrative costs for such an achievement. On the other hand, when the market is stable and the activity does not demand major efforts from different departments, there may be a low integration level, since a high intensity of integration in this situation could compromise the efficiency of tasks.

Formal integration factors, like mutual evaluation and incentive mechanisms, can increase the level of integration between functions (Kahn, 1996; Gimenez & Ventura, 2005; Jütnner et al 2007). Griffin and

Hauser (1996) highlight that the difference between the ideal level, which is the necessary integration, and the real one, forms the integration gap. If the difference between the need of integration desired by the organization and effective is large, the joint performance can be compromised because the level of integration achieved is not enough to respond to external demands. If the gap is small, it means that there was the desired integration by the organization, and this can positively affect performance.

Pagell (2004) states that the definition of the level of integration is relative, based on the semantic definition of evidences, which are often subjective. Pimenta and Silva (2012) corroborate this statement and add that, to each organization, a high or low level of integration may have different meanings, even for different people from the same organization. Thus, Pimenta (2011) states that it is important to research about what high, low or medium integration means in the perception of managers. As several different responses may arise, these can be analyzed by content and grouped according to the perception of the agents who work in the integrated functions.

According to Pimenta and Silva (2012), there are different ways of analyzing the level of integration: the amount of integration factors used, the frequency of contact, the perception of the agents about the ease to conduct joint processes and decisions.

To Bellmunt and Torres (2013), most part of the literature covers the theme of internal integration from external integration. Thus, internal and external factors of influence should be considered to measure the integration level. For internal integration, the concept most widely accepted is two-dimensional, which considers the interaction (formal aspects) and collaboration (informal aspects). According to Gupta *et al.* (1986) and Clark and Fujimoto (1991), these two dimensions form a concept where low levels of integration imply low levels of interaction and collaboration, and vice versa. On the other hand, the one-dimensional concept considers that there is an internal integration component (interaction or cooperation, for example). By studying the integration between Marketing and Logistics, Pimenta (2011) presents a classification of three levels of integration and their respective characteristics, as shown in Table 1.

Table 1: Features of different levels of integration

Integration Level	Characteristics
High	Presence of integration factors formally applied
	Trust, team spirit, and informal elements
	There are management actions to generate integration
Medium*	Great willingness to help other functions to resolve conflicts informally
	Little senior management effort
Low	Lack of integration factors **
	Unwillingness of people to integrate
	Insulation between employees and short-term contact

* There may be great efforts of senior management and unwillingness of people.
** There may be integration factors, but not in a balanced way between formal and informal.

Source: Adapted from Pimenta (2011).

Among the various definitions presented in Table 1, "conflicts" is an element that can interfere in the level of integration, depending on its type and intensity. Authors such as Pondy (1989) and Simons and Peterson (2000) argue that conflicts can disrupt the processes and decisions due to the lack of integration factors.

Pondy (1989) clarifies that organizational conflicts were seen in the past as aberrations that interrupted the normal course of processes, breaking the efficiency of the work flow. In a broader perspective, this author suggests that even the worst conflicts can be avoided with the use of management tools, such as: appropriate organizational structure, training to generate mutual understanding of perceptions and goals, or even to separate members with relationship problems.

Simons and Peterson (2000) identify two types of conflicts: 1) task conflicts (related to the content of managerial decisions due to different standpoints about the process); 2) relationship conflicts: (emotional conflicts due to the perception of personal incompatibility). For these authors, the existence of relationship conflict generates poor quality decisions. According to these authors, trust between team members is essential to avoid relationship conflicts and provide higher quality decisions.

The next section deals with the description of the methodological procedures performed in in the preparation of this paper.

3. METHODS

This study is considered qualitative and descriptive. A strategy of multiple case studies was conducted, in order to provide a higher representation than a single case study. According to Yin (2005), after obtaining the characteristics of the object of analysis, the researcher must try to replicate of the results in the analysis of other cases, identifying convergences or differences that will contribute to solving the proposed problem.

Two multinational companies, that develop and produce seeds, were studied. These organizations have processing units of seeds and experimental fields in Minas Gerais State, Brazil. As noted in the interviews, the context of these companies indicates a strong need for cross-functional integration for 1) the development of new cultivars; 2) the improvement of genetics and aspects of plant science; 3) the market positioning. Therefore, it was decided to study new product development processes, because they denote high necessity of cross-functional integration in these companies.

3.1 Data collection

Ten in depth interviews were conducted. The interview guide was based on concepts from the literature, divided into three categories: 1) integration factors (Daugherty et al., 2009; Kidron et al., 2013); 2) perception of the level of integration (Kahn & Mentzer, 1996; Pimenta, 2011; Bellmunt and Torres, 2013;Basnet, 2013); 3) impacts of the integration level on performance (Stank *et al.* 1999; Pagell, 2004;Gimenez, 2006; Jutnner *et al.*2007;Baofen, 2013). The questions were developed considering the new product development (NPD) processes, and therefore, the 10 interviewees belong to areas directly involved with the NPD process: Operations, R&D, Sales / Marketing. Table 2 shows the characteristics of the respondents.

Table 2: Characteristics of respondents

Company	Interviewed code	Function
1	TO 1	R&D
1	A2	Production
1	A3	R&D
1	A4	R&D
1	A5	Commercial
2	B1	R&D
2	B2	Production
2	B3	R&D
2	B4	Commercial
2	B5	Commercial

All participants were interviewed in their workplace. The interviews lasted around an hour and were recorded with the consent of the participants, allowing subsequent transcription to better understand the interviews.

3.2 Data analysis

The transcriptions were submitted to the technique of content analysis. Based on the guidelines of Bardin (1979), the following steps were adopted:

» Pre-analysis of the transcripts: quick read, prior identification;

» In depth analysis;

» Coding: the particular significance of each element is highlighted in frames;

» Categorization: codes are grouped into categories defined in the literature or observed in the context of the subject matter

Through these procedures, four categories of analysis related to the level of functional integration were found:

1. Integration factors: mechanisms that generate integration, related to the culture, interpersonal disposal, or formal managerial actions (Pimenta, 2011; Pimenta and Silva, 2012);

2. Perceptions of overlapping: This element was not present in the interview guide. It consists of the main theoretical contribution of this paper and emerged from the interviews and content analysis. Overlapping occurs when an employee perceives the existence of an integration factor, but another (or many others) employee involved in the same process does not perceive it. In such cases, the perception of integration is not homogeneous.

3. Formality / informality: The way the integration factors are operationalized, i.e., formal or informal processes (Ruekert and Walker, 1987; Kahn, 1996; Kahn and Mentzer, 1998).

4. Conflicts: to reduce/eliminate: conflicts between the areas of Production, Marketing and Logistics (Ballou, 2006; Ellegaard and Koch, 2014); conflicts of interests and conflicts of performance between the internal functions and organization; functional strategies not well defined or not clarified; lack of group vision and misaligned objectives (Pondy, 1989; Moses and Ahlström, 2008; Paiva, 2010); and promote trust as a way to reduce conflicts (Simons and Peterson, 2000)

These categories and their respective relationships with the level of integration are defined in the following topic.

4. RESULTS

The four categories identified in the content analysis, reinforced by quotations from the interviewees are explained in this topic. After the individual definition of each one, a set of characteristics of different levels of cross-functional integration in presented.

4.1 Integration Factors

Table 3 shows the analysis of the integration factors, i.e. mechanisms that generate integration. It also shows how these factors are operationalized in the perception of the respondents. Twenty-one integration factors were perceived in different hierarchical levels and different phases of the studied processes. In addition, the type of application of the integration factors was identified according to their formality or informality.

Table 3: Description of the integration factors and presence of formality and informality

Integration Factors	Type of Application Company 1	Type of Application Company 2	Company 1	Company 2
Adequate communication structure	Formal	Formal	There is an excess in the use of communication tools.	There is a well-defined structure.
Consideration of informal groups	Formal	Informal	Managers recognize the need to work in an integrated manner, and encourage this practice.	Managers recognize the voluntary willingness to work in an integrated manner.
Cross-functional meetings	Formal	Formal	There are too many meetings.	There are formal meetings.
Cross-functional teams	Formal	Formal and informal	Meetings are held periodically with the specific group, for alignment between areas.	There are support teams for the process to happen. There are also informal adjustments.
Cross-functional training	Formal	Formal	There is training for related areas. These sometimes occur as meetings for the development of new products.	There is training about the content of the areas and about relationship.
Goals aligned with strategy	Formal	Formal	Individual goals and departments are aligned to the objective of the company.	The employees are encouraged to think of the whole company, towards a common goal.
Group spirit	-	Informal		There is a climate of cooperation, facilitating conflict resolution.
Informal communication	-	Informal	The communication related to all processes is formalized.	People are always available for informal communication.
Information Sharing	Formal	Informal	There is information sharing by equipment and software.	People are not shy about sharing information.
Information technology	Formal	Formal and informal	The company provides modern communication mechanisms, but its use, however, is not satisfactory, which becomes a barrier.	There are ample mechanisms of information, but sometimes they hamper integration. Willingness to share helps integrate.
Integration by hierarchy	Formal	-	There are formal meetings and rules to be followed; besides, some functions depend on marketing to perform their duties.	The functions have independent managers.

Job rotation	Formal	Formal	Job rotation provides necessary skills to integrate areas.	There is job rotation, it is central to the company's development.
Joint planning	Formal	Formal	Formal processes, involving different functions in different stages of product development.	Planning together provides efficiency in the activities to be performed.
Longevity of relationships	Formal and Informal	Formal and informal	Managers acknowledge that a low turnover of employees helps to integrate functions. But there are no initiatives to reduce turnover.	The company has older employees, who create trust and integration between people.
Mutual reward / evaluation systems	Formal	Formal	There are differences in rewards but this does not generate discomfort among the areas.	The performance evaluation and reward systems and commission do not generate discomfort. There is transparency.
Mutual understanding	Formal	Informal	There is a good mechanism for information, but sometimes when there is a change of policy it is not well notified to all functions.	It happens mainly in managerial levels. Somewhat lacking in operational levels.
Non-conflicting goals	Formal	Formal	There are conflicting goals and it generates duplicate tasks.	There are common goals, based on the final customer, but the perspectives are conflicting.
Physical proximity	Formal and informal	Informal	Physical proximity is related to the company's infrastructure and encourages informal communication, which facilitates discussion and understanding of the activities.	Physical proximity is related to the company's infrastructure that facilitates integration and communication between areas.
Recognition of Interdependence	Formal	Informal	There is planning between these teams, respecting the knowledge of other areas.	There is recognition of interdependence, which facilitates cooperation.
Top management support	Formal	Formal	Top management supports the integration process.	Top management is integrated with all areas, all of which account for the risks.

Trust	Formal and informal	Formal and informal	There is trust, but some people act inappropriately. When this happens, meetings to resolve the conflict are conducted.	There is trust, but some people act inappropriately. When this happens, meetings to resolve the conflict are conducted.
Willingness to resolve conflicts	Formal	Informal	There are meetings to get in touch with other departments and discuss solutions to resolve the conflict.	There is something structured to resolve conflicts, but people end up solving them by themselves.

Among the factors above, we can highlight the planning together as fundamental to the smooth running of activities in both companies, since these factors end up encouraging other informal mechanisms. This planning often happens in the form of cross-functional meetings.

> There is a meeting to evaluate the product promotion and the new molecule requests. Too many meetings, this Company lives for meetings (A4). The impact of the planning is direct, you can optimize time, resources and get maximum efficiency in the activity that you are doing (B3). There are systematic meetings with set agendas (B4).

In both companies, goals are aligned with the strategy. "We can criticize or not the goals that the company has, but since the goals are outlined, they call people to trace the individual goals in accordance with the company's goal "(A3). For Company 2, the alignment of objectives helps to eliminate conflicts of interest. "It is explained to each employee, from when he or she starts to work here, so the company induces them to think not as an individual, but as a whole company"(B3). The meetings are also opportunities to reduce misunderstandings.

> In the annual conventions, there is opportunity to better know each other and to understand the objectives of each other (A3). People

understand the interdependence. Most part of the teams respects the knowledge of other area (A4); The cooperative work between the teams is very strong, because they acknowledge interdependence "(B3).

Based on these descriptions, one can see that, to a greater or lesser extent, the two companies have positive aspects with respect to how integration factors are applied. However, within a same company, respondents showed antagonistic perceptions with regard to the occurrence of these factors. These distortions may signal a drop in the level of integration. The next topic deals with this issue.

4.2 Overlapping of perceptions on the integration factors

There are perceptions of overlaps with regard to the existence of integration factors. For example, while an interviewee from a given company has recognized a factor, another one who has a different, opposite view, cannot recognize it. Table 4 presents all factors that have overlaps in the two companies studied. For this analysis, it was found that when a respondent perceives an integration factor within the company (Present), and the other does not (Missing), there is an overlap of perception (marked in gray). When all respondents indicate that certain factor is present or missing within the company, it means that there is no overlap of perception.

Table 4: Grouped perception showing overlap between presence and absence of integration factors

Factors	Company 1 Present	Company 1 Missing	Company 2 Present	Company 2 Missing
Adequate communication structure	X	X	X	
Consideration of informal groups	X		X	X
Cross-functional meetings	X	X	X	
Cross-functional teams	X	X	X	
Cross-functional training	X	X	X	X
Goals aligned with strategy	X	X	X	
Group spirit	X	X	X	X
Informal communication	X	X	X	X
Information sharing	X	X	X	X
Information technology	X	X	X	X
Integration by hierarchy	X	X	X	X
Job rotation	X	X	X	X
Joint Planning	X		X	
Longevity of relationships	X	X	X	X
Mutual evaluation/ rewards systems	X	X	X	
Mutual understanding	X	X	X	
Non-conflicting goals	X	X	X	X
Physical proximity	X	X	X	X
Recognition of Interdependence	X	X	X	
Top management support	X	X	X	
Trust	X	X	X	X
Willingness to resolve conflicts	X	X	X	X

It is necessary to highlight that the factor "Joint Planning" did not present overlapping perceptions in any of the companies. All respondents claimed that this factor is present within companies. To Company 1, the consideration to informal groups, is another factor present. In Company 2, the respondents highlighted eight factors: Hierarchical dependence between functions; Top management support; Adequate communication structure; Cross-functional teams; Mutual evaluation/ rewards system; Cross-functional meetings; Mutual understanding; Goals aligned with strategy.

To Company 1, three of the respondents said that the company values the longevity of relationships, contrary to respondent A4's reply, which states that

Today we have a large number of rotating people within the company. So we have a certain age gap, where we have the older people, average people we do not see much, and the younger staff. This newer staff has a very high turnover, so we're losing some of this expertise of information exchange (A4).

The same happens with Company 2, where interviewee B4 said that the organization "has a very old staff, but we have a point where the company is extremely dynamic, to move people to seek diversity, but the well-defined processes can guide us"(B2).

This overlap also happens when you ask about the top management support for integration processes. For interviewee A5 "We have done a great job to integrate various events to provide mutual understanding." However, for interviewee A3, "there is a real difficulty to integrate the team's base and the leadership does not cooperate with it".

When asked about the existence of cross-functional teams, three of the respondents from Company 1 claim that it exists. However, interviewee A3 said that "the concept is very well implemented, but in practice there is a difficulty in demanded resources and investment in time "(A3); "In the past there were temporary teams, that now are specific groups" (A4); "It existed in the past, not now" (A5).

Overlapping perceptions are even more visible when questioned on cross-functional meetings. Interviewee A3 said that "there are too many meetings, it is a negative thing, they are excessive"; while participant A5 reports that "it is not common, but it exists in the company".

Another divergence noted was about the system of evaluations/ rewards. Interviewee A2 stated that "people from an area do not aim to harm the performance of other areas" but he said that there are differences of reward policies among areas. This point of difference is also highlighted by other respondents. However, it also indicates that there are discomforts with this issue.

> The major discomfort is not the competition between the areas, but the difference between the awards. The commercial area has a prize almost six times greater than the R&D area or a marketing area (A4). Discomfort, and some actually have privileges (A3). There is a certain jealousy of the commercial part ... Then the other departments see us organizing parties, traveling... So, our award, in general, our remuneration, is far superior to other departments (A5).

Considering the willingness to resolve conflicts in Company 1, four respondents said that teams work together. However, it is important to note the response of interviewee A3, in which he states that:

> If I'm not from that area and choose to respond, and is not successful, I can be reprimanded for it. So, most of the people are shy to provide help at some points (A3).

In Company 2, interviewed B4, stated that "we have business teams, who make it very easy for problem and conflict solving". As for the B3:

> This integration exists, but when there is any more difficult problem it is directed to lead managers. However, it occurs, but only in cases where the problem is broader (B3).

Interviewee A4 said that information sharing "frequently occurs in the meetings." However, interviewees A2 and A3 informed that there is a lack of time to perform it, "the scarce time limits people, but people are willing to share, sometimes with some barriers" (A2). "The level of activities that each person manages within a private company is high. You are pressed for a result, you are very busy, so the time you have for parallel problems is scarce" (A3). The overlap also happens in Company 2, where respondent B4 says he has "open access", i.e. has no problems in sharing information. However, B3 states that "there are certain sectors within the company who work with absolute secrecy. It will only be diffused when you are very sure about the impact that such information will bring to the company's own image "(B3).

With regard to the knowledge that an area has about another, interviewee A1 states that it occurs through communication. However, A4 states: "often we have new people in the area, that do not know what is the real function of the area is. Thus, there are conflicts in which an area does the same thing as another. Then you need to have an adjustment here". The lack of mutual understanding within a given area also seems to generate difficulties in the alignment of the goals with the organization:

> The company demands what we should do, but conflicts between functions often emerge. The person does not understand his/ her function, and ends up doing duplicate work, doing the same that other teams are doing (A4). Sometimes there is a lack of clarity in the description of each function to avoid these conflicts (A2).

Taking into account the training conducted within Company 2, interviewee B3 said that this "is highly valued and encouraged." However, B2 reports:

> We have, for example, leadership training, which has several modules. People from various fields gather for a yearly meeting of company managers. Strategies are explained, sales plans, however, we don't have a specific training for Product Development, or integration (B2).

When asked if physical proximity encourages informal communication, Interviewee B3 stated that: "it happens primarily in newly built offices, where the entire space was designed to facilitate integration". However, for B2, Company 2 "has several research centers and production plants throughout Brazil, I would say that this geographic distance inhibits integration".

About the influence of hierarchy on integration in Company 2, B3 states: "this happens because hierarchical relationships are very clear and highly respected". In spite of this, B1 does not agree with that, "because the company is very horizontal and stimulates us to overcome barriers. There are few barriers, we do not see much value in it" (B1).

About Group spirit within Company 2, three interviewees stated that it exists and is well stimulated.

However, B2 opposes this view: "if all goes well, ok, however, if there is a crisis situation with regard to the area, then it simply disappears (Group spirit)" (B2).

Company 1 has more overlaps than Company 2. This irregular perception of respondents shows that cross-functional integration does not occur uniformly over the processes or between different hierarchical levels. Table 5 shows the hierarchical levels and stages of the studied processes. It was also highlights the perception about formality and informality, as well as the integration factor that corresponds to these states.

Table 5: Differences of perception of integration at different hierarchical levels at different stages of product development

		Occurrence of integration in the phases of product development		
		Early stage	**Intermediate phase**	**Final phase**
Hierarchical levels	**Management**	A1 - **formal** (cross-functional meetings, planning) **Formal establishing informal** (exchange of experience)	B2 - **formal establishing informal** (Top management support); **Formal** (hierarchical dependency between functions)	A5 - **formal** (information sharing) B4 - **informal** (Group spirit) **Formal establishing informal** (information sharing)
	Operational Level	A2 - **formal** (functional meetings) A3 - **formal** (lack of confidence, objectives sharing) A4 - **formal** (cross-functional meetings)	B1 - **formal establishing informal** (meetings creating ties through forums for discussion) B3 - **formal** (cross-functional teams)	B5- **informal** (Group spirit) **Formal establishing informal** (information sharing)

It is important to note that, according to the hierarchical position of the interviewee and phase in Product Development, perceptions of integration and occurrence of integration factors may differ. There may be integration factors in a hierarchical level and not in others. Or, these factors exist in a part of the process, and in others, no.

This is clear within Table 5, in which the functions of the interviewees A4, A3 and A2 are at the operational level. These three people presented a large volume of missing integration factors. This group also complained about the excess of formality, especially in cross-functional meetings. As for Company 2, the highlight comes from Interviewee B2, who presented more missing factors, and signs for the majority of formal processes. In addition, B2 is at the management level, which differs from Company 1, in which the interviewees that perceive lack of factors are at operating levels.

Thus, it can be considered that, a high level of cross-functional integration is related to a homogeneous existence of integration factors in all levels and at all stages of the process.

4.3 formality and informality

For Kidron et al. (2013) informal and formal mechanisms may increase the level of integration, especially the informal atmosphere. But a balance between the two is necessary. The analysis of field data revealed a complaint by respondents from Company 1 on the excessive formality, as seen in the following excerpts:

> *No, we have nothing informal within the company. All is well formalized. Emails, communications, everything is registered, nothing is informal. Because you can be here today, tomorrow you're in another area, and someone*

else comes and takes what was your decision and leaves. Then informality does not exist in the company (A5). I do not see very informal communication, but formal communication between the teams (A4). We have ground rules, there are several formal meetings or created environments to induce interaction between areas, i.e. the hierarchy operates asking us to have formal moments for it (A3).

Interviewee A3 stated: "there is a bureaucratic issue, it requires various departments interacting to solve bureaucracies and to generate confidence between areas. I would say a lot of formality is necessary within the processes to tie confidence" (A3). The same respondent states that "it is easy to share information, informally. Because we have *communicator* (a instant messenger tool) inside the company, where no formality is required for the exchange of information "(A3).

Considering this issue of informal communication and the mechanisms of information technology, participant A4 states that "often the person ends up not having a personal conversation, they prefer sending an email than to call or stop in the hall to talk. In my view, this IT issue ends up generating more formal communication than informal" (A4).

In an opposite view from Company 1, Company 2 presents more informality in their processes:

The company has a lot of informality, it has no problems in this kind of relationship. It is not bureaucratic, we can talk, talk, no problem (B2). Certainly, the company encourages it enough (B1). However, depending on the information we are seeking, communication is formal (B4). There is formal integration, but informal integration also exists and it is constant, there is a big incentive for people from different areas to seek information of what is happening in the other areas (B3).

Thus, when there are formal processes, that stimulates informal collaborative behavior, the interaction between departments and even between people. It happens in a more harmonious way, generating a high level of integration.

4.4 Conflicts

Although the two surveyed companies promote actions to manage relations between areas efficiently,

some conflicts may arise and affect negatively both the cross-functional integration and the progress of new product development processes. In Company 1, conflicts can occur for lack of planning, or when "planning is not considered in the field phases. It also happens when communication is not clear about updates of the project's progress" (A1). Conflicts can happen in the transition from one stage of NPD to another, because "some issue that occurs in the earlier stages can impact the next phase" (A2). According to interviewee A5, this creates conflicts between the functions that are part of NDP.

This type of conflict in NPD processes may also generate mistrust between the areas:

If I work in the third phase and receive a product from the second phase that has quality problems or delay, it does not reach expectations, and then you do not really believe anymore in what the area delivers, there is a distrust" (A3).

The respondent used the term *distrust* to refer to this problem, when an area does not deliver its part as it should, resulting in conflicts between them. The lack of trust is an element related to relationship conflicts and may generate management decisions of poor quality, as cited by Simons and Peterson (2000).

Interviewee A4 mentioned another conflict highlighted within Company 1:

Is the conflict of interest, they push the problems to the other department. So, a conflict of interest arises between areas. One area gains more responsibility than the other. It also happens because the areas don't know the responsibilities of each other, so, an earlier problem may affect the next phase of NPD. (A4),

In Company 2, the main problems are related to the lack of alignment between functional goals and market positioning of products.

Self-centeredness, they think that their goals are more important than the other functions (B1). There is conflict of interest in positioning of some products in the market, because today the company works with a number of different products within the agricultural line (B3).

A likely explanation for these conflicts of interest may be the system of evaluation and rewards that the company adopts. Interviewee B2, with this regard, said: "I think that indicators inhibit cooperation, sometimes it conflicts somewhat with our greater goal, which is customer service" (B2).

Considering the above, it becomes clear that conflicts can be useful elements to improve the relationship and collaboration between people. But when they turn to manifest conflicts, based on personal interest, they can lead to unilateral decisions. Relationship conflicts, as quoted by Simons and Peterson (2000), may also culminate in the same situation. These types of conflicts are perceived as being difficult to solve and may reduce the level of integration. Moreover, as cited by Pondy (1989), conflicts can be a source of enhancement, and thus contribute to the increased integration level. However, they must be managed through integration factors, such as training to generate mutual understanding of perceptions and goals, or even separating members with relationship problems.

4.5 Characterization of the level of integration

The level of cross-functional integration can be analyzed as a combination of three factors: homogeneous perception of integration factors throughout the stages of the process (as opposed to overlapping), balance between formality and informality, lack of manifest conflicts of interest, as described in the topics above.

With regard to the homogeneous perception of integration factors, Company 1 displays the highest

level of overlap. Considering the formality and informality, again, this Company presents excessive formality, as highlighted by the interviewees. The lack of balance between formal and informal integration factors indicates that the level of integration should not be high.

For Company 2, one of the most important elements to characterize its integration level is the existence of informality, encouraged by formal factors like cross-functional teams and top management support. In this company, the cross-functional teams are considered very important for the smooth running of the NPD, mainly because it facilitates the sharing of information between the areas, and reduces the incidence of manifest conflict of interest.

Based on field data, Company 2 has more consistency of its activities related to integration than Company 1, because it aligns formal and informal aspects that are critical for integration. The perception of integration factors is also more homogeneous in Company 2 than Company 1. In addition, respondents from Company 2 identify fewer situations of manifest conflicts of interest related to functional relationships than Company 1. Such evidences indicate that the level of integration in Company 2 is higher than in Company 1.

Based on the conclusions reached at the end of each subtopic of the results, we propose a definition of different levels of cross-functional integration and their respective characteristics, as shown in Table 6.

Table 6: Characteristics of functional integration levels

Integration functional level	Characteristics
High	Integration factors are perceived homogeneously by the different functions involved in the implementation of processes, throughout their initial, intermediate and final stages; Integration factors are perceived homogeneously at different hierarchical levels: strategic, managerial and operational, when the processes depend on decisions made at different levels; Existence of formal and informal integration factors that can generate collaboration without excessive bureaucracy and rigid structures; Absence of manifest conflicts of interest that are often difficult to solve through mutual cooperation between the integrated functions. The existence of team spirit and mutual understanding between the functions contributes to the solution of conflicts, strengthening the relationships. The functions are more concerned with organizational results and therefore are willing to sacrifice functional privileges.

Medium	There is some overlap about the perception of absence/presence of integration factors along different stages of the process, but that is not enough to hinder cooperation toward the common goals; There is some overlap about the perception of absence/presence of integration factors at different hierarchical levels, but that is not enough to hinder cooperation toward the common goals; Integration is achieved primarily by formal factors. There are more formal than informal factors - or - Integration is achieved primarily by informal factors. There are more informal than formal factors. There is not a balance between formality and informality. There are no formal factors that stimulate the existence of informal collaborative behaviors. There are conflicts of interest, difficult to solve, which are sometimes resolved through mutual cooperation between the integrated functions, or hierarchical order impositions.
Low	The integration factors may exist at some stages of the process, but are missing at others; There is too much formality in the application of integration factors, generating excessive bureaucracy and waste of time in meetings and standardized tasks - or - there is over-reliance on informalities to achieve integration, in which case the management does not define formal integration factors such as: meetings, planning together and cross-functional teams; Existence of manifest conflicts of interest that are often difficult to solve through cooperation between the functions. Group spirit and mutual understanding are not perceived between the functions, creating an environment in which each function is more concerned with functional results than with the result of the organization as a whole.

5. FINAL CONSIDERATIONS

This study proposes a set of characteristics to define different levels of cross-functional integration based on: homogeneous perception about integration factors throughout the stages of the process, balance between formality and informality, absence of manifest conflicts of interest. The case studies helped to identify different situations involving each of these three elements in order to define the characteristics of the three different integration levels: high, medium and low, as detailed in Table 6.

About the theoretical contribution, one relevant point of this study was to verify the existence of overlapping perceptions about integration factors, i.e., different respondents had opposing opinions on the existence or not of the same factor. When there is overlapping, integration is not perceived homogeneously among people in the same process, and that fact may indicate low level of integration. Another element related to low levels of integration is the presence of manifest conflicts. In the companies studied, the main integration problems are related to conflicts of interest and difficulty to understand its real function.

From a practical point of view, managers should observe activities in which a high level of integration can generate improvements in processes and outcomes. Firstly, they should manage the relationships between the integrated functions based on the presence of integration factors over all the phases of the process in analysis. Secondly, managers should observe the existence of balance between formal and informal integration factors. Formal factors may stimulate the existence of spontaneous cooperative behaviors. Thirdly, managers should pay attention to the motives that generate manifest conflicts of interest, once they can reduce the integration level due to their particular point of view in prejudice of the whole company's perspective. Finally, excessive application of formal factors can create a barrier to integration. Interviewees from the two surveyed companies explained that Information Technology in excess makes it difficult to integrate, since it excessively formalizes processes and cuts people from informal communications.

Due to the method of case study, this research has limitations of coverage, since its conclusions cannot be generalized. Future studies may suggest the construction of a scale for assessing the level of integration, based on each of the three defined levels and their respective characteristics. Thus, these studies may test correlations among the elements here suggested in order to identify levels of integration in different stages of several processes that require cooperation among internal functions. Especially when these processes involve decisions of different hierarchical levels for its implementation.

6. REFERENCES

Ballou, R. H. (2006). *Gerenciamento da Cadeia de Suprimentos-: Logística Empresarial*. Bookman.

Baofeng, H. (2013). *Relationship management and supply chain integration*: Literature review and research directions.

Bardin, L. (1979). *Análise de conteúdo*. Lisboa: Edições 70.

Basnet, C. (2013). The measurement of internal supply chain integration. *Management Research Review.* Vol. 36 No. 2, pp. 153-172.

Bellmunt, T. V. & Torres, P. R. (2013). Integration: attitudes, patterns and practices. *Supply Chain Management:* An International Journal 18/3, 308–323.

Clark, K. & Fujimoto, T. (1991). *Product Development Performance-Strategy, Organization, and Management in the World Auto Industry*. Boston: Havard Bussiness Scool Press.

Daugherty, P. J., Chen, H., Mattioda, D. D., & Grawe, S. J. (2009). Marketing/logistics relationships: influence on capabilities and performance.*Journal of Business Logistics*, 30(1), 1-18.

Ellegaard, C., & Koch, C. (2014). A model of functional integration and conflict: The case of purchasing-production in a construction company.*International Journal of Operations & Production Management*, 34(3), 325-346.

Ellinger, A. E. (2000). Improving Marketing/Logistics cross-functional collaboration in the supply chain. *Industrial Marketing Management*, v. 29, n. 1, p. 85-96.

Ellinger, A. E.; Keller, S. B. & Hansen, J. D. (2006). Bridging The Divide Between Logistics And Marketing: Facilitating Collaborative Behavior. *Journal of Business Logistics*, v. 27, n. 2, p. 1-28.

Gimenez, C. (2006). Logistics integration processes in the food industry. *International Journal of Physical Distribution & Logistics Management*, v. 36, n. 3, p. 231-249.

Gimenez, C. & Ventura, E. (2005). Logistics-production, logistics-marketing and external integration: Their impact on performance. *International Journal of Operations & Production Management*, v. 25, n. 1, p. 20-38.

Griffin, A. & Hauser, J. R. (1995). *The International Center for Research on the Management of Technology Integrating R & D and Marketing:* A Review and Analysis of the Literature. Cambridge, MA.

Gupta, A. K; Raj, S. P. & Wilemon, D. (1986). A model for Studying R&D-Marketing Interface in the Product Innovation Process. *Journal of Marketing.* v. 50; p. 7-17.

Jin, M.; Luo, Y. & Eksioglu, S. D. (2013). Integration of production sequencing and outbound logistics in the automotive industry. *Int. J. Production Economics*, v. 113, p. 766-774.

Jüttner, U.; Christopher, M. & Backer, S. (2007). Demand chain management-integrating marketing and supply chain management. *Industrial Marketing Management*, v. 36, n. 3, p. 377-392.

Kahn, K. B. (1996). Interdepartmental integration: a definition with implications for product development performance. *Journal of Product Innovation Management*, v. 13, p. 137-151.

Kahn, K. B. & Mentzer, J. T. (1996). Logistics and interdepartmental integration. *International Journal of Physical Distribution & Logistics Management*, v. 26, n. 8, p. 6-14.

Kidron, A. (2013). Internal integration within human resource management subsystems. *Journal of Managerial Psychology.* Vol. 28 No. 6, pp. 699-719.

Lawrence, P. R. & Lorsch, J. W. (1967). *Organization and environment:* managing differentiation and integration. 7. ed. Boston: Harvard University, p. 279.

Mentzer, J. T.; Stank, T. P. & Esper, T. L. (2008). Supply Chain Management And Its Relationship To Logistics , Marketing , Production , And Operations Management. *Journal of Business Logistics*, v. 29, n. 1, p. 31-46.

Moses, A., & Åhlström, P. (2008). Problems in cross-functional sourcing decision processes. *Journal of Purchasing and Supply Management*, 14(2), 87-99.

Onoyama, S. S.; *et al.* (2008). Integração intra e interorganizacional no desenvolvimento de produtos: estudo de caso no setor de laticínios. *Revista Gestão Industrial*, v.4, n.1, p. 68-87.

Pagell, M. (2004). Understanding the Factors that Enable and Inhibit the Integration of Operations, Purchasing and Logistics. *Journal of Operations Management*, 22, 459-487.

Paiva, E. L. (2010). Manufacturing and marketing integration from a cumulative capabilities perspective. *International journal of production economics*, 126(2), 379-386.

Pimenta, M. L. (2011). *Caracterização da dinâmica de integração interfuncional:* um estudo multicaso em Marketing e Logística. [s.l.] Universidade Federal de São Carlos.

Pimenta, M. L & Silva, A. L. da. (2012). Desafios da integração interfuncional: o papel da formalidade e da informalidade. *Anais...* XXXVI Encontro Anpad.

Pimenta, M. L. & Silva, A. L. da. (2012). Dimensões Da Integração Interfuncional: Proposta De Uma Estrutura De Análise. *Anais...* XXXII Encontro Nacional De Engenharia De Produção, Bento Gonçalves, RS.

Pondy, L. R. (1989). Reflections on organizational conflict. *Journal of Organizational Change Management*, 2(2), 94-98.

Ruekert, R. W., & Walker Jr, O. C. (1987). Marketing's interaction with other functional units: a conceptual framework and empirical evidence. *The Journal of Marketing*, 1-19.

Santos, J. B., & D'Antone, S. (2014). Reinventing the wheel? A critical view of demand-chain management. *Industrial Marketing Management*, 43(6), 1012-1025.

Silva, A. L. Da; Lombardi, G. H. V. & Pimenta, M. L. (2013). Alinhamento interfuncional: um estudo exploratório sobre os pontos de contato entre marketing, logística e produção. *Gestão & Produção*, São Carlos, v. 20, n. 4, p. 863-881.

Simons, T. L., & Peterson, R. S. (2000). Task conflict and relation-
    ship conflict in top management teams: the pivotal role of
    intragroup trust. *Journal of applied psychology*, 85(1), 102.

Stank, T. P.; Daugherty, P. J. & Ellinger, A. E. (1999). Marketing/

Logistics Integration and Firm Performance. *The International
    Journal of Logistics Management*, v. 10, n. 1, p. 11-24.

Yin, R. K. (2005). *Estudo de caso:* planejamento e métodos. Porto
    Alegre: Bookman.

10

Engineering Design Methodology for Green-Field Supply Chain Architectures Taxonomic Scheme

Petar Radanliev

Anglia Ruskin University, Lord Ashcroft International Business School

petar.radanliev@anglia.ac.uk

ABSTRACT: Supply chain engineering requires a design that possesses the flexibility of a complex adaptive system, consisting of interlinking architecture, with external dimensions and system germane internal elements. The aim of this paper is to critically analyse the key supply chain concepts and approaches, to assess the fit between the research literature and the practical issues of supply chain architecture, design and engineering. The objective is to develop a methodology for strategy engineering, which could be used by practitioners when integrating supply chain architecture and design. Taxonomic scheme is applied to consider criteria for strategy architecture, hierarchical strategy integration design, strategy engineering, and integration of supply chain as a conceptual system. The results from this paper derived with the findings that the relationship between supply chain architecture, design and engineering is weak, and challenges remain in the process of adapting and aligning operations. This paper derived with a novel approach for addressing these obstacles, through a conceptual framework diagram and a new methodology, based on the taxonomic scheme. The novelty that derives from this paper is an engineering design methodology for integrating supply chain architecture and design, with criteria that enable decomposing and building a green-field (new and non-existent) supply chain as a system. The taxonomic scheme revealed a number of tools and mechanism, which enabled the development of a new methodology for engineering integrated architecture and design. The review derived with improvements to current and existing theories for analysing interdependencies within and between their individual contexts. This issue is addressed with a hierarchical method for network design, applied for building and combining the integration criteria. The resulting methodology is field tested through a case study with the slate mining industry in North Wales.

Keywords: *Supply chain architecture, supply chain design, green-field supply chain conceptual engineering.*

1. INTRODUCTION

The progress of integrating supply chain principles is weak, specifically towards 'adapting' (Saad et al., 2002) and 'aligning' (Sakka et al., 2011). Supply chain decisions are commonly based on individual company profitability goals (Leng and Chen, 2012), undermining that supply chain is a single entity system (Mintzberg et al., 1998, Schnetzler et al., 2007, Narasimhan et al., 2008, Ivanov, 2009, Perez-Franco et al., 2010). In addition, the supply chain strategy in practice is frequently not related to the competitive strategy (Mckone et al. 2009). This findings create the rationale for further investigation on how supply chain strategies are engineered, and the overarching architectures that enable integration of operations.

Supply chain engineering has been defined as a complex adaptive system (Bozarth et al., 2009, Pathak et al., 2007), consisting of interlinking architecture and design, with external dimensions and system germane internal elements (Melnyk et al., 2013). Supply chain strategic engineering represents an effective method for implementing strategic integration (He and Lai, 2012). However, further research is required to include the relationship of change in culture and structure to integration (Nikulin, et al. 2013).

Supply chain strategy engineering as a green-field concept of non-existent until formulated supply chain, should embrace collaborative commerce and synchronisation of information flow (Frohlich and Westbrook, 2001, Vickery et al., 2003, Al-Mudimigh et al., 2004, Manthou et al., 2004, Kim, 2006).

The area of research for this paper is the field of supply chain engineering that include the external architecture and internal design, in a green-field engineering (new and non-existent supply chain). To evaluate the present approaches in supply chain practice, the paper begins with a review of existing supply chain models, which cover the relevant aspects of green-field supply chain integration. The research areas reviewed are: supply chain engineering, supply chain architecture, supply chain design, and supply chain integration.

There is a vast number of developed or proposed supply chain models focused on one or more supply chain areas. The objective of this paper is to group the factors in recognisable taxonomic scheme, and to derive with a new set of principles for green-field supply chain strategy engineering of the supply chain architecture and design.

1.1 Research Objectives

The research problems investigated are related to engineering the integration of supply chain architecture and design. The research objectives are:

1. To derive with a set of principles for a green-field supply chain architecture with multiple supply chain participants.

2. To derive with set of principles for green-field supply chain integration design.

3. To systematically integrate the supply chain engineering principles, based on the architecture and design criteria, for individual activities towards pre-defined green-field integration areas.

To relate the criteria to the methodology, the taxonomic scheme is presented in a hierarchical concept map and concept diagram methods are applied. The objectives of the paper are oriented around external and salient dimensions, which directly affect the supply chain architecture, and design, and the supply chain engineering consist of external and internal elements, forces and factors.

1.2 Structure of the paper

This paper is structured in the following order: **firstly** the research aim and objectives are defined, along with the rationale for the study; **secondly**, the literature review outlines the most prominent models and methods in this field; thirdly: the reasoning behind key tenants of the methodology are discussed in detail, with specific observations from existing literature on this topic; **fourthly**, the methodology that derived from this study is presented, followed by the principles key, containing the key tenets and abbreviations. The fourth step also relates the key tenets to existing literature and elaborates on the benefits from the methodology to practitioners and academics; and **finally**, the emerging principles are analysed to clarify how the key tenets are applied to the new methodology for engineering green-field supply chain architecture and design. To clarify how the methodology can be interpreted and applied, the methodology is field-tested through case study on the Slate Mining Industry in North Wales.

2. LITERATURE REVIEW

The literature review reveals the most prominent literature and outlines the tools and mechanisms that enabled this paper to derive with the principles for engineering green-field supply chain integration. The objective of the literature review is to analyse the key tenets that enable the architecture for inter-relating the design of supply chain operations.

Recent literature addressed the aspect of reformulating existing supply chains when problems emerge (Nikulin, et al. 2013, Melnyk et al., 2013, Perez-Franco 2010). However, those studies ignored the vast list of measurements in existing literature (Van der Vaart and van Donk, 2008) and the diverse external dimensions and the elements, factors and forces that are present in different environments (Radanliev, 2015a).

Nikulin, et al. (2013), Melnyk et al., (2013), and Perez-Franco (2010) addressed the aspect of re-engineering, while Van der Vaart and van Donk, (2008) defined the re-engineering strategic patterns. Nevertheless, the topic of formulating a supply chain strategy as a green-field concept, remains elusive and most of the closely related frameworks (Radanliev, 2015b, Schnetzler et al., 2007, Hafeez, et al. 1996, and Pettigrew, 1977) have never advanced into full working methodologies, defining the engineering in a step by step supply chain engineering design.

There is much confusion in existing supply chain literature on terminologies defining re-engineering and engineering (Radanliev, 2015c). Terms such as supply chain engineering, design or architecture are commonly used in supply chain re-engineering studies, effectively referring to re-designing. The research in this paper distances from the aspect of re-engineering and is focused on the engineering of non-existent supply chains in a green-field context. Therefore, the term green-field is a clarification concept referring to non-existent supply chains, in other words, the field is green, and there is nothing there.

3. RESEARCH METHODOLOGY

The research methodology applied in this paper was taxonomy of approaches from literature review. The selected papers have been related to supply chain strategy, distancing from supply chain management. Recent literature clearly separated between the topics of supply chain management and supply chain strategy (Perez-Franco et al., 2010, Schnetzler et al., 2007, Martínez-Olvera and Shunk, 2006). Supply chain management has been defined as the process of transforming materials into a finished product, presenting a long term objective where validation should expand over a long period

of time (Saad et al., 2002, Mentzer et al., 2001). The supply chain strategy was considered as an investigation into how the supply chain should operate efficiently to compete, by evaluating costs, benefits and trade-offs in the supply chain operational components (Perez-Franco et al., 2010, Schnetzler et al., 2007, Martínez-Olvera and Shunk, 2006).

In exception of a few cases, the papers have been selected with a research time horizon over the last 10 years (2005-2015), covering literature published on the topic of supply chain strategy engineering. A limited number of most prominent papers from earlier literature have also been reviewed, because of their specific contribution to the topic of green-field supply chain strategy engineering.

By distancing from the area of supply chain management, the number of relevant papers was reduced dramatically. This focused the review of literature specific to the engineering aspect of a supply chain strategy, and building a methodology for green-field supply chain strategy engineering.

Over seventy papers have been reviewed, covering empirical techniques (case/field study, survey, archival research, action research, conceptual models) or modelling techniques (optimisation, simulation, algorithms, systems). What united all the papers reviewed is their singular focus on supply chain strategy, was identified as a topic far less covered in existing literature than supply chain management.

Multiple methods have been used to search for appropriate literature, to provide transparency, and to reduce risk of missing out on important literature. The databases used include the Web of Science and the Business Source Complete. In addition, Google Scholar was used to ensure the literature selected provides a wide coverage of the topic. The initial results produced more results than a single study can handle. The process of selecting the most pertinent literature involved applying selection criteria. The selection criteria are based on deriving with keywords and scanning first the titles for those word. Secondly, the selected literature was further reduced by scanning the abstract to ensure direct relevance to the topic.

The complexity of the subject, the multiple environments, dimensions, elements and concepts, required a research that does not set any limits to categorising the conceptual, analytical or empirical nature of the existing approaches. Many of the approaches identified in literature are focused on resolving singular supply chain problems, and are not relating to other aspects of supply chain engineering. This presented the rational for applying a taxonomic scheme to investigate, interrelate and group the attitudes, practices and patterns, present in existing literature on the topics of supply chain: engineering, integration, architecture and design. The taxonomic scheme enabled categorising concepts into different clusters. The categorisation enabled the process of recognising, differentiating and understanding different attitudes, practices and patterns for engineering supply chain strategy, and interrelating them in accordance to positive relationships between different concepts.

But in general, many of the studies have hardly built on previous work. The taxonomic scheme enabled combing and pairing factors and elements from different papers, because they were based on the same aspect of research, and discussed the same constructs and items in terms of supply chain strategy engineering. As a result of the taxonomic scheme, the analysis derived with the most prominent attitudes, patterns, and practices for supply chain engineering, and the   interactions, or interrelationships between these factors.

The synthesised knowledge is then applied for building a methodology integrating the approaches in existing literature on supply chain strategy engineering.

The papers have been analysed around a taxonomy of characteristics, to map and evaluate green-field supply chain strategy engineering. The different approaches have been categorised in hierarchical methodology.

The case study method was applied to field-test the resulting methodology on formulating a green-field supply chain strategy for the Slate Mining Industry in North Wales.

4. TAXONOMIC SCHEME

4.1 Green-field strategic integration

The process of merging distinct green-field operational areas into the supply chain area, creates an urgency to integrate the information and physical flow into relationships that link these areas and fosters 'trust and commitment' (TC) with supply chain partners (Bozarth et al., 2009). Pathak et al. (2007) designed a set of principles based on TC, however,

the principles would benefit from being tested with case study, in a similar way that other frameworks are field-tested (Perez-Franco et al., 2010, Narasimhan et al., 2008, Martínez-Olvera, 2008, Martínez-Olvera and Shunk, 2006). In addition, these frameworks would benefit from criteria to evaluate and measure performance of integrating supply chain participants into a 'networked organisation' (NO) (Sukati et al., 2012). Where performance depends on 'identification of best candidates' (IBC) (Lee and Billington, 1992), and requires measurement system for 'interdependence and organisational compatibility' (IOC) in supply chain design (Beamon, 1998).

4.2 Characterising green-field integration

'Supply chain strategy integration' (SCI) is described as a 'single entity system' or a 'confederation' (Mentzer, 2001) and a 'networked organisation' (Ivanov, 2009). The 'single entity system' should be focused on 'capturing the essence and forecasting the effect' of supply chain integration and performance (CEFE) (Mentzer, 2001), through combining resources and capabilities (Narasimhan et al., 2008). In addition, to 'characterise greenfield supply chain strategy and integration' (CGSI) the functional activities should be investigated to identify actual instead of desired strategy outcomes (Cigolini et al., 2004).

Strategic integration represents an effective method for implementing strategic choices and further research is required to include the 'architecture implementation' (FI) in integration (He and Lai, 2012). To address this, an algorithm has been described for selecting best supply chain integration strategy through separation in 'space, time, parts and conditions' (STPC) for scenarios when problems occur (Nikulin et al. 2013). The soundness and the logic behind Nikulin et al. (2013) approach could be applied as a tool to build upon a framework for supply chain strategy architecture. Such framework should embrace collaborative commerce and synchronisation of supply chain information flow, promoting flexibility and effectiveness (Frohlich and Westbrook, 2001, Vickery et al., 2003, Al-Mudimigh et al., 2004, Manthou et al., 2004, Kim, 2006).

4.3 Categorising green-field integration activities

Supply chain competences lead to diverse performance advantages in various business environments (Closs and Mollenkopf, 2004), but the same practices and patterns cannot be applicable in every industry context to achieve superior performance (Nikulin et al., 2013, Van der Vaart and van Donk, 2008, Vickery et al., 2003). Factors that improve supply chain integration and performance have been categorised into attitudes, practices and patterns (Van der Vaart and van Donk, 2008). The relationship between these clusters remains elusive and the number of 'architecture elements' (FE) and 'architecture concepts' (FCo), should be validated through further research. Formulating supply chain strategies in the context of 'green-field architecture' (GF) with a singular focus on integration and performance (Frohlich and Westbrook, 2001), presents limitations (Childerhouse and Towill, 2011, Perez-Franco et al., 2010, Rosenzweig et al., 2003), because various supply chain aspects should be considered in the design and architecture stage, and supply chain integration activities have a unique set of benefits (Swink et al., 2007).

A holistic framework for supply chain design (Melnyk et al. 2013) concluded that supply chain design must consider the 'external dimension' (ExD). The study recommended a process for uncovering the various pieces that orchestrate the overall supply chain architecture and design, through investigating the 'underlying factors' (UF) and 'salient dimensions'(SaD), such as 'external elements' (EE), 'factors' (EFa), and 'forces' (EFo) (Melnyk et al. 2013).

4.4 Green-field supply chain decomposition design

Supply chain design is a dynamic process and interdependencies should be analysed 'within' and 'between' in individual context (Dubois et al., 2004). One approach for building and combining the criteria is a hierarchical method for network design (Dotoli et al., 2005). This approach can be strengthened by building upon the principles from 'Analytical Target Cascading' in context of decomposing a complete supply chain hierarchical tree (Qu et al., 2010), similarly to 'decomposing supply chain into hierarchical tree' (DSCHT) (Schnetzler et al. 2007). The DSCHT combined with the techniques from the customer–product–process–resource (CPPR) (Martínez-Olvera and Shunk, 2006) and 'analytical target cascading' (ATC), provide the background for designing a new engineering method that would include the process of getting from the 'present to (the) required' stage (PR).

The design process could apply a 'conceptual approach for supply chain inter-organisational integration' (CSCIOI) (Perez-Franco et al., 2010). Alter-

natively, conceptual system can be verified with system dynamics and mathematical modelling (Ivanov, 2009), however, mathematical modelling could hardly calculate with precision the perceptions of the individual decision maker perceptions.

Engineering systems literature integrated a system dynamics principles to decompose supply chain and tested the approach though dynamic analysis (Hafeez et al., 1996). The engineering system approach could be applied as a visualisation tool for presenting and interlinking multiple supply chain areas with external business dimensions (Lertpattarapong, 2002), but such approach could hardly comprehend the supply chain complexities and multiple variables in 'integration as a method for integrating strategic choices' (IMSC), leading to the conclusion that conceptual architectures and supply chain decomposition design are stronger visualisation tools.

Nevertheless, engineering design techniques such as the Pugh Controlled Convergence (Pugh, 1990), the Enhanced Quality Function Deployment (Clausing, 1992), the Design Structure Matrix (Eppinger et al., 1994) the Engineering System Matrix (Bartolomei et al., 2007), and the 'techniques tool matrix' (Cigolini et al., 2004), can be applied in combination with 'cascading strategy' (Narasimhan et al., 2008), to case study, to build the supply chain strategy engineering architecture and design as a conceptual system (Perez-Franco et al., 2010). Such an approach can be combined with supply chain decomposition (Schnetzler et al., 2007) to address the 'architecture criteria' (FCr) problem.

4.5 Green-field conceptual engineering

'Conceptual model' approach (CM) has been applied for strategy architecture to evaluate decision makers strategic goals (Perez-Franco et al., 2010, Narasimhan et al., 2008, Cigolini et al., 2004). Therefore, 'a conceptual system for supply chain decomposition' (CSSCD), could integrate operational level employees to identify relationship between the vision and goals and for explaining the relationship between concepts (Platts et al., 1996, Menda and Dilts, 1997).

4.6 Ontological semantic alignment for green-field design

Alternatively, an 'ontological approach can be applied for semantic alignment' (OASA) where knowledge elicitation, containing, mapping and merging should represent the foundations for adapting or aligning supply chain principles (Sakka et al., 2011). The process should conceptualise strategy as a system of choices, patterns or decisions to address the phenomenon of 'strategy absence' (SA) in strategy architecture (Inkpen and Choudhury, 1995). The process should start by reaching a consensus on the 'preliminary salient dimensions' (PSaD) and strategic objectives (Platts et al., 1996, Menda and Dilts, 1997). The process can be further clarified by applying 'architecture criteria' (FC), such as: procedure, process and participation, which require communication mechanisms to enable concept understanding (Inkpen and Choudhury, 1995). The concept understanding should apply design 'integration criteria' (EC) through systematic innovation (Sheu and Lee, 2011), as a method for distilling innovation to strategy. However, strategy absence must be addressed through the architecture criteria prior to applying the integration criteria, because systematic innovation brings strategy dynamics through the 'process chain and virtual eChain' (PC-VC) feedback mechanisms, whereas strategy absence effectively disables the feedback mechanisms and reduces the 'supply chain agility' (SCA).

The feedback mechanisms enable the process of: (1) anticipating the demand for a product, market standards and influencers, product variety and life cycle (Fisher, 1997); (2) investigating the internal and external factors (Narasimhan et al., 2008); (3) determine the supplier or customer focus and level of integration (Frohlich and Westbrook, 2001); and (4) enable building trust and commitment, or interdependence and organisational compatibility (Mentzer, 2001). These feedback mechanisms enable building upon the supply chain architecture criteria and until present, the architecture criteria has not been combined with the 'integration criteria' (EC): visibility (Inkpen and Choudhury, 1995, Fisher, 1997), acceptance (Saad et al., 2002), participation (Menda and Dilts, 1997, Zhou and Chen, 2001, Qureshi et al., 2009), communication (Tracey et al., 1999), formality (Andrews et al., 2009), adaptability (Sakka et al., 2011, Saad et al., 2002), integration (Bozarth et al., 2009), effectiveness (Fisher, 1997) flexibility (Kim, 2006) and responsiveness (Fisher, 1997). Building upon and combining the criteria would represent a novel contribution from synthesising existing knowledge for deriving new findings.

4.7 Green-field supply chain engineering in uncertain environments

Recent literature are the indications that supply chain engineering and competitive strategy are commonly not linked to the 'corporate strategy' (CS) (Mckone et al., 2009). Adding to these concerns are the findings that challenges still remain in the processes for 'adapting and aligning' (AA) supply chain engineering (Saad et al., 2002) and operations (Sakka et al., 2011). The strategy architecture represents a process of 'capabilities integration' (CE) and accepting the reality and acting upon that reality in a given business environment (Miller and Friesen, 1978). The supply chain engineering topic remains inconclusive and there are remaining 'barriers to change and approaches to overcome' (BCAO) (Mckone et al., 2009, Saad et al., 2002, Sakka et al., 2011).

In a similar context, various algorithms have been applied to several supply chain problems, however, in some environments the 'participants aims and objectives' (PAO) problem is larger than the test data and optimal solutions cannot be found in reasonable time frame (Lee et al., 2010) leading to 'strategy absence' (SA). Metaheuristic algorithms could in the future provide a solution for identifying optimal logistic solution for supply chain strategy design (Griffis et al., 2012). Such a method would be useful for addressing the logistics as a specific problem in strategy architecture. However, metaheuristics would hardly anticipate aspects such as the individual decisions of decision makers in the vast numbered dimensions in multiple business environments. In this context, the conceptual system approach has been proven effective for 'supply chain strategy articulation' (SCSA) and optimal solution detection (Perez-Franco et al., 2010).

4.8 Supply chain efficiency of green-field architectures

The process of determining the underlying factors of salient dimensions in supply chain engineering, should be focused on preserving core-activities and outsource non-core activities (Gilley and Rasheed, 2000). For example, in the 'transport and logistics strategy' (TLS) third party logistic partnerships enable cost reduction combined with improvement in service and operational efficiency (Sheffi, 1990), bringing into focus the 'transportation and logistics integration strategic elements' (TLISE). In this context, further investigation of a potential 'fit' between companies outsourcing intensities and vertical strategic integration could strengthen existing understanding of the 'outsourcing through abstention' (OTA) problem (Gilley and Rasheed, 2000). Since greater collective operational activities need to be advanced through supply chain alliances, then the strategic problem of 'integration as a method for integrating strategic choices' (IMSC) grows into one of a degree (Frohlich and Westbrook, 2001), however, the right level of 'fit, intensity and integration' (FOI) should be identified to optimise performance (Jayaram and Tan, 2010).

4.9 Engineering the performance of green-field architectures

Existing frameworks such as Kaplan and Norton (1996), which was expanded by Brewer and Speh (2000), are applicable to specific supply chain categories 'supply chain performance measures and integration' (SCPME). These frameworks are not applied to evaluate strategy architecture that can be defined as 'green-field performance measures' (GPM), where measuring performance in effect refers to forecasting performance. The most advanced performance measurement system identified is the SCOR model (SCC, 2001) because the model is applied to industry and has evolved through feedback from industry. However, in an uncertain market demand and continuous new product development, flexibility and feasibility should also be included in the performance measures (Perez-Franco et al., 2010).

4.10 Engineering the environmental dimensions for green-field architectures

Supply chain engineering must anticipate 'product and product family' (PF) in the design process, while supply chain architecture must be designed in accordance to the 'best product operating cost' (BPOC) (Liu and Hipel, 2012, Lo and Power, 2010, Lamothe et al., 2006). The supply chain design must anticipate 'design for environment', and 'design for disassembly' (DE-DD) (Clendenin, 1997). Supply chain strategy architecture should be focused on: (1) optimising the company strategy and service elements through 'postponement strategy and market demand' (PS-MD) (Korpela et al., 2001b); (2) the relationship between buyer and supplier in the 'strategy dimensions' (StD) (Van der Vaart and van Donk, 2008, Closs and Mollenkopf, 2004); (3) the supply chain functions must be based on the 'business environment' (BE); (5) the supply chain integration strategy must be based on the 'market and distribution planning' (MDP) strategies (Narasimhan and Kim, 2002).

5. FORMULATING THE METHODOLOGY

The taxonomic scheme applied, is aimed at addressing various problems emerging in formulating a green-field supply chain strategy. These are critically appraised above, with specific observations against each approach, to identify limitations and areas applicable to designing a methodology for green-field supply chain strategy engineering. The taxonomy of literature resulted in identifying, categorising and cataloguing the main themes (Table 1) necessary for generating a new methodology.

The methodology is transcribed into a concept diagram (Figure 1), before the findings from the taxonomy of literature are summarised into building blocks, and drawn into diagram of problems related to practical aspects of supply chain engineering (Figure 2). The concept diagram and the building blocks are related to the identified gaps in existing literature.

The process of categorising, cataloguing and relating the key tenets from existing literature enabled the development of a new methodology (Figure 2 and Figure 3). The approach is compliant with Eisenhardt (1989), Glaser and Strauss (1967) and Yin (2009) guidance on theory building. The methodology contains different aspects, which interrelate to define and interpret the process of engineering a green-field supply chain integration strategy. Different aspects of the taxonomy are interrelated to define the methodology. Interrelated aspects are interpreted in the following building blocks.

In the supply chain engineering methodology, the architecture of a green-field project integration strategy is interpreted as: articulation of the external dimensions, elements, forces and factors out of the control of the business and supply chain strategy. The critical analysis of the factors and problems derived with emerging categories of external dimensions, elements, forces and factors.

The methodology interrelates the architecture, through evaluating salient dimensions in relation to the external elements, forces and factors. In the process of interrelating these aspects, different problems emerge from the salient dimensions in relation to the external elements, forces and factors. The taxonomy of approaches determined the importance of dimensions, elements, forces and factors in relation to key tenets for green-field strategy integration (Table 1).

The priority of the supply chain engineering methodology is placed on designing a method for systematic prioritising of activities towards green-field integration areas. The design aspect is defined through applying the key tenets (Table 1), to designing hierarchical concept map (Figure 1), for identifying and organising individual operational activities towards integrated supply chain strategy engineering.

The second aspect of the methodology is the designing of evaluation criteria for the integrated supply chain strategy. The priority of this aspect of the design was, to investigate how conflict of interests can be identified and eliminated. This was addressed though designing a diagram interrelating the con-

cepts that emerged from the taxonomy of approaches (Figure 2). The objective of the diagram was to enable supply chain participants to visualise individual business objectives and gaps in interrelating the supply chain strategy. The diagram should be interpreted in individual context of the supply chain scenario in accordance to the concepts defined in the taxonomy (Table 1). The design of conceptual diagram related to the specific supply chain scenarios, enables visualising individual activities and gaps in integration of supply chain operations, specific to individual supply chain activities.

Table 1: Taxonomy of key tenets for engineering a green-field supply chain integration strategy

Taxonomic Scheme			
StD: Strategy Dimensions BE: Business environment ExD: External dimension SaD: Salient dimension **GF: Greenfield supply chain Architecture** SA: Strategy absence CS: Corporate strategy SCSA: Supply chain strategy articulation PAO: Participants aims and objectives	**FE: Architecture Elements** FCr: Architecture criteria NO: Networked organisation TC: Trust and commitment IOC: Interdependence and organisational compatibility IBC: Identification of best candidates CSCIOI: Conceptual supply chain inter-organisational integration	**FCo: Architecture Concepts** CE: Capabilities integration EE: External element EFa: External factor EFo: External force UF: Underlying factor **FI: Architecture Implementation** AA: Adapting and aligning OASA: ontological approach for semantic alignment	DSCHT: Decomposing supply chain into hierarchical three PR: process of getting from the present to the required stage CSSCD: Conceptual system for supply chain decomposition CF: Framework approach
PSaD: Preliminary salient dimensions PF: product and product family BPOC: best product operating cost DE-DD: design for environment and design for disassembly PS-MD: postponement strategy and market demand MDP: market and distribution planning	**TLS: Transport and logistics strategy** TLISE: transportation and logistics integration strategic elements SCA: supply chain agility **SCPME: Supply chain performance measures and integration** GPM: Greenfield supply chain performance measures	**SCI: Supply chain integration** OTA: Outsourcing through abstention FOI: fit, intensity and integration CEFE: Capture the essence and forecast the effect of supply chain integration and performance CGSI: Characterise Greenfield supply chain supply chain strategy and integration	BCAO: Barriers to change and approaches to overcome IMSC: integration as a method for integrating strategic choices STPC: Separation in space, time, parts and conditions PC-VC: Process chain and virtual eChain

Principles emerging from the Taxonomic Scheme

The process of building methodology (Figure 2) is relying on a number of key tenets (Table 1) presented as supply chain engineering principles:

» First principle: in supply chain architecture, to understand the companies' real strategies the architecture must be interacting with the design (activities) (Sukati et al., 2012, Perez-Franco et al., 2010, Bozarth et al., 2009, Cigolini et al., 2004, Porter, 1996, Andrews, 1982).

» Second principle: to understand how supply chains are designed, 'tacit knowledge' should be

considered as instrumental in distinguishing between the engineering the strategy and the design of the activities (Sukati et al., 2012, Perez-Franco et al., 2010).

» Third principle: supply chain can be engineered as a conceptual system, where the architecture is based on a conceptual design (Melnyk et al. 2013, Perez-Franco et al., 2010, Bozarth et al., 2009).

» Fourth principle: the supply chain activities are sufficient for conceptualising the architecture, design and engineering (Melnyk et al. 2013, Perez-

Franco et al., 2010, Bozarth et al., 2009, Cigolini et al., 2004).

» Fifth principle: supply chain engineering contains architecture and design, where the engineering is the central idea of the external architecture and internal design (Perez-Franco et al., 2010), but the design is representative of the integrated objectives and the design determines the architecture (Melnyk et al. 2013, Narasimhan et al., 2008, Mentzer, 2001).

» Sixth principle: the supply chain engineering relies on the integrated design and the design is the based on the external architecture, but while the architecture is influenced, it is not determined by the integrated design (Nikulin et al. 2013, Sukati et al., 2012, Inkpen and Choudhury, 1995). The design represent a set of ideas incorporated in the engineering that; supplement, assist and enable the architecture (Melnyk et al. 2013, Perez-Franco et al., 2010, Martínez-Olvera, 2008, Schnetzler et al., 2007, Martínez-Olvera and Shunk, 2006).

The next step in interpreting and applying the taxonomic scheme (Table 1), was to design a conceptual framework diagram identifying the gaps in literature on engineering a green-field integration strategy (Figure 1). The conceptual framework

Defining the conceptual framework diagram and the methodology

The conceptual framework diagram (Figure 1) represents the supply chain architecture and integration design, and is based on supply chain activities identified in existing literature and presented in a taxonomic scheme (Table 1). The architecture and design relates the activities to the predetermined supply chain integration areas from the taxonomic scheme (Table 1). These are evaluated with combining the evaluation criteria from existing literature (Table 1) and interrelated to the conceptual framework (Figure 2).

Figure 1 represents the architecture and design, and the gaps that are identified in literature. Those gaps represent problems that could create negative effects on green-field supply chain engineering. Thus, they need to be addressed in a systematic process when engineering the green-field supply chain strategy. Figure 2 represents that systematic process for supply chain engineering, and should be interpreted as the process for interrelating the attitudes, practices and patterns present in existing literature. The full list of attitudes, patters, and practices is outlined in the taxonomic scheme (Table 1).

An important conclusion based on the taxonomic scheme (Table 1) is that there is little consensus on how to engineer green-field supply chain strategy integration, or on how to measure the effects of supply chain architecture on integration and performance. In Figure 1, we take this concern as a starting point to create a conceptual framework diagram from existing research studies on the topic of supply chain architecture and design. In the Figure 2, the findings derived from the taxonomic scheme (Table 1) are applied as a discussion focused on the interrelationships between the various supply chain strategic factors, on the relationship between supply chain architecture and design, and on the attitudes, practices and patterns that have an impact on supply chain engineering.

Examining the relationship between supply chain architecture and design, without concrete set of evaluation criteria of the interrelationships between the different supply chain engineering factors, seems inconclusive. Given the complex interactions between attitudes, patterns and practices, outlined in Table 1, it seems necessary to take into account these interactions when investigating the process of engineering supply chain architecture and design.

For example, one would anticipate an interaction between architecture (e.g. external elements, factors and forces) and practices (e.g. corporate strategy). Similarly, we would expect there to be a relationship between corporate strategy and the integrated business strategy.

Figure 1: Conceptual framework for engineering a green-field supply chain integration

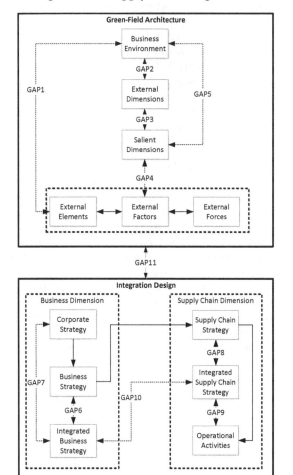

Figure 2: Methodology for engineering a green-field supply chain integration strategy

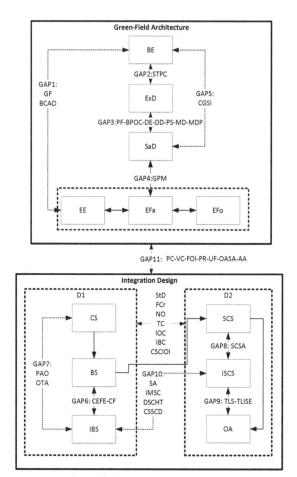

In line with the finding from the taxonomic scheme (Table 1), it seems logical, especially from a conceptual point of view, to focus on systematically engineering the holistic supply chain, by focusing on the interrelationship between supply chain architecture and integration design in individual context. Many authors instead focus on individual problems in individual context. It is not sufficient to have a solution to one problem and to ignore other supply chain problems. The objective of methodology (Figure 2) is to systematically address multiple problems in the same time.

The methodology (Figure 2) measures the interrelationships within a single relationship and then to relate the supply chain engineering of the architecture and design. The advantage of relating individual interrelationships is that it is relatively easy to acquire reliable, evaluation criteria for single interrelationship. By doing that, it becomes clearer about what is exactly being engineered (Figure 2) and interrelated to the multiple relationships (Table 1).

To ensure validity of these findings, the methodology is field tested with a case study of the Mining Industry. Before field testing the methodology, a set of six principles are defined. The set of principles enable academics and practitioners to interrelate different aspects of the methodology and to help them in interpreting Table 1, Figure 1 and Figure 2.

Field testing the new methodology with a case study

The case study was performed on the Slate Mining Industry in North Wales (Figure 3), to formulate a green-field supply chain strategy, integrating the complete supply chain. The case study included a Slate Mining Quarry, Civil Engineering Company, Logistics Company, Rail Terminal Company, Wholesalers (Virtual Quarries) and Retailers (Gardening and Building Materials Shops). The final

result of the engineering is expressed in Figure 3, detailing how different aspect are interrelated in practice and interpreting the practical contributions from the methodology.

The supply chain engineering in the case study was performed by applying the methodology and assembling the Pugh controlled convergence (PuCC) conceptual design (Pugh, 1990), in combination with the mechanisms for capturing, evaluating and reformulating a supply chain strategy (Perez-Franco et al. 2010). These methods are applied in combination with: the supply chain design decomposition pyramidal arrangements (Schnetzler et al., 2007) and the engineering system dynamics for supply chain design (Hafeez et al., 1996).

Figure 3: Application of the methodology on the Slate Mining Industry in North Wales.

Practical Application of the Methodology for Engineering a Green-Field Supply Chain Architecture

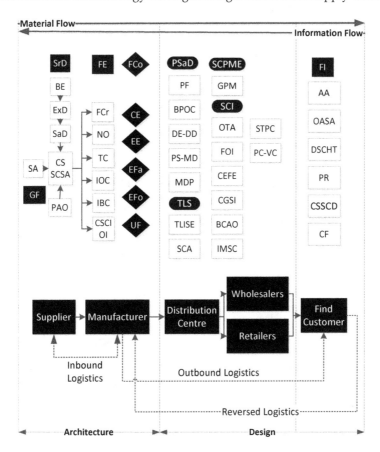

6. DISCUSSION AND IMPLICATIONS

The attention of many researchers outlined in this paper, has often focused on a single area of supply chain strategy. They have generally neglected research on the whole performance of the supply chain strategy engineering, which includes the architecture and design aspects. Considering these gaps, this paper established a methodology, which used the concept of strategic decision making levels and supply chain integration processes, as the approach to the study of the holistic supply chain strategy engineering. In the theory generation stages, the methodology was designed towards green-field strategy engineering for integrating multiple participants. The concept of green-field integration sets this apart from existing methods, which are designed to re-formulate existing strategies of individual companies.

The implications of this study are focused on the strategic operational activities, and on avoiding prescriptive and descriptive approaches, and addressed the operationalisation aspects of supply chain engineering. While validating the methodology with a case study, the methodology guided the development of integrated strategy, and addressed multiple supply chain complexities, which represented testing the theory in a real life phenomenon with multiple variables.

7. CONCLUSION

The paper revealed a new methodology for engineering, architecting, and designing integrated green-field supply chain. The methodology derived with the conclusion that green-field supply chain architecture, design and engineering represents a dynamic process, and should be analysed in individual contexts. The critical summary of literature reviewed resulted in identifying the main themes in a summary map (Table 1), necessary for generating a new methodology (Figure 1). The main themes are categorised in key tenants (Table 1). The key tenants are catalogued for addressing several problems present in engineering the architecture and design of green-field supply chains. These are critically appraised, with specific observations, to identify and catalogue the key tenants that function as principles for building the methodology.

The hierarchical method for network design was applied for building and combining the architecture, design and engineering criteria. This approach was supported with principles from DSCHT, and combined with the techniques from ATC. The new principles contribute to knowledge with: (1) architecting the supply chain elements from multiple supply chain participants; (2) designing the participants' main aims and objectives, and (3) engineering the process of getting from the present to the required stage. The supply chain principles are also aimed at anticipating operational capabilities through internal competencies and by considering inter-organisational integration in combination with operations re-engineering.

The concept verification applied architecture and integration criteria as a method for strategy engineering. The new methodology enables building upon the supply chain engineering criteria that until present, has not been built upon and combined with the process engineering design criteria: visibility, acceptance, participation, communication, adaptability, integration, effectiveness, flexibility, and responsiveness. Combining the criteria represents a holistic approach for supply chain architecture and result in deriving new understandings of green-field supply chain engineering that can be applied by supply chain practitioners.

7.1 Limitations and future research

The methodology contributes to and enriches the existing literature and provides background for further academic research in this subject. However, this methodology was verified with a single case study on the mining industry, and while it is anticipated that the proposed methodology is suitable for other sectors, the findings would need to be delimited through further testing and research.

Further research is required into the topic of addressing strategy absence. In scenarios of high strategy absence the engineering and evaluation criteria of this methodology would be difficult to implement. In that respect, the main challenge for future research is in extracting supply chain strategy tacit knowledge and converting it into explicit. There is a strong preference in practice towards desired over feasible objectives. This issue becomes one of a degree in an integration, because of avoidance of criticism, conflict, disagreement, and controversy. Future research studies should be aware that these challenges.

8. References

Abdur Razzaque, M., and Chen Sheng, C. (1998). Outsourcing of logistics functions: a literature survey. *International Journal of Physical Distribution and Logistics Management*, 28(2), pp.89–107.

Al-Mudimigh, A. S., Zairi, M., and Ahmed, A. M. M. (2004). *Extending the concept of supply chain: The effective management of value chains*. International Journal of Production Economics, 87(3), pp.309–320.

Andrews, K. R. 1982. The Concept of Corporate Strategy. In C.R. Christensen, K. R. Andrews, J. L. Bower, R. G. Hamermesh And M. E. Porter (Eds.), Business Policy: Text And Cases, Irwin, Homewood, Il.

Andrews, R. B., George A. Law, J. W., Richard, M., (2009). Strategy Formulation, Strategy Content and Performance: An Empirical Analysis. *Public Management Review*, 11, pp.1-22.

Beamon, B.M., 1998. Supply Chain Design and Analysis: Models and Methods. International Journal of Production Economics, 55(3), pp. 281–294

Bogataj, M., and Bogataj, L. (2001). Supply chain coordination in spatial games. *International Journal of Production Economics*, 71(1-3), pp.277–285.

Bozarth, C.C., Warsinga, D.P., Flynnb, B.B., Flynn, E.J., 2009. *The impact of supply chain complexity on manufacturing plant performance. Journal of Operations Management*, 27(1), pp.78–93.

Brewer, P. C., and Speh, T. W. (2000). Using the balanced scorecard to measure supply chain performance. *Journal of Business Logistics*, 21(1), 75–94.

Childerhouse, P., and Towill, D. R. (2011). Arcs of supply chain integration. *International Journal of Production Research*, 49(24), pp.7441–7468.

Cigolini, R., Cozzi, M., and Perona, M. (2004). A new framework for supply chain management. *International Journal of Operations and Production Management*, 24(1), pp.7–41.

Clausing, D. (1992). Enhanced quality function deployment (EQFD). [Cambridge, Mass.] : Massachusetts Institute of Technology, *MIT Center for Advanced Engineering Study*, MIT Press.

Clendenin, J. A. (1997). Closing the Supply Chain Loop: Reengineering the Returns Channel Process. *The International Journal of Logistics Management*, 8(1), pp. 75–86.

Closs, D. J., and Mollenkopf, D. A. (2004). A global supply chain framework. *Industrial Marketing Management*, 33(1), pp.37–44.

Dotoli, M. Fanti, M. P., Melonia., and Zhoub, M.C., 2007. A multi-level approach for network design of integrated supply chains. Interna-tional Journal of Production Research. 43 (20), pp 4267-4287

Dubois, A., Hulthén, K., and Pedersen, A.C. (2004). Supply chains and interdependence: a theoretical analysis. *Journal of Purchasing and Supply Management*, 10(1), pp.3–9.

Eisenhardt, K. M. (1989). Building Theories From Case Study Research. *Academy Of Management Review*, 14(4), pp. 532-550.

Eppinger, S. D., Whitney, D. E., Smith, R. P., and Gebala, D. A. (1994). A model-based method for organizing tasks in product development. *Research in Engineering Design*, 6(1), pp.1–13.

Frohlich, M. and Westbrook, R., 2001. *Arcs of Integration: An International Study of Supply Chain Strategies*. Journal of Operations Management. 19 (2001), pp. 185–200.

Gilley, K. M., and Rasheed, A. (2000). Making More by Doing Less: An Analysis of Outsourcing and its Effects on Firm Performance. *Journal of Management*, 26(4), pp.763–790.

Glaser, B. S., and Stauss, A.L. (1967). The Discovery of Grounded Theory, London, Weidenfeld & Nicolson.

Griffis, S. E., Bell, J. E., and Closs, D. J. (2012). Metaheuristics in Logistics and Supply Chain Management. *Journal of Business Logistics*, 33(2), pp.90–106.

Hafeez, K., Griffiths, M., Griffiths, J., and Naim, M. M. (1996). Systems design of a two-echelon steel industry supply chain. *International Journal of Production Economics*, 45(1-3), pp.121–130.

He, Y., and Lai, K. K. (2012). Supply chain integration and service oriented transformation: Evidence from Chinese equipment manufacturers. *International Journal of Production Economics*, 135(2), pp.791–799.

Hipel, K. W. (2012). A Hierarchical Decision Model to Select Quality Control Strategies for a Complex Product. *IEEE Transactions on Systems, Man, and Cybernetics - Part A: Systems and Humans*, 42(4), pp.814–826.

Inkpen, A., and Choudhury, N. (1995). The seeking of strategy where it is not: Towards a theory of strategy absence. *Strategic Management Journal*, 16(4), pp.313–323.

Ivanov, D. (2010). An adaptive framework for aligning (re)planning decisions on supply chain strategy, design, tactics, and operations. *International Journal of Production Research*, 48(13), pp.3999–4017.

Jayaram, J. and Tan, K.C., 2010. Supply Chain Integration with Third-Party Logistics Providers. *International Journal of Production Economics*, 125 (2), pp. 262–271.

Kaplan, R. and Norton, D., 1996. Using the balanced scorecard as a strategic management system. Harvard Business Review, 74 (1), pp. 75-85

Kim, D. (2006). Process chain: A new paradigm of collaborative commerce and synchronized supply chain. *Business Horizons*, 49(5), pp.359–367.

Korpela, J., Lehmusvaara, A., and Tuominen, M. (2001). An analytic approach to supply chain development. *International Journal of Production Economics*, 71(1-3), pp.145–155.

Korpela, J., Lehmusvaara, A., Tuominen, M., Lamothe, J., Hadj-Hamou, K., Aldanondo, M., Siferd, S. P. (2001). Customer service based design of the supply chain. *International Journal of Production Economics*, 69(2), pp.193–204.

Lamothe, J., Hadj-Hamou, K., and Aldanondo, M. (2006). An optimization model for selecting a product family and designing its supply chain. *European Journal of Operational Research*, 169(3), pp.1030–1047.

Lee, H. and Billington, C., (1992). Managing supply chain inventory: pitfalls and opportunities. Sloan management review, 33(3), pp.64–73.

Lertpattarapong, C. (2002). Applying System Dynamics Approach to the supply chain management problem, *MSc Thesis, Massachusetts Institute of Technology*, MIT Press.

Lee, H., Padmanabhan, V. and Whang, S., (1997). The bullwhip effect in supply chains1. *Sloan management review*, 38(3), pp.93–102.

Lo, S. M., and Power, D. (2010). An empirical investigation of the relationship between product nature and supply chain strategy. *Supply Chain Management: An International Journal*, 15(2), pp.139–153.

Manthou, V., Vlachopoulou, M., and Folinas, D. (2004). Virtual e-Chain (VeC) model for supply chain collaboration. *International Journal of Production Economics*, 87(3), pp. 241–250.

Martínez-Olvera, C. (2008). Methodology for realignment of supply-chain structural elements. *International Journal of Production Economics*, 114(2), pp.714–722.

Martínez-Olvera, C., and Shunk, D. (2006). Comprehensive framework for the development of a supply chain strategy. *International Journal of Production Research*, 44(21), pp.4511–4528.

Mckone-Sweet, K., and Lee, Y.T. (2009). Development and Analysis of a Supply Chain Strategy Taxonomy. *Journal of Supply Chain Management*, 45(3), pp.3–24.

Melnyk, S. A., Narasimhan, R., and DeCampos, H. A. (2013). Supply chain design: issues, challenges, frameworks and solutions. *International Journal of Production Research*, 52(7), pp.1887–1896.

Menda, R. and Dilts, D., (1997). The manufacturing strategy formulation process: linking multifunctional viewpoints. Journal of Operations Management, 15(4), pp.223–241.

Mentzer, J.T., DeWitt, W., Keebler, J.S., Min. S., Nix, N.W., Smith, C.D., Zacharia, Z.G. (2001). *Defining Supply Chain Management*. Journal of Business Logistics, 22(2), pp.1–25.

Miller, D. and Friesen, P.H., 1978. Archetypes of Strategy Formulation. Management Science, 24(9), pp.921–933.

Narasimhan, R., Kim, S.-W. and Tan, K.-C., 2008. An Empirical Investi-gation of Supply Chain Strategy Typologies and Relationships to Performance. *International Journal of Production Research*, 46(18), pp.5231 – 5259.

Nikulin, C., Graziosi, S., Cascini, G., Araneda, A., and Minutolo, M. (2013). An Algorithm for Supply Chain Integration based on OTSM-TRIZ. *Procedia - Social and Behavioral Sciences*, 75, pp.383–396.

Pathak, S. D., Day, J. M., Nair, A., Sawaya, W. J., and Kristal, M. M. (2007). Complexity and adaptivity in supply networks: building supply network theory using a complex adaptive systems perspective. *Decision Sciences*, 38(4), pp.547–580.

Perez – Franco, R. J, Sheffi, Y. Silbey, S., Frey, D., Singh, M., Leveson, N. 2010. A methodology to capture, evaluate and reformulate a firm's supply chain strategy as a conceptual system. PhD Thesis, *MIT Press*

Platts, K., Mills, J. and Neely, A., (1996). Evaluating manufacturing strategy formulation processess. International Journal of Production Economics: Proceedings of the 8th International Working Seminar on Production Economics, 46-47, pp. 233–240

Porter, M. (1996). What is Strategy? *Harvard Business Review*, 61-78.

Pugh, S. (1990). Total Design: Integrated Methods for Successful Product Engineering, *Addison-Wesley* Wokingham, UK.

Radanliev, P., (2015a) 'Green-field Architecture for Sustainable Supply Chain Strategy Formulation', *International Journal of Supply Chain Management*, 4(2), pp.62-67.

Radanliev, P., (2015b) 'Supply Chain Systems Architecture and Engineering Design: Green-field Supply Chain Integration' *Operations and Supply Chain Management: An International Journal*, 9(1), pp. 22-30.

Radanliev, P., (2015c) 'Architectures for Green-Field Supply Chain Integration: Supply Chain Integration Design', *Journal of Supply Chain and Operations Management*, 13(2), pp.56-78.

Qu, T., Huang, G. Q., Cung, V.-D., and Mangione, F. (2010). Optimal configuration of assembly supply chains using analytical target cascading. *International Journal of Production Research*, 48(23), pp.6883–6907.

Qureshi, M. N., Kumar, P., and Kumar, D., 2009. Selection of Transportation Company: An Analytic Network Process Approach. *Icfai Journal of Supply Chain Management*, 6(2), pp.26-38.

Rao, P., and Holt, D. (2005). Do green supply chains lead to competitiveness and economic performance? *International Journal of Operations and Production Management*, 25(9), pp.898–916.

Rosenzweig, E. D., Roth, A. V, and Dean, J. W. (2003). The influence of an integration strategy on competitive capabilities and business performance: An exploratory study of consumer products manufacturers. *Journal of Operations Management*, 21(4), pp.437–456.

Saad, M., Jones, M., and James, P. (2002). A review of the progress towards the adoption of supply chain management (SCM) relationships in construction. *European Journal of Purchasing and Supply Management*, 8(3), pp.173–183.

Sakka, O., Millet, P.-A., and Botta-Genoulaz, V. (2011). An ontological approach for strategic alignment: a supply chain operations reference case study. *International Journal of Computer Integrated Manufacturing*, 24(11), pp.1022–1037.

Scc. (2001). Supply-Chain Operations Reference-Model. Pittsburgh: Supply Chain Council, Inc., Retrieved From The World Wide Web: Http://Www.Supply-Chain.Org.

Schnetzler, M. J., Sennheiser, A., and Schönsleben, P. (2007). A decomposition-based approach for the development of a supply chain strategy. *International Journal of Production Economics*, 105(1), pp. 21–42.

Shah, J., and Singh, N. (2001). Benchmarking Internal Supply Chain Performance: Development of a Framework. *The Journal of Supply Chain Management*, 37(1), pp.37–47.

Sheffi, Y., (1990). Third party logistics: present and future prospects. *Journal of Business Logistics*, 11(2), pp.27–39.

Sheu, D. D., and Lee, H.-K. (2011). A proposed process for systematic innovation. *International Journal of Production Research*, 49(3), pp.847–868.

Soni, G., and Kodali, R. (2010). Internal benchmarking for assessment of supply chain performance. *Benchmarking: An International Journal*, 17(1), pp.44–76.

Sukati, I., Hamid, A. B., Baharun, R., and Yusoff, R. M. (2012). The Study of Supply Chain Management Strategy and Practices on Supply Chain Performance. *Procedia - Social and Behavioral Sciences*, 40, pp.225–233.

Swink, M., Narasimhan, R., and Wang, C. (2007). Managing beyond the factory walls: Effects of four types of strategic integration on manufacturing plant performance. *Journal of Operations Management*, 25(1), pp.148–164.

Tracey, M., Vonderembse, M. A., and Lim, J.S. (1999). Manufacturing technology and strategy formulation: keys to enhancing competitiveness and improving performance. *Journal of Operations Management*, 17(4), pp.411–428.

Van der Vaart, T., and van Donk, D. P. (2008). A critical review of survey-based research in supply chain integration. *International Journal of Production Economics*, 111(1), pp.42–55.

Van Donk, D. P., and van der Vaart, T. (2005). A case of shared resources, uncertainty and supply chain integration in the process industry. *International Journal of Production Economics*, 96(1), pp.97–108.

Vickery, S. K., Jayaram, J., Droge, C., and Calantone, R. (2003). The effects of an integrative supply chain strategy on customer service and financial performance: an analysis of direct versus indirect relationships. *Journal of Operations Management*, 21(5), pp.523–539.

Yin, R. K. 2009. Case study research: Design and methods, Sage Publications, Inc.

Zhou, S., and Chen, R. (2001). A decision model for selecting participants in supply chain. *Journal of Shanghai University (English Edition)*, 5(4), pp.341–344.

Zsidisin, G. A., and Siferd, S. P. (2001). Environmental purchasing: a framework for theory development. *European Journal of Purchasing and Supply Management*, 7(1), pp.61–73.

11

A Stochastic Two-Echelon Supply Chain Model for the Petrol Station Replenishment Problem

Kizito Paul Mubiru

Kyambogo University

kizito.mubiru@yahoo.com

ABSTRACT: In this paper, a new mathematical model is developed to optimize replenishment policies and inventory costs of a two-echelon supply chain system of kerosene product under demand uncertainty. The system consists of a fuel depot at the upper echelon and four petrol stations at the lower echelon. The petrol stations face stochastic stationary demand where inventory replenishment periods are uniformly fixed over the echelons. Adopting a Markov decision process approach, the states of a Markov chain represent possible states of demand for the inventory item. The replenishment cost, holding cost and shortage costs are combined with demand and inventory positions in order to generate the inventory cost matrix over the echelons. The matrix represents the long run measure of performance for the decision problem. The objective is to determine in each echelon of the planning horizon an optimal replenishment policy so that the long run inventory costs are minimized for a given state of demand. Using weekly equal intervals, the decisions of when to replenish additional units are made using dynamic programming over a finite period planning horizon. A numerical example demonstrates the existence of an optimal state-dependent replenishment policy and inventory costs over the echelons.

Keywords: *Petrol station, supply chain, replenishment, stochastic, two-echelon*

1. INTRODUCTION

The goal of a supply chain network is to procure raw materials, transform them into intermediate goods and then final products. Finally, delivery of products to customers is required through a distribution system that includes an echelon inventory system. The system spans procurement, manufacturing and distribution with inventory management as one key element. To cope with current turbulent market demands, there is still need to adopt coordinated inventory control across supply chain facilities by establishing optimal replenishment policies in a stochastic demand environment. In practice, large industries continually strive to optimize replenishment policies of products in multi-echelon inventory systems. This is a considerable challenge when the demand for manufactured items follows a stochastic trend. One major challenge is usually encountered: determining the most desirable period during which to replenish additional units of the item in question given a periodic review production-inventory system when demand is uncertain.

In this paper, a two-echelon inventory system is considered whose goal is to optimize replenishment policies and the inventory costs associated with kerosene product. At the beginning of each period, a major decision has to be made, namely whether to replenish additional units of fuel or not to replenish and keep fuel at prevailing inventory position in order to sustain demand at a given echelon. The paper is organized as follows. After reviewing the relevant literature §2, a mathematical model is described in §3 where consideration is given to the process of estimating the model parameters. The model is solved in §4 and applied to a special case study in §5.Some final remarks lastly follow in §6.

2. LITERATURE REVIEWS

Rodney and Roman (2004) examined the optimal policies study in the context of a capacitated two-echelon inventory system. This model includes installations with production capacity limits, and demonstrates that a modified base stock policy is optimal in a two-stage system when there is a smaller capacity at the downstream facility. This is shown by decomposing the dynamic programming value function into value functions dependent upon individual echelon stock variables. The optimal structure holds for both stationary and non stationary customer demand.

Axsater S (2005) formulated a simple decision rule for decentralized two-echelon inventory control. A two-echelon distribution inventory system with a central warehouse and a number of retailers is considered. The retailers face stochastic demand and the system is controlled by continuous review installation stock policies with given batch quantities. A back order cost is provided to the warehouse and the warehouse chooses the reorder point so that the sum of the expected holding and backorder costs are minimized. Given the resulting warehouse policy, the retailers similarly optimize their costs with respect to the reorder points. The study provides a simple technique for determining the backorder cost to be used by the warehouse.

Cornillier F,Boctor F,Laporte G and Renand J(2008) developed an exact algorithm for the petrol station replenishment problem. The algorithm decomposes the problem into a truck loading and routing problem. The authors determine quantities to deliver within a given interval of allocating products to tank truck compartments and of designing delivery routes to stations. In related work by Cornillier F,Boctor F,Laporte G and Renand J(2009) , a heuristic for the multi-period petrol station replenishment problem was developed. In this article, the objective is to maximize the total profit equal to the revenue minus the sum of routing costs and of regular and overtime costs. Procedures are provided for the route construction, truck loading and route packing enabling anticipation or the postponement of deliveries. The solution procedure to the problem was extended by Cornillier F,Boctor F,Laporte G and and Renand J(2009). The authors analyzed the petrol station replenishment problem with time windows. In this article, the aim is to optimize the delivery of several petroleum products to a set of petrol stations using limited heterogeneous fleet of trucks by assigning products to truck compartments, delivery routes and schedules.

In related work by Haji R (2011), a two-echelon inventory system is considered consisting of one central warehouse and a number of non-identical retailers. The warehouse uses a one-for-one policy to replenish its inventory, but the retailers apply a new policy that is each retailer orders one unit to central warehouse in a predetermined time interval; thus retailer orders are deterministic not random.

Abhijeet S and Saroj K (2011) considered a vendor managed Two-Echelon inventory system for an integrated production procurement case. Joint economic lot size models are presented for the two supply situations, namely staggered supply and uniform supply. Cases are employed that describe the inventory situation of a single vendor supplying an item to a manufacturer that is further processed before it is supplied to the end user. Using illustrative examples, the comparative advantages of a uniform sub batch supply over a staggered alternative are investigated and uniform supply models are found to be comparatively more beneficial and robust than the staggered sub batch supply.

2.1 The Stochastic Two-Echelon Supply chain Model versus Petrol Station   Replenishment Models

The literature cited provides profound insights by authors that are crucial in analyzing two-echelon inventory systems. Existing models that address the petrol station replenishment problem are similarly presented. Based on the existing models by scholars, a new stochastic dynamic programming approach is sought in order to relate state-transitions with customers, demand and inventory positions of the item over the echelons. This is done with a view of optimizing replenishment policies and inventory costs of the supply chain in a multi-stage decision setting.

As noted by Cornillier F,Boctor F,Larporte G and Renand J(2008,2009,2009),the three models address the petrol station replenishment problem from the transportation and logistics perspective. The source (depot) is not vividly known and the overall goal is to minimize transportation costs of petroleum products. Randomness of demand is not a salient issue or not discussed at all. However, demand uncertainty has a direct bearing in answering the inventory question of "when to deliver or replenish" at minimum inventory costs.

On a comparative note, the stochastic Two-Echelon supply chain Model incorporates demand uncertainty in determining optimal replenishment decisions where "shortage" or "no shortage" conditions are catered for when calculating total inventory costs over the echelons. The Model can assist inventory managers of petroleum products in answering the question of "when to replenish" at minimum costs under demand uncertainty. Petrol stations within a supply chain framework that share a common fuel depot can consider adopting the stochastic Two-Echelon supply chain model. As cost minimization strategy, the model provides a practical solution to replenishment decisions of petroleum products under demand uncertainty.

3. MODEL FORMULATION

3.1 Notation and assumptions

i,j	=	States of demand
F	=	Favorable state
U	=	Unfavorable state
h	=	Inventory echelon
n,N	=	Stages
Z	=	Replenishment policy
N^Z	=	Customer matrix
N^Z_{ij}	=	Number of customers
D^Z	=	Demand matrix
D^Z_{ij}	=	Quantity demanded
Q^Z	=	Demand transition matrix
Q^Z_{ij}	=	Demand transition probability
C^Z	=	Inventory cost matrix
C^Z_{ij}	=	Inventory costs
e^Z_i	=	Expected inventory costs
a^Z_i	=	Accumulated inventory costs
c_r	=	Unit replenishment costs
c_h	=	Unit holding costs
c_s	=	Unit shortage costs

$i,j \; \varepsilon \; \{F,U\} \; h \; \varepsilon \; \{1,2\} \; Z \; \varepsilon \; \{0,1\} \; n=1,2,\ldots\ldots\ldots\ldots\ldots\ldots N$

We consider a two-echelon inventory system consisting of a fuel depot storing kerosene fuel for a designated number of petrol stations at echelon 1.At echelon 2; customers demand kerosene at petrol stations. The demand during each time period over a fixed planning horizon for a given echelon (h) is classified as either *favorable* (denoted by state F) or *unfavorable* (denoted by state U) and the demand of any such period is assumed to depend on the demand of the preceding period. The transition probabilities over the planning horizon from one demand state to another may be described by means of a Markov chain. Suppose one is interested in determining an optimal course of action, namely to replenish additional units of kerosene (a decision denoted by Z=1) or not to replenish additional units of kerosene (a decision denoted by Z=0) during each time period over the planning horizon, where Z is a binary decision variable. Optimality is defined such that the minimum inventory costs are accumulated at the end of N consecutive time periods spanning the planning horizon under consideration. In this paper, a two-echelon (h =2) and two-period (N=2) planning horizon is considered.

3.2 Finite - period dynamic programming problem formulation

Recalling that the demand can either be in state F or in state U, the problem of finding an optimal replenishment policy may be expressed as a finite period dynamic programming model.

Let $g_n(i, h)$ denote the optimal expected inventory costs accumulated during the periods $n, n+1, \ldots, N$ given that the state of the system at the beginning of period n is $i \in \{F, U\}$. The recursive equation relating g_n and g_{n+1} is

$$g_n(i, h) = min_Z[Q_{iF}^Z(h)C_{iF}^Z(h) + g_{n+1}(F, h), Q_{iU}^Z(h)C_{iU}^Z(h) + g_{n+1}(U, h)] \qquad (1)$$

$i \in \{F, U\}$, $h=\{1,2\}$, $n= 1,2,\ldots\ldots\ldots\ldots\ldots N$

together with the final conditions

$g_{N+1}(F, h) = g_{N+1}(U, h) = 0$

This recursive relationship may be justified by noting that the cumulative inventory costs $C_{ij}^Z(h) + g_{N+1}(j)$ resulting from reaching state $j \in \{F, U\}$ at the start of period n+1 from state i $\in \{F, U\}$ at the start of period n occurs with probability $Q_{ij}^Z(h)$.

Clearly, $e^Z(h) = [Q_{ij}^Z(h)] [R^Z(h)]^T$, $Z \in \{0,1\}$, $h \in \{1,2\}$ \qquad (2)

where 'T' denoted matrix transposition, and hence the dynamic programming recursive equations

$$g_N(i, h) = min_Z[e_i^Z(h) + Q_{iF}^Z(h)\ g_{N+1}(F) + Q_{iU}^Z(h)\ g_{N+1}(U)] \qquad (3)$$

$$g_N(i, h) = min_Z[e_i^Z(h)] \qquad (4)$$

result where (4) represents the Markov chain stable state.

3.2.1 Computing $Q^Z(h)$ and $C^Z(h)$

The demand transition probability from state $i \in \{F, U\}$ to state $j \in \{F, U\}$, given replenishment policy $Z \in \{0,1\}$ may be taken as the number of customers observed over echelon h with demand initially in state i and later with demand changing to state j, divided by the sum of customers over all states. That is,

$$Q_{ij}^Z(h) = N_{ij}^Z(h)/((N_{iF}^Z(h) + (N_{iU}^Z(h))$$

$i \in \{F, U\}, Z \in \{0,1\}$, $h= \{1, 2\}$ \qquad (5)

When demand outweighs on-hand inventory, the inventory cost matrix $C^Z(h)$ may be computed by means of the relation

$$C^Z(h) = (c_r + c_h + c_s)[D^Z(h) - I^Z(h)]$$

Therefore,

$$C_{ij}^Z(h) = \begin{cases} (c_r + c_h + c_s)[D_{ij}^Z(h) - I_{ij}^Z(h)] & if \ \ D_{ij}^Z(h) > I_{ij}^Z(h) \\ c_h[I_{ij}^Z(h) - D_{ij}^Z(h)] & if \ \ D_{ij}^Z(h) \le I_{ij}^Z(h) \end{cases}$$

(6)

for all i,je{ F, U }, h e{1,2} and Ze{0,1}.

The justification for expression (6) is that D_{ij}^Z(h) – I_{ij}^Z(h) units must be replenished to meet excess demand. Otherwise replenishment is cancelled when demand is less than or equal to on-hand inventory.

The following conditions must, however hold:

Z=1 when c_r > 0 and Z=0 when c_r = 0

c_s > 0 when shortages are allowed and c_s= 0 when shortages are not allowed.

4. OPTIMIZATION

The optimal replenishment policy and profits are found in this section for each period over echelon h separately.

4.1 Optimization during period 1

When demand is favorable (ie. in state F), the optimal replenishment policy during period 1 is

$$Z = \begin{cases} 1 & if \ \ e_F^1(h) < e_F^0(h) \\ 0 & if \ \ e_F^1(h) \ge e_F^0(h) \end{cases}$$

The associated inventory costs are then

$$g_1(F, h) = \begin{cases} e_F^1(h) & if \ \ Z = 1 \\ e_F^0(h) & if \ \ Z = 0 \end{cases}$$

Similarly, when demand is unfavorable (ie. in state U), the optimal replenishment policy during period 1 is

$$Z = \begin{cases} 1 & if \ \ e_U^1(h) < e_U^0(h) \\ 0 & if \ \ e_U^1(h) \ge e_U^0(h) \end{cases}$$

In this case, the associated inventory costs are

$$g_1(U, h) = \begin{cases} e_U^1(h) & if \ \ Z = 1 \\ e_U^0(h) & if \ \ Z = 0 \end{cases}$$

4.2 Optimization during period 2

Using (2),(3) and recalling that a_i^Z(h)denotes the already accumulated inventory costs at the end of period 1 as a result of decisions made during that period 1, it follows that

$$a_i^Z(h) = e_i^Z(h) + Q_{iF}^Z(h)min[e_F^1(h), e_F^0(h)]$$

$$+ Q_{iU}^Z(h)min[e_U^1(h), e_U^0(h)]$$

$$a_i^Z(h) = e_i^Z(h) + Q_{iF}^Z(h) \ g_2(F, h)$$

$$+ Q_{iU}^Z(h) \ g_2(U, h)$$

Therefore when demand is favorable (ie.in state F),the optimal replenishment policy during period 2 is

$$Z = \begin{cases} 1 & if \ \ a_F^1(h) < a_F^0(h) \\ 0 & if \ \ a_F^1(h) \ge a_F^0(h) \end{cases}$$

while the associated inventory costs are

$$g_2(F, h) = \begin{cases} a_F^1(h) & if \ \ Z = 1 \\ a_F^0(h) & if \ \ Z = 0 \end{cases}$$

Similarly, when the demand is unfavorable (ie. in state U), the optimal replenishment policy during period 2 is

$$Z = \begin{cases} 1 & if \ \ a_U^1(h) < a_U^0(h) \\ 0 & if \ \ a_U^1(h) \ge a_U^0(h) \end{cases}$$

In this case the associated inventory costs are

$$g_2(U, h) = \begin{cases} a_U^1(h) & if \ \ Z = 1 \\ a_U^0(h) & if \ \ Z = 0 \end{cases}$$

5. CASE STUDY

In order to demonstrate use of the model in §2-3, real case applications from *Total(U)Ltd*, a fuel company for kerosene product and four Total petrol stations in Uganda are presented in this section. The fuel depot supplies kerosene at petrol stations (echelon 1), while end customers come to petrol stations for kerosene (echelon 2).The demand for kerosene fluctuates every week at both echelons. The fuel depot and petrol stations want to avoid excess inventory when demand is Unfavorable (state U) or running out of stock when demand is Favorable (state F) and hence seek decision support in terms of an optimal replenishment policy and the associated inventory cost of kerosene in a two-week planning period. The network topology of a two-echelon inventory system for kerosene is illustrated in Figure 1 below:

Figure 1: A two-echelon supply chain for kerosene product

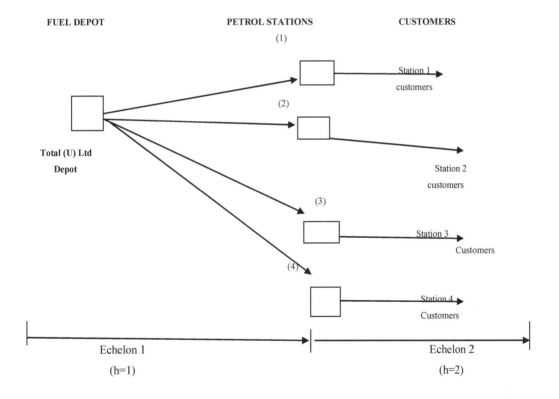

5.1 Data collection

Samples of customers demand and inventory levels were taken for kerosene product (in thousand litres) at echelons 1 and 2 over the state-transitions and the respective replenishment policies for twelve weeks as shown in Table 1.

**Table 1: Customers, demand and replenishment policies
given state-transitions, and echelons over twelve weeks**

STATE TRANSITION (i,j)	ECHELON (h)	REPLENISHMENT POLICY (Z)	CUSTOMERS $N^z_{ij}(h)$	DEMAND $D^z_{ij}(h)$	INVENTORY $I^z_{ij}(h)$
FF	1	1	91	156	95
FU	1	1	71	15	93
UF	1	1	64	107	93
UU	1	1	13	11	94
FF	1	0	82	123	43.5
FU	1	0	30	78	45
UF	1	0	55	78	46.5
UU	1	0	25	15	45.5
FF	2	1	45	93	145
FU	2	1	59	60	40
UF	2	1	59	59	35.5
UU	2	1	13	11	79.5
FF	2	0	54	72	81
FU	2	0	40	77	78.5
UF	2	0	45	75	79.5
UU	2	0	11	11	78.5

In either case, the unit replenishment cost (c_r) is \$1.50, the unit holding cost per week (c_h) is \$0.50 and the unit shortage cost per week (c_s) is \$0.75

5.2 Computation of Model Parameters

Using (5) and (6), the state transition matrices and inventory costs (in million UGX) at each respective echelon for week1 are

$$Q^1(1) = \begin{bmatrix} 0.5617 & 0.4383 \\ 0.8312 & 0.1688 \end{bmatrix} \qquad C^1(1) = \begin{bmatrix} 167.75 & 39 \\ 38.5 & 41.5 \end{bmatrix}$$

$$Q^1(2) = \begin{bmatrix} 0.4327 & 0.5673 \\ 0.8194 & 0.1806 \end{bmatrix} \qquad C^1(2) = \begin{bmatrix} 26 & 55 \\ 64.63 & 34.25 \end{bmatrix}$$

for the case when additional units were replenished (Z=1) during week 1, while these matrices are given by

$$Q^0(1) = \begin{bmatrix} 0.7322 & 0.2678 \\ 0.6875 & 0.3125 \end{bmatrix} \qquad C^0(1) = \begin{bmatrix} 218.63 & 90.75 \\ 86.63 & 15.25 \end{bmatrix}$$

$$Q^0(2) = \begin{bmatrix} 0.5745 & 0.4255 \\ 0.8036 & 0.1964 \end{bmatrix} \qquad\qquad C^0(2) = \begin{bmatrix} 4.5 & 0.75 \\ 2.25 & 33.75 \end{bmatrix}$$

for the case when additional units were not replenished   (Z=0) during week 1.

When additional units were replenished (Z = 1), the matrices Q^1 (1), C^1 (1) , Q^1 (2) and C^1(2) yield the inventory costs(in million UGX)

$$e_F^1(1) = (0.5617)(167.75) + (0.4383)(39) = 111.32$$

$$e_U^1(1) = (0.8312)(38.5) + (0.1688)(41.5) = 39.01$$

$$e_F^1(2) = (0.4327)(26) + (0.5673)(55) = 42.45$$

$$e_U^1(2) = (0.8194)(64.63) + (0.1806)(34.25) = 59.14$$

However, when additional units were *not* replenished   (Z=0), the matrices Q^0 (1), C^0(1) , Q^0 (2) and C^0(2) yield the inventory costs(in million UGX)

$$e_F^0(1) = (0.7322)(218.63) + (0.2678)(90.75) = 184.25$$

$$e_U^0(1) = (0.6875)(86.63) + (0.3125)(64.32) = 15.25$$

$$e_F^0(2) = (0.5745)(4.5) + (0.4255)(0.75) = 2.90$$

$$e_U^0(2) = (0.8036)(2.25) + (0.1964)(33.75) = 8.44$$

When additional units were replenished (Z=1), the accumulated inventory costs at the end of week 2 are calculated as follows:

Echelon 1:

$$a_F^1(1) = 111.32 + (0.5617)(111.32) + (0.4383)(39.01) = 190.95$$

$$a_U^1(1) = 39.01 + (0.8312)(111.32) + (0.1688)(39.01) = 138.12$$

Echelon 2:

$$a_F^1(2) = 42.45 + (0.4327)(111.32) + (0.5723)(39.01) = 112.94$$

$$a_U^1(2) = 59.14 + (0.8194)(111.32) + (0.1806)(39.01) = 157.40$$

When additional units were *not* replenished (Z=0), the accumulated inventory costs at the end of week 2 are calculated as follows:

Echelon 1:

$$a_F^0(1) = 184.25 + (0.7322)(184.25) + (0.2678)(39.01) = 329.60$$

$$a_U^0(1) = 64.32 + (0.6875)(184.25) + (0.3125)(39.01) = 203.18$$

Echelon 2:

$$a_F^0(2) = 2.90 + (0.5745)(184.25) + (0.4255)(39.01) = 125.35$$

$$a_U^0(2) = 8.44 + (0.8036)(184.25) + (0.1964)(39.01) = 164.16$$

5.3 The Optimal Replenishment Policy

Week1: Echelon 1

Since 111.32 < 184.25, it follows that Z=1 is an optimal replenishment policy for week 1 with associated inventory costs of \$111.32 for the case of favorable demand. Since 39.01 < 64.32, it follows that Z=1 is an optimal replenishment policy for week 1 with associated inventory costs of \$39.01 for the case when demand is unfavorable.

Week1: Echelon 2

Since 2.90 < 42.45, it follows that Z=0 is an optimal replenishment policy for week 1 with associated inventory costs of \$2.90 when demand is favorable. Since 8.44 < 59.14, it follows that Z=0 is an optimal replenishment policy for week 1 with associated inventory costs of \$8.44 when demand is unfavorable.

Week 2: Echelon 1

Since 190.95 < 329.0, it follows that Z=1 is an optimal replenishment policy for week 2 with associated accumulated inventory costs of \$190.95 when demand is favorable. Since 138.12 < 203.18, it follows that Z=1 is an optimal replenishment policy for week 2 with associated accumulated inventory costs of \$138.12 when demand is unfavorable.

Week 2: Echelon 2

Since 112.94 < 125.35, it follows that Z=1 is an optimal replenishment policy for week 2 with associated accumulated inventory costs of \$112.94 for the case of favorable demand. Since 157.40 < 164.16, it follows that Z=1 is an optimal replenishment policy for week 2 with associated accumulated inventory costs of \$157.40 for the case of unfavorable demand.

6. CONCLUSION

A two-echelon supply chain model with stochastic demand was presented in this paper. The model determines an optimal replenishment policy and inventory costs of kerosene product under demand uncertainty. The decision of whether or not to replenish additional units is modeled as a multi-period decision problem using dynamic programming over a finite planning horizon. Results from the model indicate optimal replenishment policies and inventory costs over the echelons for the given problem. As a cost minimization strategy in echelon-based inventory systems, computational efforts of using Markov decision process approach provide promising results for the petrol station replenishment problem. However, further extensions of research are sought in order to analyze replenishment policies that minimize inventory costs under non stationary demand conditions over the echelons. In the same spirit, the model developed raises a number of salient issues to consider: Lead time of kerosene during the replenishment cycle and customer response to abrupt changes in price of the product. Finally, special interest is thought in further extending our model by considering replenishment policies for minimum inventory costs in the context of Continuous Time Markov Chains (CTMC).

7. REFERENCES

Rodney P & Roman K, 2004, "Optimal Policies for a capacitated Two-Echelon Inventory system", *Operations Research*, 152(5), 739-747.

Axsater S, 2005, A simple decision rule for decentralized two-echelon inventory control, *International Journal of Production Economics*, 93-94(1), 53-59.

Cornillier F,Boctor F,Laporte G & Renand J,2008,"An Exact Algorithm for the Petrol station Replenishment Problem", *Journal of Operations Research Society*,vol.59,No.5,pp.607-615.

Cornillier F,Boctor F,Laporte G & Renand J,2009,"The Petrol station Replenishment Problem with Time Windows", *Computers and Operations Research,* vol.56,No.3,pp.919-935.

Cornillier F,Boctor F,Laporte G & Renand J,2009,"A Heuristic for the multi-period Petrol station Replenishment Problem", *European Journal of Operations Research,* vol.19,No.2,pp.295-305.

Haji R & Tayebi H,2011,"Applying a new ordering policy in a two-echelon inventory system with Poisson demand rate retailers and transportation cost", *International Journal of Business Performance and Supply chain Modeling,*20-27.

Abhijeet S & Saroj K, 2011, A Vendor-managed Two-Echelon Inventory system for an integrated procurement case", *Asia Pacific Journal of Operations Research,* 28(2), 301-322.

Modelling Collaborative Transportation Management: Current State And Opportunities For Future Research

Liane Okdinawati
School of Business and Management, Bandung Institute of Technology
aneu.okdinawati@sbm-itb.ac.id

Togar M. Simatupang
School of Business and Management, Bandung Institute of Technology
togar@sbm-itb.ac.id

Yos Sunitiyoso
School of Business and Management, Bandung Institute of Technology

ABSTRACT: Collaborative Transportation Management (CTM) aims to reduce inefficiency, improve services, and provide mutual outcome to all parties. CTM has raised significant interest of both researchers and practitioners. Sharing information is the most basic form of coordination in supply chains to integrate CTM models at strategic, tactical, and operational levels. However, little has been known about the state of the art of CTM models. This paper presents a comprehensive review on the current state of CTM models. The overview of the CTM models is organized by classifying the previous literatures on different collaborative structures and different levels of planning. This paper also presents the relevant solution techniques used for each planning level. A review on the current state of CTM models concludes by highlighting the unaddressed areas or the gaps existing in the current literatures and by suggesting directions for future research in CTM.

Keywords: Collaborative Transportation Management (CTM), collaborative structure, planning level, solution method, supply chain management, information sharing, model.

1. INTRODUCTION

Logistics nowadays is influenced by globalization in responding to changing demand of the consumer, mass production, and customization (Gereffi, 2001). The globalization increases business competitiveness and provides competitive advantages to different parties in the supply chain, especially in the transportation area. These situations along with the rising operating costs cause fierce competition among transportation companies and force them to run an efficient operation. An efficient operation requires a type of collaboration where each party involved in the transportation area has the same objective to get a better operation result and is more concerned with the optimization objectives for all of the parties involved rather than for an individual one (Mason et al., 2007).

Collaborative Transportation Management (CTM) is an emerging model of collaboration in the transportation area (Tyan et al., 2003). VICS (2004) and Li and Chan (2012) define CTM as a holistic process that not only does it bring all parties together in the supply chain to drive inefficiencies out of the transportation planning and execution process but also it improves the operating performances of all parties through collaboration. Some of the benefits of CTM are the reduction in increase load capacity usage, the travelling time, and reduction in transportation costs, particularly the back-haul costs, when two transportations combine to minimize the distance (VICS, 2004). Several researchers such as Browning and White (2000), Sutherland (2003), Esper and Williams (2003), and Bishop (2004) state the needs to incorporate CTM into logistics to avoid logistics bottlenecks, reduce inefficiency, and provide mutual benefits for all collaborative parties. In addition, CTM can reduce the inventory-holding cost, increase the responsiveness, and synchronize the activities in logistics efficiently (Ozener, 2008).

CTM in the supply chain has become a topic of great interest to researchers and practitioners. Many researchers have developed models of CTM in the supply chain that emphasizes different issues, such as on operation efficiency, cost minimization, profit maximization, or a combination of them as their objectives. However, the issues on behavioral aspects that arise from the collaborative transportation have not been explored. Although the CTM models could be used in different types of collaboration, depending on the subject and scope of collaboration, many researchers have only used the CTM models in the

scope of vertical collaboration and operational level. In consequence, there are still many research areas that could be addressed to effectively consider and evaluate any possible applications of the models in different scopes of collaboration to create optimal scenarios for collaborative parties in different planning levels.

Due to the lack of CTM literatures and the aim to develop a better understanding on CTM, a systematic literature review that can point out both the importance of CTM in the supply chain and the exploration of various CTM models is required. This paper provides a literature review on the state of the art in the CTM areas, the unaddressed CTM areas, and the research gaps in CTM by classifying the previous literatures into several categories, which are based on four dimensions, such as collaborative structure, general characteristics, collaborative planning levels, and solution methodologies.

This paper is organized as follows. First, CTM is defined based on the summary of the previous literatures. Second, the methods for the systematic review are described. Third, the classification of the existing literatures is also described. Fourth, the previous literatures are examined based on the classification. Next, the discussion on the results of the systematic review is presented. Finally, the conclusion and research opportunities are presented.

2. COLLABORATIVE TRANSPORTATION MANAGEMENT (CTM)

In logistics and transportation areas, many opportunities arise from developing collaboration when firms work together to achieve common goals that bring mutual benefits to all parties (Min et al., 2005). Similar to that, Simatupang and Sridharan (2002) state that a better result for all collaborative parties can be achieved by working together through data information sharing, a joint decision making, and benefit sharing.

Under the Voluntary Inter-industry Commerce Standards (VICS, 2004), it is stated that CTM complements logistics collaboration after an order is generated via Collaboration Planning Forecasting Replenishment (CPFR). CPFR requires trading partners to collaborate on sales and demand planning activities as well as on an order placement that uses technologies to improve both the accuracy of sales order forecast and the subsequent replenishment orders. Several transportation and distribution activities that are not included in CPFR, such as: ship-ments, modes or carrier assignments, scheduling, tracks, and traces can be done by CTM (VICS, 2004). CTM represents a new application of logistics col-laboration to ensure that the benefits of CPFR are properly executed and expanded in the transporta-tion area.

According to Tyan et al. (2003), CTM is a new busi-ness model, which is based on information sharing in which carriers, as a strategic partner in logistic collaboration, is included. Esper and Williams (2003) state that CTM adds value to a collaborative rela-tionship and an entire collaboration process, includ-ing transportation that provide services. In addition, Feng and Yuan (2007) and Chan and Zhang (2011) state that CTM is based on an interaction among lo-gistics parties in order to improve the flexibility in the physical distributions and to minimize the inef-ficiency in the transportation components.

In this paper, CTM is defined as a transportation process which is based on the interaction, coordina-tion, and collaboration among the shippers, receiv-ers, and transportation service providers involved in the logistics process. The aims of CTM are not only to reduce inefficiency and cost in the transportation but also to provide mutual benefits to all parties.

3. METHOD

The research method for conducting the systematic review on CTM in the supply chain can be seen in Figure 1. The first step was conducting the web-based search from Proquest, Science Direct, SpringerLink, Taylor and Francis database, and recommendation from peers to identify the potential relevant articles,

raging from Dissertation Abstracts, Papers, and Sci-ences Citation Index (SCI). The search used different combinations of keywords, such as: "supply chain" and "supply chain collaboration"; "transportation" and "collaborative transportation"; "collabora-tive formation" and "collaborative structure"; and "planning level" and "planning horizon". In addi-tion, the keywords such as "solution method" were used to find every related article in this field. From these keywords combinations, 228 articles from dif-ferent journals and publications were found. In the second step, to search for the relevant publications, the key word "CTM" was used. With the keyword, 65 articles were obtained. In this step, both irrelevant articles and the same articles were removed (some articles were obtained by using different search en-gines). These articles come from the database con-taining abstracts and the full papers.

In the third step, an in-depth content analysis to the 65 articles was performed. Based on the analysis of the titles as well as the abstracts of both the ar-ticles and the full papers, 27 of the 65 articles were selected. The 27 articles were selected because they contained the topic concerning the significance of CTM, the implementation of CTM, the contribution of various CTM models, the planning levels of CTM, and methodologies of CTM. The articles that did not contain the relevant topic on CTM were therefore excluded. The remaining 38 articles were excluded because they focused on urban transportation, not on CTM models. Figure 2 shows the distribution of the CTM literatures by year. It can be seen that in the last couple of years the number of articles has been increased. However, there has been no relevant con-tribution to the CTM models between 2014 and 2015.

Figure 1. Methods of Literature Review

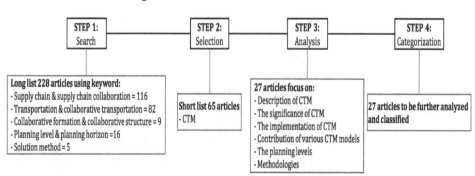

Figure 2. Literature Review by Year

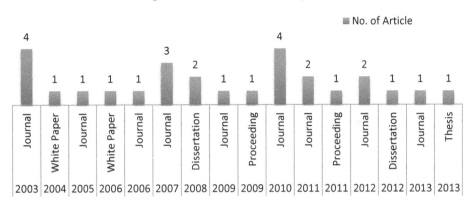

3.1 The Classification of CTM Models

Based on analysis of literatures, to systematically classify the literatures the classification framework for the literature review of CTM is based on four dimensions. The four dimensions of the classification namely collaborative structure, general characteristics, collaborative planning level, and solution methodologies. The classification of the literatures can be seen in Figure 3.

The first dimension describes the distinction between the parties involved and the scope of the collaboration made under the collaborative structure categories, i.e., vertical, horizontal, and lateral collaboration. This refers to CTM definition where the parties of supply chain as receiver, shipper, and carrier establish collaboration in transportation in several collaborative structures based on the interaction between logistics parties. The second dimension reflects the general characteristics of each collaboration and CTM models. In the previous literatures, each collaboration and CTM model were developed

to understand the transportation problem and to evaluate the benefits of collaboration in transportation area for all collaborative parties. Each collaboration also caused several problems in the process. Based on analysis of literatures, CTM also employed the planning horizon and decision-making process in the collaboration process to coordinate the plans of several partners to achieve CTM objectives. Planning and decision-making process in CTM can be formulated into different planning levels, depending on the time horizon and the importance of the problem. Therefore, the third dimension of collaborative planning perspective is based on the planning decisions level, such as: strategic, tactical, and operational planning level.

The fourth dimension is used to review and classify the literatures according to the relevant solution method of each CTM model. Several methods are used to optimize and solve complicated problems related to CTM. It is very important and very challenging to find a solution method for the problems related to CTM.

Figure 3: The Classification of CTM Models

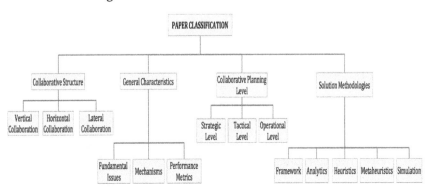

3.1.1 Collaborative Structure

According to VICS (2004) CTM focuses on enhancing the interaction and collaboration not only between the three principal parties: a shipper, a receiver, and a carrier, but also among the secondary participants such as the third-party logistics service providers (3PL). In this paper, CTM among the parties is classified into three categories: vertical, horizontal, and lateral collaboration based on a collaborative structure, depending on the parties involved and the scope of the collaboration (Simatupang and Sridharan, 2002; Soosay et al., 2006; and Zamboni, 2011).

Vertical Collaboration concerns two or more organizations, such as a receiver, a shipper, and a carrier, which share their responsibilities, resources, and data information to serve relatively similar end customers. *Horizontal Collaboration* concerns two or more unrelated or competing organizations that cooperate by sharing their private information or resources such as joint transportation mode between two carriers. *Lateral Collaboration* aims to gain more flexibility by combining and sharing capabilities both vertically and horizontally.

3.1.2 General Characteristics

CTM is formulated based on several general characteristics such as fundamental issues, mechanisms, and performance metrics. Certain issues arising from the logistics process are recorded in the previous literatures. The issues are on increasing an efficient and reliable product delivery, increasing a usage capacity, reducing cost, and increasing competitiveness. Furthermore, the mechanisms of CTM by both resources and information sharing are developed to ensure a common unity of effort and ensure benefits for all collaborative parties. Engaging the parties in CTM not only gives significant benefits for them but also improve their understanding on CTM and management of CTM. The performance metrics used by previous researchers covered cost, transportation parameters, inventory investment, and inventory level reduction.

3.1.3 Collaborative Planning Level

Several problems could be arising during the collaboration process. Because of these problems, the third category is based on the collaborative planning levels among the collaborative parties. This type of category would potentially help distinguish all par-

ties' proper planning, decision-making, and coordination of decisions in achieving their expected goals of CTM. There are three levels of a collaborative planning proposed for each transportation problem that represent decision making process depending on the time horizon (VICS, 2004; Ilyas et al., 2005; and Meyr et al., 2005).

The first level is the *strategic level*. It functions as the front-end agreement, the foundation for the entire supply chain process, and as an essential part of supply chain management. Strategic level is classified into *strategic partnership model* and the *network model*. *Strategic Partnership Model* is a formalized agreement to develop a collaboration relationship. To make the relationship works, benefit, risk, and commitment sharing are determined, and limitations that could reduce potential benefits are identified. *Network Model* uses static route/continuous movement programs to optimize the loading management. Carriers may collaborate either with shippers and or with other carriers.

The second collaborative planning level is the *tactical level* that focuses on shipment requirements to improve transportation utilization and efficiency. Tactical level is classified into *order and shipment forecasting model* and *carrier assignment model*. The purpose of *Order and Shipment Forecasting Model* is to improve the efficiency and utilization of transportation mode, while the purpose of *Carrier Assignment Model* is to map different carrier used in the logistics process. *Carrier Assignment Model* is developed based on a shipment order.

The third collaborative planning level is the *operational level*, which covers the process flow to fulfill the customer's orders on daily basis, and it is concerned with the efficient operation. This level has three models: *scheduling model, route model,* and *order processing model*. *Scheduling Model* is developed on a daily basis based on a carrier assignment in the tactical planning level by optimizing shipments. *Route Model* is developed based on the network model in the strategic level to reduce transportation costs effectively through reduced distances and traveling time. *Order Processing Model* is developed based on an information system and a technology used to support information exchange.

3.1.4 Solution Methodologies

The current literatures indicate that many techniques have been proposed to solve problems and calculate optimization in the CTM area. These proposed solution techniques could be classified into five categories. *Framework* as the first solution technique is divided into a theoretical framework and a conceptual framework. The aim of the framework is to improve the understanding on how CTM concepts perform. *Analytics* as the second solution technique uses mathematical models that have a closed form of solution and is used to describe changes in a system. The third solution technique is *heuristics*. Heuristics is not guaranteed to be an optimal solution, but it is used to speed up the process of finding an optimal solution. The fourth solution technique is *metaheuristics*. It is a higher-level solution procedure that provides a sufficiently good solution for an optimization problem, especially for a problem with incomplete or imperfect information and having a limited computation capacity. The last solution technique is *simulation*. This technique is used to show the effects of an action on either a system or a real life.

4. FINDINGS

The review of literatures is divided into three major groups. The first group of literature review examines the state of the art of the previous literatures, which are essential for the development of the vertical collaboration. The second group of literature review examines the state of the art of the horizontal collaboration, and the last group of literature review examines the lateral collaboration. The previous literatures of each group are summarized in Appendix 1. To differentiate one group of literature review from another one, the general characteristics as decision variables, CTM models in three collaborative planning levels, and solution methods are used as the classification bases, can be seen in Table 1.

Table 1. Classification of Literature Review

AUTHOR	GENERAL CHARACTERISTICS			CTM MODEL			SOLUTION METHOD
	FUNDAMEN-TAL ISSUES	COLLABORA-TION MECHA-NISM	PERFORMANCE INDICATORS	STRATEGIC LEVEL	TACTICAL LEVEL	OPERATION-AL LEVEL	
Tyan et al. (2003)	Capacity issue, improving service levels, reducing cost, and increasing competitiveness	Information and data sharing, sharing benefit	Transportation parameters			Order Processing Model	ANALYTICS (Empirical Research)
Esper and William (2003)	Reducing cost, inefficient and unreliable product delivery	Information and data sharing	Cost saving, transportation parameters			Order Processing Model	ANALYTICS (Empirical Research)
Caplice and Seffi (2003)	Reducing cost, and increasing competitiveness	Information and data sharing, sharing benefit	Cost saving, transportation parameters	Strategic Partnership Model			ANALYTICS (Optimization-Based Procurement)
Feng et al. (2005)	Capacity issue, reducing cost, inefficient and unreliable product delivery	Information and data sharing	Cost saving, transportation parameters, inventory level/cost		Carrier Assignment Model		SIMULATION (Beer Game)
Audy et al. (2006)	Reducing cost, inefficient and unreliable product delivery	Sharing resources, information and data sharing		Strategic Partnership Model			FRAMEWORK (Business Model Coalition)
Ergun et al. (2007)	Reducing cost	Sharing resources	Cost saving, transportation parameters	Network Model			HEURISTICS (Greedy Merge Heuristics)

VERTICAL COLLABORATION

Table 1. Classification of Literature Review (Cont.)

AUTHOR	GENERAL CHARACTERISTICS			CTM MODEL			SOLUTION METHOD
	FUNDAMENTAL ISSUES	COLLABORATION MECHANISM	PERFORMANCE INDICATORS	STRATEGIC LEVEL	TACTICAL LEVEL	OPERATIONAL LEVEL	
			VERTICAL COLLABORATION				
Feng and Yuan (2007)	Improving service levels and reducing cost	Information and data sharing	Cost saving, transportation parameters			Order Processing Model	ANALYTICS (Empirical Research)
Kayikci (2009)	Improving service levels, reducing cost, and increasing competitiveness	Information and data sharing	Cost saving, revenue, customer satisfaction, inventory level/cost	Strategic Partnership Model			ANALYTICS (Partial Least Square)
Chen et al. (2010)	Reducing cost	Information and data sharing	Cost saving, inventory level/cost			Order Processing Model	ANALYTICS (Transcendental Logarithmic)
Silva et al. (2011)	Reducing cost	Information and data sharing, sharing benefit, and managing trust	Revenue	Strategic Partnership Model			SIMULATION (Agent-Based & System Dynamic)
Gonzalez-Feliu and Morana (2011)	Reducing cost	Sharing resources, information and data sharing, sharing risk		Strategic Partnership Model			FRAMEWORK (Logistics Sharing)
Li and Chan (2012)	Improving service levels, reducing cost, inefficient and unreliable delivery	Information and data sharing, sharing risk	Cost saving, transportation parameters, revenue, and inventory level/cost			Order Processing Model	SIMULATION (Agent-Based)

Table 1. Classification of Literature Review (Cont.)

AUTHOR / FUNDAMENTAL ISSUES	GENERAL CHARACTERISTICS			CTM MODEL		SOLUTION METHOD
	COLLABORATION MECHANISM	PERFORMANCE INDICATORS	STRATEGIC LEVEL	TACTICAL LEVEL	OPERATIONAL LEVEL	
VERTICAL COLLABORATION						
Moll (2012)	Improving service levels and increasing competitiveness	Information and data sharing, sharing benefit	Cost saving, transportation parameters, and revenue		Scheduling Model	ANALYTICS (Empirical Research)
Wen (2012)	Increasing competitiveness, inefficient and unreliable product delivery	Information and data sharing		Strategic Partnership Model		ANALYTICS (Factor Analysis)
HORIZONTAL COLLABORATION						
Song and Regan (2003)	Reducing cost and increasing competitiveness	Sharing resources, sharing benefit	Cost saving	Strategic Partnership Model		ANALYTICS (Quasi Linier)
Nadarajah (2008)	Reducing cost and increasing competitiveness	Sharing resources	Cost saving, revenue		Route Model	METAHEURISTICS (Tabu Search & Guided Local Search)
Asawasakulsorn (2009)	Capacity issue and reducing cost	Sharing resources, managing trust		Strategic Partnership Model		ANALYTICS (Simple & Multi Regression)
Fisk et al. (2010)	Reducing cost, inefficient and unreliable product delivery	Sharing resources, sharing benefit	Cost saving, transportation parameters	Strategic Partnership Model		ANALYTICS (Linier Programming)

Table 1. *Classification of Literature Review (Cont.)*

AUTHOR FUNDAMENTAL ISSUES	GENERAL CHARACTERISTICS			CTM MODEL		SOLUTION METHOD
	COLLABORATION MECHANISM	PERFORMANCE INDICATORS	STRATEGIC LEVEL	TACTICAL LEVEL	OPERATIONAL LEVEL	
HORIZONTAL COLLABORATION						
Liu et al. (2010)	Reducing cost, increasing competitiveness	Sharing resources, sharing benefit	Cost saving	Strategic Partnership Model		SIMULATION (Weighted Relative Savings Model)
Audy et al. (2010)	Reducing cost	Sharing resources, sharing benefit	Cost saving	Strategic Partnership Model		SIMULATION (Game Theory-Equal Profit Method)
Peeta and Hernandez (2011)	Capacity issue, reducing cost, inefficient and unreliable product delivery	Sharing resources, information and data sharing	Cost saving, transportation parameters, revenue		Route Model	SIMULATION (Mixed Logit-Simulation Based Maximum Likelihood)
Taherian (2013)	Reducing cost, inefficient and unreliable product delivery	Sharing resources	Cost saving, transportation parameters, revenue	Strategic Partnership Model		ANALYTICS (Empirical Research)
LATERAL COLLABORATION						
VICS (2004)	Capacity issue, improving service level, reducing cost, increasing competitiveness, inefficient delivery	Sharing resources, information and data sharing, managing trust, sharing benefit, sharing risks	Cost saving, transportation parameters, revenue, customer satisfaction, inventory level/cost	Strategic Partnership Model		FRAMEWORK (Selecting Partner)

AUTHOR / FUNDAMENTAL ISSUES	GENERAL CHARACTERISTICS			CTM MODEL		SOLUTION METHOD
	COLLABORATION MECHANISM	PERFORMANCE INDICATORS	STRATEGIC LEVEL	TACTICAL LEVEL	OPERATIONAL LEVEL	
LATERAL COLLABORATION						
Sutherland (2006)	Capacity issue, improving service level, reducing cost, increasing competitiveness, inefficient and unreliable product delivery	Sharing resources, information and data sharing, managing trust, sharing benefit, sharing risks	Cost saving, transportation parameters, revenue, customer satisfaction, inventory level/cost	Strategic Partnership Model		FRAMEWORK (Selecting Partner)
Mason et al. (2007)	Reducing cost, inefficient and unreliable product delivery	Sharing resources, information and data sharing, sharing benefit	Cost saving, transportation parameters, revenue, customer satisfaction, inventory level/cost		Order Processing Model	ANALYTICS (Empirical Research)
Ozener (2008)	Reducing cost	Sharing resources, information and data sharing, sharing benefit	Cost saving	Network Model	Route Model	HEURISTICS (Shapley Value & Mixed Integer Linier Programming)
Gonzalez-Feliu et al. (2013)	Reducing cost	Sharing resources, sharing benefit	Cost saving	Strategic Partnership Model		SIMULATION (Clustering Phase)

4.1 Vertical Collaboration

In this section, the collaboration among parties in the same supply chain, known as the vertical collaboration will be discussed. Each collaborative planning level will be discussed separately. In addition, the general characteristics and the variety of solution methodologies will be discussed.

4.1.1 Strategic Level

The strategic planning model to improve performances takes into account the long-term interests of all collaborative parties and their decisions on both suitable businesses and operational policies. Audy et al. (2006) and Gonzalez-Feliu and Morana (2011) used a similar approach to develop a framework for the strategic partnership model. Audy et al. (2006) proposed a series of business models to build a collaborative transportation coalition. Also, Gonzalez-Feliu and Morana (2011) developed a conceptual framework model that summarizes the organizational model and sharing analysis factors, including information sharing in the context of the press distribution sector in France.

The models in the above-mentioned research (Audy et al., 2006; Gonzalez-Feliu and Morana, 2011), need to be implemented and their performance indicators need to be measured to facilitate the evaluation of the strategic decisions. In Audy et al. (2006), managing trust and sharing risk were not included as a mechanism of collaboration. On the other hand Gonzales-Feliu and Morana (2011) included several types of risk (financial risk, technology risk, and policy risk) but still did not include how the collaborative parties interact and how the collaborative parties manage a trust.

Caplice and Seffi (2003) discussed the network model in which shippers could procure transportation services by underpinning the optimization of a conditional bidding for carriers so that the shippers can quantify and compare the levels of services with the carriers' rates. The approach introduced by Caplice and Seffi (2003) can be used as a marketing tool by carriers to help a better understanding for shippers' clients on how to place value on their specific services. The limitation of this research is that they only used one aspect of the process, which is a procurement that uses a bidding method. Therefore, the sharing information process, the impact of the bidding method, the interaction, and the synergies among collaborative parties are still not covered.

Wen (2012) on the other hand, used the Exploratory Factor Analysis to identify the key factors associated with CTM practices, such as the logistics capability and competitive advantage for carriers. Similarly, Kayikci (2009) showed the impact of CTM's implementation process on intermodal freight transportation by developing a path model. Both studies provide empirical evidence to support a conceptual framework regarding the impact of CTM for carriers and the implementation of CTM practices. The limitation of the research (Wen, 2012 and Kayikci, 2009) is that quantifying the benefits and impacts of CTM for carriers and supply chain partners was not carried out.

Ergun et al. (2007) used heuristics as a solution method to assist the identification of dedicated truckload's continuous moving tours for the time-constrained lane-covering problem. Ergun et al. (2007) conducted computational experiments on slightly simplified instances, in which they did not consider loading and unloading times, and they used the algorithm that ignored Hours of Service regulations. In addition, Silva et al. (2011) studied the problem of reducing freight costs in the export process between the industries of manufacture goods and the maritime carriers. They used the strategic scope of relationship to see the collaboration role of each party in response to either party-to-party interactions or each party's interaction with the environment. They used the System Dynamics (SD) and Agent Based Modeling and Simulation (ABMS) as their solution methodologies. Due to the limitation of factual data in this research, the suggested results did not represent the real world's negotiations and information sharing in them. Silva et al. (2011) also omitted both the risk and trust mechanism in the model.

4.1.2 Tactical Level

Companies make medium-term decisions at the tactical level to define the process based on a general planning at a strategic level. Feng et al. (2005) proposed a concept of CTM and a framework for evaluating CTM. They also elaborated how CTM affects the supply chain's total costs and transportation capacity utilization. The simulation of beer game model was used to consider transportation capacity. The limitation of this research is that it had no complete analysis of actual CTM to obtain more real effects on the supply chain.

4.1.3 Operational Level

The operational level deals with the day-to-day process, a decision-making, and a planning that make supply chain process run smoothly, achieve maximum benefits, and increase performances. Moll (2012) shows that a short-term timetable planning in an operational process could achieve high productivity of freight railways. However, the potential benefits are not equally divided for all collaborative parties, due to a heterogenic transportation planning process. This research contributes to a better understanding of operational level of Switzerland's rail freight and shows the applicability of research in practices. Because the approach is incompatible with the operational process of the freight railways in Europe, this research could not be used as the foundation for the implementation of collaboration on an operational strategy.

Many researchers (Tyan et al., 2003; Esper and William, 2003; Feng and Yuan, 2007; and Chen et al., 2010) pointed out that information sharing and information technology in CTM could increase performances. Feng and Yuan (2007), Tyan et al. (2003) and Chen et al. (2010) used Notebook industry in Taiwan as their case study. Tyan et al. (2003) pointed out the benefits of CTM in three performance indicators, such as: shipment volume, delivery performance, and delivery cycle time. However, Feng and Yuan (2007) used different performance indicators, such as: on-time delivery, shipment visibility, transportation cost, and tracking cycle time to emphasize the benefits of CTM. Chen et al. (2010) tried to use a different approach by developing the cost function based on an actual operation. Chen et al. (2010) showed that the higher accuracy of CTM and the higher degree of information sharing resulted in saving costs in the supply chain.

In addition, Esper and William (2003) used a different industry to point out information sharing and information technology in CTM by measuring transportation cost, on-time performance, asset utilization, and administrative cost. The limitations of this research (Tyan et al., 2003; Esper and William, 2003; Feng and Yuan, 2007; Chen et al., 2010) are that both the interaction among collaborative parties and collaborative parties' problems related to trust, technology risk, and operational risk, when associated with information technology in CTM, were not explored.

Li and Chan (2012), on the other hand, proposed the interactions among different supply chain partners under a demand disruption. This research showed that CTM was efficient to handle risk in the supply chain when a demand disruption occurred. However, this research only used a virtual company as its calculation basis. Therefore, a company that uses reliable data needs to be explored to provide better evidence on the benefits of information sharing in CTM. The limitation of conducting research in this operational level is that there is no previous studies that point out how each collaborative party interact with another party in making its decision on a delivery route.

4.2 Horizontal Collaboration

In horizontal collaboration, the total cost of supply chain is used as a key issue in performance measurement (Prakash and Deshmukh, 2010).

4.2.1 Strategic Level

The strategic level provides an overall direction by determining the objectives, developing policies, and plans based on the consideration of resource allocation and environment (Nag et al., 2007). With the same direction, Song and Regan (2003) proposed the feasibility of the auction as a basis for the procurement in the horizontal collaboration. They conclude that the auction method is more efficient than both the long-term agreement and the spot market. The limitations of this research were that Song and Regan (2003) did not explore how information sharing process in the auction process was conducted and how transportation companies could separate profitable opportunities from unprofitable ones in the auction procurement.

Asawasakulsorn (2009) developed five selection criteria, based on economic concept, to select partners to join the collaboration. There are some limitations in this research, i.e., using a non-probabilistic sampling. Therefore, the relationship among all collaborative parties could not be measured, and the benefits of collaboration could not be evaluated. Taherian (2013) developed a practical guideline for companies that intend to engage in the horizontal collaboration. Taherian (2013) evaluated the benefits of the total savings by a network synergy of 6 companies that were engaged in the horizontal collaboration. The limitation of this research is that Taherian (2013) did not evaluate the performance indicators other than the cost savings.

Audy et al. (2010) and Frisk et al. (2010), on the other hand, used a different approach to develop a policy in the strategic level by proposing an agreement among collaborative parties on how cost savings could be shared among them. Both research pointed out the cost could be shared among collaborative parties, and the impact of cost sharing could be evaluated. The limitation of the research conducted by Audy et al. (2010) is that they excluded the evaluation on how cost savings could be shared among collaborative parties. On the other hand, Frisk et al. (2010) evaluated the impact of cost sharing more comprehensively on backhauling, time periods, geographical distributions, and coalition sizes. The limitation of the research (Audy et al., 2010; and Frisk et al., 2010) is that they excluded the negotiation process when the companies have different negotiating powers. They also did not evaluate how information was shared among collaborative parties,, how collaborative parties interacted, and how trust among collaborative parties is maintained, and how cost was shared equally.

Liu et al. (2010) demonstrated a profit allocation mechanism among collaborative parties to ensure the establishment and sustainability of the alliance for small and medium sized LTL carriers. The results of the simulation for the real-life data showed the effectiveness of the proposed model. However, due to the limitation of the horizontal collaboration in the transportation industry, the research conducted by Liu et al. (2010) only used three carrier companies as its samples. Therefore, this research needs to adopt the model that is proposed for the practical application.

4.2.2 Operational Level

The decisions in this level include taking orders for shipment and the movement of goods from a point of origin to a destination point. Only two researchers (Peeta and Hernandez, 2011; and Nadarajah, 2008) developed a route models for the operational level. Peeta and Hernandez (2011) explored the LTL collaboration from the perspective of small to medium-sized LTL carriers. This research indicated that the carrier collaboration increased the capacity utilization thereby increasing the revenue of empty-haul trips and decreasing the impacts to the fuel cost. Peeta and Hernandez (2011) used a combination of multivariate techniques and the mixed logit model to determine the probability of a carrier. The significance of variables illustrates that LTL carriers are concerned with the potential economic impacts and the possibility of forming collaborative alliances. The limitation of this research is that it did not quantify and explore the impact of performance indicators of collaborative parties on the benefits for the parties engaged in the horizontal collaboration.

Nadarajah (2008), on the other hand, proposed a carrier collaboration framework in order to reduce deadhead miles and to increase carriers' revenue. In addition, this research explores CTM related to green transportation by showing that CTM can reduce congestion and pollution by using metaheuristics as its solution method. However, Nadajarah (2008) did not explore how the collaborative parties interact to one another in order to align each collaborative party's own objectives.

4.3 Lateral Collaboration

Many companies get involved in either the vertical collaboration or horizontal collaboration. However, combining both the vertical and horizontal collaboration into practice is not easy to implement. The objective of the lateral collaboration is to get the benefits from both the vertical collaboration and horizontal collaboration (Mason et al., 2007).

4.3.1 Strategic Level

VICS (2004) and Sutherland (2006) used the framework model to describe the variables that are relevant to the transportation problems by using the CTM approach as a guidance to solve the problems. According to VICS (2004) and Sutherland (2006) there are four key variables for CTM, and they explain what key enablers that facilitate the success of CTM. Both research also reported the performance benefits of CTM's pilot initiatives in various companies and settings in the U.S. starting in 1999.

Ozener (2008) developed the network model and combined it with the routing model. Ozener (2008) developed his research in three stages. At the first stage, the shippers offered continuous move routes to the carriers in return for the reduction in per mile charges. Both the second stage and the third stage will be explained on the operational level. The limitation of this study is that Ozener (2008) did not explore the negotiation process and did not explore the risk that could be arising in an uncertain condition in both the network and route model.

On the other hand, Gonzalez-Feliu et al. (2013) developed an integrated approach between the vertical and horizontal collaboration in transportation and proposed a framework to support the main strategic planning decisions from a group viewpoint. This framework evaluates a strategic planning decision based on a hierarchical cluster analysis and a decision ranking method by using five possible strategies for collaborative transportation. Gonzales-Feliu et al. (2013) showed that the method could be applied to support a group of heterogeneous decision makers in implementing collaboration strategy. However, the method was not able to capture both the real interactions and the real negotiations in the process. Its other performance criteria, such as the quality and service accuracy in a strategic decision-making also needs to be evaluated

4.3.2 Operational Level

Both the second stage and the third stage of the research conducted by Ozener (2008) relate not only to the development of the route model to reduce both the transportation and distribution cost but also to the evaluation of fair benefits sharing among them. The example is the carriers exchange loads among themselves to reduce empty repositioning and to increase truck utilization. At the third stage, under the vendor management inventory, the replenishment among customers due to their locations, usage rates, and storage capacities, may be exploited to reduce the distribution costs. This model was developed to serve the nearby customers on the same route at the same time. One result of the research done by Ozener (2008) showed that the proposed methods performed significantly better than the proportional allocation methods used in practice. Another result also demonstrated that the proposed methods are computationally efficient.

Mason et al. (2007) conducted three case studies to illustrate the advantages of collaboration among supply chain partners that used information technology system, such as: Internet and RFID. Several performances that were evaluated in this research were cost reduction, service levels, visibility, end customer satisfaction, and many others. The limitations of this research are that Mason et al. (2007) did not evaluate the transportation performance indicators, the risk arising from the information sharing and information technology, and the interaction among the parties who were engaged, and how trust was developed and maintained by each party.

5. DISCUSSION

This paper reviews 27 articles gathered from Proquest, Science Direct, Taylor and Francis database. This paper also includes athe recommendation from peers that relate to the description, implementa-

tion, planning levels, and methodologies of CTM, and contribution of various CTM models. From 27 articles reviewed show the benefits of CTM on the vertical, horizontal, and lateral collaboration. Various performance indicators are evaluated to point out the benefits of implementing CTM. Even though all of the articles point out the benefits of CTM, there are still some limitations of the previous research.

The vertical collaboration, also known as the traditional collaboration, is the most well formed type collaboration used in the area of CTM. However there are several limitations existing in the current literatures. Wen (2012), Caplice and Seffi (2003), and Kayikci (2009) developed a strategic partnership model although quantifying the benefits and impacts of CTM on the carriers and supply chain partners was not integrated into it. However, previous researchers only identified the benefits and impacts of CTM by indicating several performance indicators without analyzing the interactions and relationships of a partnership's elements, such as: commitment, trust management of collaborative parties, conflict resolution, and risk sharing. On the other hand, Silva et al. (2011) tried to explore the shortcomings of previous literatures by examining the interactions among collaborative parties and benefits of CTM.

In tactical level, only one article was found. It was written by Feng et al. (2005). They developed a carrier assignment model to evaluate effects of CTM on the supply chain, such as: total costs and transportation capacity utilization. Nevertheless, there is no complete analysis of actual CTM in evaluating upstream suppliers of manufacturers and downstream retailers or customers of the distributors to obtain more real effects of CTM on the supply chain. Moreover, no literature discusses the research in the order and shipment forecasting model.

Some research has been dedicated to develop order-processing models to point out the benefits of CTM (Tyan et al., 2003; Esper and William, 2003; Feng and Yuan, 2007; and Chen et al., 2010). However, pointing out the benefits of CTM is not enough only by presenting how CTM works in the operational level. Li and Chan (2012), on the other hand, seem to answer the shortcomings of the previous research by showing the operational interactions among supply chain partners under a demand disruption. This research only explored one risk in the supply chain and used a virtual company as its calculation basis. Several risks, such as technology risks and operational risks, arise from the collaborative transportation, particularly when it relates to the order processing model was not explored.

The horizontal collaboration has been gaining attention as a new business model that can make the transportation and logistics sector more efficient, effective, and sustainable. However, until today there are still limitations related to the horizontal collaboration in practice and research area due to its complex nature. All previous research focused on the horizontal collaboration at the strategic level only developed strategic partnership models. Asawasakulsorn (2009) and Taherian (2013) did not evaluate the performance indicators except for the cost savings on the horizontal collaboration. Audy et al. (2010), Fisk et al. (2010), and Liu et al. (2010) provided the evaluation of performance indicators on the horizontal collaboration. However, they did not evaluate information sharing process, interactions among collaborative parties, and trust management that related to information sharing among collaborative parties in order to share the cost equally.

On the other hand, Peeta and Hernandez (2011) developed a route model, but this research did not quantify and explore the impact and the benefits of CTM in the horizontal collaboration. In addition, the research done by Nadarajah (2008) showed that by conducting CTM, congestion and pollution could be reduced. The limitation of the research in the horizontal collaboration, particularly at the operational level, is that the research emphasized neither on the interaction and information sharing among all parties in the collaboration nor on how the uncertainty in operational process could impact the decision-making.

In order to manage the transportation within the supply chain setting, it is important to understand the characteristics of modern supply chain management by combining both the horizontal and vertical forms of collaboration (Mason et al, 2007). The lateral collaboration is also being exploited as a new collaboration approach to create superior value adding solutions to many supply chains. In the strategic level, VICS (2004) and Sutherland (2006) used the framework model to give guidance for a decision-making to use the CTM models in each planning level and in selecting partners for CTM, as one of the stages in the strategic level. In addition, Gonzalez-Feliu et al. (2013) developed a decision-making model in the strategic level. However, Gonzalez-Feliu et al. (2013) did not take into account the negotiation process, information sharing, interactions among collaborative

parties, trusts management, and risk management as the foundations in a decision-making process.

Concerning the operational level, Mason et al. (2007) illustrates that the use of information technology will increase the performance indicators in CTM. However, he did not quantify the performance indicators. Therefore, it is difficult to evaluate how significant the advantages of collaboration for each party are. Mason et al. (2007) also did not evaluate the risks arising from the information sharing and information technology that were used by all parties, the interactions that happened among the collaborative parties, and the trust management that was built in the collaboration process. In addition to several limitations explained previously, no one has done research in the tactical level both in the horizontal and lateral collaboration. For this reason, any research in this area will give a better understanding on how CTM can be developed in the tactical level.

Based on the above-mentioned categories, there are six research gaps that are found from previous literatures. The first research gap is that many of the previous research only focused on the optimization of CTM, causing a gap in the exploration of the behaviors and the interactions among parties involved in CTM. Therefore this gap prevents a more realistic understanding on the CTM. The behaviors and interactions among the collaborative parties may significantly influence how operating systems work, perform, and improve (Gino and Pisano, 2008). The second research gap is the limitations regarding the integration of an information structure, based on information sharing, into CTM. Such integration is necessary to formulate a foundation to develop a decision in each planning level and each stage of the collaboration process in order to improve the visibility and the accuracy of a decision-making.

The third research gap is that all previous research did not explore the integration of decision-making into the models in order to get a better result in implementing CTM. Distributed decision-making among collaborative parties leads to increasing agility by synchronizing decisions for each collaborative party that has different objectives and different perspectives (Wadhwa and Rao, 2003).

The fourth research gap is that the previous literatures did not explore how to integrate different stages of the collaboration process into CTM. Interdependent stages of collaboration process among collaborative parties are necessary to be developed in order to capture the interactions among the collaborative parties involved in a transportation planning and execution processes.

The fifth research gap is that all previous literatures did not explore and evaluate the incentive alignment to share risks and benefits for all collaborative parties equally. The incentive alignment can be used as an instrument for motivating and inducing all collaborative parties involved in CTM to join the collaboration by sharing costs, risks, and rewards.

The last research gap is that all the previous literatures already explored several performance indicators to capture the benefits of CTM for all collaborative parties. However, the previous literatures did not explore and evaluate how value co-created among collaborative parties, based on customer value and customer expectations, become the benefits of CTM other than the performance metrics.

To address these research gaps, a proposed framework is developed based on the characteristics of behavior, hierarchical decision-making processes, a soft system approach, and collaborative approach.

Behavioral in Operation Management is defined as the study of human behavior and cognition and their impacts on operating systems and processes (Gino and Pisano, 2008). Carter et al. (2007) also mention that the aim of behavior in Operation Management is to understand people's decision-making processes in order to improve the operation of the supply chain. *A hierarchical decision-making process* is a decision system in which multiple decision makers are involved in a business process and in which it

has a strategic, tactical, and operational levels (Liu, 2010). This hierarchical decision-making process is designed by decisions of each level based on certain rules and behaviors of each individual involved in each collaborative structure. *Soft system* is also used when facing a dynamic and unpredictable situation as well as when goals and objective cannot clearly qualify (Checkland, 2001). Soft system is applied to analyze problem situations in which human perceptions, behaviors, or actions are dominating factors so that the goals can be negotiable (Checkland, 2001). In addition, *collaboration approach*, in several stages, is used in order to capture the interactions, actions, and the effects of decision-making in CTM. The collaboration stages, namely forming, preparation, design, planning, implementation, and evaluation stage, were adopted from Dwyer et al. (1987).

The behaviors of multi-agent's hierarchical decision-making process, as the proposed framework, can be seen in Figure 4. The proposed framework helps to understand and explore the behaviors of the collaborative parties in CTM, the interaction with other parties, and the parties' abilities to make decision in strategic, tactical, and operational level in meeting the goals in each collaboration structure (i.e. vertical, horizontal, and lateral). The behavioral aspect for hierarchical decision-making process in CTM is developed in order to deliver services that lead to value co-creation of collaborative parties. In addition, the proposed framework is also developed to gain a systematic understanding of how and when different objectives and perspectives of collaborative parties affect decision-making process in each collaborative structure.

Figure 4. The Proposed Framework of The Behaviors of Multi-agent's Hierarchical Decision-Making Processes

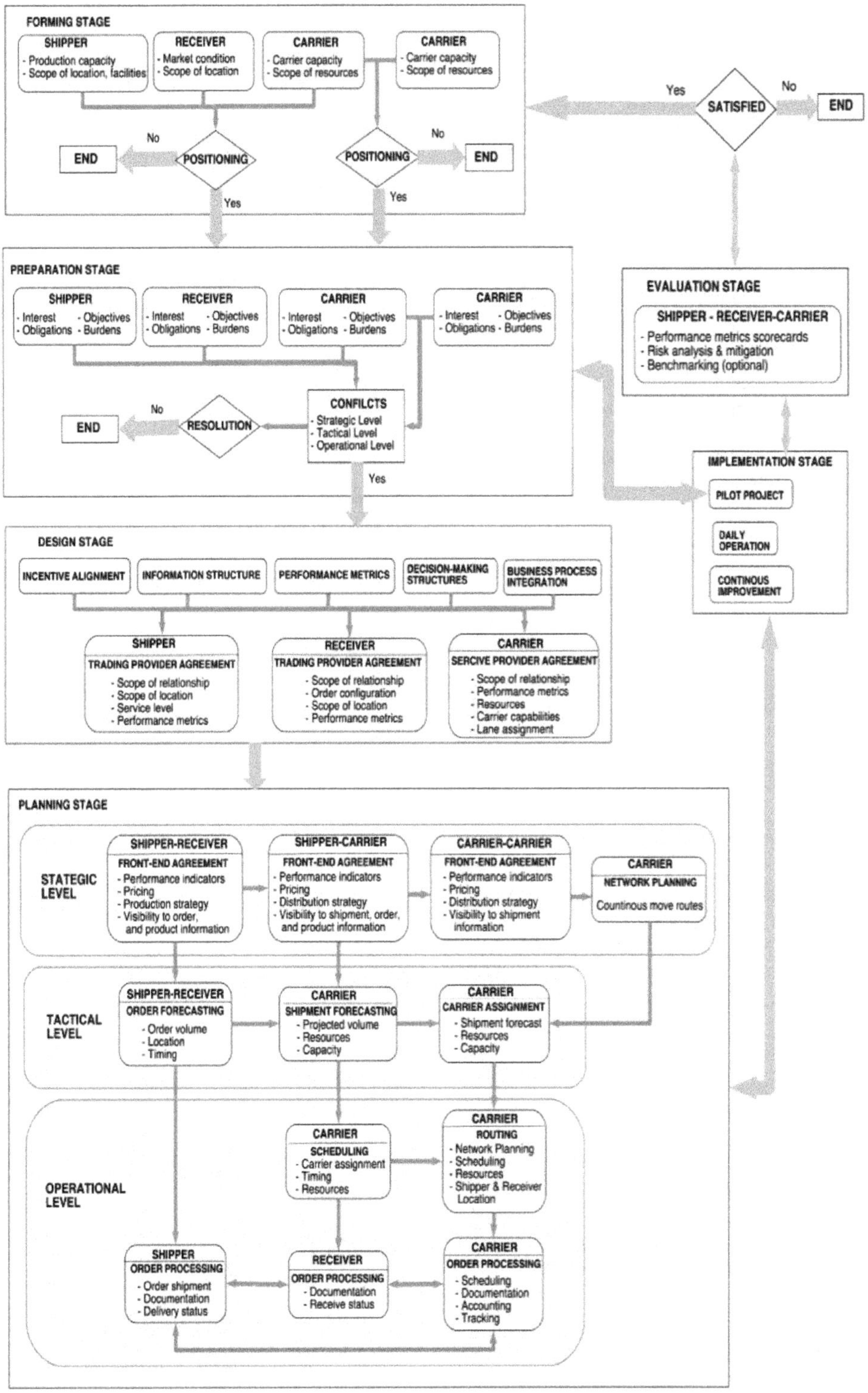

6. CONCLUSIONS

Academics and practitioners recognize CTM as a business strategy to eliminatie inefficiencies in the transportation component. Despite the growing interest in CTM, there are several issues that remain unaddressed. There are 27 articles that have been reviewed and classified based on four categories. The first category is based on the different collaborative structures, namely: the vertical, horizontal, and lateral collaboration. The second category is based on the general characteristics of fundamental issues and collaboration mechanisms. The third category is based on the time horizons of collaborative planning levels such as the strategic, tactical, and operational level. The last category is based on the solution method used to solve the problems that are approached by CTM models. Based on the systematic reviews, several research gaps have been outlined.

Future research on CTM could be taken by developing behavioral models in order to capture the interactions among collaborative parties. Future research should also be focused on the integration of the information structure into both a collaboration process and a hierarchical decision-making. Future research can also be focused on using an incentive alignment to persuade collaborative parties to behave in ways that are best for all by distributing the risks, costs, and rewards fairly among the involved parties. In addition, how useful is the value co-creation of CTM for all collaborative parties can be evaluated.

For future research an agent-based simulation can be proposed as a solution method for a CTM model. This simulation can be used to represent all the details and behaviors of collaborative parties in each collaborative planning level. Furthermore, this simulation can also be used to re-create and enhance the ability to understand, predict, and control a decision-making for the CTM that uses a behavioral approach.

7. REFERENCES

Asawasakulsorn, A. (2009). Transportation Collaboration: Partner Selection Criteria and Inter-Organizational System (IOS) Design Issues for Supporting Trust. *International Journal of Business and Information*, 4 (2), 199–220.

Audy, J.F., D'Amours, S. & Rönnqvist, M. (2006). Business Models for Collaborative Planning in Transportation: An Application to Wood Products. *Frontiers of E-Business Research*.

Audy, J.F., D'Amours, S., &. Rousseau, L.M. (2010). Cost allocation in the establishment of a collaborative transportation agreement-an application in the furniture industry. *The Journal of the Operational Research Society*, 62 (6), 960–970.

Bishop, S.B. (2002). Collaborative transportation management benefits. *2001 Annual Conference Proceedings*.

Browning, B., & White, A. (2000). Collaborative Transportation Management. Logility Inc. http://www. vics. Org (accessed October 4, 2013).

Caplice, C., & Sheffi, Y. (2003). Optimization-Based Procurement For Transportation Services. *Journal of Business Logistics*, 24 (2), 109–128.

Carter, C. R., Kaufmann, L., & Michel, A. (2007). Behavioral Supply Management: A Taxonomy of Judgment and Decision-Making Biases. *International Journal of Physical Distribution and Logistics Management*, 37(8), 631–669.

Chan, F.T.S., & Zhang, T. (2011). The impact of collaborative transportation management on supply chain performance: A simulation approach. *Expert Systems With Applications*. March 38 (3), 2319-2329.

Chen, D.J., Chen, H.C., & Lai, S.H. (2010). The Effect of Adopting Collaborative Transportation Management by Taiwanese Computer Manufacturers- Model Building and Empirical Studies. *International Journal of Information and Management Sciences*, 21, 481-499.

Checkland, P.B. (2001). *Soft Systems Methodology in Action*. John Wiley & Sons. England.

Dwyer, R.F., Schurr, P. H., & Oh, S. (1987). Developing Buyer-Seller Relationships. *The Journal of Marketing*, 51 (2), 11-27.

Ergun, O., Kuyzu, G., & Savelsbergh, M. (2007). Reducing Truckload Transportation Costs Through Collaboration. *Transportation Science*, 41(2), 206–221.

Esper, T.L., & Williams, L.R. (2003). The value of Collaborative Transportation Management (CTM): its relationship to CPFR and Information Technology. *Transportation Journal*, 42 (4), 55–65.

Feng, C.M., Yuan, C.Y., & Lin, Y.C. (2005). The System Framework For Evaluating The Effect Of Collaborative Transportation Management On Supply Chain. *Journal of the Eastern Asia Society for Transportation Studies*, 6: 2837–2851.

Feng, C.M., & Yuan, C.Y. (2007). Application of collaborative transportation management to global logistics: An interview case study. *International Journal of Management*, 24 (4), 623–636.

Frisk, M., Gothe-Lundgren, M., Jornsten, K., & Ronnqvist, M. (2010). Cost Allocation in Collaborative Forest Transportation. *European Journal of Operational Research*, 205 (2), 448–458.

Gereffi, G., Humphrey, J., & Kaplinsky, R. (2001). Introduction: Globalisation, value chains and development. *IDS bulletin*, 32 (3), 1-8.

Gino, F., & Pisano, G. (2008). Toward a Theory of Behavioral Operations. *Manufacturing & Service Operations Management*, 10 (4), 676–691.

Gonzales-Feliu, J., & Morana, J. (2011). Case study from France. *Technologies for Supporting Reasoning Communities and Collaborative Decision Making: Cooperative Approaches*, 252–271.

Gonzalez-Feliu, J., Morana, M., Grau, J.M.S., & Ma, T.Y. (2013). Design and scenario assessment for collaborative logistics and freight transport systems. *International Journal of Transport Economics*, 207–240.

llyas, R.M., Shankar, R., & Banwet, D. K. (2005). Interventional Roadmap for Digital Enablement Leading to Effective Value-chain Management in the Manufacturing Sector. *Global Business Review*, 6 (2), 207–229.

Kayikci, Y. (2009). Performance Improvement In Intermodal Freight Transportation System Through Efficient Collaborative Transportation Management. *Proceedings of the 14th International Symposium on Logistics*, 701–709.

Li, J., & Chan, F.T.S. (2012). The impact of collaborative transportation management on demand disruption of manufacturing supply chains. *International Journal of Production Research*, 50(19), 5635–5650.

Liu, P., Wu, Y., & Xu, N. (2010). Allocating Collaborative Profit in Less-than-Truckload Carrier Alliance. *Journal of Service Science & Management*, 3 (1), 143–149.

Mason, R., Lalwani, C., & Boughton, R. (2007). Combining vertical and horizontal collaboration for transport optimization. *Supply Chain Management: An International Journal*, 12 (3), 187–199.

Meyr, H., Wagner, M., & Rohde, J. (2005). Structure of Advanced Planning Systems" *Supply Chain Management and Advanced Planning*, 109–116. Springer Berlin Heidelberg.

Min, S., Roath, A.S., Daugherty, P.J., Genchev, S.E., Chen, H., Arndt, A.D., & Richey, R.G. (2005). Supply chain collaboration: what's happening. *The International Journal of Logistics Management*, 16 (2), 237–256.

Moll, S.M. (2012). Productivity Improvement For Freight Railways Through Collaborative Transport Planning. Dissertation ETH ZURICH.

Nadarajah, S. (2008). Collaborative Logistics in Vehicle Routing. University of Waterloo.

Nag, R., Hambrick, D.C., & Chen, M.J. (2007). What is strategic management really? Inductive derivation of a consensus definition of the field. *Strategic Management Journal*, 28 (9), 935–955.

Ozener, O. (2008). Collaboration in Transportation. Georgia Institute of Technology.

Peeta, S., & Hernandez, S.H. (2011). Modeling of Collaborative Less-than-truckload Carrier Freight Networks. USDOT Region V Regional University Transportation Center Final Report.

Prakash, A., & Deshmukh, S.G. (2010). Horizontal Collaboration in Flexible Supply Chains: A Simulation Study. *Journal of Studies on Manufacturing*, 1(1), 54-58.

Silva, V.M.D., Coelho, A.S., & Novaes, A.G.N. (2011).The role of collaboration through manufactured goods' exportation process under System Dynamics analysis. *Proceedings of the 29th International Conference of The System Dynamics Society*, 24–28.

Simatupang, M.T., & Sridharan, R. (2002). The Collaborative Supply Chain. *The International Journal of Logistics Management*, 13(1),15–30.

Song, J., & Regan, A.C. (2003). An Auction Based Collaborative Carrier Network. *Transport Research Part E: Logistics and Transportation Review*, 2.

Soosay, C.A., Hyland, P., & Mario, F. (2006). Supply chain collaboration: capabilities for continuous innovation. *Supply Chain Management: An International Journal*, 13 (2), 160–169.

Sutherland, J.L. (2003). Collaborative transportation management– creating value through increased transportation efficiencies. Business Briefing – Pharmagenerics.

Sutherland, J.L. (2006). Collaborative transportation management: A solution to the current transportation crisis. CVCR white paper 602. Lehigh University, Pennsylvania, U.S.A.

Taherian, H. (2013). Outbound Transportation Collaboration-Do It Yourself (DIY). Thesis Engineering System Division, MIT.

Tyan, J.C., Wang, F.K., & Du, T. (2003). Applying collaborative transportation management in global third party logistics. *International Journal of Computer Integrated Manufacturing*, 16(4-5), 283–291.

VICS (CTM sub-committee of the voluntary inter-industry commerce standards logistic committee). (2004). Collaborative Transportation Management White Paper. Version 1.0. http://www.vics.org (accessed October 4, 2013).

Wadhawa, S., & Rao, K.S. (2003). Flexibility and agility for enterprise synchronization: knowledge and innovation management towards flexibility. *Studies in Informatics and Control*, 12 (2), 111-128.

Wen, Y.H. (2012). Impact of collaborative transportation management on logistics capability and competitive advantage for the carrier. *Transportation Journal*, 51 (4), 452–473.

Zamboni, S. (2011). Supply Chain Collaboration and Open Innovation: Toward a New Framework for Network Dynamic Innovation Capabilities. Universita Degli Studi Di Bergamo.

APPENDIX 1. A List of Previous Literatures Review

AUTHOR	MAIN OBJECTIVE OF THE PAPER	APPLICATION OF THE MODELS
VERTICAL COLLABORATION		
Tyan et al. (2003)	Analyze an effective collaboration in global supply chain (GSC) execution to reduce delivery time and improve delivery reliability.	3PL provider in a notebook computer GSC
Esper and William (2003)	Portray the holistic value of supply chain collaboration by discussing CTM and the role of information technology and its benefits.	Case study: 3PL Transplace
Caplice and Seffi (2003)	Analyze the optimization-based procurement process to securing and managing a strategic relationship.	US truckload (TL) transportation
Feng et al. (2005)	Evaluating the benefits of CTM by simulating 3-scenario model on the manufactures, distributions and carriers in supply chain.	Manufacturer-Carier-Distributor in Taiwan
Audy et al. (2006)	Design a framework to describe collaboration in transportation, and a different business models associated with collaboration in transport are proposed.	Five industrial application in wood fiber transportation
Ergun et al. (2007)	Generate optimization technology to assist in the identification of repeatable, dedicated truckload continuous move tours with little truck repositioning.	US Industry
Feng and Yuan (2007)	Analyze the application integrating CTM with enterprise resource planning (ERP) via information technology (IT) to facilitate transportation capacity planning and achieve prompt delivery within the shortest time possible.	First International Computer Inc and UPS Taiwan branch
Kayikci (2009)	Evaluate performance outcomes depend on the communication quality, long-term orientation and satisfaction, the quality of information and the intensity of joint information sharing.	Different industries in Europe both transport users and transport service providers
Chen et al. (2010)	Explore the cost difference after the computer industry introduced CTM and the association analysis between the inventory element and the transportation element.	TFT–LCD

APPENDIX 1. A List of Previous Literatures Review (Cont.)

AUTHOR	MAIN OBJECTIVE OF THE PAPER	APPLICATION OF THE MODELS
VERTICAL COLLABORATION		
Silva et al. (2011)	Analyze the behavior of the collaboration in order to reduce freight costs.	Maritime logistics of manufacture export companies in Brazil
Gonzalez-Feliu and Morana (2011)	Develop a conceptual schema focus on socio-economic and legislative aspects in order to define the main concepts related to logistics sharing agreements that representing the most important organizational aspects.	French press distribution sector
Li and Chan (2012)	Determine the impact of CTM on the performance of manufacturing supply chains using two supply chain models (with and without CTM) in order to show the impact of CTM under demand disruption.	Virtual Companies
Moll (2012)	Identified and assessed twelve potential forms of collaborative approaches in order to improve the efficiency of locomotives and train drivers, the effectiveness of single wagon load trains, and also increase freight rail productivity.	SBB Cargo-Swiss Freight Railway
Wen (2012)	Examine the impacts of CTM on logistics capability and competitive advantage of carriers within a supply chain, and analyzes the relationships between logistics capability and competitive advantage.	The carriers and transportation service providers in Taiwan
HORIZONTAL COLLABORATION		
Song and Regan (2003)	Examine and develop a new auction based carrier collaboration mechanism for complex decision problems associated with subcontracting, bidding, and bid selection are investigated.	Trucking industry in US
Nadarajah (2008)	Develop simple examples where a firm can enhance its transportation efficiencies through Less-than-Truckload collaboration to reduced cost and improved customer service.	Less-Than-Truckload (LTL)

APPENDIX 1. A List of Previous Literatures Review (Cont.)

AUTHOR	MAIN OBJECTIVE OF THE PAPER	APPLICATION OF THE MODELS
HORIZONTAL COLLABORATION		
Asawasakulsorn (2009)	Develop partner selection criteria during the formation stage based on economic, social perspectives, and inter-organizational system (IOS) design factors regarding trust.	Shipper and carrier company in Thailand
Fisk et al. (2010)	Evaluate sharing mechanisms and propose a new allocation method, with the aim that the participants relative profits are as equal as possible.	Forest industry in Sweden
Liu et al. (2010)	Develop the LTL collaboration game and propose allocation method to distribute profits/savings among the participants that are fair, reasonable, and easy to implement.	LTL industry
Audy et al. (2010)	Evaluate different coordination mechanisms scenarios to ensure cost and delivery time reductions as well as gain in market geographic coverage.	Canadian furniture industry
Peeta and Hernandez (2011)	Modeled LTL collaborative paradigms from the supply and demand perspectives to identify potential collaborative opportunities and encourage collaboration by increasing capacity utilization for member carriers.	Less-Than-Truckload (LTL)
Taherian (2013)	Design a practical guideline to engage in collaboration by Do-It-Yourself (DIY) approach and focus on passive collaboration by addressing how to qualify potential collaboration partners, how to evaluate the associated savings, and how to make it work.	LTL and TL shipments
LATERAL COLLABORATION		
VICS (2004)	Provides an overview of CTM, a process for bringing trading partners and transportation service providers together for the sake of "win-win" outcomes among all parties.	Various companies in US as pilot project
Sutherland (2006)	Demonstrate how supply chain partners collaborate on transportation process become more adaptable to day-to-day demand changes as well as resilient in the event of major supply chain disruptions	Various companies in US as pilot project

APPENDIX 1. A List of Previous Literatures Review (Cont.)

AUTHOR	MAIN OBJECTIVE OF THE PAPER	APPLICATION OF THE MODELS
LATERAL COLLABORATION		
Mason et al. (2007)	Demonstrate that lateral collaboration are emerging for better transport optimization, that exploit the competitive power of collaboration, both vertically with supply chain partners and horizontally with other logistics service providers (LSPs).	The road freight transport industry in the UK and Europe
Ozener (2008)	Develop framework and evaluate collaborative approaches to identify collaborative opportunities among shippers and among carriers to reduce transportation cost and distribution cost.	Industrial gas company in US
Gonzalez-Feliu et al. (2013)	Determine collaborative freight transport, its links with supply chain management, and aims at framing an assessment method to help decision makers in strategic collaborative logistics, transport design, and planning.	LTL transport operators

Building Resilient Supply Chains Through Flexibility: a Case Study in Healthcare

Marcelo Bradaschia
Fundação Getulio Vargas - EAESP
mbradaschia@gmail.com

Susana Carla Farias Pereira
Fundação Getulio Vargas – EAESP
Susana.pereira@fgv.br

ABSTRACT: This research seeks to understand how the capability of flexibility manifests itself for the formation of resilience in service supply chains. The survey was conducted through a single case study of a hospital chain that was impacted by the H1N1 pandemic in 2009. This analyzed chain was formed by the hospital, doctors, nurses, the Ministry of Health, State Secretary of Health of São Paulo and the pharmaceutical industry. As a result, the following categories of flexibility manifestation were identified: redesign, alteration/creation, prioritization, redundancy/availability/robustness and elimination.

1. INTRODUCTION

The increased competition and pressure for constant innovations led companies to seek efficiency in its operations and chains (CHRISTOPHER; PECK, 2004). Because of that, companies have become leaner in their processes, reducing inventories and activities with fewer maneuver options; increased the outsourcing activities in order to focus on its core business, thus increasing the amount of links in the chains, making it longer and more complex; and, sought lower costs and higher quality, causing several activities to be located in other countries, fragmenting the chains in political contexts, economics and diverse societies (BLACKHURST et al., 2011; CRAIGHEAD et al., 2004; PETTIT et al., 2013; PETTIT et al., 2010).

The mere existence of supply chains already make them exposed to suffering disruptions, and since these factors described serve to increase their vulnerability, negative reflexes can appear in all their links, even to the final consumer (CRAIGHEAD et al., 2007; PONOMAROV; HOLCOMB, 2009).

Generally speaking, in recent years the research related to Supply Chain Risk Management focused on the study of strategies for risk mitigation either by reducing the probability of the occurrence of adverse events to the chain or on mitigating its effects once they happen, with the understanding that they can be anticipated (JÜTTNER; MAKLAN, 2011). On the other hand, the increasing occurrence of disrupting events has led researchers and executives to question this traditional look of risk management, where normally they do not consider risks with low probability of occurrence or uncertainty, or events that cannot be anticipated (JÜTTNER; MAKLAN, 2011; PETTIT et al., 2013; PETTIT et al., 2010). In addition, the strategy to evaluate and develop plans for mitigating each of the potential risks could prove to be expensive and time consuming, often times not taking priority in a day to day corporate schedule (PETTIT et al., 2010).

In this regard, recent research has been devoted to understanding factors that make a supply chain resilient in different situations, in order to cover this gap in traditional research of risk (JÜTTNER; MAKLAN, 2011; PETTIT et al., 2013; PETTIT et al., 2010). Resilience of supply chains is defined as "The adaptive capacity of the supply chain to prepare for unexpected events, respond to disruptions, and recover from them by maintaining continuity of operations at the desired level of connectedness and control over structure and function" (PONOMAROV; HOLCOMB, 2009, p. 131). Despite the increase in the number of written works on the topic, understanding the factors that enable or form the resiliency is still in its infancy (BLACKHURST et al., 2011).

Recent work has positioned resilience as a characteristic of the company or supply chain, originated from capabilities (BRANDON-JONES et al., 2014; JÜTTNER; MAKLAN, 2011; PETTIT et al., 2013; PETTIT et al., 2010), formed in an idiosyncratic manner from practices and resources (WU et al., 2010). Also under this vision of capabilities, there are still different views about which are responsible for forming a resilient supply chain, being the most cited collaboration, visibility and agility (CHRISTOPHER; PECK, 2004A; JÜTTNER; MAKLAN, 2011; SCHOLTEN et al., 2014). On the other hand, there are other capabilities in the literature that do not have share consensus among different authors, such as the ability to re-design the supply chain (Christopher & Peck, 2004), velocity (JÜTTNER; MAKLAN, 2011), agility and flexibility (PETTIT et al., 2013b).

However, the capability of flexibility is considered by many authors as fundamental to the formation of resilient chains as it is responsible for creating options for the supply chain and the different nodes involved to deal with problems (JÜTTNER; MARKLAN, 2011; SCHOLTEN et al., 2014; BLACKHURST et al. 2011; TANG; TOMLIN, 2008; PETTIT et al., 2010). On the other hand, as far as has been verified, there are no studies focused on the forms of manifestation of this capability.

This research seeks to answer the following question: how does the capability of flexibility manifest itself contributing for the formation of resilient supply chains?

As context, a healthcare chain that was affected by the H1N1 pandemic that struck Brazil in 2009 was analyzed. The study is based on a single case study of a healthcare supply chain from a well-recognized hospital in the city of São Paulo, that was positioned as the focal company of the supply chain, and other links, such as the Ministry of Health, State Secretary of Health of São Paulo and the pharmaceutical industry responsible for the production and commercialization of the anti-viral medicine used for prophylaxis and the treatment of the disease.

2. REVIEW OF THE LITERATURE

This section will present the theoretical review related to resilience and the capability of flexibility.

2.1 Resilience in Supply Chains

In recent years, some authors began to argue that traditional models of risk management are not capable of addressing risks of disruption since many of them cannot be anticipated or a specific strategy to mitigate them can be economically unviable (JÜTTNER; MAKLAN, 2011; JÜTTNER et al., 2003; MITROFF; ALPASLAN, 2003; PETTIT et al., 2010). For this reason, another line of research has been deepening in the understanding of resilience in order to understand what allows certain chains to pass through situations of disruption, suffering less impact than others, and rapidly returning their operations to the desired situation.

According to the vision of Jüttner and Maklan (2011) the reduction of the probability of occurrence of risk, although it also may lead to a reduction in vulnerability, does not necessarily have an effect on the increasing of the resilience since, in the event of risk becoming reality, the company can suffer from drastic consequences. Thus, according to these authors, resilience is related to the mitigation of the effects of risk, whether in relationship to its gravity or its recovery time, and not to the reduction of the likelihood of its occurrence.

The essential factor for resiliency of a supply chain is its ability to adapt so that it can return the operations to the desired state (PONOMAROV; HOLCOMB, 2009). In this sense, some works position resilience as a multidimensional capability.

The discussion of the concept of capabilities has been refined in recent years, inserted into the theoretical lens of RBT (Resource Based Theory) (BARNEY 1991; PETERAF 1993) and its evolutions (TEECE et al., 1997; BARNEY 1996, 2001; PETERAF; BARNEY, 2003).

Although there is no consensus about the capabilities that form resilient supply chains, several works consider that flexibility is one of the most essential to its formation (CHRISTOPHER; PECK, 2004; SHEFFI; RICE, 2005; JÜTTNER; MARKLAN, 2011; PETTIT et al., 2013; SCHOLTEN et al., 2014).

2.2 Flexibility

Jüttner and Marklan (2011) define the capability of flexibility as "The ease with which a supply chain can change its range number (i.e. the number of possible "options") and range heterogeneity (i.e. the degree of difference between the "options") in order to cope with a range of market changes/ events while performing comparably well" (p. 251). Skipper and Hanna (2009) discuss that flexibility is usually related to the immediate ability of adapting to new situations. Therefore, the existence of flexibility in disrupting events is important since it offers alternatives for the supply chain to circumventing situations which hamper the implementation of activities that are essential to its operation.

For example, Pettit et al. (2013, p. 49) point out that flexibility in the provision and execution of orders are important to the supply chain. For provisioning, flexibility is defined as the ability of the supply chain or its entities to quickly change its sources or ways of receiving input. Flexibility in the execution of orders is the ability of the chain or its entities to quickly change the outputs or the way it delivers its orders. The authors also describe adaptability, defined as the ability to modify operations, as important to resilience, reinforcing the definition of flexibility presented earlier of Jüttner and Marklan (2011).

In order for flexibility to exist, it is necessary that resources are available and there is ability to coordinate them so they may become options to the situation. The coordination of resources, according to Craighead et al. (2007), can occur before or after the occurrence of the disruptive event, which suggests that flexibility can be planned and have its execution previously operationalized or articulated. In this sense, the existence of contingency plans can increase the level of flexibility of a company, reinforcing its importance in the mitigation phase of disruption (SKIPPER; HANNA, 2009).

The modularization of processes and design of products, for example, is a way to increase the agility and flexibility, to the extent that it can bring alternatives for reassessing the production lines (KLEINDORFER & SAAD, 2005; TANG 2006).

Various practices described by Tang et al. (2006) can increase the flexibility of companies and supply chains, as for example: the postponement of production; the implementation of strategic stocks; the use of a flexible supplier base; the use of the approach of make or buy; the planning of transport alternatives; and the active management of revenue and price, directing the consumption to products with greater availability.

The resources used to achieve flexibility in supply chains can be both tangible and intangible. An example presented by Pettit et al. (2013) are financial resources, which are important for the absorption of oscillations in chains.

The use of security stocks is also described in the literature as being important for the formation of flexibility in disruptive situations. One of the strategies for self-protecting from disruptive events described by Bode et al. (2011) is called buffering. This strategy has a built-in view of the focal company, in the creation of self-protection mechanisms for dealing with external events, working as a buffer to absorb shocks. According to the authors, this can be based, for example, in the use of security stocks, flexible production processes, redundant suppliers, and the design of products that are not dependent on just one supplier.

Differently, Sheffi and Rice (2005) believe that the use of emergency stocks do not refer to the construction of flexibility but for redundancy, which they regard as distinct concepts. They argue that, although both have a positive relationship with resilience, flexibility entails lower costs and could become a source of competitive advantage. The argument comes from the vision that flexibility does not involve the need for idle resources, while redundancy does. Some common examples in companies are the use of emergency/security stocks, the use of a multiple base of suppliers, even while causing a higher cost, or the maintaining of slack operations. Similarly, Scholten et al. (2014) distinguishes flexibility of redundancy.

Tang and Tomlin (2008) have already presented that the existence of operational buffer enables flexibility. In this paper, the authors perform simulations to identify the amount of flexibility necessary to deal with risks of supply, demand and of process. In their study, flexibility is positioned as a quantitative variable, relating it to different practices, such as the use of multiple vendors, the use of flexible supply contracts, the use of flexible manufacturing processes, the postponement of products in production lines and the use of flexible pricing politics to influence demand. The result shows that even the existence of small levels of operational buffer is sufficient to increase flexibility. This occurs once the existence of this buffer reveals the interoperability of the opera-

tion, i.e. that different processes can be executed in different locations. Jüttner and Marklan (2011) also hold the view that the redundancy "is one of the routes for flexibility."

Christopher and Peck (2004) argue that the definition of supply risk mitigation is not only about the decision to keep multiple vendors within the base, but to understand the implications for the business, since, in some situations, establishing a relationship with a deep bond with the supplier may be the safest strategy (BODE et al., 2011). The possibility of conversion of an operation is also related to flexibility, as in the case of migrating the operation to different locations in case there is a problem with one of them (CHRISTOPHER; PECK, 2004). The authors point out the necessity of structuring supply chains that maintain various open options in case a disruptive event happens. Additionally, they reinforce that the search for efficiency may not be the best decision, but that maintaining redundancy in key processes can be a better alternative.

At the individual level, Weick (1993) shows that the ability of improvisation is important so that an organization can go through stressful situations, as will be the case of a disruption. Improvisation involves the ability to recombine available resources for a specific task. In this vision of improvisation, the author also includes creativity, defining it as the ability to use what you already know in different situations. In this way, creativity and, consequently, improvisation, are related to flexibility, to the extent that they are responsible for the increase in available options for dealing with a given situation.

Sheffi and Rice (2005) argue that risk perception as well as collaboration, play an important part in flexibility, since you usually cannot recover from a disruptive situation without the involvement of different areas of the business and entities of the supply chain, no matter how close one is to the direct effects that affect it.

In addition to the points described related to the construction of flexibility, there are others that can difficult its existence, such as strict internal and external regulations, as well as the complexity and requirements of materials that make the amount of available options limited (BLACKHURST et al., 2011).

3. METHODOLOGY

The study on resilience in supply chains is still in its infancy (BLACKHURST et al., 2011), therefore, there is still a great deal of disagreement about the concept and what composes the theme. This empirical research was carried out by a single case study of a healthcare chain in Brazil. Single case studies, despite having a smaller external validity, allow the researcher to go deeper into the case (SIGGELKOW, 2007). In addition, single cases are especially relevant when they are regarded as critical, extreme and revelatory of the question posed by the research (MILES et al., 2013; YIN 2014).

For this research, the unit of analysis considered was the service supply chain. The service supply chain chosen for this research is embedded in the context of health management and refers specifically to a hospital chain. As the main objective of this chain is to provide care for patients, the hospital is positioned as the focal company, considered as the service provider (BALTACIOGLU et al., 2007). Additionally, the context in which the unit of analysis is embedded is the pandemic of the H1N1 virus that struck Brazil in 2009.

The links that were selected were chosen in order to represent the entities most affected or that influenced by actions the H1N1 outbreak in 2009. The entities selected were validated based on preliminary interviews with health professionals involved in H1N1 pandemic in 2009.

Hospital: the focal company to be studied from the chain. Responsible for the care of patients, the hospital is the last link in the supply chain, since problems that occurred in previous links have the potential to impact patient care and, consequently, their goal of treating them.

Doctors: responsible for the diagnosis and medication of patients. Along with the nurses, they are on the front line of care and have to deal with the day-to-day situations.

Nurses: responsible for the treatments of the patient, focused on their physical, social and mental well-being.

In this context, doctors and nurses are being considered as links in the chain and not only as hospital staff workers, since in many situations these professionals provide services to more than one entity.

Pharmaceutical Industry: responsible for the supply of medicines for the treatment of patients. In the case of this study, interviews were conducted with industry professionals responsible for the supply of Oseltamivir Phosphate, the main antiviral used for the treatment of the H1N1 virus.

Secretary of Epidemiological Surveillance of the Ministry of Health: responsible for the management of the National System of Epidemiological Surveillance and Environment in Health. There are attributes of this body that should be highlighted: the national coordination of epidemiological actions and disease control; technical assistance to the states; provision of diagnostic kits; management of epidemiological information systems, including the consolidation of data from the states and the dissemination of information and epidemiological analyses; monitoring, supervision and control of the implementation of the actions related to epidemiology including the evaluation of the epidemiological surveillance systems of the states (CONASS 2003).

State Secretary of Health of São Paulo (SES-SP)/ Center for Epidemiological Surveillance: the state body that sets state health policies, in accordance with the guidelines defined by the Unified Health System (Sistema Único de Saúde – SUS) (CONASS 2003). The SES-SP has eight company departments, including the Coordination of Disease Control (CCD), whose mission is to "Coordinate the state response to disease, aggravations and existing or potential risks, within the framework of public health, with emphasis on planning, monitoring, evaluation, production and the dissemination of knowledge, for the promotion, prevention and the control of the health conditions of the population, in line with regional characteristics and the principles and guidelines of SUS" (CONASS , 2003, p. 2). Within this organization, you find the Epidemiological Surveillance Center.

3.1 Sample Selection

Unlike quantitative analysis for the case studies, the selection of the sample should not be random, as in the case of quantitative research, but instead in a theoretical way (EISENHARDT, 1989; YIN, 2014). The choice of the object is related to the possibility of the case contributing to the research question (STUART et al., 2002), whereas the generalization sought with the findings obtained through case studies is not statistic, as in the case of quantitative research, but analytical (YIN, 2014).

A hospital in São Paulo, considered to be highly complex, was chosen for this work. This hospital is considered to be one of the main Brazilian centers of the dissemination of techno-scientific information, known for being a center of excellence and reference in the field of teaching, research and service. It has more than 2,000 beds and 15,000 professionals in different areas of expertise. According to the social reaction related to the H1N1 virus, this and other high complexity hospitals were widely sought after by a large volume of people for diagnosis and treatment of the disease, raising the risk of disruptions in the chain and becoming a relevant context to the study.

The health professionals who provide services to the hospital were selected after interviews with the administration team, so that professionals indicated had a relevant participation in the defined context.

As in the hospital, so in the other links, the interviewed professionals were protagonists with relevant roles in the preparation of mitigation plans or during the pandemic of 2009. The specific positions are not described in order to ensure the confidentiality of the respondents, but all possessed roles as directors, managers or supervisors of areas related to the event. In total, sixteen semi-structured interviews were conducted.

One concern that existed in the conception of this study was the fact that the H1N1 pandemic studied took place almost five years ago, which could lead to inaccuracies in the data collected. To mitigate these problems, we used a large number of interviews, apart from the information collected from different links allowing triangulation of information. The completion of the analysis with secondary information also contributed to minimizing this problem.

3.2 Data Collection

In order to answer the research questions, the collection of data was conducted through semi-structured interviews. The interviews lasted from 30 to 120 minutes, and on average, they were 75 minutes long. All the interviews were conducted in person and recorded with previous authorization and subsequently transcribed for use as sources of analysis. There was only one exception that was not recorded due to technical problems. In this case, a memo was written right after the interview in order to reduce the probability of losing content.

The transcripts were produced as close as possible to the actual interviews by outsourced capable professionals. That allowed the analysis to happen in parallel with the other interviews (Eisenhardt & Graebner, 2007; Miles et al., 2013; Yin 2014).

The interview protocol was based on the theoretical review performed. The goal of the protocol was to guide the interview, with the objective of assisting the researcher in covering the relevant issues.

The research protocol was previously validated with academics of operations management as well as health professionals in order to ensure that it was adherent to the theme and context studied (YIN, 2014). All of the information was analyzed with the support of the Atlas TI software, version 7 for Mac.

Table 1 summarizes the information pertaining to persons who were interviewed, describing to which link they belonged, the relationship they had with the entity in 2009, as well as the name that will be used during the analysis to identify the information presented.

Table 1: Relationships of the Interviewees

Responsibility	Name	Relationship this 2009 H1N1 outbrake
Hospital		
Crisis management committee	HP_CGC_1	Related to hospital infection control and member of the crisis management committee
	HP_CGC_2	Related to hospital infection control and member of the crisis management committee
Administration	HP_ADM	Related to departments responsible for security, cleaning and supplies
	HP_SPR	Related to supply management, including purchases and internal logistics
	HP_EMG	Related to emergential purchases
Infectologist pysician	HP_UTI	Related to infectious diseases ICU - Intensive Care Unit
	HP_DMI	Related to infectious disease care
ER	HP_PSC	Related to ER management
Nurses	HP_ENF	Related to the nursing team management
Supplier		
Pharmaceutical industry	IF_MED	Related to antiviral product management
	IF_GOV	Related to government relationship
Governo		
Health Ministry	MS_VEP_1	Related to federal epidemiological surveillance group
	MS_VEP_2	Related to federal epidemiological surveillance group
	MS_VEP_3	Related to federal epidemiological surveillance group
Health Secretary of the State of São Paulo	SE_VEP_1	Related to state epidemiological surveillance group
	SE_VEP_2	Related to state epidemiological surveillance group

Source: Original Compilation

3.3 Data Analysis

The data analysis protocol was adapted from Scholten et al. (2014), which in turn, was derived from Miles et al. (2013). This approach is based on the reduction and analysis of data in a process called encoding.

As described in Miles et al. (2013), codes are assigned to the descriptive or inferred information during a study, which are represented symbolically as a phrase or word that refers to the original idea. In the words of the authors, "the code is a construct generated by the researcher that symbolizes and assigns the meaning interpreted for each individual piece of data for future purposes of detection of patterns, categorizations, generation of theory and other analytical processes" (MILES et al 2013). The data to be classified can vary from words, sentences, paragraphs, even entire pages. According to the authors, the encoding is an activity of data condensation, and is part of the process of analysis, which they recommend performing in two steps:

The first coding cycle deals with the raw data, and has the main function of reducing the information so they can be later sorted in the second cycle. Three

of the most common strategies described by Miles et al. (2013) are: a) descriptive encoding, where the aim is to summarize the topic in question with a word (usually a noun) or short sentence; b) encoding in vivo, which uses literal words or phrases used by respondents who reflect their own language, and; c) encoding processes, where typically gerunds are used to describe actions observed in the data or the interaction with time, showing trends or issues which are emerging, for example.

Miles et al. (2013), suggests two approaches for the first cycle of coding, the inductive and deductive, that could happen at the same time. In the deductive approach, the researcher starts with an initial list of codes that may have been based on an initial conceptual model, a list of research questions, hypotheses or variables that the researcher brings to the study.

The second cycle of encoding usually deals with the generated code in the first cycle, in order to group them in a smaller amount and more parsimonious categories that symbolize themes and constructs (Miles et al., 2013; Scholten et al., 2014). The identification of these patterns allow the researcher to condense a large volume of data (Miles et al., 2013).

The analysis process followed the steps detailed in Table 2.

Tabel 2: Analysis protocol

Literature Review: based on a review of the literature, the main capabilities responsible for forming the resilience have been identified. Codes have been created for each of these items in the Atlas TI software.
Coding based on Literature: the data was coded using the codes created based on the literature (item 1)
Inductive Coding: throughout the process of analysis and understanding of the case, additional codes were created that were relative to the observed events, such as: protection stock, organizational structure, lack of preparation, support from senior management, etc.
Grouping of the Codes: the codes created in item 3 were grouped according to the objective of the research,
Linking with the capability of flexibility: the codes created in the groups of item 4 were linked with the capability of flexibility,
Consistency with the literature: the result of the analyses was contrasted with the literature to ensure its consistency.

Source: Original compilation

4. DISCUSSION

During the 2009 pandemic, the chain had to deal with various situations where their usual processes and resources were not prepared to deal with the new context. So, it was necessary to create options.

Through the process of analysis, various forms of manifestation of flexibility were identified, where the prior existence of resources was a common element (TANG, 2006). The various forms identified are summarized in Figure 1.

Figure 1: Manifested forms of flexibility

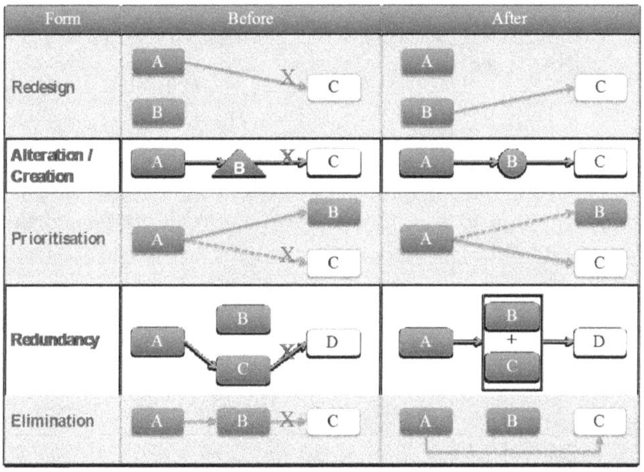

Source: Original compilation

The letters in Figure 1 could refer to entities, processes or activities, depending on the situation. To simplify the explanation of the forms of manifestation (Table 3), the letters will be simply referred as resources, with the proper explanation already made. The letters that are in the white square refer to the objective to be achieved, and the "X" shows the path that is not feasible in the particular context. Table 3 presents the 5 forms of manifestation of flexibility identified in the analysis and examples presented during the interviews

Table 3: Forms of manifestation of flexibility and examples

Form of Manifestation	Example
Redesign: the ability of the supply chain to adapt by changing the resource that is obstructing its operation. In the figure, this is illustrated by the exchange of the resource A for the resource B. An example is the use of a different supplier to provide specific input.	*Whomever said that they wouldn't be able to attend the demand, went looking for partners. - HP_ADM* *The alternative that we have left are the emergency purchases, which are acquired though the Foundation funds. What is verified is the possibility of acquiring this material from a second or third party vendor. - HP_SUPR*
Alteration /Creation: In this case, for example, a resource B is adapted, turning this resource into a resource more appropriate than the original one. An example of this is the training of professionals to carry out additional activities not foreseen initially. The composition of different resources can also lead to creation of a new one.	*Disposable masks were used by different professionals including the doormen, who were the first [people] to come in contact with [suspected patients]. [...] at that time, they [doormen] had also been trained on what to ask, how to act when a sick person arrived... They were lay people. They didn't have this ability to investigate and it wasn't even their role. - HP_ENF* *[...]then we processed in the [Hospital] in a weekend 2000 bottles. We got the antiviral powder and made the medication for the children. - SE_VEP_1* *We said that we were playing MacGyver here in the Hospital. - HP_UTI*
Prioritization: In this situation, a resource C is prioritized at the expense of resource B, since it was more important at that moment, as was the case with the prioritization of ICU beds in the Hospital for H1N1 patients.	*[...] at the time, everybody, regardless if you were ICU of Cardiology, ICU of Pneumology, ICU of Surgery, when they had a bed, the first thing they do was to call me. "Someone needs ICU?" We would transfer someone there in order to receive other patients. - HP_UTI* *The [laboratory] [...] practically stopped all other functions. All was geared for just H1N1 analysis [...] We worked through the weekend - SE_VEP_1*
Redundancy: in this case, existing resources have buffer or the ability to bear a greater load, enabling the resource D.	*[...]We had enough stock to get going. We will use it and later replenish it. You have to keep an eye on the stock so it doesn't zero out. - HP_ADM* *So what we did, basically, all States had emergency stocks, so you used it, you replaced it later. Whenever ran out of the product. - MS_VEP_2* *They were asking for people to put in extra On-Calls "Contribute by giving an extra On-Call". - HP_CGC_2*
Elimination: The elimination of an intermediate resource B can be the solution for enabling a determined option C that was not initially available.	*[...] when the pandemic started, we had some blisters available in the States that were close to reach their expiration date. Then ANVISA did the revalidation. We performed tests and validated it. - MS_VEP_3*

Source: Original compilation

In the next few sessions, these categories related to the forms of manifestation of flexibility identified from the analysis of the data will be explored in depth.

4.1 Redesign

The possibility of changing the design of the chain is a factor that allows the entities impacted to increase the amount of options available at the time of crisis (Christopher and Peck, 2004a).

The most usual way, as identified within the literature, is the possibility of changing the suppliers (CHRISTOPHER; PECK, 2004; PETTIT et al., 2013; PETTIT et al., 2010). This was also identified during the research at the healthcare chain.

According to the bidding law, contracts which are performed between the Hospital and its suppliers possess a very hard character. In this way, the replacement of suppliers could prove complex, even though there was evidence of redesign of the chain at the level of suppliers.

On the other hand, the importance of processes that enable this redesign when necessary were also identified. In the case of the Hospital, there is the possibility that certain purchases with a nature of emergency will be carried out using the funds of the Foundation its is linked to. In this context, the purchases are not made through bidding law, which would give more flexibility.

Through the use of the Foundation, a resource that the Hospital has (BARNEY, 1996; WU et al., 2010), it was possible that the redesign of the chain could happen in order to create a new option for the situation.

4.2 Alteration and Creation of Resources

Within the analysis of the case, situations were encountered in which a given resource was not available, or the way that it was available was not adequate to deal with a particular situation.

In these situations, there is a possibility that these resources could be altered or recombined in a way that will carry a new function creating options for the supply chain or its entities to deal with disruptive situations, increasing their resilience. Pettit et al. (2010), for example, refers to the adaptability of processes and Christopher and Peck (2004) to conversion.

These situations usually involve a certain degree of courage and pioneering spirit on the part of its em-

ployees, since often times, the alternatives created had not been previously tested, in particular when these alternatives are experimented during the crisis.

One of the main factors for the resilience of the Hospital during the pandemic was the accomplishment of the tests internally for verifying the infection of patients by the H1N1, as it was the critical path for several other decisions concerning movements, hospitalizations and treatment of patients

The network of laboratories set up by the Government had no capacity to deal with the volume of tests needed to support the health units of the State. The Hospital adapted its available resources, such as the existing laboratory and its professionals to perform the tests internally. This decision was considered one of the key elements to reduce operational impacts. In addition to the physical location and the technical expertise of the professionals involved, there was a resource, a relationship between the CDC (Centers for Disease Control and Prevention, in Atlanta, USA) and the Hospital laboratory professionals (DYER; SINGH, 1998), which made it possible to access the specific knowledge needed to prepare the exams (HARDY et al., 2003).

Some resources, such as human resources, presented itself possessing a high degree of adaptability to different situations and roles. During the 2009 pandemic, the preparation of professionals to perform functions which they were not initially prepared was an important factor that increased the amount of options available to deal with the events. Two cases that exemplify this statement were: training the doormen to perform screenings of patients at the entrance of the Hospital, since they were the first people to come in contact with them; and the training of nurses in the emergency room to conduct sample collection of materials for examination through the use of a swab in patients suspected of infection with H1N1.

With regards to improvisation, as pointed out by Weick (1993) its existence proved to be relevant to the construction of flexibility in the case analyzed. The improvisation implicitly contains the concept of creativity, which is related to the ability to adapt previous knowledge to new situations (WEICK, 1993). For this reason, improvisation is an element capable of providing new options in situations of disruptions, thereby increasing the flexibility and consequently, resilience.

An event that exemplifies the use of improvisation during the 2009 pandemic was the need for defining the dosages of the drug Oseltamivir to be administered to patients in specific situations, for example, with renal failure, since the knowledge was not available in the literature. In order to define this dosage, a medical board was formed to discuss the issue and, in this way, make the decision based on knowledge available at that point.

Several professionals at the Hospital that were interviewed described the necessity to improvise on a daily basis and not just during disruptive events. Therefore, the prior existence of the ability to improvise was accessed during the 2009 pandemic, proving its importance in that situation.

4.3 Prioritization

In the study, there were situations where necessary resources existed, but were allocated to other functions or activities. This allocation, at the time of the disruption, can be of minor importance and, in this way, may be replaced by another of greater relevance (CRAIGHEAD et al., 2007).

During the 2009 pandemic, for example, the ICU beds in the different departments of the Hospital were prioritized for the infectious diseases department. This way, if there were any beds available in other departments, they would be provided as a priority to patients infected with the H1N1 virus.

Activities that often trigger prioritization cause adverse effects in activities for which the resources were originally allocated. Often times, these resources belong to other areas or even entities within the chain. In this way, the existence of a chain of command proved to be important so that decisions can be executed (CHRISTOPHER; PECK, 2004; CRAIG HEAD et al., 2007).

Another example within the supply chain was the prioritization given to performing tests in the main laboratory of the government. Craighead et al. (2007) reinforces the importance of the coordination of resources for building resilient supply chains. Flexibility through prioritization proved possible by the existence of resources and by the existence of decision-making mechanisms, thusly proving to be an important way of making feasible alternatives during the 2009 pandemic.

4.4 Redundancy, Availability and Robustness

Although authors like Sheffi and Rice (2005) argue that there is a difference between flexibility and redundancy, empirically, these concepts proved to be difficult to separate. Several authors have argued that the existence of very lean processes increase risk (BLACKHURST et al., 2011; CRAIGHEAD et al., 2007; PETTIT et al., 2013; PETTIT et al., 2010), as they diminish the possibilities of maneuverability. The evidence of the case studied show that the existence of idle resources, even in a small degree, is an important factor for resilience.

The most common example in the literature (BODE et al., 2011; SHEFFI; RICE, 2005) also identified in the case analyzed was the existence of emergency stocks, which allowed, especially in the case of the Hospital, to get past the disruptive situation with little impact related from the lack of supplies. In general, the professionals interviewed stressed that there was no lack of supplies to treat patients, such as the personal protection equipment (PPE), during the pandemic, despite many problems that the suppliers were facing to deal with the demand.

Despite the suppliers having an important role of ensuring that the Hospital had the needed supplies available, the existence of emergency stock was important in allowing time for adaptation. In addition to the existence of stockpiles in the central warehouse of the Hospital, it was possible to use materials from others departments' warehouses.

In the case of the distribution of medicines between the Ministry of Health and State Secretaries, the existence of stocks also proved to be an important factor by giving time for the supply chain to adjust.

The availability of materials from suppliers or distributors can also be considered as an element of redundancy or availability of resources (SHEFFIE; RICE, 2005). This availability of resources from other entities was also used as an alternative by the government when the decision was made to withdraw the drugs available in drug stores so that they could be distributed by the Health Ministry. The existence of these drugs was a key factor so that the Ministry could meet the demand allocating it according to the necessity in the early months of the pandemic in the country, since the process of distributing the medicine powder was not yet ready.

The use of available time from human resources also contributed to the resiliency during the 2009 pandemic. Two examples, the increasing workload of professionals through overtime or alternative forms of work, and the use of physical resources in times that are idle. In respect to the time of the professionals, it was common in the Hospital to offer overtime in order to meet the increased demand for attending patients. On-Call shifts by phone were transformed into in-person shifts in order to increase the number of people working at the hospital.

Another point that does not have consensus in the literature, are the differences between resilience and robustness (BRANDON-JONES et al., 2014; CHRISTOPHER; PECK, 2004A; WIELAND; WALLENBURG, 2013). The evidence identified in the research suggests that the existence of robust processes can be a viable factor of resilience, once robust processes allow to increase the load on them, such as including new activities.

An example is the prior existence of a structure for emergency purchases in the Hospital. This structure was essential in enabling the purchase of materials for the institution in order to meet the sudden increase in demand. Another example was the use of existing logistics processes in the Ministry of Health to distribute the drugs to the States.

In this way, these processes can be considered as available options and can be framed in the definition of capability of flexibility.

4.5 Elimination

The ability to eliminate existing processes also presented itself as a way to create flexibility, to the extent that it enabled options that initially were not available.

Blackhurst et al. (2011) reinforces that the existence of regulations and rigid processes work against resilience. In this way, it is possible to conclude that the elimination of these factors could increase resilience. In the case study, an example that corroborates with this statement was the elimination of bureaucratic barriers, such as the one that occurred by the government when it worked together with Anvisa, to validate lots of drugs that were close to their expiration date.

This enabled a considerable volume of medicine, which was suitable for use, to be made available to the service network, at a time when there was a shortage.

5. CONCLUSION

The capability of flexibility has a main function of generating new options for the chain and its entities in order to deal with situations of disruption, and thus plays an important role for resilience (JÜTTNER; MARKLAN, 2011; SCHOLTEN ET AL., 2014). In this research, the importance of the capability of flexibility for the formation of resilience in service chains was verified, as well as the different forms of manifestation in disruptive situations.

The redesign allows the entity or the supply chain to access other options by exchanging one resource for another one available (CHRISTOPHER; PECK, 2004). An example that represents this manifestation is the use of another supplier when there are problems with the original.

The change and creation of resources is achieved from knowledge and skills present in the members of the chains or its entities (FAISAL et al., 2006). The ease with which resources can be modified and the ability of the members to improvise were important alternatives in the case analyzed.

Prioritization became apparent in the case analyzed when a resource that was allocated to a given function could be allocated to another more relevant function during the disruptive event. As there may be a trade off, because this change could lead to negative effects to the original function, the importance of decision-making mechanisms proved to be important in the case studied, corroborating with Christopher and Peck (2004).

Redundancy, availability and robustness also proved important for the formation of flexibility. The existence of buffers, which can be evidenced, for example, by the existence of emergency stocks, is an important option for the entities of the supply chain studied. The possibility of using resources beyond the original planned, as the allocation of extra time by the professionals or the existence of robust processes that allow scalability are also important for the formation of flexibility (JÜTTNER; MARKLAN, 2011). In this way, this work also argues that mechanisms for redundancy and robustness are important for the formation of resilience, positioning them as part of the capability of flexibility and not as unrelated concepts.

Finally it was found that the flexibility is also favored by the possibility of the elimination of processes, resources or activities that impede the objective, such as the elimination of rules or bureaucracy.

As was shown, there are several categories with potential to contribute to the formation of flexibility. The common factor is the previous existence of resources for it to manifest. A proposition which can be made in this regard is that, the choice or construction a priori of resources is important for the formation of flexibility, just as is the recruitment of qualified professionals.

6. LIMITATIONS AND FUTURE RESEARCH

In spite of the care given to methodology, as is in all research, this also presents some limitations that need to be considered.

A first limitation refers to the elapsed time since the occurrence of the event that took place approximately 5 years ago. In addition to the difficulty of identifying professionals from the different entities that were in the functions of interest in this period, at various times it was noted the difficulty of these informants to remember with accuracy the dates and events. To mitigate these effects, interviews were conducted with various people involved in order to triangulate the data. The use of some documentary sources also assisted in this matter, since the event was deeply covered by the media. It is important to consider that there might be inaccuracies related to the data collected.

The second limitation relates to the single case study. Several authors reinforce the limitations involved in only one case study (EISENHARDT, 1989; MILES et al., 2013; YIN, 2014), since the conclusions may reduce the external validity of the survey. Nevertheless, it is worth mentioning that some entities are analyzed only in relation to the context in question, such as, for example, the Health Ministry, the pharmaceutical industry, and the Secretary of State, as in the case of São Paulo.

7. BIBLIOGRAPHY

Baltacioglu, T., Ada, E., Kaplan, M. D., Yurt And, O., E Cem Kaplan, Y. (2007). A new framework for service supply chains. The Service Industries Journal, 27(2), 105-124.

Barney, J. (1991). Firm resources and sustained competitive advantage. Journal of Management, 17(1), 99-120.

Barney, J. (1996). The resource-based theory of the firm. Organization Science.

Barney, J. (2001). The resource-based view of the firm: Ten years after 1991. Journal of Management, 27(6), 625-641. doi:10.1177/014920630102700601

Blackhurst, J., Dunn, K. S., E Craighead, C. W. (2011). An empirically derived framework of global supply resiliency. Journal of Business Logistics, 32(4), 374-391.

Bode, C., Wagner, S. M., Petersen, K. J., Ellram, L. M. (2011). Understanding responses to supply chain disruptions: Insights from information processing and resource dependence perspectives. Academy of Management Journal, 54(4), 833-856.

Brandon-Jones, E., Squire, B., Autry, C., E Petersen, K. J. (2014). A contingent resource-based perspective of supply chain resilience and robustness. Journal of Supply Chain Management.

Braunscheidel, M. J., E Suresh, N. C. (2009). The organizational antecedents of a firm's supply chain agility for risk mitigation and response. Journal of Operations Management, 27(2), 119-140. doi:10.1016/j.jom.2008.09.006

Christopher, M., Peck, H. (2004). Building the resilient supply chain. International Journal of Logistics Management, the, 15(2), 1-14.

CONASS (2003). Para entender a gestão do SUS. Brasília, Brasil: CONASS - Conselho Nacional de Secretários de Saúde.

Craighead, C. W., Blackhurst, J., Rungtusanatham, M. J., Handfield, R. B. (2007). The severity of supply chain disruptions: Design characteristics and mitigation capabilities. Decision Sciences, 38(1), 131-156.

Craighead, C. W., Karwan, K. R., E Miller, J. L. (2004). The effects of severity of failure and customer loyalty on service recovery strategies. Production and Operations Management, 13(4), 307-321.

Dyer, J. H., E Singh, H. (1998). The relational view: Cooperative strategy and sources of interorganizational competitive advantage. Academy of Management Review, 23(4), 660-679.

Eisenhardt, K. M. (1989). Building theories from case study research. The Academy of Management Review, 14(4), 1-19. doi:10.2307/258557

Ellram, L. M., Tate, W. L., Billington, C. (2004). Understanding and managing the services supply chain. Journal of Supply Chain Management, 40(4), 17-32.

Faisal, M. N., Banwet, D. K., E Shankar, R. (2006). Supply chain risk mitigation: Modeling the enablers. Business Process Management Journal, 12(4), 535-552.

Hardy, C., Phillips, N., E Lawrence, T. B. (2003). Resources, knowledge and influence: The organizational effects of interorganizational collaboration*. Journal of Management Studies, 40(2), 321-347.

Jüttner, U., Maklan, S. (2011). Supply chain resilience in the global financial crisis: An empirical study. Supply Chain Management: An International Journal, 16(4), 246-259.

Jüttner, U., Peck, H., Christopher, M. (2003). Supply chain risk management: Outlining an agenda for future research. International Journal of Logistics: Research and Applications, 6(4), 197-210.

Miles, M. B., Huberman, A. M., E Saldaña, J. (2013). Qualitative data analysis: A methods sourcebook. SAGE Publications, Incorporated.

Mitroff, I. I., Alpaslan, M. C. (2003). Preparing for evil. Harvard Business School Pub.

Peteraf, M. A. (1993). Intra-Industry structure and the response toward rivals. Managerial and Decision Economics, 14(6), 519-528.

Peteraf, M. A., Barney, J. B. (2003). Unraveling the resource-based tangle. Managerial and Decision Economics, 24(4), 309-323.

Pettit, T. J., Croxton, K. L., Fiksel, J. (2013). Ensuring supply chain resilience: Development and implementation of an assessment tool. Journal of Business Logistics, 34(1), 46-76.

Pettit, T. J., Fiksel, J., Croxton, K. L. (2010). Ensuring supply chain resilience: Development of a conceptual framework. Journal of Business Logistics, 31(1), 1-21.

Ponomarov, S. Y., E Holcomb, M. C. (2009). Understanding the concept of supply chain resilience. The International Journal of Logistics Management, 20(1), 124-143.

Scholten, K., Scott, P. S., E Fynes, B. (2014). Mitigation processes – antecedents for building supply chain resilience. Supply Chain Management: An International Journal, 19(2), 211-228.

Seuring, S. A. (2008). Assessing the rigor of case study research in supply chain management. Supply Chain Management: An International Journal, 13(2), 128-137.

Sheffi, Y., Rice Jr, J. B. (2005). A supply chain view of the resilient enterprise. MIT Sloan Management Review, 47(1).

Siggelkow, N. (2007). Persuasion with case studies. Academy of Management Journal, 50(1), 20-24.

Skipper, J. B., Hanna, J. B. (2009). Minimizing supply chain disruption risk through enhanced flexibility. International Journal of Physical Distribution & Logistics Management, 39(5), 404-427.

Stuart, I., McCutcheon, D., Handfield, R., McLachlin, R., E Samson, D. (2002). Effective case research in operations management: A process perspective. Journal of Operations Management, 20(5), 419-433.

Tang, C. (2006). Robust strategies for mitigating supply chain disruptions. International Journal of Logistics, 9(1), 33-45.

Tang, C., Tomlin, B. (2008). The power of flexibility for mitigating supply chain risks. International Journal of Production Economics, 116(1), 12-27.

Teece, D. J., Pisano, G., E Shuen, A. (1997). Dynamic capabilities and strategic management. Strategic Management Journal, 18(7), 509-533.

Weick, K. E. (1993). The collapse of sensemaking in organizations: The mann gulch disaster. Administrative Science Quarterly, 628-652.

Wieland, A., E Wallenburg, C. M. (2013). The influence of relational competencies on supply chain resilience: A relational view. International Journal of Physical Distribution E Logistics Management, 43(4), 300-320.

Wu, S. J., Melnyk, S. A., E Flynn, B. B. (2010). Operational capabilities: The secret ingredient. Decision Sciences, 41(4), 721-754.

Yin, R. K. (2014). Case study research: Design and methods. Sage publications.

Permissions

The contributors of this book come from diverse backgrounds, making this book a truly international effort. This book will bring forth new frontiers with its revolutionizing research information and detailed analysis of the nascent developments around the world.

We would like to thank all the contributing authors for lending their expertise to make the book truly unique. They have played a crucial role in the development of this book. Without their invaluable contributions this book wouldn't have been possible. They have made vital efforts to compile up to date information on the varied aspects of this subject to make this book a valuable addition to the collection of many professionals and students.

This book was conceptualized with the vision of imparting up-to-date information and advanced data in this field. To ensure the same, a matchless editorial board was set up. Every individual on the board went through rigorous rounds of assessment to prove their worth. After which they invested a large part of their time researching and compiling the most relevant data for our readers.

The editorial board has been involved in producing this book since its inception. They have spent rigorous hours researching and exploring the diverse topics which have resulted in the successful publishing of this book. They have passed on their knowledge of decades through this book. To expedite this challenging task, the publisher supported the team at every step. A small team of assistant editors was also appointed to further simplify the editing procedure and attain best results for the readers.

Apart from the editorial board, the designing team has also invested a significant amount of their time in understanding the subject and creating the most relevant covers. They scrutinized every image to scout for the most suitable representation of the subject and create an appropriate cover for the book.

The publishing team has been an ardent support to the editorial, designing and production team. Their endless efforts to recruit the best for this project, has resulted in the accomplishment of this book. They are a veteran in the field of academics and their pool of knowledge is as vast as their experience in printing. Their expertise and guidance has proved useful at every step. Their uncompromising quality standards have made this book an exceptional effort. Their encouragement from time to time has been an inspiration for everyone.

The publisher and the editorial board hope that this book will prove to be a valuable piece of knowledge for researchers, students, practitioners and scholars across the globe.

List of Contributors

Ingridi Vargas Bortolaso
Unisinos

Alsones Balestrin
Unisinos

Rafael Teixeira
Unisinos

Kadigia Faccin
Unisinos

Angel Díaz
IE Business Schoolangel

Elcio Mendonça Tachizawa
Universidad Carlos III

Felipe de Mattos Zarpelon
Universidade do Vale do Rio dos Sinos –
UNISINOS

Iuri Gavronski
Universidade do Vale do Rio dos Sinos –
UNISINO

Minelle Enéas da Silva
Federal University of Rio Grande do Sul

Daiane Mulling Neutzling
Universidade Feevale

Ana Paula Ferreira Alves
Federal University of Rio Grande do Sul

Patrícia Dias
Federal University of Rio Grande do Sul

Carlos Alberto Frantz dos Santos
Federal University of Rio Grande

Luis Felipe Nascimento
Federal University of Rio Grande do Sul

Ely Laureano Paiva
FGV-EAESP

Cristiane Biazzin
FGV-EAESP

Luiz Carlos Di Serio
FGV-EAESP

Marta Cleia Ferreira de Andrade
Faculdade de Ciências e Educação de
Rubiataba

Flávio Jorge Freire D Andrade Battistuzzo
Universidade Nove de Julho

Marcos Roberto Piscopo
Universidade Nove de Julho

Edson Júnior Gomes Guedes
FGV-EAESP

Alexandre de Vicente Bittar
FGV-EAESP

Luiz Carlos Di Serio
FGV-EAESP

Luciel Henrique de Oliveira
FGV-EAESP

Yeongling H. Yang
San Diego State University

Ana Cristina Ferreira
Federal University of Uberlândia

Franciele Olivo Bertan
Federal University of Uberlândia

Marcio Lopes Pimenta
Federal University of Uberlândia

Petar Radanliev
Anglia Ruskin University, Lord Ashcroft
International Business School

Kizito Paul Mubiru
Kyambogo University

Liane Okdinawati
School of Business and Management, Bandung
Institute of Technology

Togar M. Simatupang
School of Business and Management, Bandung
Institute of Technology

Yos Sunitiyoso
School of Business and Management, Bandung
Institute of Technology

Marcelo Bradaschia
Fundação Getulio Vargas – EAESP

Susana Carla Farias Pereira
Fundação Getulio Vargas – EAESP

Index

CPSIA information can be obtained
at www.ICGtesting.com
Printed in the USA
BVHW061220170622
640058BV00004B/79

9 781682 854